Education in Spite of Polic

CW00544946

A national system of education cannot function without policy. But the path to practice is seldom smooth, especially when ideology overrules evidence or when ministers seek to micromanage what is best left to teachers. And once the media join the fray the mixture becomes downright combustible.

Drawing on his long experience as teacher, researcher, government adviser, campaigner and international consultant, and on over 600 published sources, Robin Alexander expertly illustrates and illuminates these processes. This selection from his recent writing, some hitherto unpublished, opens windows onto cases and issues that concern every teacher.

Part 1 tackles system-level reform. It revisits the Cambridge Primary Review, an evidence-rich enquiry into the condition and future of primary education in England, which challenged the UK government's policies on curriculum, testing, standards and more besides. Here the reform narratives and strategies of successive governments are confronted and dissected.

Part 2 follows the development of England's current National Curriculum, exposing its narrow vision and questionable use of evidence and offering a more generous aims-driven alternative. This section also investigates the expertise and leadership needed if children are to experience a curriculum of the highest quality in all its aspects.

Part 3 reaches the heart of the matter: securing the place in effective pedagogy of well-founded classroom talk, a mission repeatedly frustrated by political intervention. The centrepiece is dialogic teaching, a proven tool for advancing students' speaking, thinking, learning and arguing, and an essential response to the corrosion of democracy and the nihilism of 'post-truth'.

Part 4 goes global. It investigates governments' PISA-fuelled flirtations with what they think can be adapted or copied from education elsewhere, examines the benefits and pitfalls of international comparison, and ends with the ultimate policy initiative: the United Nations mission to ensure 'inclusive and equitable quality education' for all the world's children.

Education in Spite of Policy is for all those teachers, students, school leaders and researchers who value the conversation of policy, evidence and practice, and who wish to explore the parts of education that policy cannot reach.

Robin Alexander is Fellow of Wolfson College at the University of Cambridge, Professor of Education Emeritus at the University of Warwick, and Fellow of the British Academy. His five-nation *Culture and Pedagogy* (2001) won the Outstanding Book Award of the American Educational Research Association, while *Children, their World, their Education* (2010), and his work as director of the Cambridge Primary Review, won the SES Book Awards First Prize and the BERA/Sage Public Impact and Engagement Award. His most recent book, *A Dialogic Teaching Companion* (2020), is a summation of many years of work on the quality of talk in teaching and learning.

Education in Spite of Policy

Robin Alexander

Routledge
Taylor & Francis Group

LONDON AND NEW YORK

Cover image: R A Kearton / Getty Images

First published 2022
by Routledge
2 Park Square, Milton Park, Abingdon, Oxon OX14 4RN

and by Routledge
605 Third Avenue, New York, NY 10158

Routledge is an imprint of the Taylor & Francis Group, an informa business

British Library Cataloguing-in-Publication Data
A catalogue record for this book is available from the British Library

Library of Congress Cataloging-in-Publication Data
A catalog record for this book has been requested

ISBN: 978-1-138-04986-4 (hbk)
ISBN: 978-1-138-04987-1 (pbk)
ISBN: 978-1-315-16937-8 (ebk)

DOI: 10.4324/9781315169378

Typeset in Bembo
by Apex CoVantage, LLC

Full circle, almost:

for Fiona, Gavin and Karen.

Contents

Acknowledgements

For generous funding which sustained projects drawn upon in this book I would like to thank: the Education Endowment Foundation (Cambridge Primary Review Trust/University of York Dialogic Teaching Project, 2014–17); Esmée Fairbairn Foundation (Cambridge Primary Review, Cambridge Primary Review Network and Cambridge Primary Review Archive, 2006–13); Leverhulme Trust, the British Council and the University of Warwick (Culture and Pedagogy, 1994–8 and 2002–3); Pearson Education (Cambridge Primary Review Trust, 2013–17).

Chapters that started as conference keynote lectures benefited from invitations, and in many cases generous hospitality, from the following: Barndrømmen, Copenhagen (Chapter 12); British Association for International and Comparative Education (BAICE) (Chapter 20); Cambridge Primary Review Trust (Chapter 6); The College of Teachers (part of Chapter 2); CPPS Westminster Seminars (Chapter 10); Curious Minds (Chapter 12); European Association for Research in Learning and Instruction (EARLI) (Chapter 18); Gabriela Mistral University, Santiago, Chile (parts of Chapters 2, 8 and 21); National College for School Leadership (Chapter 14); National Institute of Education, Singapore (part of Chapter 4); Scottish Educational Research Association (Chapter 21); University of Edinburgh and the Godfrey Thomson Trust (Chapter 7); University of Melbourne (parts of Chapters 4 and 8); University of Oslo in conjunction with UNICEF (Chapter 22); Van Leer Foundation, Jerusalem (part of Chapter 21).

Cambridge Primary Review assigned copyright for its publications to the University of Cambridge, so I thank my *alma mater* and former employer for permission to reproduce pp 245–51 from Alexander, R.J. (ed) (2010) *Children, Their World, Their Education: final report and recommendations from the Cambridge Primary* Review, Routledge. Also, three of the Cambridge Primary Review Briefings written by myself: *Community Soundings* (2007), *The Final Report* (2009), and *Policy Priorities for Primary Education* (2010).

The following articles have been reproduced with the permission of the publishers concerned, some of them in part and re-edited or augmented rather than in their original form:

Where there is no vision. . . *Forum 49(1/2)*, 187–200 (2007).

Testaments to the power of 10, *Times Education Supplement* (16 May 2008).

Towards a comparative pedagogy, in R. Cowen and A.M. Kazamias (ed) *International Handbook of Comparative Education*, Springer, 922–41 (2009).

Ministers fail to learn lessons, *The Guardian* (24 October 2009).

'World class schools' – noble aspiration or global hokum? *Compare 40(6)*, 801–17 (2010). Reprinted by permission of Taylor & Francis Ltd on behalf of the British Association for International and Comparative Education.

Evidence, rhetoric and collateral damage: the problematic pursuit of 'world class' standards, *Cambridge Journal of Education 41(3)*, 265–86 (2011). Reprinted by permission of Taylor & Francis Ltd on behalf of the University of Cambridge Faculty of Education.

Legacies, policies and prospects: one year on from the Cambridge Primary Review, *Forum 53(1)*, 71–92 (2011).

Neither national nor a curriculum? *Forum 54(3)*, 369–84 (2012).

Moral panic, miracles cures and educational policy: what can we really learn from educational comparison? *Scottish Educational Review 44(1)*, 4–21 (2012).

Evidence, policy and the reform of primary education: a cautionary tale, *Forum 56(3)* (2014).

Teaching and learning for all: the quality imperative revisited, *International Journal of Educational Development 41(1)* 250–58 (2015).

Developing dialogic teaching: genesis, process, trial, *Research Papers in Education 33(5)*, 561–98 (2018).

Whose discourse? Dialogic pedagogy for a post-truth world, *Dialogic Pedagogy Journal 7*, E1–19 (2019).

1 Introduction

In February 2021, the UK government appointed England's first Education Recovery Commissioner. His task was to 'advise on the design and implementation of potential interventions. . . [to] help students catch up learning lost due to the pandemic'.[1] The Commissioner was Kevan Collins, formerly Chief Executive of the Education Endowment Foundation. The pandemic was Covid-19, which during 2020 and 2021 swept across the world, and by the time this book went to press had caused over 150,000 deaths in the UK,[2] 600,000 in the United States and 500,000 in Brazil.[3] It also severely disrupted the education of millions of children.

Collins resigned after just four months, having had his £15 billion recovery plan rejected. The government allowed less than one tenth of that, which Collins said fell 'far short of what is needed', and was 'too narrow, too small and [would] be delivered too slowly'. He added that the average primary school [would] receive just £6,000 a year, equivalent to £22 per child,[4] and in evidence to the House of Commons Education Committee he tersely dismissed the government's plan as 'feeble'.[5]

Meanwhile, apparently following a similar trajectory,[6] the Education Policy Institute (EPI) published its own report on how children's lost education should be reclaimed, costing its proposals at £13.5 billion. Anticipating that this figure might be deemed unrealistic, EPI compared the £984 million needed for the first year of its educational recovery programme with the £840 million released in just one month to support the economic recovery of the hospitality industry, daring politicians to disagree that the nation's children and schools deserved no less than the nation's cafés, restaurants and pubs.[7]

EPI calculated that by the first half of the 2020 autumn term the pandemic had cost England's primary and secondary school students up to two months' progress in reading and, among primary students, up to three months in mathematics, and that these learning losses would result in comparable reductions in lifetime earnings. The losses were even greater for socio-economically disadvantaged pupils, among whom the pandemic greatly exacerbated existing inequalities.

Simultaneously, and confirming that these inequalities extended far beyond education, a study by the Institute of Health Equity (IHE) reported that in the

DOI: 10.4324/9781315169378-1

13 months to March 2021 the Covid-19 death rate was 25 per cent higher in the Manchester City Region than in England as a whole; and that this high death rate contributed to a decline in life expectancy which was significantly larger in England's disadvantaged north-west than nationally.[8]

The EPI report argued that recovery should address children's mental health and wellbeing as well as their progress in reading and mathematics, while IHE insisted that achieving health and wellbeing equity should be prioritised alongside the narrower economic goals in which the government was chiefly interested. EPI's recommended recovery strategy included extended school hours, summer wellbeing programmes, targeted individual tuition, extension of the Pupil Premium for disadvantaged pupils, incentives for teachers working in 'challenging areas', guidance on inclusion, lower stakes accountability measures, tightly-focused professional development, and the option for pupils to repeat school years in extreme cases of 'learning loss'.[9]

This episode, prominent in the media and at Westminster as this book goes to press, vividly illustrates two of its central themes: the all-too-frequent mismatch between what is needed educationally and what policymakers permit or dictate; and the precarious place in the policy process of evidence and expertise, both of which were required by the Commissioner's job specification but in the end counted for little.[10]

★ ★ ★

The papers in this volume span the period 2006–21 and in one sense may be viewed as completing a trilogy initiated by two earlier Routledge collections, *Versions of Primary Education* (1995) and *Essays on Pedagogy* (2008). Like these, *Education in Spite of Policy* includes conference papers, some hitherto unpublished, and journal articles. Source-wise, however, the present volume is much more diverse and eclectic than its predecessors, and alongside the more substantial journal and conference pieces readers will encounter newspaper articles, blogs and briefings. There is geographical diversity too. Appearing here in their original or edited forms are keynotes from conferences in England, Scotland, Australia, Chile, Denmark, Finland, Israel, Norway and Singapore, and although the book begins locally, its canvas becomes progressively more international.

Readers will also note, but I hope not be irritated by, variation in style and tone. Some chapters are of the discursive academic kind, while the newspaper articles and blogs aim for journalistic immediacy and the conference keynotes retain some of the tenor of the spoken word. But such deviations from the stylistic conventions of academic writing should not be mistaken for frivolous intent. The book's themes are as serious as they are constant, and over 600 published sources are cited.

Here, then, is the bottom line: education matters, policy matters, evidence matters; but the relationship between them is rarely straightforward, especially when ideology overrules evidence or when ministers try to micromanage what is best left to teachers. And once the media join the fray the mixture becomes downright combustible.

If, as Clifford Geertz famously asserted, culture is 'the stories we tell ourselves',[11] this applies *a fortiori* to the culture of education. Narrative is one of this book's leitmotifs, and in its pages we witness the power of political and media narratives about education, and their frequent collisions with those of students, teachers and researchers.

The opening chapter illustrates one such collision by reminding us of the journey of the Plowden report from harbinger of cross-party progress to target of right-wing abuse. Comparable encounters surface in later chapters, notably in relation to the Cambridge Primary Review, educational standards and testing, the national curriculum, international educational comparisons, and the place in children's education of language in general and spoken language in particular. Within the book's timescale Britain has experienced Labour, Coalition and Conservative governments, and in matters such as these there may be little to choose between political parties once they gain power. Shaping and dominating the narrative is, for any government, an almost sacred duty.

But one of the casualties of this single-minded quest may be truth as others understand it. Indeed, here we seem to be spiralling rapidly downwards. Three decades ago people thought it clever and entertaining to invert the politicians' slogan 'evidence-based policy'. 'Policy-based evidence' held that what politicians were really interested in was finding evidence to justify what they had already decided. Yet the jibe was genial and even the cynics presumed the good intentions of most policymakers, if not their competence. By 2021 the traumas of Brexit, MAGA[12] and Covid had changed everything. Trust in politicians had fallen to an all-time low.[13] Political leaders in both Britain and the United States were accused of serial lying on an industrial scale, and by following the fact-checkers we can see that the accusers had a point.[14] In consequence, the phrase 'post-truth' is now used so frequently that its devastating implications for what were once regarded as democratic, legal and moral obligations are merely shrugged off as 'the new normal'. And in Britain the Ministerial Code ('Ministers who knowingly mislead Parliament will be expected to offer their resignation to the Prime Minister'[15]) is no longer observed or enforced – partly because the offenders may not have the moral compass that the Code presumes, but mainly because the prime minister may not be the exemplar of integrity on which the Code's entire validity depends.

But normal this can never be allowed to be. In a scrupulously-sourced analysis of the words and conduct of the man who at the time of writing is Britain's prime minister, Peter Oborne documents lie after insouciant lie on Brexit, the National Health Service, Russian interference in British elections, immigration, the Covid-19 pandemic and – notably over the examination chaos of 2020 – education. Other ministers, including a former education secretary, fare little better.[16]

Oborne also exposes the means whereby these people sought to discredit their colleagues as well as opponents, and their attacks on the public institutions, including the judiciary and Parliament itself, that exist to hold the line against corruption and autocracy. He shows how these tendencies are part of a wider pattern of growing disdain for rules-based systems of national and international order which were designed to recover human dignity, progress and rights from the slaughter and ashes of the second world war. But international lawyer Philippe Sands shows how this process began some time before the arrival of Trump and Johnson, reaching back to a succession of American-led international 'adventures' under Presidents Reagan and Clinton, and he rates the 'war on terror' of US President George W. Bush and UK Prime Minister Tony Blair as, in effect, a 'war on law'.[17]

★ ★ ★

This, then, is where we are. In its own consideration of competing narratives this book chronicles, samples and reflects upon four major points of intersection between education practice, research and policy.

Part 1 is about systemic reform. It revisits the Cambridge Primary Review, a major national enquiry into the condition and future of primary education in England, and its sequel, the Cambridge Primary Review Trust. These pinned faith in the power of evidence and argument to inform debate, policy and practice in this vital phase of education. Government responded defensively and then aggressively; teachers were much more welcoming. From the Review's wealth of published material these chapters sample context, content and consequence, before stepping back to dissect the reform narratives and strategies of this and subsequent governments.

Part 2 focuses more specifically on the curriculum. It examines the properly contested questions of what children should learn and why, explores tensions between political partisanship and cultural diversity, exposes again the problem of evidence, tests the limits of a 'national' curriculum, and contrasts ministers' opportunistic pursuit of fads like 'grit and resilience' with their perennial failure to give due weight to the arts and creativity. Along the way Part 2 encounters the curriculum building blocks or stumbling blocks of subjects, knowledge and skills.

Part 3 is about pedagogy, and specifically the pedagogy of the spoken word, the importance in learning and teaching of well-founded classroom talk, and the frustration of that mission by its politicisation. The section's centrepiece is dialogic teaching and argumentation. Now successfully evaluated by the Education Endowment Foundation, this is a vital tool for student learning and empowerment, especially in contexts of social disadvantage, and it is an essential response to the epistemic nihilism of 'post-truth' and the growing crisis of democracy.

Part 4 goes global. After a brief excursion into the possibilities of comparative education we investigate the PISA-driven preoccupation with what can be learned, adapted or copied from education elsewhere, a theme already touched on in Part 2. The book ends with reservations about the grandest of all education policy initiatives: the United Nations mission to secure education for all the world's children by 2030. Here the problem is the way that the UN's monitoring paradigm seems simply not up to the task of engaging with what is, or should be, at the heart of its effort: the quality of teaching and learning.

Notes at the head of each chapter briefly sketch background and context, so that readers can follow without too much difficulty the narrative threads.

★ ★ ★

Providing content and impetus for all this have been two parallel strands of my work during the past two decades or so. The first is research. All the chapters here post-date the comparative, historical and ethnographic study of primary education in five cultures – England, France, India, Russia and the United States – which between 1994 and 2000 I undertook with the support of the Leverhulme Trust and which resulted in the book *Culture and Pedagogy* (2001). But that work laid intellectual trails which I follow to this day, and some of them are readily detectable in this book. Next came the Cambridge Primary Review (2006–9), supported by the Esmée Fairbairn Foundation and producing 31 interim reports, the final report, *Children, Their World, Their Education* (2010) and *The Cambridge Primary Review Research Surveys* (2010). This independent national enquiry led to the Cambridge Primary Review Network (2010–12), also supported by Esmée Fairbairn, and the Pearson-funded Cambridge Primary Review Trust (2013–17). Then, straddling both projects, came my work on pedagogy in general and classroom talk in particular. This yielded the development, refinement and trialling of what I have called 'dialogic teaching', culminating to date in the Education Endowment Foundation's 2014–17 randomised control trial of my dialogic teaching framework, and the re-thinking of that framework and contingent issues and evidence for *A Dialogic Teaching Companion* (2020).

The other contributory strand has been my proximity to the policy process itself. Here I am fortunate in being able to write from the inside as well as the outside, so I hope that my commentary will not be seen as mere armchair carping, and although I am frequently critical of policy, I also recognise its dilemmas – not least in the matter of post-Covid educational recovery. Before the period covered by this volume, but mentioned in it from time to time, I was part of the then government's so-called 'three wise men' enquiry into primary education (1991–2). This was prompted by media sensationalising of my evaluation of primary education reform in Leeds (1986–91) and led to the short but controversial government report *Curriculum Organisation and Classroom Practice in Primary Schools* (1992). This was something of a baptism of fire for a naive academic, but it taught me a lot about how education is politicised within the academy as well as outside it, and about the fraught but symbiotic relationship between policymakers and the media. I wrote in detail about this episode in the second edition of *Policy and Practice in Primary Education* (1997).

Meanwhile, I found myself serving on government advisory bodies and hence dealing directly and frequently with ministers and officials: the Council for the Accreditation of Teacher Education (CATE) from 1989–94, and the Qualifications and Curriculum Authority (QCA) from 1997 to 2002. CATE accredited all courses of initial teacher education and advised government on teacher education reform, while QCA had charge of the national curriculum and statutory assessment. Both of these 'arm's length' non-departmental public bodies were later replaced by others over which ministers were able to exert unfettered and unaccountable control.

In addition to these formal roles, I have discussed education matters with ministers, officials, Downing Street special advisers and members of Parliament and the House of Lords. So, for example, during the course of the Cambridge Primary Review I had 15 meetings with ministers and officials, 12 with government advisory bodies, 12 with education spokespersons from other political parties in both houses and four with the House of Commons Education Select Committee.[18] After the completion of the Review, and throughout its dissemination and networking phases (2010–12) and the life of the Cambridge Primary Review Trust (2013–17), regular meetings with officials, and occasional meetings with ministers, took place by agreement with the Secretary of State. These covered, for example: strategies for tackling disadvantage; implementing the national curriculum; assessment; schools and research; primary schools' curriculum capacity; and the handling of children's spoken language in schools and national policy. And both through the Review and the Trust and on an individual basis I have made a point of responding to government consultations, pointless though, apropos 'policy-based evidence', this has sometimes seemed.

On the international front, the three-level *Culture and Pedagogy* research entailed my interviewing policymakers and officials in the five chosen countries as well as working intensively in schools and classrooms. In one of them, India, I found myself as a consequence drawn from 1994 onwards into the programmes of primary education reform and universalisation under DPEP and SSA[19] on behalf of the UK Department for International Development (DfID) and the European Commission, both of which were among the international donor agencies that worked with the Government of India to support its reforms. This entailed regular periods of work at every level of India's vast education system from the ministry in Delhi to individual states, districts and schools, often in remote rural areas. Through this activity I became involved in the larger global conversations about UN Millennium Development Goal 2 (universal primary education, 2001–15) and Sustainable Development Goal 4 (Quality education, 2015–30). These provide the focus for the book's final chapter.

★ ★ ★

So what, if anything, should be read into the title *Education in Spite of Policy*? I show how in respect of a number of government interventions it may well be fair to assert, in the words of those four leading academics who wrote an open letter to the press in 2008, that 'government policy is no longer the solution to the difficulties we face but our greatest problem'.[20] Yet I do not argue that this is always or inevitably the case, and am slightly uneasy about its Reaganite echoes.[21] For a public system of schooling cannot exist, let alone succeed, without a framework of policy, and there are many instances where government has intervened to the benefit of all concerned. Labour's London Challenge (2003–11), which raised standards in underperforming secondary schools above those of the rest of England, and whose impact is still evident, provides one striking example.[22]

Here, the 'policy balance sheet' drawn up by the Cambridge Primary Review on the basis of its evidence is instructive. It deals with policy between 1997 and 2009, but its themes are generic and many of them are contemporary.[23] Broadly, policies in support of children's development, health, wellbeing and access to good early childhood education fared better than those that sought to determine precisely what and how children should be taught and assessed. It would be interesting to re-run that part of the Cambridge enquiry from time to time, in all phases of education. Governments urge teachers to apply the criterion 'what works' in classrooms. They may be less inclined to submit to discussion about 'what works' in policy.

To pre-empt criticism of what the book fails to do, I should add that it neither claims nor attempts to be an exercise in sustained policy analysis of the kind so skilfully undertaken by, say, my colleague Stephen Ball, who in relation to the idea of the policy balance sheet agrees that there are both situations where policy interventions are needed and those where schools and local communities are better placed to decide, but that in recent years 'the state has both interfered too much and not enough'.[24] Ball concludes that, as a result, state education in England is riddled by incoherence, inconsistency and even contradiction.

Though such a conclusion may also be merited in the light of what follows, I reach it by a different route to that taken by Ball: here we have a series of linked snapshots of encounters between policy, research, practice and – critically – the media, in aspects of education in which I have been personally involved. But the chapters combine showing and illustrating with telling and explaining, and some of them venture analysis of the policy process and its impact, always bearing in mind the need to distinguish between policy as promulgated and policy as enacted.[25] For schools respond to policy in different ways, domesticating it to fit their circumstances and sometimes changing it almost beyond recognition.

Policymakers themselves are aware of this untidy tendency, and 1960s/1970s curriculum developers used to talk wistfully of a day when teachers would unswervingly and unquestioningly follow the recipes in 'teacher-proof' curriculum cookery books and achieve identical results. Former government adviser Tim Oates gained the patronage of Secretary of State Michael Gove in part because he produced a list of 'control factors' that would ensure that teachers would 'deliver' the national curriculum precisely as specified by ministers, without deviation.[26] But as with the earlier efforts of Michael Barber, creator of the science or pseudo-science of 'deliverology',[27] this was a forlorn hope, and Stephen Ball shows how a long succession of ad hoc policies and overweening government faith in performativity has produced an education 'system' that is scarcely a system at all.[28]

There is also the matter of the fleeting nature of high office. I became professionally involved in education in September 1964, leaving university to teach in the first of several schools before eventually moving back into universities as an academic. When I met my first class of 9–10-year-olds the Minister of Education was Quintin Hogg (Conservative). A mere month later it was Michael Stewart (Labour). Three months after that it was Anthony Crosland (Labour). And so it went on: 27 ministers or, as they are now, secretaries of state, in 57 years, or an average tenure of just over two years each. In fact, because a few of them – Margaret Thatcher, Shirley Williams, Keith Joseph, Kenneth Baker, David Blunkett and Michael Gove – served for longer, the more usual term of office was between one and two years and in some cases only a few months. (The latter three individuals have been interviewed for a new book by Tim Brighouse and Mick Waters, and it will be interesting to see what they say about the episodes and issues discussed here.)[29]

Brevity of office concentrates ambition. Each of the 27 was determined or required to make his or her mark, and each had a prime minister to impress. Given the rapid turnover, each also needed to act quickly and come up with ideas that were sufficiently and eye-catchingly different to what had gone before to justify the label 'reform'. But from 1997 or so, 'reform' wasn't enough: policies had to be 'tough' and 'new', to be 'rolled out', to mark a 'step change', to rout the 'educational establishment', to produce 'the highest standards ever'. Apart from the historical implausibility of the latter claim, 'tough' and 'new' often meant undoing the work of one's ministerial predecessor before it had been fully implemented, let alone evaluated. This endless parade of careerist and sometimes contradictory initiatives was hardly a basis for considered, cumulative and coherent policy, or for the development of a properly-functioning national education system.

Finally, I should make it clear that the umbrella term 'policy', as used throughout this book, covers the process, context and politics of policy as well as its content; and the transmission, reception and translation of policy as well as its creation.

Notes

1 DfE 2021.
2 https://coronavirus.data.gov.uk/details/deaths. The official figures on 10 June 2021 were between 127,860 and 152,289. The disparity reflects the application of alternative criteria (deaths within 28 days of a positive test/deaths with Covid-19 on the

death certificate). The figures exclude deaths indirectly attributable to Covid-19 (for example when the pressure on hospitals prevented patients from being treated for other conditions).

3 https://coronavirus.jhu.edu/map.html (accessed 20 June 2021).

4 As reported by the BBC: www.bbc.co.uk/news/education-57335558 and *The Guardian* www.theguardian.com/politics/2021/jun/02/education-recovery-chief-kevan-collins-quit-english-schools-catch-up-row (accessed June 2021).

5 www.theguardian.com/education/2021/jun/29/recovery-plan-pupils-england-feeble-kevan-collins-says (accessed June 2021).

6 I say 'apparently' because Kevan Collins's education recovery proposals were leaked in part rather than published in full.

7 EPI 2021.

8 Marmot *et al* 2021.

9 Crenna-Jennings *et al* 2021.

10 'The Commissioner will use evidence to focus the work on the potential interventions of greatest impact for children and young people, society and the economy . . . The Commissioner will be expected to engage with education experts to improve implementation and refine proposals' (DfE 2021).

11 Geertz 1973.

12 MAGA: 'Make America Great Again'. Trump's slogan was chanted at his rallies and emblazoned on the headgear, clothes, bodies and minds of his supporters, including many of the mob that stormed the Capitol on 6 January 2021 in an attempt to overturn his defeat in the 2020 presidential election. Others saw it as the nadir of divisive, racist, dog-whistle politics, and a repudiation of the rules-based international order to which the USA had been ostensibly committed since the second world war.

13 Sippitt 2019, 3: 'Politicians are one of the least trusted professions, with about 19% of people in the UK saying they trust them to tell the truth . . . Trust in journalists to tell the truth is a little higher, with 26% of Brits saying they trust them.'

14 CNN, *Washington Post, New York Times, Huffpost, BuzzFeed* and other media fact checked President Trump's public utterances throughout his term of office from 2017–21 and arrived at the extraordinary tally of 30,000 lies over the four years, or an average of 21 a day www.independent.co.uk/news/world/americas/us-election-2020/trump-lies-false-presidency-b1790285.html (accessed May 2021). In the UK we have Full-Fact https://fullfact.org/ and Fact Check UK https://theconversation.com/uk/topics/fact-check-uk-15076 (accessed June 2021) and, focusing specifically on Prime Minister Boris Johnson, the record of habitual mendacity compiled by his former colleague Peter Oborne (2021).

15 www.gov.uk/government/publications/ministerial-code (accessed June 2021).

16 Oborne comments: 'Though this [i.e. his] book has concentrated on the integrity of the prime minister, Gove was another habitual liar' (Oborne 2021, 117).

17 Sands 2005.

18 See the meeting record in Alexander 2010a, 537–8.

19 District Primary Education Programme (DPEP), the limited programme of increasing primary education access, recruitment and retention initiated in 1994; and Sarva Shiksha Abhiyan (SSA), the more ambitious scheme for universalising elementary education for all of India's children aged 6–14, which took over from DPEP in 2001.

20 Coffield *et al* 2008.

21 From President Ronald Reagan's inaugural address, January 1981: 'Government is not a solution to our problem; government is the problem.' www.reaganfoundation.org/ronald-reagan/reagan-quotes-speeches/inaugural-address-2/ (accessed May 2021).

22 Ofsted 2010a. See chapter 4.

23 Alexander 2010a, 469–71.

24 Ball 2012, see also 2018, 209; Bowe *et al* 2017.

25 Ball *et al* 2011.
26 Oates 2012. See this volume, Chapter 10.
27 Barber 2011.
28 Ball 2018.
29 Brighouse and Waters 2022.

Part 1

Above the parapet

2 A tale of two reviews

During the past century there have been many enquiries into aspects of state education, some official, others independent. Whether governments take notice of the resulting reports seems to depend more on their political convenience than on the validity or authority of their findings, and contrary to what one might expect, government-commissioned reports may fare no better than their independent counterparts. Indeed, it is a testament to the imperviousness of education policymakers to new ideas, let alone well-founded critique, that most such documents sink without trace. But in the history of English primary education two government-commissioned enquiries – Hadow (1928–31) and Plowden (1963–7) – have in their different ways exerted considerable influence and they therefore provided points of reference for the Cambridge Primary Review, the large-scale independent enquiry into the condition and future of primary education in England whose progress and aftermath are sampled in the next few chapters. Here, looking back to Plowden and forward to the Cambridge Review, we have extracts from *Forum 49:1/2* (2007), *Forum 53:1* (2011) and *Education Today 59:3* (2009). The idea that there was not one Plowden but several first featured, under the title *Plowden, Truth and Myth: a warning*, at the College of Teachers Honorary Award Ceremony in May 2009. On that occasion members of the late Lady Plowden's family were present.

Though the 1931 Hadow Report[1] paved the way, it took Plowden's happily timed appearance at the crest of 1960s optimism finally to propel English primary education into the political mainstream. This imposing document[2] – two volumes, 1189 pages, 46 plates, 197 recommendations and much evidence exhaustively discussed – confirmed the profound importance to children and society of what hitherto had been regarded as little more than a sideshow to the grander enterprises of secondary and higher education.

The price paid for this elevation was the rapid collapse of the cross-party consensus that had attended Plowden's progress – a Conservative minister had commissioned it, a Labour minister welcomed its final report – and the burial of its true messages in the mire of professional misunderstanding, media mythologising and political scapegoating. For Plowden had transformed primary education into something worth arguing about, indeed fighting for. The report undoubtedly liberated and inspired some exceptional teaching, and it is essential that this be duly recalled and properly recorded;[3] as indeed we should recall that tradition of rigorous but sympathetic attention to children's thinking, feeling and learning which in the hands of teacher-scholars like Sybil Marshall, Michael Armstrong and Mary-Jane Drummond was far more searching than

DOI: 10.4324/9781315169378-3

the lazy rhetoric of generalised child-centredness allowed.[4] And distinguished BBC education correspondent Mike Baker was in no doubt about Plowden's positive impact:

> Plowden had a huge influence on education policy, from the support for 'positive discrimination' in 'education priority areas' to the expansion of nursery education. It influenced school building design, classroom layout, teaching methods, the introduction of a more flexible school starting age, and greater involvement of parents.[5]

But Plowden also unleashed a discourse which in debilitating measures combined the simplistic, muddled and doctrinaire. Academics speedily exposed Plowden's philosophical and evidential frailties,[6] while classroom researchers revealed the prosaic truth that post-Plowden pedagogy was all too often notable less for the inspirational shock of the new than the ideologically convoluted persistence of the old.[7] Meanwhile, emboldened by the 'Black Paper' movement, the political and media right began to blame Plowden for declining standards of reading, behaviour, public morality, imperial ambition and much else besides,[8] elevating this toxic discourse to one of the Conservative government's central themes in the 1992 general election.

By that point the attacks had taken on an increasingly personal tone, with Lady Plowden herself singled out for abuse. Thus, as one example among many, the *Daily Telegraph's*: 'Look on your works, Lady Plowden, and despair'.[9] Writing in the *Times Educational Supplement* after the publication of the so-called 'three wise men' report, which I had co-authored,[10] I commented:

> Few episodes in recent educational journalism have been more disgraceful than the vilification of Lady Plowden, and our report explicitly distances itself from such behaviour: 'It is fashionable to blame the Plowden Report for what are perceived as the current ills of primary education. However, if ill-conceived practices have been justified by reference to Plowden, this reflects far more damagingly on those who have used the report in this way than on Plowden itself . . . If things have gone wrong – and the word "if" is important – then scapegoating is not the answer. All those responsible for administering and delivering our system of primary education need to look carefully at the part they may have played.'[11]

I still have the letter I received from Lady Plowden thanking me for this intervention. By then in her 80s, she was understandably distressed by the way she – and the rest of her family – were being hounded by the press, egged on by sections of the Conservative Party. But not all of them. In 1993 Sir Malcolm Thornton, Conservative chair of the House of Commons Education Committee, stepped spectacularly and courageously out of line:

> I believe that both the wider debate and the ears of ministers have been disproportionately influenced by extremists . . . And who are they to foist

upon the children of this country ideas which will only take them back-wards? What hard evidence do they have to support their assertions? How often do they go into schools and see for themselves what is happening? What possible authority can they claim for representing the views of 'the overwhelming majority of parents'? . . . Their insidious propaganda must be challenged . . . The extreme right-wing think-tanks . . . are the spindle and loom of chaos; the offspring of bigoted minds and muddy understandings.[12]

As we shall see, the discourse Thornton deplored in 1993 was no passing phase. It is true that in 1997 crude Plowden-bashing gave way to New Labour's chill-ing edict that the preceding era should be not so much excoriated as simply written off as one of 'uninformed professional judgement'.[13] But the old nar-rative persisted, and even now the other side of the routinely recycled 'back to basics' mantra is an equally predictable lampooning of a cartoon version of the cautious progressivism for which Plowden stood: 'a generation of wasted time' . . . 'very peculiar practice' . . . 'an anarchic ideology' . . . 'much play but little learning' . . . 'trendy teaching' . . . 'back to the blackboard for prima-ries' . . . 'progressive teaching gets a caning' . . . 'children of nine still counting on fingers' . . . 'trendies produce a lesson in failure' . . .[14]

In celebrating Plowden's anniversary it is therefore essential to distinguish between three different versions of the report: what it actually said, what peo-ple claimed it said, and what they did in its name; and further to differentiate the second version: Plowden as sanctified, Plowden as demonised.

The gulf between the various Plowdens could be alarmingly wide. So, for example, though it was taken by both teachers and detractors (for ideologi-cally opposing reasons) to pronounce the death of a subject-based curriculum, Plowden actually favoured (para. 555) a measured progression from a relatively open curriculum in the early years to a subject-differentiated one by age 12, which was hardly revolutionary; and its discussion of that curriculum (paras 558–721) was anyway contained within the traditional subject framework and indeed offered an elaboration of Hadow's 1931 account rather than anything startlingly new. (This isn't the only continuity: read both reports and you'll discover just how much Plowden owes to Hadow's misleadingly dour little document.)

Again, though it was held to advocate unbridled individualism, Plowden actually recommended (para. 1243, subsection 96) 'a combination of individ-ual, group [*sic*] and class work'. The absence of a serial comma here didn't help the cause of clarity, but the general thrust of Plowden's advocacy of 'mixed methods' was pretty evident, and Plowden itself acknowledged (para. 754) what it took the combined efforts of several major classroom research studies finally to bring home many years later: the essentially unrealistic nature of any aspiration towards the complete individualisation of learning in classrooms of 30 or more children.[15]

Yet that particular aspiration, and others supposedly but not actually author-ised by Plowden, took root. I use 'authorised' advisedly, for the third version of Plowden – what people did in its name – was all too often associated with a professional climate in which messianic zeal, absolute head teacher authority and local authority patronage combined to make impossible the realisation of another of Plowden's clearly signalled intentions. This was to sustain as 'one of the mainsprings of progress in primary schools . . . the willingness of teachers to experiment, to innovate and to change' (para. 1151) and to do so by attending closely to evidence from published research, for 'research and practice are parts of a whole, and neither can flourish without the other' (para. 1152).

As John Dewey noted in relation to the American progressive experience and the fate of his own writing: 'An educational idea which professes to be based on the idea of freedom may become as dogmatic as ever was the traditional education which was reacted against.'[16] Later, his widow complained to comparativist Edmund King that Dewey's followers 'could not see their idol for the incense they sent up'.[17]

Something of this fate certainly befell Plowden, as anyone who worked in primary education during that period can testify. Lady Plowden was an unlikely guru, but then the real priesthood here was not the chair or members of the Plowden Committee but those who anointed themselves as interpreters and guardians of its truths for a dependent and compliant teaching force. What came to matter, as I've said, were Plowden versions 2 and 3 rather than the all-important version 1, the *Urtext* of Plowden as published. Regrettably, the sacerdotal imagery I've employed here is not at all far-fetched, for at this time it was sufficient in some quarters to assert 'Plowden says. . .' to block all further discussion.[18]

So this is one cautionary tale for anyone embarking on a new enquiry into primary education. Another is the time which it takes to implement even those changes which seem both sensible and urgent. True, the Educational Priority Area (EPA) scheme was a Plowden success story, the prototype for a succession of socio-educational interventions in poverty and disadvantage culminating in the Pupil Premium and the work of the Education Endowment Foundation, both launched in 2011. But Plowden also recommended as an adjunct to its strategy for tackling social disadvantage the immediate and substantial expansion of pre-school education (para. 343) – yet how long did it take England to come anywhere close to catching up with its continental neighbours in this regard? Relatedly, and pressing home the theme of giving every child the best possible start in life, Plowden argued (para. 215) for close collaboration between educational, social and medical services, but only with the 2004 Children Act and Every Child Matters did seamless multi-agency activity approach becoming a reality, and it took several cases of children suffering the harrowing consequences of agency disarticulation to achieve what common sense as well as Plowden had long demanded.

Beyond these important examples are habits of thought and practice which have survived not just the decades since Plowden but the century which preceded it as well, and have resisted each and every challenge to their hegemony: the class-teacher system (from which Plowden encouraged more deviation than many realise) (paras 752-777); the infant/junior separation (now KS1/2); the two-tier curriculum ('basics' vs. the rest, later repackaged as 'core' and 'other foundation', later as 'excellence and enjoyment'); the defining of those 'basics' as proficiency in the 3Rs but little else, despite all that we know, for instance, about the cognitive and cultural power of talk or the rooting of truly civilised human relations in the capacity to imagine and empathise.

Forty years on: the Cambridge Primary Review

The Cambridge Primary Review was conceived in 1997, the year which in unintended juxtaposition witnessed Tony Blair's 'new dawn' of 'education, education, education' and Plowden's 30th anniversary. The conception was shelved while I worked on the five-nation *Culture and Pedagogy* project, then revisited in 2004 when preparation and the quest for sponsorship began in earnest. The Review was finally launched in October 2006, after seven years of gestation and two years of planning and consultation.

The Review was supported by a major UK charity, the Esmée Fairbairn Foundation, and this gave it the independence from public funding and government interference which was essential to its freedom and credibility. Its remit was to investigate, report and make recommendations on the condition and future of primary education in England. Its scope was broad – three overarching perspectives, ten themes, 23 sub-themes and 100 questions covering every aspect of primary education from aims, curriculum, pedagogy and assessment to school organisation, staffing, teacher training, funding, governance and of course policy. These strictly educational questions were to be framed by others about children, childhood, parenting and caring, the society, cultures and world in which today's children are growing up, and about how all these bear on the education that young children receive. Hence the Review's strapline, which later became the title of its final report: *Children, their World, their Education.*[19]

About each theme we asked 'What is?' and 'What ought to be?' and these descriptive and normative questions were addressed through four complementary strands of evidence. First, and following the usual convention of public enquiries, we invited formal written submissions, and received well over 1000 of them from most of the country's educational organisations, both official and voluntary, and from groups and individuals. The submissions alone yielded a vast compendium of experience and insight. Next, we commissioned 28 surveys of published research relating to the Review's themes and sub-themes: 66 academics in 20 university departments were involved in this strand,[20] and between them they distilled the implications of over 3000 published research sources. Simultaneously we undertook our programme of 'soundings': 250 meetings all over the country with major educational organisations and official bodies including government, opposition parties and quangos, but also and especially with children, parents, teachers, heads, local authorities, voluntary agencies, religious leaders, community representatives, police and others offering perspectives on children and their primary education. Meanwhile, in the

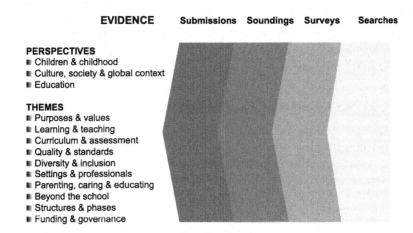

Figure 2.1 The Cambridge Primary Review: perspectives, themes and evidence

'searches', we assembled and re-assessed official demographic and statistical data relevant to our task.

Some reviewers found the Review's methodology opaque. Actually, it was straightforward. The ten designated themes were viewed through the four complimentary lenses I have mentioned – submissions, surveys, soundings and searches. Why that particular combination? Well, the range of themes and the kinds of questions about them that we posed – about fact and value, present and future, policy and practice – demanded it. Opinion surveys on their own would not have been sufficient; nor, despite their empirical scope and depth, would research reviews; nor would official documents. Our evidence needed to draw on, compare and triangulate both official sources *and* academic research; individual or collective opinion *and* the real or aspired-to objectivity of systematic enquiry; unmediated viewpoints *and* face-to-face exploratory discussion; the voices of primary education's many stakeholders (for want of a better term), especially children, teachers and parents; and, providing an essential comparative and global perspective, evidence and insight from other parts of the UK and the wider world (Figure 2.1).

Where did all this lead? Between October 2007 and March 2009 the Review published 31 interim reports, including an account of what had emerged from the 87 regional community soundings, 28 reports on the commissioned surveys of published research, and a two-volume special report on the curriculum. These, with their accompanying four-page briefings and media releases, were published in groups on ten occasions over that 17-month period.[21] Each publication event was preceded by a press conference and hence provoked media attention. Independent media analysis commissioned by our communications director Richard Margrave showed that on five of those ten occasions the Review was top UK news story overall.

In that recurrent media exposure, I suggest, more than in what we actually reported, lay the seeds of the Labour government's growing impatience with the Review and its decision to reject our reports rather than engage with them. In suffering that fate we were not alone. Between 2007 and 2009 I followed the progress of other enquiries on a whole range of topics, some independent, some commissioned by government itself, and came to realise that all of them – all of us – were members of a rather special club. Each of us had produced reports which BBC Radio 4 'Today' deemed important enough to feature before adding, with monotonous but predictable regularity, 'The government has dismissed the findings.'

In October 2009 we published the 600-page final report together with an 850-page companion volume containing revised versions of the 28 research surveys.[22] Between them, the two volumes drew on over 4000 published sources as well as all the other evidence from the submissions, soundings, surveys and searches. Copies of the final report, published by Routledge, were sent to selected great and good, while a 42-page illustrated booklet about the Review and its outcomes prepared by journalists Diane Hofkins and Stephanie Northen[23] was sent to every school in the UK (not just England and not only primary), to every MP and their Scottish, Welsh and Northern Ireland counterparts, to every member of the House of Lords, and to all major educational organisations and teaching unions, a distribution of 44,000 copies.

The final report was prepared by a group of 14 authors led by myself, drawing on data which had been sorted and analysed by the 18 full- and part-time members of the Cambridge team.[24] Commentators like to personalise these things, and in our case the government dragged personalisation down to the unworthy depths of personal smear and flagrant misrepresentation, but the report's conclusions and recommendations were finalised only when we had secured the full agreement of all 14 authors and all 20 members of the Review's distinguished advisory committee, which had been chaired throughout by Dame Gillian Pugh.[25] It remains important to stress that what the Review concluded and recommended was very much a collective matter.

After the final report's publication we entered an intensive phase of dissemination, discussion and debate. We gave the usual political, professional and media briefings, responded to numerous speaking invitations, and organised ten major events of our own: a national launch conference at the Royal Society of Arts (RSA), eight regional conferences for teachers, teacher educators and others, and a national seminar which took stock of the comments and concerns which all these events had generated. From this we distilled 11 policy priorities for primary education which were published in the national press and sent to political and educational leaders shortly before the 2010 general election.[26]

After the 2010 general election dissemination morphed into the establishment of regionally-located professional discussion and implementation networks, and in 2012, when the final grant from the Esmée Fairbairn Foundation ended, Pearson came forward to fund the continuation and expansion of this work until 2017 under the banner of the Cambridge Primary Review Trust.

Themes and perspectives

A national system of primary education offers to an enquiry such as the Cambridge Primary Review, if that enquiry is properly conceived, a dauntingly vast canvas. It is *national*, so it raises questions about culture, values, identities, the condition of English and indeed British society, and the lives and futures of the groups and individuals of which that society is constituted. It is a *system*, so there are questions about policy, structure, organisation, finance and governance to consider. And being an *education* system, it raises a distinctively educational array of questions about the children whose needs, along with those of society, the system claims to address, and about schools, what goes on in them, and the contexts within which they operate. Equally, ostensibly discrete and practical matters such as curriculum, teaching, assessment, leadership and workforce reform raise larger questions of purpose, value and social context. Thus, a curriculum is much more than a syllabus: it is a response to culture and hopes or assumptions about the future; and British culture today is nothing if not complex, while even optimists recognise that the future is highly problematic. Similarly, teaching is not merely a matter of technique, but reflects ideas about thinking, knowing, learning and relating. Assessment, for better or worse, has become as much a political as a professional activity. In turn, all of these are framed, enabled and/or constrained by policy, structure and finance.

So in any national educational review breadth is essential. At the same time, it is impossible to cover everything, and choices must be confronted and made. The coverage of the Cambridge Primary Review was therefore expressed as a hierarchy of 'perspectives', 'themes' and 'questions' so that we could keep constantly in mind what matters most.[27] (See Figure 2.1).

We started with three broad *perspectives* or metathemes: children and childhood; culture, society and the global context; and of course education. In other words, children, the world in which they are growing up, and the schooling which mediates that world and prepares them for it. These were the Review's core concerns and together they provided the framework for its more specific themes and questions. They also anticipated the title of the final report: *Children, their World, their Education*.

Next, ten *themes* attended to those particular matters on which it is agreed that the Review should concentrate: purposes and values; learning and teaching; curriculum and assessment; quality and standards; diversity and inclusion; settings and professionals; parenting, caring and educating; beyond the school; structures and phases; funding and governance.

Finally, for every theme there were sets of 'is' and 'ought' *questions*. These – 100 questions in all – indicated in more precise terms what we needed to investigate, and what we wished to encourage those providing evidence to comment upon.

Space does not permit us to set out the full list of questions we identified under each theme, but it is worth spelling out the three perspectives in full.

Children and Childhood. What do we know about young children's lives in and out of school, and about the nature of childhood, at the start of the twenty-first century? How do children of primary school age develop, think, feel, act and learn? To which of the myriad individual and collective differences between children should educators and related professionals particularly respond? What do children most fundamentally need from those charged with providing their primary education?

Culture, Society and the Global Context. In what kind of society and world are today's children growing up and being educated? In what do England's (and Britain's) cultural differences and commonalities reside? What is the country's likely economic, social and political future? Is there a consensus about the 'good society' and education's role in helping to shape and secure it? What can we predict about the future – social, economic, environmental, moral, political – of the wider world with which Britain is interdependent? What, too, does this imply for children and primary education? What must be done in order that today's children, and their children, have a future worth looking forward to?

Education. Taking the system as a whole, from national policy and overall structure to the fine detail of school and classroom practice, what are the current characteristics, strengths and weaknesses of the English state system of primary education? To what needs and purposes should it be chiefly directed over the coming decades? What values should it espouse? What learning experiences should it provide? By what means can its quality be secured and sustained?

These perspectives also demonstrate some of the most striking conceptual or thematic differences between the Cambridge Primary Review and Plowden. The trail marked by Plowden's chapters starts with 'The Children: their growth and development', progresses to 'The Children and their Environment' and thence into 'The Structure of Primary Education' and onward to aims, learning, curriculum and so on. In as far as Plowden looked outward it addressed – albeit very persuasively – essentially local questions to do with the relationship of community, home and school, especially in the context of social disadvantage. In this it was very much of its time, for the 1960s was the decade of celebrated studies like those of Douglas and Jackson[28] and Educational Priority Areas (EPAs) merely awaited Plowden's nod to spring into life.

The Cambridge Primary Review was also concerned with this vital relationship. Indeed to help us unravel it we met parents and children as well as those who usually purport to speak for them and act in their interests. Yet the Review's perspectives were no less national and international than local. Further, while Plowden seemed to fuel a tendency to see children and society as in opposition – 'children vs. society' became as common a dichotomising slogan as 'children vs. subjects', and perhaps a more damaging one – we regarded the two as inseparable. Partly this arose from acceptance that the child/society duality is untenable because children are members of society and childhood is anyway a social construct; partly it reflected a Vygotskian understanding that culture is an essential ingredient in human development, and that in such development the 'natural' and 'cultural' lines reinforce one another.[29]

There were other reasons to broaden the perspective of a new enquiry into primary education beyond the nexus of child, family, community and school. First, in place of the laissez-faire localism that attended primary education during the 1960s, England in 2006 had one of the more centralised education systems in the developed world and from 1997 it became one of the more tightly policed, especially under Ofsted's second chief inspector, the combative Chris Woodhead.

The language is indicative: Plowden's benign opening maxim 'At the heart of the educational process lies the child' was soon challenged in what was surely a deliberate way – 'The school curriculum is at the heart of education'[30] – when the Thatcher government gave early warning of its intention to take greater control. In turn, with control of curriculum and testing secured by the 1988 Education Reform Act, this generalised repositioning gave way from 1997 to the New Labour machismo of standards, targets, step changes, league tables, task forces, best practice and failing schools, and the endless parade (or 'rolling out') of initiatives and strategies, each habitually but implausibly qualified by 'tough' or 'new', or more commonly by both. From 2003 to 2010 the entire edifice was crowned by a Primary National Strategy[31] with a designated Strategy 'manager' in every local authority.

And it was a culmination. Ten years or so after Plowden, and acting on that report's recommendation, Her Majesty's Inspectors had undertaken a survey of 542 primary schools to see how the system was progressing. They highlighted problems of curriculum breadth, quality, expertise and management and encouraged discussion on ways of using teachers' curriculum specialisms to achieve more even curriculum quality across the school as a whole.[32] But the curriculum itself remained firmly in the hands of schools and local education authorities (LEAs), who indeed responded with rather unwise reluctance to the then government's not unreasonable request for information on how they were fulfilling their statutory curriculum responsibilities.[33]

Ten years on again, in 1988, LEA bluff had been called, England had its National Curriculum, national standards and national tests, and power in these and other matters had been transferred from local authorities to London,[34] though not yet entirely to Downing Street.

Fast forward another decade, to 1998-9: the final frontier had been breached, and the same Labour Party that had raised its hands in horror at the Conservatives' seizure of educational power in 1988 now took to itself powers beyond even Margaret Thatcher's wildest dreams – not just over curriculum and assessment but over the minute-by-minute conduct of teaching itself, as closely-prescribed literacy and numeracy lessons were laid down for every classroom in the land.

It follows, then, that one of the Cambridge Primary Review's central tasks was to establish from both official and independent sources exactly what had happened to the quality of primary education after the defining of educational quality became the prerogative of national government rather than schools and an independent inspectorate. But – and this takes us to the second main justification for the Review – the debate could not stop there, for educational quality and standards are culturally, philosophically and indeed empirically much more complex notions than their political arbiters may admit. Certainly they can no more be exclusively equated with test scores at age 11 than the 3Rs can be defined as the totality of a rounded education.

Thus, beyond the no-nonsense Westminster slogans about standards and a 'real-world' and 'relevant' curriculum lay a country whose real-world consciousness was strikingly permeated by questions of cultural diversity and identity, a country which in one estimate was sleepwalking into racial segregation and communal strife,[35] and which in another had allowed its democratic processes to become dangerously undermined by a combination of public apathy and political chicanery.[36] Such pathologies have as direct a bearing on how we define quality in primary education as do the rituals of national test results, school league tables and Ofsted inspection reports by which quality is officially defined.

In its proper resonances 'quality' is no less international than national or local. Globalisation is hardly a new phenomenon, but the way that by 2006 its absolute primacy as economic and hence educational imperative was insisted upon would surely have startled Lady Plowden's committee. In this matter, the UK's global economic competitiveness, and the country's position in the OECD league tables of student attainment, were undoubtedly important yet only part of the story. The gap between the world's rich and poor continued and continues to widen, while there was and is a fast-growing consensus that escalating climate change and global warming may make this the make-or-break century for humanity as a whole, and that these trends – and whatever can be done to bring them under control – are rooted as directly in public economic policy as in private attitude and aspiration.[37]

To some it may seem far-fetched to link primary education with national identity, democracy, global poverty and climate change, though people are happy enough to link primary education via skill development to global economic competitiveness. Yet such matters bear directly on what we mean, or might mean, by educational quality. Education helps to shape both consciousness and culture, and hence the good society. Today's children will need the knowledge, skills and dispositions not only to cope with the world others have created, but to act on that world in its interests as much as their own.

Meanwhile, there's increasing concern that childhood here and now is being fast eroded by a whole raft of social changes ranging from increased marital breakdown to precocious consumerism, the loss of intergenerational contact and the poverty of the inner lives of those children whose days outside school are dominated by social media, internet games, television, and electronic toys which leave little to the imagination. And today's security-obsessed primary schools, with their reinforced doors, keypads, Criminal Records Bureau-vetted adults and anxious parents waiting in their no less fortress-like SUVs to hurry their children home to tea and texting contrast all too tellingly with the physical openness of schools during the 1960s and 1970s (even though the much-vaunted curricular and pedagogical openness of those schools was often illusory).

It is a statement of the painfully obvious that today's children, and their children, rather than the adults and politicians who confidently make the decisions which affect their futures, will reap the environmental, economic and social whirlwind that many now predict as a certainty rather than a mere possibility; and that such concerns cannot but raise daunting questions about the kind of education which schools should provide and the values they should pursue. Political vision is notoriously short term. Educational vision cannot afford to be: today's primary children will live well into the twenty-first century and on current life-expectancy projections some of them will make the twenty-second. Education cannot conceivably cater for every life-chance contingency, let alone when so much is fluid and uncertain, but it can at least strive to lay an appropriate foundation for a challenging future, and in doing so acknowledge that its agency is moral no less than instrumental.[38]

Such concerns shaped the rationale for the Cambridge Primary Review. These, and the need to take stock of the impact for better or worse of 20 years of growing government intervention in a sector which during the Plowden era had been left very much to its own devices – maybe too much for its own good. And, too, there was a need to bring together and make sense of the extensive evidence which by then was available.

Can a national enquiry make a difference?

Nothing can be guaranteed, and even if the Review's interim and final reports were to make a media splash there was no guaranteed route thence to thoughtful consideration and appropriate application of the Review's analysis, findings and recommendations. The mixed fate of Plowden and the premature demise of many other deserving enquiries provided a constant warning of how difficult it can be to make a difference outside one's local patch, especially if one's messages go against the political or cultural grain.

What we could say at the outset, though, was that the Review took nearly three years to plan and that much of that time was devoted to careful consultation with a wide range of interested individuals and groups. As a result, though the Review's independence was everywhere understood, its team established constructive working relationships with the Department for Education and Skills, Office for Standards in Education, Qualifications and Curriculum Authority, Teaching and Development Agency and the General Teaching Council, with the two main opposition parties, and with the all-party Commons Education and Skills Committee; and, beyond such official bodies, with the teaching unions, with major faith groups, and with a large number of professional organisations. And it is worth recording that on the day of the Review's formal launch in October 2006 I received a personal note from Alan Johnson MP, the then Secretary of State for Education and Skills, welcoming the Review, wishing it every success and promising his department's co-operation. Regrettably, he was replaced eight months later by the much less accommodating Ed Balls, shortly before the publication of the Review's first interim report. Balls remained in post from June 2007 until Labour's defeat in the May 2010 general election.

Unlike Plowden, ours was not an officially commissioned enquiry and, notwithstanding the cordial working relations we thought we had secured with government and statutory agencies, we could presume nothing about the level of official support which our findings and recommendations might secure. On the other hand, some predicted that because these days no Secretary of State would risk giving a government-commissioned enquiry into primary education the freedom which Sir Edward Boyle granted to Lady Plowden's committee in August 1963 ('to consider primary education in all its aspects'), a genuinely independent enquiry might attract attention precisely because it could ask what it wanted, and say what needed to be said in light of the evidence it received.

Unlike Plowden again, we were not staking everything on a single final report, but decided to put our evidence into the public domain as soon as it emerged in order to stimulate debate and provide a feedback loop for the preparation of our final report. In this, also unlike Plowden, we had the enormous resource of electronic communications to assist us. For the rest, we hoped that there were sufficient people of goodwill who shared our concern about the importance of primary education and the world in which our children were growing up. We hoped that they would be prepared to join the debate, submit evidence and help us to construct an accurate and illuminating account of the strengths and weaknesses of contemporary English primary education; and that on this basis we might formulate a vision for the future which lifted educational horizons above the prevailing preoccupation with government initiatives, and reinstate a vision of teaching as more than mere compliance.[39]

Notes

1 Board of Education 1931.
2 Central Advisory Council for Education 1967.
3 Cunningham 1988.
4 Marshall 1963; Armstrong 1980, 2006, 2011; Drummond 1989, 2003.
5 Baker 2009.
6 Peters 1968; Dearden 1976.
7 Simon 1981a; Alexander 1984.
8 Cox and Dyson 1971. See also media and political responses to the 1986–91 Leeds Primary Needs Evaluation Project and the subsequent 1991–2 'three wise men' government initiative (Alexander 1997).
9 *Daily Telegraph*, 7 November 1991.
10 Alexander *et al* 1992.
11 Alexander 1992. The embedded quotation is from Alexander *et al* 1992, 10.
12 Thornton 1993.
13 Barber 2001, 13-14.
14 Newspaper headlines quoted in Alexander 1997, xiii–xv.
15 Galton and Simon 1980; Alexander *et al* 1992; Simon 1992.
16 Ravitch 1983, 59.

17 King 1979, 343.
18 Alexander 1984, chapter 1.
19 Alexander 2010a.
20 Listed in Alexander 2010a, 519–20.
21 All this media material can be found at https://cprtrust.org.uk/cpr/cpr-media-cover-age/ (accessed May 2021).
22 Alexander 2010a; Alexander *et al* 2010.
23 Hofkins and Northen 2009.
24 Listed in Alexander 2010a, 518–9.
25 Listed in Alexander 2010a, 520–1.
26 Cambridge Primary Review 2010.
27 The Review's perspectives, themes and questions are in Alexander 2010a, Appendix 2, 522–6.
28 Douglas 1964; Jackson and Marsden 1962
29 Vygotsky 1981.
30 CACE 1967, para 9; Department of Education and Science 1981, 1.
31 Department for Education and Skills 2003.
32 Department of Education and Science 1978.
33 Department of Education and Science 1977.
34 Actually, for a while the National Curriculum Council was based in York, but London soon reasserted itself.
35 Phillips 2005
36 Power Enquiry 2006.
37 Stern 2007.
38 Alexander 2006b.
39 Alexander 2004b.

3   Health of a nation

Each of the interim reports from the Cambridge Primary Review, like its final report, was accompanied by a four-page leaflet-style briefing modelled on those produced by the 1993 National Commission on Education.[1] The briefings publicised each report's main findings and concerns in compressed and, we hoped, accessible form.[2] This chapter samples just three of the 41 briefings released between 2007 and 2010. *Community Soundings* (October 2007) summarised from the report of that name the hopes and concerns of teachers, parents, children and community representatives at the 87 focus group sessions convened in different parts of England during the Review's first few months.[3] Two years later, *The Final Report* (October 2009) did the same job with the full range of Review evidence and the much more substantial *Children, their World, their Education: final report and recommendations of the Cambridge Primary Review.*[4] Then, with the May 2010 general election in sight, *Policy Priorities for Primary Education* (April 2010) drew on the Review's initial period of dissemination to highlight major issues of primary education policy requiring attention by the incoming government, whether Labour or Conservative – or, as it turned out, a rather unequal coalition of Conservatives and Liberal Democrats. The latter briefing also featured at the New Visions for Education Group's National Forum on Education and the Election (London, March 2010), and the annual conference of the National Union of Teachers (Liverpool, April 2010), and was reprinted in *The Guardian* on 27 April 2010.

This chapter's title alludes less to Adam Smith than to Ernest Boyer's maxim 'A report card on public education is a report card on the nation'.[5]

Community soundings (2007)

The community soundings were regionally-based one- or two-day events. Their aim was to discuss matters central to the Review's remit with those at the education system's point of delivery; to explore the relationship between school and community; to uncover key areas of consensus and divergence across both constituencies and venues; and to identify issues and questions to take forward to the Review's national soundings and, in combination with other evidence, into the final report.

The soundings, which took place between January and March 2007, included meetings with those involved in the day-to-day work of primary schools and representatives of the wider community: teachers, teaching assistants and other support staff, teachers, heads, and children themselves; parents, school governors, local authority officials and elected members, representatives of statutory and voluntary agencies concerned with children's welfare, employers, religious leaders, community leaders, the police, legal officers; and members of groups who are perceived to be marginalised by the education system, such as migrants

DOI: 10.4324/9781315169378-4

and Gypsy, Roma and Traveller communities. There were nine sets of community soundings in different parts of England, some of them multi-site, with 87 sessions attended by over 750 witnesses.

The full report *Community Soundings* summarises, constituency by constituency, what emerged from these witness sessions, starting with children and moving out from the classroom to the school and the wider community. Regional differences are noted, and the report ends by identifying issues and questions for the National Soundings, which in autumn 2007 initiated the process of assessing evidence from all of the Review's sources, not just this one.

Community Soundings covers a wide range of themes, and this briefing cannot do justice to all of them. About the data as a whole, however, we record three striking findings:

- In spite of our careful attempts to elicit and record differences among the witnesses, there is a substantial measure of agreement on key issues such as the aims of primary education, the curriculum, assessment, the condition of childhood and society, and the world in which today's children are growing up. This consensus transcends both constituency and location.
- Although witnesses – especially children themselves – had much to say which was positive, the responses overall reveal a pervasive anxiety about the current educational and social contexts, including significant areas of recent policy, and a deeper pessimism about the world in which today's children are growing up.
- Despite this, the schools themselves provided optimistic and caring settings for children's development and learning, and were highly valued by children, parents and their communities.

The views which we most frequently heard were these:

- that today's children are under intense and perhaps excessive pressure from the policy-driven demands of their schools and the commercially-driven values of the wider society;
- that family life and community are breaking down;
- that respect and empathy both within and between generations are in decline;
- that life for young children outside the school gates is increasingly insecure and, in many areas, dangerous (though for many parents the chief perceived danger is traffic);
- that the wider world is changing rapidly and in ways which it is not always easy to comprehend, though on balance the changes give cause for alarm, especially in respect of global warming, environmental sustainability and geo-political stability;
- that the primary curriculum is too rigidly prescribed and, because of the pressure of SATs, too narrow;

- that primary pupils' educational careers are being distorted by the dominance of the national tests, especially in Years 5 and 6;
- that though some government initiatives, notably *Every Child Matters*, are to be warmly welcomed, others – especially in the domains of curriculum, assessment and pedagogy – may constrain and disempower rather than enable;
- that the task facing teachers and other professionals who work with children is, for these and other reasons, much more difficult now than it was a generation ago.

Negative responses might suggest negative questioning, or that respondents have been unduly influenced by the gloomy tenor of the news stories of the day. *Community Soundings* examines both of these possibilities and finds that the line of questioning was open rather than leading, that witnesses frequently referred to specific local issues by way of illustration, and that the voices represented here are both authentic and – in view of their consistency across 87 sessions and nine very different regional venues – representative of a wider national mood.

Pessimism turned to hope when witnesses felt they had the power to act. Thus, the children who were most confident that climate change might not overwhelm them were those whose schools had decided to replace unfocused fear by factual information and practical strategies for energy reduction and sustainability. Similarly, the teachers who were least worried by national initiatives were those who responded to them with robust criticism rather than resentful compliance, and asserted their professional right to go their own way. There is a lesson from such empowerment for government as well as schools. Of course, not even the most enterprising school can reverse some of the social trends which worried many of our witnesses. That being so, these community soundings have implications for social and economic policy more generally, and for public attitudes and values, not merely for government and the schools.

Among the locally specific issues, which across the soundings represented differences more of emphasis than of substance, were the following:

- The loss of local employment opportunities, and educational routes to such employment, for what are often referred to as the 'less academic' children.
- The aggravation of the gap between high and lower achievers, already greater in England than in many other countries, by both local circumstances and an inflexible national curriculum.
- The extent to which the retention of selective secondary education in some areas adds to the difficulties faced by the lower achievers.
- The need to re-assess the case for the three-tier system of education, and for middle schools in particular, before they are finally phased out (a strong case for their retention was made on developmental grounds).

- Differences in the way schools are perceived, valued and used in affluent and less affluent areas, with more affluent families establishing 'parallel' systems of coaching and other out-of-school support for their children, while less affluent families see the school itself as the best available resource, socially as well as educationally.
- Variation, within a common framework of deep concern about parenting and home-school relations, in respect of the form that such relations should take, the best ways to support parents of children with special needs, and ways that schools can engage with parents who are hard to reach or who have low aspirations for their children.
- The challenge of balancing respect for difference with the fostering of a shared sense of identity, especially in communities where there are concentrations of what in national terms are defined as ethnic and/or religious minorities.
- The failure of an essentially urban-oriented education system to address the distinctive challenges and needs of small and rural primary schools, and the difficulty which small schools have in responding positively to pressure towards school clustering for mutual support when the national system places them in competition with each other.
- The essential unreliability of national data on migration, and the failure of resourcing to match local educational need in areas with growing migrant populations, especially when such groups are dispersed rather than concentrated.
- The need for an education system historically premised on stability to be more responsive to change and transience in school intakes, which for demographic and cultural reasons are now a fact of national life.

The report identifies 47 significant questions generated by the community soundings on which we agreed to consult during the National Soundings and to probe through evidence from the Review's other strands. These are grouped under eight headings:

- *Changing national and global contexts.* The question of how primary schools should respond to: climate change, environmental sustainability and global poverty; increasingly uncertain employment prospects; the perceived decline in community, social cohesion and intergenerational empathy and respect; the perceived growth in selfishness, materialism and anti-social behaviour; migration and growing ethnic and religious diversity; children's personal safety in increasingly dangerous urban environments; the benefits and dangers of the information society.
- *Children and childhood.* Children and childhood under pressure. The myth or reality of 'childhood innocence' lost. Strengthening and resourcing the implementation of Every Child Matters. Attending to the needs of mobile children (looked-after, migrant, and Gypsy, Roma and Traveller children) in a system premised on stability of pupil intake. Coping with a profile of

special needs in which behavioural difficulties are increasingly prominent. Making school councils more than tokenistic and making 'children's voice' a genuinely equitable movement which empowers children as learners and future citizens.

- *Parenting, caring and educating.* Parenting in decline: reality or myth? Strengthening home-school partnership and building the necessary relationship of mutual trust and respect. Addressing the perennial challenge of parents who have low educational aspirations for their children, and/or are hard to reach. Securing parental interest and involvement in children's education throughout compulsory schooling, not just in the early years.
- *Aims, values and the curriculum.* Reassessing the aims of primary education and the values by which it is underpinned. Shifting from the currently narrow view of utility to one which is based on a more comprehensive and humane analysis of what is necessary for a productive adult life. The place of creativity and alternative views of a rounded and balanced primary education. The balance of knowledge and skills and the current vogue for reconfiguring the curriculum in terms of the latter. The place of religious faith in the primary school. The early and later years curriculum: different in degree or nature? The relationship of the foundation stage to KS1.
- *Assessment.* How best to address the perceived problems of SATs: excessive pressure on children and teachers; distortion of the primary curriculum. The uses and abuses of tests. The relationship and balance of assessment for accountability and assessment for learning. Establishing who needs to know what about children's progress and achievement.
- *Learning, teaching and teachers.* The relationship between common sense and research-based views of effective learning and teaching. Reassessing the pedagogical basis of recent official interventions in primary teaching. The adequacy of primary teacher training for the job which primary teachers perform; standards of entry to training courses and to the profession. The adequacy of continuing professional development (CPD) arrangements for supporting primary teachers' transition from novice to expert roles. The relationship between the roles of teacher and teaching assistant, and the training and remuneration of the latter. The impact of workforce reform.
- *Schools, structures, ages and stages.* Starting compulsory schooling: is age five too young? Revisiting the three-tier system in light of children's developmental and social needs. De-stressing school transfer. The tasks and roles of primary heads: are they too many and too diverse, and on what should they really concentrate? Supporting small schools: balancing support through clustering with respect for individuality.
- *Funding and governance.* Eliminating funding inequities and anomalies between local authorities and schools. Making funding more responsive to the uncertain demographics of migration. Achieving qualitative consistency between local authorities. The National Literacy, Numeracy and Primary Strategies: what is the truth about their quality, implementation and impact? Centralisation, national agencies and the balance of control and

responsibility between national government, local authorities and schools. The reality of recently announced 'flexibilities' and 'freedoms' offered by government to schools.

The final report (2009)

Context and content

Since October 2006, with the support of the Esmée Fairbairn Foundation, the Cambridge Primary Review has been investigating the condition and future of primary education in England. Between October 2007 and February 2009 the Review's 31 interim reports examined matters as diverse as childhood, parenting, learning, teaching, testing, educational standards, the curriculum, school organi-sation, teacher training and the impact of national policy. Many of these reports provoked considerable media and public interest and have influenced both policy and the wider debate.

Now the Review presents *Children, their World, their Education: final report and recommendations of the Cambridge Primary Review.*[6] This 608-page report draws on over 4000 published sources as well as commissioned research surveys, writ-ten submissions, face-to-face soundings and searches of official data. It aims to combine evidence about what *is* with a vision of what *might be.*

Part 1 sets the scene and tracks primary education policy since the 1960s. Part 2 examines children's development and learning, their lives outside school and their needs, aspirations and prospects in a changing world. Part 3 explores what goes on in primary schools, from the formative early years to aims, curriculum, pedagogy, assessment, standards and school organisation. Part 4 deals with the system as a whole: ages and stages; schools and other agencies; teacher training, leadership and workforce reform; governance, funding and policy. Part 5 draws everything together with 78 formal conclusions and 75 recommendations for future policy and practice.

A report of the length and complexity of *Children, their World, their Education* is not readily compressed into a four-page briefing, so here, by way of taster rather than summary, are some key points from the report's concluding chapter.

The bottom line: how good is English primary education and where is it heading?

Primary schools: how well are they doing?

The Review finds England's primary schools under intense pressure, but in good heart and in general doing a good job. Investment in primary education has risen dramatically and many recent policies have had a positive impact. Highly valued by children and parents, primary schools now represent, for many, stability and positive values in a world where much else is changing and uncertain. Contrary to populist claims, schools are not in danger of subversion by 1970s ideologues and they do not neglect the 3Rs. The real problems are very different: on these, and on what genuinely requires reappraisal and improvement, the Cambridge report points the way.

What is primary education for?

For too long the aims of primary education have been confused or tokenistic; and, too often, aims tend to set off grandly in one direction while the curriculum follows a much narrower path. The school system requires a coherent set of aims uniting its various phases, but each phase is developmentally and educationally so distinct that it needs its own vision too. The report proposes a framework of 12 aims grounded in its evidence on the imperatives of childhood, society and the wider world today. Such aims should drive curriculum, pedagogy and school life rather than be tagged on as an afterthought. The Review wants its proposed aims to be properly debated, and presents them as a carefully-considered alternative to the more usual 'off the shelf' approach.

Childhood, society, policy: three recurrent and pervasive themes

Empowering children, respecting childhood

There are legitimate concerns about the quality of children's lives, and about the transient values and materialist pressures to which they are subject, but the 'crisis' of contemporary childhood may have been overstated, and children themselves were the Review's most upbeat witnesses. The truly urgent crisis concerns not the pursuit of shallow celebrity but the fate of those children whose lives are blighted by poverty, disadvantage, risk and discrimination, and here governments are right to intervene. Meanwhile, among the many positives of modern childhood, the report celebrates the research evidence on just how much young children know, understand and can do, and argues for an education which heeds their voices and empowers them for life as both learners and citizens. The report also argues that childhood's rich potential should be protected from a system apparently bent on pressing children into a uniform mould at an ever-younger age.

A world fit to grow up in?

While governments equivocate on global warming and climate change, parents and children do not. The condition of British society and the wider world generated considerable anxiety among the Review's witnesses, the more so as they noted that today's primary school pupils will be only in their forties when the world reaches what some predict as the tipping point for climate change. This, allied with concerns about the loss of identity, community, social cohesion and mutual respect, made many witnesses deeply pessimistic about the future. But again the antidote was empowerment: pessimism turned to hope when witnesses felt they could take control and make a difference, whether in relation to environmental sustainability and active citizenship or in the face of the latest official initiative.

Policy: solution or problem?

The report assesses reaction to the many recent policies and initiatives for primary education and finds that while the childhood agenda is applauded, the standards agenda is viewed less favourably; not because of opposition to high standards or accountability – far from it – but because of the way the apparatus of targets, testing, performance tables, national strategies and inspection is believed to distort children's primary schooling for questionable returns. There is also concern about the policy *process*, and in this education appears to mirror the wider problems recorded by those who see British democracy in retreat. In common with other recent studies, the report notes the questionable evidence on which some key educational policies have been based; the disenfranchising of local voice; the rise of unelected and unaccountable groups taking key decisions behind closed doors; the 'empty rituals' of consultation; the authoritarian mindset; and the use of myth and derision to underwrite exaggerated accounts of progress and discredit alternative views.

Standards, structures, curriculum, testing and teaching

Standards: beyond the rhetoric

For over two decades the word 'standards' has dominated educational politics. The report re-assesses both the prevailing concept of standards – finding it restricted, restrictive and misleading – and the national and international evidence on what has happened to primary school standards in recent years. From this evidence we conclude that the picture is neither as rosy nor as bleak as opposing camps tend to claim. Subject to the limitations of the conventional definition, many of the positive claims about standards can be sustained, but so too can some of the negatives; there are methodological problems with some of the test procedures and data; and several of the more spectacular assertions (such as that in 1997 English primary education was at a 'low state', or that testing of itself drives up standards, or that SATs are the only way to hold schools to account) have little or no basis in evidence.

Children's needs: equalising provision in an unequal society

The Review supports initiatives like Every Child Matters, the Children's Plan and Narrowing the Gap, which seek to make the lives of all children more secure and to reduce the gap in outcomes between vulnerable children and the rest. But England remains a country of massive inequality, and the persistent 'long tail' of underachievement, in which Britain compares unfavourably with many other countries, maps closely onto gross disparities in income, health, housing, risk and wellbeing. Reducing these gaps must remain a priority for social and economic policy generally, not just for education. There is also excessive local variation in provision for children with special educational needs, and the report calls for a full SEN review.

Matching ages, stages and structures

The English insistence on the earliest possible start to formal schooling, against the grain of international evidence and practice, is educationally counterproductive. The Early Years Foundation Stage should be renamed and extended to age six, and early years provision should be strengthened in its quality and staffing so that children are properly prepared – socially, linguistically and experientially – for formal learning. The Key Stage 1/2 division should be replaced by a single primary phase, yielding seamless progress through Foundation (0–6) and Primary (6–11). The desirability of raising the school starting age in line with these changes should then be examined, though we are more concerned with the content of early education than structure.

The curriculum: not there yet

There is much unfinished business from previous national curriculum reviews. The report disputes the Rose Review's claim that the central problem is 'quarts into pint pots' and shows how the quality of the curriculum, as well as its manageability, reflect patterns of staffing and notions of professional expertise which have survived since the nineteenth century and have skewed the entire discourse of curriculum. The report also rejects the claim that schools can deliver either standards in the 'basics' or a broad curriculum but not both, and argues that in any case the notion of 'basics' should reflect twenty-first-century realities and needs. The report proposes a curriculum which is driven by the proposed 12 aims (see 'What is primary education for?') and is realised through eight clearly-specified domains of knowledge, skill and enquiry, central to which are language, oracy and literacy. It also guarantees entitlement to breadth, balance and quality; combines a national framework with an innovative and locally-responsive 'community curriculum'; encourages greater professional flexibility and creativity; demands a more sophisticated debate about subjects and knowledge than currently obtains; and requires a re-think of primary school teaching roles, expertise and training.

Assessment: reform, not tinkering

The report unequivocally supports both public accountability and the raising of standards, but – like several others – it is critical of prevailing approaches to testing in primary schools, and the collateral damage they are perceived to have caused. It commends not the marginal adjustment of recent proposals but a total re-think. Summative assessment at the end of the primary phase should be retained, but assessment for accountability should be uncoupled from assessment for learning. The narrow focus of SATs, which treat literacy and numeracy as proxies for the whole of primary education, should be replaced by a system which reports on children's attainment in all areas of their education, with minimal disruption and greater use of teacher assessment. School and system performance should be monitored through sample testing and an improved model of inspection.

A pedagogy of evidence and principle, not prescription

The report finds support for the claim that national tests, national teaching strategies, inspection, centrally-determined teacher training and ring-fenced finance have together produced a 'state theory of learning'; and it views as suspect some of what has been imposed. The report argues for a pedagogy of repertoire and principle rather than recipe and prescription, and proposes reforms in teacher training to match. It wants teaching to be fully rather than selectively informed by research, especially by pedagogical, psychological and neuroscientific evidence which clarifies the conditions for effective learning and teaching. The principle that it is not for government or government agencies to tell teachers how to teach, abandoned in 1997, should be reinstated.

Expertise for entitlement: re-thinking school staffing

The report commends recent increases in the numbers of teachers and teaching assistants (TAs), and efforts to give primary teachers status, incentives and support. But there is a historic and growing mismatch between the tasks primary schools are required to undertake and the professional resources available to them. TAs are no substitute for teachers, or for the expertise which a modern curriculum requires. At issue is the viability of a system which continues to treat the generalist class-teacher role as the default. The report calls for a full review of primary school staffing which properly assesses the nature of the expertise which a modern primary education requires, taking account of the full diversity of schools' work. The report particularly underlines the importance of teachers' domain or subject knowledge – the point at which the class-teacher system is most vulnerable – because research shows that it is the teacher's depth of engagement with what is to be taught, allied to skill in providing feedback on learning, that separates expert teachers from the rest. It argues for training and resources which enable schools to mix the undeniably important role of class teacher with those of semi-specialist and specialist, so that every school can meet the Review's definition of educational entitlement as access to the highest possible standards of teaching in all curriculum domains, regardless of how much or how little time is allocated to them. The report supports moves to distributed school leadership, but urges that heads be given more support, especially in their non-educational tasks, and that they should be helped to concentrate on the job for which they are most needed – leading learning.

From novice to expert: reforming initial teacher training (ITT) and continuing professional development (CPD)

While applauding the dedication of the primary teaching force, the report contests the claim that England's teachers are 'the best-trained ever' on the grounds that it cannot be proved and encourages complacency, and that certain vital aspects of teaching are neglected in ITT. In line with its recommendations on school staffing, the report wants ITT to prepare teachers for a greater variety of classroom roles. It rejects training for mere 'delivery' or 'compliance' and urges that more attention be given to evidence-based pedagogy, subject expertise, curriculum analysis and the open exploration of questions of value and purpose. It queries the value and empirical basis of the current TDA standards for professional certification and advancement, finding them out of line with research as well as too generalised to discriminate securely between the different professional levels, and recommends their replacement by a framework which is properly validated against research and pupil learning outcomes. It urges the end of 'one-size-fits-all' CPD and commends an approach which balances support for inexperienced and less secure teachers with freedom and respect for the experienced and talented.

Local and national

Schools in communities, schools as communities

The report supports government initiatives to encourage multi-agency working across the boundaries of education and care, and argues for greater use of mutual professional support through clustering, federation, all-through schools and the exchange of specialist expertise. It highlights the considerable communal potential of schools, and wants this to be enacted through curriculum and pedagogy as well as through 'joined-up' relations with parents, carers and community groups. The proposed community curriculum partnerships could be catalysts for this activity. With their strong educational record and vital community role in mind, the report urges that small and rural schools be safeguarded against cost-cutting closure. It also warns against the closure of middle schools, commending attention to witnesses' developmental arguments for their retention at a time of anxiety that children are growing up too soon. In the matter of funding, too, the Review believes that the historic primary-secondary funding differential, which has defied the recommendations of official enquiries since 1931, and from which 7–11 schools suffer particular disadvantage, should finally be eliminated.

Decentralising control, redirecting funds, raising standards

The Review finds a widespread perception that notwithstanding the delegation of school budgets and staffing, the centralisation of the core educational activities of curriculum, assessment, teaching, inspection and teacher training has gone too far. The report calls for the responsibilities of government, national bodies, local authorities and schools to be re-balanced; and for top-down control and edict to be replaced by professional empowerment, mutual accountability and proper respect for research and experience.

Policy priorities (2010)

Since the publication of its final report in October 2009, the Cambridge Primary Review has organised and contributed to numerous regional, national and international events convened to consider the Review's findings. Simultaneously, the media, politicians and public figures have joined the debate on matters within the Review's orbit: childhood, the social and cultural conditions in which today's children are growing up, the curriculum, classroom practice, standards, testing, teacher training, leadership, school organisation, educational ages and stages . . . and much more.

Public and professional reaction to the Review has been overwhelmingly positive, political reaction rather less so, initially at least. But in approaching the general election, party leaders should be aware that the Review and its final report are widely perceived to have captured as well as prompted a general desire for change: change not just in the way primary education is conceived and practised but also in the way that those who shape educational policy go about their business.

Perhaps the most frequent observation of teachers at our initial dissemination events was this: 'We're impressed by the Cambridge Primary Review's evidence. We like the ideas. We want to take them forward. But we daren't do so without permission from Ofsted and our SIPS' (local authority school improvement partners). Fortunately, not all teachers say this and not all Ofsted inspectors or SIPs give them cause; and the Cambridge Primary Review (CPR) has now launched a network linking those who are keen to build on the report and in many cases have begun to do so – without permission. Yet the fact that some of our most senior education professionals fear to act as their training, experience, judgement and local knowledge dictate is a symptom of what has gone wrong. The Westminster reforms which electorally-attentive parliamentary candidates are queuing up to endorse must be about much more than parliamentary expenses.

Drawing on both its final report and the dissemination events during 2009–10, CPR has identified 11 policy priorities for primary education. But here's the proviso: we commend these not just to the incoming Prime Minister and Secretary of State, but also to schools. For if schools assume that reform is the task of government alone, then compliance will not give way to empowerment, and dependence on unargued prescription will continue to override the marshalling and scrutiny of evidence.

Thus, from the list that follows, government can and should lead on matters like assessment reform, the long-overdue primary staffing review and enhanced teacher education. These are the keys that together can unlock the door to both a richer curriculum and higher educational standards. For, as the Review's evidence shows, the two go hand in hand. Government must also lead, as to its credit it has done, on striving to tackle the multiple crises of childhood poverty, social disadvantage and educational underachievement, for these too are closely linked and they demand action across a much wider spectrum of public policy than education alone.

But in taking the lead on such pressing matters government must not presume that they can be fixed by setting up compliant 'expert groups' from which the real experts are excluded, or by dismissing evidence other than that which supports the party line. Assessment is perhaps the most prominent instance where much-needed reform has been blocked by dogma and politically-filtered evidence, and even by attempts to portray those who argue for reform as opponents of standards and accountability. This, then, takes us to the political sea-change on which much else depends: a radical overhaul of the policy process itself and the relationship between government and national agencies on the one hand and schools, researchers, teacher educators and local authorities on the other.

This political transformation will not happen voluntarily or overnight. It requires those in the educational front line to take hold of the agenda and make it their own; and it requires sustained effort and, for some, professional re-education. For, as the Review's final report notes, 'a process which over the course of two decades has concentrated so much power at the centre . . . cannot be instantly unpicked . . . Centrally-determined versions of teaching are all that many teachers know.'

Thus, many of the priorities listed later will be advanced only if teachers, and the communities they serve, seize the opportunity and the evidence provided by initiatives such as the Cambridge Primary Review, and use them to debate the central educational questions which too often go by default: what primary education is for; what constitutes an enabling and balanced curriculum; how research on learning and teaching can be translated into effective classroom practice that engages every child; in what kinds of decisions about their lives and learning young children can or should be involved; how educational quality and standards should be defined and assessed; and how – individually and in partnership – schools should be organised. Equally, these questions are the stuff of an initial teacher education which, while not deviating one jot from the vital task of building young teachers' classroom knowledge and skill, helps them to become thinking professionals rather than unquestioning operatives.

So the alternative to prescription and micro-management is not unaccountable license. CPR is very clear that teachers should always be able to give a coherent justification for their decisions, citing evidence, principle and aim, and this requires reforms in their training, continuing development and leadership to produce a more convincing articulation of research and practice.

Here, then, are the policy priorities that our dissemination partners distilled from the 75 recommendations with which the Cambridge Primary Review's final report ends. It is not exclusive, for the report identifies much more that needs to change than can be summarised here. But this, we suggest, is where reform should concentrate its attention.

Accelerate the drive to reduce England's gross and overlapping gaps in wealth, well-being and educational attainment, all of them far wider in England than most other developed countries. Understand that teachers can do only so much to close the attainment gap for as long as the lives of so many children are blighted by poverty and disadvantage. Excellence for all requires equity.

Make children's agency and rights a reality in policy, schools and classrooms. Apply the UN Convention on the Rights of the Child in ways that reinforce what we now know about how children most effectively learn, but do so with common sense and an understanding of context so that 'pupil voice' does not degenerate into tokenism or fad.

Consolidate the Early Years Foundation Stage, extending it to age six so as to give young children the best possible foundation for oracy, literacy, numeracy, the wider curriculum and lifelong learning. And if there is still any doubt about what CPR said on this matter, let it be understood that this is about the character of the early years and early primary *curriculum,* not the school starting age.

Address the perennially neglected question of what primary education is for. The Mrs Beeton approach – first catch your curriculum, then liberally garnish with aims – is not the way to proceed. Aims must be grounded in a clear framework of values – for education is at heart a moral matter – and in properly argued positions on childhood, society, the wider world and the nature and advancement of knowledge and understanding. And aims should *shape* curriculum, pedagogy, assessment and the wider life of the school, not be added as mere decoration.

Replace curriculum tinkering by genuine curriculum reform. Seize the opportunity presented by the dropping of the primary curriculum clauses from the Children, Schools and Families Bill and the launch of the new national curriculum review. Understand that the Rose Review's narrow remit prevented it from addressing some of the problems of the primary curriculum which are most in need of attention, especially the counterproductive sacrificing of curriculum entitlement to a needlessly restricted notion of 'standards', the corrosive split between the 'basics' and the rest, the muddled posturing on subjects, knowledge and skills, and the vital matter of the relationship between curriculum quality, expertise and staffing; and that the curriculum debate therefore remains wide open. But don't think that the minimalism of the 1950s (or 1870s) is an adequate alternative. Look instead at the Cambridge model: an aims-driven entitlement curriculum of breadth, richness and contemporary relevance, which secures the basics and much more besides, and combines a national framework with a strong local component.

Abandon the dogma that there is no alternative to SATs. Stop treating testing and assessment as synonymous. Stop making Year 6 tests bear the triple burden of assessing pupils, evaluating schools and monitoring national performance. Abandon the naive belief that testing of itself drives up standards. It doesn't: good teaching does. Initiate wholesale assessment reform drawing on the wealth of alternative models now available, so that we can at last have systems of formative and summative assessment – in which tests certainly have a place – which do their jobs validly, reliably and without causing collateral damage. Adopt the CPR's definition of standards as excellence in *all* domains of the curriculum to which children are statutorily entitled, not just the 3Rs. And understand that those who argue for reform are every bit as committed to rigorous assessment and accountability as those who pin everything on the current tests. The issue is not *whether* children should be assessed or schools should be accountable – they should – but *how* and in relation to *what*.

Replace the pedagogy of official recipe by pedagogies of repertoire, evidence and principle. Recognise that this is no soft option, for in place of mere compliance with what others expect, we want teachers to be accountable to evidence so that they can justify the decisions they take. Note that the CPR's evaluation of over 4000 published sources shows how far that evidence differs from some versions of 'best practice' which teachers are currently required to adopt. As the Cambridge report says: 'Children will not learn to think for themselves if their teachers are expected merely to do as they are told.'

Replace the government's professional standards for teachers, which have limited evidential provenance, by a framework validated by research about how teachers develop as they progress from novice to expert. Retain guidance and support for those who need it, but liberate the nation's most talented teachers – and hence the learning of their pupils – from banal and bureaucratic prescriptions. Balance the need to give new teachers the necessary knowledge, skill and confidence for their first appointment with the vital ingredient that teacher educators have been forced to drop: critical engagement with the larger questions of educational context, content and purpose.

Grasp at last the primary school staffing nettle. Recognise that the generalist classteacher system inherited from the nineteenth century confers undoubted educational benefits, but that in terms of the range and depth of knowledge required by a modern curriculum it may demand more than many teachers can give. Initiate a full review of primary school staffing, assessing expertise, roles and numbers against the tasks which primary schools are required to undertake. Consider more flexible ways of staffing primary schools using a mix of generalists, semi-specialists and specialists, and exploit opportunities for professional partnerships and exchanges, especially for small schools. Re-assess, too, the balance of teachers, teaching assistants and other support staff. Give head teachers time and support to do the job for which they are most needed: leading learning and assuring quality.

Help schools to work in partnership with each other and with their communities rather than in competition, sharing ideas, expertise and resources – including across the primary/secondary divide – and together identifying local educational needs and opportunities. End the league table rat race and – since Finland is the country whose educational standards policymakers seek to match – note Finland's paramount commitment to social and educational equity through a genuinely comprehensive school system of consistently high quality.

Re-balance the relationship between government, national agencies, local authorities and schools. Reverse the centralising thrust of recent policy. End government micro-management of teaching. Require national agencies and local authorities to be independent advisers rather than political cheerleaders or enforcers, and to argue their cases with due rigour. Re-invigorate parental and community engagement in schools and the curriculum. Abandon myth, spin and the selective use of evidence. Restore the checks and balances which are so vital to the formulation of sound policy. Exploit the unrivalled compendium of evidence and ideas which the Cambridge Review has provided on this and the other matters outlined earlier.

Notes

1 National Commission on Education (1993).
2 All Cambridge Primary Review reports and briefings are listed at https://cprtrust.org. uk/cpr/cpr-publications/ (accessed May 2021). The briefings and interim reports may also be viewed and downloaded. The final report and companion research volume are published by Routledge: Alexander 2010a; Alexander *et al* 2010.
3 Cambridge Primary Review 2007; Alexander and Hargreaves 2007.
4 Cambridge Primary Review 2009; Alexander 2010a; Alexander *et al* 2010.
5 Boyer 1983, 6.
6 Alexander 2010a.

4 Success, amnesia and collateral damage

This chapter looks into just one of the issues examined by the Cambridge Primary Review, albeit one that remained controversial throughout: the evidence on educational standards over time, the means by which such standards are defined, measured and improved, and the role in these matters of national policy. The chapter draws on the author's Miegunyah Lecture at the University of Melbourne, Australia, and his C.J. Koh Lecture at the National Institute of Education, Singapore, both in March 2010. Some of it appeared later in *Cambridge Journal of Education*, 41(3), 265–86 (2011).[1] A note has been added about London Challenge, a strikingly successful initiative whose lessons the government failed to apply.

Of all the so-called 'levers' of systemic reform, tests are the instrument of choice in policymakers' efforts to do the two things which they believe they must always be seen to do: raise educational standards and call schools to account. This means that tests are high stakes not just for children and teachers but also for politicians, and that they are as much about accruing electoral capital as making educational progress.

Not surprisingly, there is now a counter-culture. From the United States comes a burgeoning literature on the role of high-stakes tests in initiatives such as A Nation at Risk in 1983 and NCLB, the 2001 No Child Left Behind Act of President George W. Bush. It's from one of the most powerful critiques of NCLB, by Sharon Nichols and David Berliner[2] (2007), that I coin for the title of this chapter that chilling battleground euphemism beloved of four-star generals, 'collateral damage'. More recently, Diane Ravitch – erstwhile advocate of marketisation and standards-based federal reforms, and former assistant education secretary to President George Bush senior – has witheringly repudiated NCLB in a book subtitled *How testing and choice are undermining education*. As reviewers have been quick to point out, when such criticisms come from the left they tend to be dismissed; but coming from someone so closely identified with conservative administrations they cannot be ignored. Ravitch concludes that 'at the present time, public education [in the United States] is in peril. Efforts to reform public education are, ironically, diminishing its quality and endangering its very survival.'[3]

In England, the testing of 7- and 11-year-olds was introduced along with the national curriculum in 1988 and then made pivotal to the Labour government's post-1997 standards drive. Inevitably, therefore, tests and testing loomed large

DOI: 10.4324/9781315169378-5

in the evidence to the Cambridge Primary Review, a three-year independent enquiry into the condition and future of English primary education which, *inter alia*, examined this strand of policy in some detail and whose final report was released in October 2009.[4]

Smarting from the media's massaging of the report's conclusions (it was immediately clear that nobody in or close to government had actually read the report itself) and for political reasons unable to acknowledge the possibility that its standards strategy may have been less than completely successful, the Labour government summarily rejected the final report of the Cambridge Primary Review in its entirety. In this, the Cambridge Review's experience was far from unique. In May 2008, the House of Commons Children, Schools and Families Select Committee had published an authoritative but critical report about the government's approach to assessment and testing.[5] This too was dismissed, as were other reports on the same subject from the teaching unions and various distinguished experts and commentators. Thus, from the DCSF press office:

> The Government does not share the view that children are over-tested[6] . . . The testing process is rigorously monitored. If there was a problem, this close scrutiny and monitoring would pick that up[7] . . . Parents do not want to go back to a world where schools were closed institutions. Transparency and accountability are here to stay.[8]

Far from being reassured, members of two of Britain's teaching unions increased the pressure by voting to boycott the SAT tests for 11-year-olds. Meanwhile, the Assessment Reform Group had sustained a 21-year campaign for approaches to assessment which align more closely with both research evidence and the imperatives of learning and teaching.[9]

By 2009, tests so dominated educational discourse in England that of the ten themes, 23 sub-themes and 100 research questions addressed by the Cambridge Primary Review, the press mostly concentrated on just three: what the Review said – or, rather, did not say – about the school starting age, the tests for 11-year-olds, and government micro-management of what goes on in schools; or how primary schooling should start, how it should end and who should control it. There was much less media interest in the educational process itself, in what happens during the vital formative years between children's entering primary school at age 4 or 5 and being tested just before they leave it at age 11. The clear implication was that input and output are what matter most: manipulate one, measure the other, and education is sorted.

In fairness, media editors were only responding to what they claimed the public wanted. Yet precisely because the debate about assessment has been so media-driven, many have found it difficult to gain a hearing for the self-evident truths that there's more to assessment than tests, and that criticising the post

1997-test regime does not mean that one is soft on standards or accountability. On the contrary, as the Cambridge Review final report insists:

> We take it as axiomatic that in a public system of education teachers and schools should be fully accountable to parents, children, government and the electorate for what they do. We reject any suggestion that our proposals for the reform of assessment and inspection imply otherwise. For us, the issue is not whether schools should be accountable, but for what and by what means, and the evidence shows that current approaches are in certain respects unsatisfactory. By insisting on a concept of standards which extends across the full curriculum rather than part of it, we are strengthening rather than weakening school accountability.

And:

> It is no less important that others involved in primary education, including central and local government, are fully accountable for their part in the process. When responsibilities are shared, accountability should also be shared so that the precise cause and location of problems can be speedily and accurately diagnosed and appropriate remedial action can be taken.[10]

English primary education: a strategy for reform

The Blair government swept to power in 1997 with the slogan 'education, education, education'. It promised to raise standards in England's 17,300 primary schools and launched a programme of unprecedented investment and intervention. The chosen instruments of reform were:

- national literacy and numeracy strategies which prescribed in detail not just the content but also the methods of daily literacy and numeracy lessons to be taught in every primary school and classroom in the country;
- a sustained sequence of supporting publications and materials – 459 government documents on the teaching of literacy alone were issued to schools during the eight years from 1996 to 2004,[11] or over one a week – not to mention comparable material on numeracy and much else besides;
- the extension of the existing national test regime at age 7 and 11 to include targets for the percentage of 11-year-olds who should achieve specified literacy and numeracy levels by 2002 and each year after that;
- the publication of annual school-by-school test results and inter-school league tables;
- a national inspection system which checked schools for compliance with the strategies and 'named and shamed' those not up to scratch;
- competencies and standards for initial teacher training and in-service professional development which were closely aligned with this agenda;

- ring-fenced funding to support in-service courses for teachers in areas of policy priority;
- local authority school improvement partners (SIPs) charged with checking on each school's measured outcomes and ensuring that they followed the prescribed or preferred routes to improvement, again as measured by the tests;
- the extension of the powers of national bodies, and the tightening of government control over them.

The standards agenda was classic stick and carrot. The intrusiveness of the instruments listed here was ostensibly made more palatable by improving primary teachers' working conditions: over the period 1997–2009, 35,000 additional teachers and 172,000 teaching assistants were appointed and government sanctioned a 27 per cent increase in teachers' pay and a 55 per cent increase in per-pupil funding. Averaged at 2.25 per cent per annum the pay increase looked less spectacular, while the increase in support staff was undeniably impressive, if of doubtful efficacy.[12]

Standards in primary education 1997–2008

We turn now to the question of the degree of success achieved by the post-1997 standards agenda. The then Secretary of State for Education, David Blunkett, upped the ante when he launched the standards drive in 1997, promising that he would resign if the 2002 literacy and numeracy targets were not met. They were not, but by then he had been moved to another ministry, so his successor resigned instead. Yet by 2006–7, despite the failure to meet the targets, the government was claiming that its standards agenda had been an untarnished success. Thus, in the words of ministers and their advisers:

> Today's newly qualified teachers are the best trained ever.[13] . . . Standards stayed the same for 50 years before rising sharply in the late 1990s[14] . . . Primary standards are at their highest ever levels. This is not opinion: it is fact[15] . . . Primary standards are at their highest ever levels . . . This huge rise in standards since 1997 follows 50 years of little or no improvement in literacy and represents a very good return on our investment in the literacy strategy.[16] . . . Independent inspections show there have never been so many outstanding and good primary schools, and Key Stage 2 results show huge progress over the last decade.[17]

Note the gung-ho relationship with eternity – the speakers here use the words 'ever' or 'never' four times. To test these and similar claims the Cambridge Primary Review commissioned six independent surveys of the test and inspection data, together with the contingent research and policy literature, by groups of senior academics at five universities and the National Foundation for Educational Research (NFER). At Durham, Peter Tymms and

Christine Merrell concentrated on the national tests. At NFER, Chris Whetton, Graham Ruddock and Liz Twist examined the international achievement surveys featuring England – TIMSS, PISA, PIRLS and so on. Wynne Harlen of Bristol University and the Assessment Reform Group considered both the trends in these data and the wider assessment issues. Peter Cunningham and Philip Raymont of Cambridge looked at the national school inspection system under Ofsted. Working with Dominic Wyse from Cambridge, Harry Torrance and Elaine McCreery of Manchester Metropolitan University reviewed literature and data across the post-1997 standards drive as a whole, taking in curriculum, assessment, inspection and the national strategies. Meanwhile, Maria Balarin and Hugh Lauder of Bath University set the entire standards agenda in the context of national educational policy and governance.

The three reports on the test data were published in November 2007.[18] They were duly sensationalised by the media with headlines sharply at odds with the confident claims of ministers and advisers just quoted:

> Primary tests blasted by experts . . . Too much testing harms primary school pupils . . . Literacy drive has almost no impact . . . Literacy drive is flop, say experts . . . Millions wasted on teaching reading.[19]

Matters were not helped when in February 2008 the Review published the other three reports, on inspection, governance and the overall trajectory of post-1988 reform.[20] 'Failed!' shouted the newspaper headlines:

> Political interference is damaging our children's education . . . An oppressive system that is failing our children . . . School system test-obsessed . . . England's children among the most tested . . . Our children are tested to destruction . . . A shattering failure for our masters . . . Primary pupils let down by Labour . . . Primary schools have got worse.[21]

On this basis one might conclude that a meeting of minds on the government's standards drive was beyond reach. However, the truth of the matter lay somewhere between the political hype and media scaremongering, and indeed each of the reports cited was careful to give credit where it was due and, taken together, the six studies were considerably more positive about the government's record than was compatible with the media maxim 'Simplify, then exaggerate'.[22]

In fact, the Cambridge Primary Review offered the one thing with which few politicians or sub-editors can cope: a mixed message. In its final report, the Review combined the findings of the six commissioned research surveys cited earlier with its other relevant data to offer an overview of trends up to 2008. It reported that the national and international evidence on standards in England's primary schools was both positive and negative, but also in certain respects problematic.[23]

Positive evidence on standards of primary pupils' attainment up to 2008

Thus, within the limitations and variations of the measures used, standards of tested pupil attainment were fairly stable over time. Pupils' attitudes to their learning in the tested areas were generally positive, though they appeared to decline with age. The national data showed modest improvements in primary mathematics standards, especially after 1995 – a trajectory that started well before Labour's national literacy and numeracy strategies and which cannot therefore be attributed to it – though different datasets told different stories. The international data also showed substantial improvements in primary mathematics from 1995 to 2003. The international data from 2001 showed high standards in reading among English pupils by comparison with those from other countries, but the later data (from 2006 onwards) suggested that the 2001 results may have been misleading (England appeared to be above the international average but not exceptionally so). The international data showed considerable improvements in primary science by comparison with other countries, though there were methodological reservations about the studies in question.

Negative evidence on standards

However, the Blair government's national literacy strategy had a far less pronounced impact on reading standards than might have been expected from the level of investment (the national strategies in combination cost GBP 2 billion of taxpayers' money during the decade 1998–2008), and gains in reading skills were sometimes at the expense of pupils' enjoyment of reading. There was some evidence of an increase in test-induced stress among primary pupils, and much firmer evidence of stress among their teachers; at the same time, the primary curriculum narrowed in direct response to the perceived demands of the testing regime and the national strategies, to the extent that in many schools children's statutory entitlement to a broad and balanced curriculum was seriously compromised. Confirming and perhaps tacitly condoning this tendency, there was no reliable evidence on national standards in areas of children's learning outside those aspects of literacy, numeracy and science which were tested, other than that in many schools such learning had been squeezed out by the post-1997 standards drive itself.

Meanwhile, England's historically wide gap between high and low attaining pupils in reading, mathematics and science persisted throughout the period in question. Already evident at a very young age, it widens as children move through the primary phase, and it is more pronounced in Britain and the United States than in most other developed countries. This attainment gap maps closely onto indicators of inequality in other aspects of children's lives, notably income, health, housing, risk, ethnicity and social class; and it confirms that tackling inequalities in educational outcome requires action across a broad range of public policy, including much that lies outside the control of schools.

Methodological problems with national testing and inspection

Beyond this balance sheet, and serving to compromise many of the public claims about standards, there were methodological problems with the evidence on which judgements about standards were based. Up to the year 2000, for example, England's national system of assessment had a low level of dependability both in relation to results for a given year and as a basis for tracking trends over time. After 2000, the quality of the data improved, but overall this means that claims about long-term trends must be treated with scepticism. There were similar reservations about data from school and teacher-training inspections during the same period, where the methodology changed too frequently to allow year-on-year comparison, and there were problems of validity in relation to what was inspected and of reliability in the inspection process. Though in some respects the international comparative evidence on trends in pupil attainment was encouraging, overall it was rather thin, and there were – and are – considerable challenges in the devising of international measures and the interpretation of international data. Finally, as Mansell argues, Labour's concept of 'standards' was highly problematic yet was routinely presumed to be straightforward.[24]

Questionable claims and assumptions

On the basis of its reassessment of the standards data, the Cambridge Primary Review's final report went on to challenge claims and assumptions by which the Labour governments of 1997–2010 had sought to justify their standards drive and their insistence that national tests of literacy and numeracy were the only way forward. Here are some examples:

Testing of itself drives up standards. Formative assessment embedded in good teaching has a much greater impact, while the impact of national tests on standards is at best oblique.

Parents support testing. Many parents who were interviewed or submitted written evidence to the Review were as worried about high-stakes testing as were teachers. All of them wanted to know how their children were getting on, but unlike government they did not see such information as synonymous with high-stakes tests.[25]

Tests are the only way to hold schools to account and monitor the performance of the system as a whole. Tests are one way among several, and in fact are less suited to this purpose than, for example, inspection and sample achievement surveys.

The pursuit of standards in the 'basics' is incompatible with a broad, balanced and enriching curriculum. Official inspection evidence and test data show the exact opposite, and primary schools which deliver high standards in the 'basics' do so in the context of a broad and well-managed curriculum.[26] Interestingly, both children and parents told the Cambridge Primary Review that literacy and numeracy, though paramount, must not be pursued at the expense of the wider curriculum.[27]

Literacy and numeracy are valid proxies for the curriculum as a whole. Numeracy and – especially – literacy are foundational, but they do not encompass all that the rest of the curriculum embodies. In any case, the exclusive concentration on literacy and numeracy has compromised schools' wider educational purposes, so awarding them proxy status is self-defeating.

England has the best-trained teachers ever. Much repeated by Ofsted, the TDA and the government, but empirically unsustainable, as the available measures of newly-qualified teacher competence go back only a few years, offering a somewhat eccentric definition of 'ever'.

England has the highest standards ever. By the same token, a meaningless claim. It can be neither proved nor refuted.

Looming over the entire standards drive and the debate about what it is legitimate to infer from the available standards data is the problematic nature of the term 'standards'. As Mansell argues:

> The word 'standards' . . . has been routinely abused in the last few years, by politicians and others. 'Raising standards' . . . is implied to stand for improving the overall quality of education in our schools. That, in the public mind . . . is what the phrase means. The reality in schools, however, is that 'raising standards' means raising test scores, as measured by a set of relatively narrow indicators laid down more or less unilaterally by ministers . . . The two meanings are not interchangeable, and should not be treated as such.[28]

The Cambridge Review's evidence shows how, over the period 1997–2010, the pursuit of this narrow concept of 'standards' at the primary stage seriously compromised children's legal entitlement to a broad and balanced curriculum and – exacerbating the problem and tacitly condoning the neglect – provided the central and in many cases sole criteria for the work of local authority school improvement partners (SIPs). It is also possible – I stress 'possible', because the evidence is strong but oblique – that because HMI and Ofsted have shown a close association between standards in literacy/ numeracy and the scope and quality of the wider curriculum,[29] the narrowing of the curriculum in pursuit of an even more restricted definition of standards may have had the opposite result to that intended, depressing standards in 'the basics' rather than raising them.

Educational standards, the Cambridge Review argues – and this argument is central to its proposals on curriculum and pedagogy as well as those on assessment and standards – should be redefined as the quality and outcomes of learning in the entire curriculum to which children are entitled by law.[30] This definition is closer to what Mansell (as quoted) takes to be the public perception.

There is a further twist. England has performance standards for teachers as well as pupils. From 2007, these were specified as behaviours required of teachers at different stages of development from novice to expert, or what were called 'newly qualified', 'post-induction', 'post-threshold', 'excellent' and 'advanced skills'.[31] But the nominated standards had no obvious empirical basis, and indeed ran counter to what we know, mainly from American research, about the way professionals develop in their thinking and practice as they acquire greater expertise.[32] The crucial point is that professionals move from a condition of needing external support to one of self-regulation in which, through experience, precedent and practice, they internalise an extensive operational repertoire on which they draw almost unconsciously and which can yield ways of working which to outsiders may look idiosyncratic but which in fact are very securely grounded. The British government's framework for teachers' professional development did not acknowledge or even permit this possibility. It required teachers at every stage to operate within an externally-defined set of competencies, while the national literacy, numeracy and primary strategies of 1998, 1999 and 2003 expected every teacher, regardless of age, experience or situation, to teach the prescribed four-part literacy lesson and three-part numeracy lesson every day of the week.

Thus the Cambridge Review was forced to conclude that far from raising standards of teaching this approach may actually have depressed or at least contained standards by constraining the work of the country's most talented teachers – even assuming the prescribed teaching strategies to be well-founded empirically, which in the case of the national teaching standards and national literacy strategy they were not. The TDA framework may have worked tolerably well for novices, because it gave them the support they needed, but the nation's best teachers may have been constrained and diminished by it: that, indeed, is what senior teachers claimed in their evidence to the Review. Thus is the circle of learning and teaching closed. As the Cambridge report noted: 'Children will not learn to think for themselves if their teachers are expected merely to do as they are told.'[33]

Collateral damage, myth and other policy ailments

By now we are firmly in the arena of collateral damage. The Cambridge Primary Review's evidence shows that the post-1997 drive to raise standards in literacy and numeracy in England's primary schools undoubtedly yielded positive gains, but at considerable cost, educationally and professionally as well as financially. The tests impoverished the curriculum. The national strategies and professional standards impoverished pedagogy in both conception and practice – a trend evident from the outset.[34] In many primary schools a professional culture of excitement, inventiveness and healthy scepticism was supplanted by one of dependency, compliance and even fear. And the approach may in some cases have depressed both standards of learning and the quality of teaching.

One of the Cambridge Review's commissioned research surveys suggested that Labour's standards package amounted to what its authors called a 'state theory of learning'.[35] This combined the repeated high-stakes testing of pupils and a national curriculum and mandated pedagogy in literacy and numeracy, to which can be added requirements for inspection, initial teacher training, continuing professional development and so-called 'school improvement' by which compliance with the theory is secured.

The Review's final report quoted this argument but warned against the Stalinist overtones of the phrase 'a state theory of learning', insisting that such a charge needed to be carefully tested rather than unthinkingly adopted.[36] Ignoring the warning but joyously seizing on the epithet, the *Daily Mail* launched a stinging attack on the government's 'Stalinist control of teaching'.[37]

But of more fundamental concern is what the Review's evidence revealed not just about the *substance* of policy on matters such as educational standards but also about the way such policy is created and sustained. The Review took place against a backdrop of growing concern about the condition of democracy in Britain. The Power enquiry sponsored by the Joseph Rowntree Trust reported 'high and widespread alienation' towards politicians, the main political parties and the country's key institutions. Dismissing claims that the public had voluntarily disengaged from formal political processes out of apathy, the 2006 Power report concluded:

> Citizens do not feel that the processes of formal democracy offer them enough influence over political decisions . . . the main political parties are widely perceived to be too similar and lacking in principle . . . people feel they lack information or knowledge . . . The political parties are widely held in contempt . . . Voting is simply regarded as a waste of time.[38]

No less seriously, the Power report talked of a 'crisis of disengagement': a 'loss of mandate and legitimacy'; a 'loss of dialogue between government and governed'; the growth of a 'quiet authoritarianism' . . . where 'policy is made in consultation with a small coterie of supporters . . . and general elections become empty rituals'.[39]

The *Power* analysis was shared by eminent political commentators and historians such as Anthony Sampson and Eric Hobsbawm,[40] and it spoke to a malaise which was more profound than the scandal of MPs' expenses which exercised the British press during 2009–10. These are the conditions which ensure that an independent enquiry like the Cambridge Primary Review, however authoritative and evidentially well founded it is, will make little headway if it says what a government does not wish to hear.

Afterword: the strategic anomaly of London Challenge

The same Labour government that was responsible for the primary school 'standards' regime discussed here oversaw a very different strategy to tackle standards in London's underperforming secondary schools (some primary schools joined the project later). Initiated in 2003 and led by Tim Brighouse, London Challenge helped secondary schools in the capital rapidly to transform their fortunes. By 2010, Key Stage 4 examination results had moved from among the worst in England to the best, and 30 per cent of London Challenge schools were rated 'outstanding' by Ofsted compared with 17.5 per cent nationally. The improvements also included the poorest pupils, and by 2010 London had the smallest gap between children receiving free schools meals (FSM) and the rest.[41]

What was no less striking than the dramatic and rapid success of London Challenge was its contrast with Labour's educational improvement strategy for primary schools as discussed. Personalities helped: Tim Brighouse had an impressive record of educational leadership in schools and in the local authorities of Buckinghamshire, Oxfordshire and Birmingham, and – crucially – genuinely respected teachers and was trusted by them. And, unusually, the Secretary of State who announced London Challenge was Estelle Morris, herself a former teacher and one of the very few holders of her office to gain professional respect. She resigned in 2002 and teachers were sorry to see her go, but her stance remained influential, and it was she who persuaded Brighouse to become London Schools Commissioner. Then the government appointed, again unusually, a minister with a local brief. Stephen Twigg became Minister for London Schools and he too worked with the professional grain. Finally, the lead civil servant for the scheme, Jon Coles, was able to uncouple from mainstream departmental thinking and with a small group of young fast-track officials looked for fresh analyses and solutions.

The study of London Challenge by Kidson and Norris notes that although it was embedded in wider Labour education policies its leaders conspicuously distanced it and themselves from some of these. For example:

> One of the distinctive contrasts between London Challenge and other education policies, both before and since, was the deliberate decision not to 'name and shame' schools as failing. Such negative language and a tendency to write-off struggling schools as 'basket cases', said one official, had been prevalent within the department and was part of the rhetoric around academies.[42]

And, as Tim Brighouse told me:

> Gradually they all came into an understanding that language matters enormously . . . For example, I insisted that the term 'failing school' should never be used. We called them 'Keys to success' schools. If these schools succeed, I argued, then any school can.[43]

The pessimistic mindset and negative language that Brighouse resisted were deeply engrained, not least in the inspection system. In 2001, comparing

England's education ministers and inspectors with their counterparts in other countries in the way they spoke about schools, I wrote:

> During the 1990s schools in England were seldom allowed to be just schools. Each must face the world wearing its obligatory judgemental tag – 'outstanding', 'effective', 'improving', 'failing', 'weak' or the ominous 'requiring special measures' – as if to suggest that schools would do a good job only if they lived in constant fear of being named, praised or shamed.[44] For its part, the UK government took to spinning even its most benign policies as 'tough' – as if to signal that schools would regress to a natural state of fecklessness or incompetence unless they were whipped into line. English primary schools in the 1990s were regarded rather as English elementary school pupils were regarded in the 1870s – as irredeemably tainted by original sin.[45]

There were other features that made London Challenge something of a policy outlier. The programme was preceded by careful analysis of the nature and causes of school under-performance, in which locally-specific as well as generic factors were identified. In this and throughout, evidence was sought and acted on. Then, instead of a 'one-size-fit-all' national strategy, London Challenge offered tailored support for individual schools and London boroughs. There was a strong emphasis on local partnerships and the sharing of ideas and experiences rather than imposed top-down 'solutions'. A model of leadership was encouraged which centred on co-ownership, networking and moral purpose rather than compliance with somebody else's requirements, and here the Ofsted evaluation commended leaders' 'skill in matching people and schools, creating a sense of mutual trust'.[46] Tim Brighouse appointed to the vital support roles of London Challenge Adviser individuals with experience and credibility in the task of addressing the challenges in question. He also took the decision to work as far as possible 'below the radar' so as to avoid the risk that the mission might be destabilised by the wrong kind of media treatment[47] – as was the Cambridge Primary Review's relationship with the government.

As I noted in the introduction, 'Education in spite of policy' should not be interpreted as a rejection of government intervention in education, but rather as an invitation to examine its purposes, content, processes and impact, and to assess when policy interventions are appropriate and when they are not. London Challenge repays such examination, and provides an important corrective to some of the problems that this chapter has identified. From a wider policy standpoint, what is intriguing about this initiative is its strategic dislocation from Labour's main reform effort, and indeed the contradictions between the two approaches. For his part, Tim Brighouse is clear on why London Challenge was different:

> The reason it was different was that those were the terms on which I agreed to do it. Estelle [Morris] was a Yardley MP who had therefore seen at close hand, and as a former teacher, what I had done, and more significantly

how I had created a certain culture in Birmingham. She said, 'Just do in London what you did and how you did it in Birmingham.'[48]

It is less obvious why Downing Street failed to apply to its subsequent efforts the lessons of this strikingly successful initiative. Chronology may have been part of the problem. The national literacy and numeracy strategies were launched in 1998 and 1999, so Labour was already committed to centralised pedagogy and punitive performativity well before London Challenge, and would have found it politically difficult to change tack. But London Challenge also fell into the unwritten but acknowledged Downing Street category of promising initiatives that could not be mainstreamed into national policy because they were 'not invented here'.[49]

Notes

1 Alexander 2011a.
2 Nichols and Berliner 2007.
3 Ravitch 2010.
4 Alexander 2010a.
5 House of Commons 2008.
6 DCSF spokesperson, quoted by Press Association, 12.10.07.
7 Schools Minister Lord Adonis, quoted by Reuters, 02.11.07.
8 DCSF spokesperson quoted in *The Times Educational Supplement*, 02.11.07.
9 Mansell and James 2009.
10 Alexander 2010a, recommendation 25, p 500.
11 Moss 2007.
12 Blatchford *et al* 2008.
13 Day 2007; Revell 2006.
14 Barber 2007, 150.
15 Adonis 2007.
16 DCSF 2007.
17 Coaker 2009.
18 Tymms and Merrell 2007; Whetton *et al* 2007; Harlen 2007.
19 Sample media headlines from 2 November 2007: (i) *The Independent* and Sky News, (ii) *The Daily Telegraph*, (iii) *The Guardian, The Daily Mail* and ITN, (iv) *The Times*, (v) *Daily Mirror*.
20 Cunningham and Raymont 2008; Balarin and Lauder 2008; Wyse *et al* 2007.
21 From 2, 8 and 29 February 2008: (i), (ii) and (iii) *The Independent*, (iv) *Daily Express* and BBC News, (v) *The Times* and BBC News, (vi) and (vii) *The Independent*, (viii) *The Daily Telegraph*, (ix) BBC News.
22 Usually attributed to Geoffrey Crowther, editor of *The Economist* from 1938 to 1956.
23 The four sub-sections which follow compress information presented in detail in Alexander 2010a, 328–42 and 471–4; Alexander *et al* 2010, 431–520 and 727–817.
24 Mansell 2007.
25 Alexander and Hargreaves 2007, 25.
26 DES 1978, 1985; Ofsted 1997, 2002a, 2008, 2009.
27 Alexander and Hargreaves 2007, 13, 25 and 35.
28 Mansell 2007, 25.
29 See 24.
30 Alexander 2010a, recommendations 47, 70, 81 and 125.

31 TDA 2007.
32 Dreyfus and Dreyfus 1986; Ericsson 1996; Bond *et al* 2000; Berliner 2004; Galton 1995, 2007.
33 Alexander 2010a, 496.
34 Alexander 2004a.
35 Balarin and Lauder 2008.
36 Alexander 2010a, 291.
37 *Daily Mail* 2009.
38 Joseph Rowntree Charitable Trust 2006, 16–17.
39 Joseph Rowntree Charitable Trust 2006, 33–5.
40 Sampson 2004; Hobsbawm 2007.
41 Ofsted 2010a.
42 Kidson and Norris 2015, 7.
43 Tim Brighouse, personal communication, June 2021.
44 The School Inspections Act 1996 stated that 'Special measures are required to be taken in relation to a school if the school is failing or likely to fail to give its pupils an acceptable standard of education' (OFSTED 1999, 166).
45 Alexander 2001a, 175.
46 Ofsted 2010a, 6.
47 Kidson and Norris 2015.
48 Tim Brighouse, personal communication, June 2021.
49 During a discussion with a senior Downing Street official in the early days of the Cambridge Primary Review, I was told that this phrase was shorthand for structural antipathy towards good ideas for which ministers could not take the credit. The trick, according to another informant, was to flatter the minister by contriving to suggest, not too obviously, that he/she was the inventor.

5   Triumph of the eristic

Times Educational Supplement (TES), 16 May 2008, and *The Guardian*, 24 October 2009.[1] These two newspaper articles – one marking the publication of the last of the 31 Cambridge Primary Review interim reports, the other commenting on ministers' reaction to the final report – illustrate how media coverage aggravated the Government's growing hostility towards the Review, and finally spurred its no-holds-barred misrepresentation of the Review's findings.

The interim reports (2007–8)

With today's three research surveys on learning and teaching in primary schools, the Cambridge Primary Review completes dissemination of its interim reports and enters its next phase: preparation of the final report.

After the Review's launch in October 2006, the Cambridge team traversed the country, talking to teachers, parents, children and community representatives. We invited written submissions and received them in abundance and detail. We trawled official data to keep track of changing policy and demographics. We met all manner of stakeholders. Our 66 academic consultants undertook exhaustive surveys of published research on the Review's ten themes, between them covering many thousands of published sources, national and international. We contributed to public events, sometimes – as with the GTC and the Children's Society – in collaboration with others. Latterly, sessions with practitioners and national organisations considered implications of our emerging evidence.

As far as the Review's public face was concerned, the first year, though busy for us, was quiet. All that changed in October 2007, when we published our report on the 87 regional community soundings. The report was wide-ranging, but just one issue translated instantly into banner headlines: children under stress. A few weeks later our three commissioned research surveys on standards, testing and assessment were billed as a 'searing indictment' of the government's standards drive and SATs regime, matters seldom out of the news since then.

We might cavil at distorted findings and the sensationalising of complex issues, but we are grateful that the media have found in the Cambridge Primary Review not an ephemeral event but an unfolding and important narrative: about children's development, needs and learning, and their lives outside as well as inside school; about parenting and caring;

DOI: 10.4324/9781315169378-6

about primary school aims, curriculum, assessment, standards and teaching; about teacher training, development and leadership; and about educational structures, funding, governance, policy and reform. All of these have been placed in the context of larger questions about the economy, the fabric of national life and the condition of the world in which our children are growing up.

Some teachers tell us that what they particularly value in the Review's reports and briefings are persuasive alternatives to the official view. This is important, for there now remain few aspects of primary education which have not become the subject of government policy. One vivid measure of this political investment is the continuing deluge of documents from DCSF to schools. Another is how government chooses to respond to an independent enquiry like ours.

Matters started well, for alongside the opposition parties, statutory organisations and teaching unions DCSF agreed to cooperate with the Review and in that spirit joined us in fruitful meetings and exchanges. We worked hard for this, not just for pragmatic reasons but because we respected the seriousness of the government's commitment to improving primary education.

But the Review's contentious media profile has put the relationship under undeniable strain, for DCSF has found itself having to respond to media accounts of our reports in which government itself has been the main story. Further, though our reports have conveyed the mixed messages about recent policy that are inevitable in a large and complex system undergoing substantial change, much of the press coverage has concentrated on the negative. In turn, it is to this negative gloss, rather than to what our reports actually say, that government has felt obliged to respond.

Presumably on the principle that attack is the best form of defence, DCSF has opted against the engagement which our reports warrant and the nation's children and teachers deserve, and to which it initially agreed. Instead, in a three-pronged assault on the Review's probity, the work of the 66 leading academics who have written these interim reports has been summarily dismissed as 'a collection of recycled, partial or out of date research';[2] the Review's Cambridge team has been accused of 'being out of touch with the concerns of parents';[3] and to the Review's director DCSF has attributed views of an extreme and ludicrous kind which neither he nor anyone else involved in the Review actually holds or has expressed. A choice and arguably libellous example is this: 'We need parents to make books available, read to their children and take an interest in their homework. Many parents already do this, and unlike Professor Alexander, we think they are right to do so.'[4]

Conspiracy theorists go further, questioning the government's motives for launching its own primary (curriculum) review with an email address almost identical to ours, a suspicion which is confirmed rather than refuted by those closest to the action.[5] Be that as it may, what started as one press story, the Cambridge Primary Review, has now spawned a second: the Government versus the Cambridge Primary Review.

The difficulty is this. Policy is now so all-pervasive, and education has become so intensely politicised, that a well-researched independent finding is not the positive contribution to the cause of improving public services which in a saner world would be welcomed with open arms, but a political threat to be neutralised by whatever means possible, fair or foul. Far from being unique, the Review's case is part of a consistent pattern of official reaction, across the full spectrum of public policy, to anything deemed off-message. This is hardly healthy, for education or for democracy.

Yet things are not necessarily what they seem, for we have also witnessed subtle changes in tone and direction on some of those very issues on which in relation to the Review government has been most defiant: early childhood, school starting age, curriculum – even testing. It could be that you don't need to wait until the Review's final report: it is already making a difference, though nobody cares to admit it.

Equally, even in a centralised system policy is not all that matters. Teachers do, and must, exercise professional judgement on the basis of what only they know about the children they teach; and a national education system belongs not to ministers and officials but to all of us.

The final report (2009)

The government's instant dismissal of the final report of the Cambridge Primary Review has become as a big a story as the report itself. The Review's email in-boxes are overflowing with messages not just about the findings that the press focused on – starting age, testing, centralisation – but with expressions of spluttering outrage shading into quiet despair at last week's statement from schools minister Vernon Coaker.[6] Nor was dismay confined to what some call 'the educational establishment': among those voicing disquiet about the Government's behaviour were teachers, parents, academics, members of other political parties, members of the House of Lords, and an archbishop.[7]

Thus is the circle of centralisation closed, sadly to the detriment of a government which has done an enormous amount for young children and primary education, as our report makes clear. If the report finds that primary schools 'are in good heart . . . highly valued by children and parents and in general doing a good job . . . the one point of stability and positive values in a world where everything else is changing and uncertain. . .'[8] this is a tribute to government as well as teachers. But when things go wrong in a micro-managed system the finger of blame points in one direction only, and in such a situation this government allows itself only one response: lash out wildly.

So Vernon Coaker said that by virtue of having started three years ago the report was out of date. What a strange and desperate ploy. One would have thought that its length testifies to its depth and thoroughness, especially as when pressed this week by the Select Committee to justify the DCSF accusation, Ed Balls wrongly claimed that the report had ignored the Williams maths enquiry (mentioned on pages 38, 46, 49, 433, 434, 436, 506 and 575), the 'expert group' on assessment (mentioned by name on pages 47, 497 and 513, and by its findings in several other places) and the Lamb special needs review (the report argues for an SEN review with a broader and different remit).

That was not all the minister got wrong. Like many others, he misrepresented as a bid to raise the school starting age our proposal that the government's Early Years Foundation Stage should be extended to age six, thus confusing curriculum (which is what the EYFS is about) with organisational structure. Though we said that in light of international evidence the starting age needs to be discussed, that was as far as we went. Get the early years curriculum right, we argued, and school starting age is no longer an issue.

The government claimed we wanted to scrap the English and maths tests (and by implication all assessment) and deny accountability. We said, emphatically and repeatedly, that children must be assessed at the end of their primary schooling and that schools should be fully accountable. Our evidence pointed to the *reform* of assessment and external school inspection, not their abolition – who in their right minds would argue for the latter? The imperative is to have a system of summative assessment which covers all aspects of the curriculum to which children are statutorily entitled, does not treat literacy and numeracy as proxies for the whole, builds on cumulative teacher assessment, does not distort the very thing it is trying to assess, and is externally moderated. The minister said the new report cards will provide the necessary breadth. In respect of matters like wellbeing they may, but the proposed report card measure of a child's entire primary school *attainment* remains precisely as now – test scores in the 3Rs at age 11.

On standards, the minister had us claiming that 'primary standards have not risen across the board'. Our report goes into detail on this vital matter and its conclusions are nuanced. If 'across the board' means all children, then we know that the attainment gap remains as wide as ever. If it means across the curriculum then we know about pupils' attainment only in a very narrow spectrum of their learning and the official definition of 'standards' is restricted and misleading. We looked carefully at what the national tests, international achievement surveys, school inspection and independent research tell us. We separated those claims about standards, positive and negative, which can be sustained from those which cannot, and we identified the methodological problems which get in the way of secure judgements. The true picture on standards is much more complex than the minister's rhetoric allows.

And so it goes on. What was especially rich about the DCSF response was its indignation over what our report 'failed to mention' (on which, as I've shown, it was wrong anyway). This from a government which has rejected every one of our 31 carefully-researched interim reports and now our 600-page final report, and has 'failed to mention' in its own work our evidence from over 4000 cited publications, 28 specially-commissioned research surveys and the views and experience of the thousands of individuals and organisations who, through written submissions, emails and face-to-face meetings, gave evidence to the Cambridge Primary Review in the hope that it would make a difference.

Nobody expects ministers to have the time to read every massive report that lands on their desks, not overnight anyway. But serious questions must now be asked about the advice on which the government's response was based, the advisers who provided the minister with such a hopeless script, and the wisdom of approaching a general election as the government which refuses to listen, engage and learn, let alone observe the basic conventions of reasoned argument. Children, parents and teachers deserve better than this.

Notes

1 Alexander R.J. 2008a, 2009a.
2 DCSF spokesperson, quoted in *The Times Educational Supplement*, 29.02.08.
3 Secretary of State Ed Balls, quoted in *The Independent*, 29.02.08.
4 Ed Hawkesworth, DCSF Press Office briefing, 23.11.07.
5 Mick Waters, former QCA Director of Curriculum, quoted in Bangs *et al* 2010, 157.
6 Schools Minister Vernon Coaker, quoted in DCSF press release, 16.10.09.
7 In May 2021 Coaker himself became a member of Britain's ultimate establishment, the unelected House of Lords.
8 Alexander 2010a, 488.

6 What works and what matters

This chapter looks back over the decade of the Cambridge Primary Review and Cambridge Primary Review Trust, 2006–16. Edited version of keynote for 'Primary Education: What Is and What Might Be', the final conference of the Cambridge Primary Review Trust, London, 18 November 2016.

This conference marks the tenth anniversary of the launch of the Cambridge Primary Review (CPR), and anticipates the fourth of its successor, the Cambridge Primary Review Trust (CPRT). In celebrating these events I pay tribute to the Esmée Fairbairn Foundation, whose five consecutive grants supported the Review from 2006 to 2012, and to Pearson, who have supported the Trust since then.

Awards from the National Union of Teachers, the Association of Managers in Education, the Society of Educational Studies, the British Educational Research Association and Sage have testified to the Review's significance for teachers and researchers, but its impact on national policy is debatable. Yet on one measure, media coverage, its success cannot be contested. The Review achieved extensive press coverage throughout, and independent media analysis shows that on five of the ten occasions when the Review published its reports it was the top UK news story overall.

But such exposure came at a price, for despite the evidential wealth of our reports, and what we hoped was their measured tone, the headlines they provoked frequently sensationalised our findings. Those who were prepared to read beyond the headlines could find even-handed reporting, but overall the media narrative was Review *versus* Government, or in respect of the Labour Government's curriculum review Alexander *versus* Rose.[1]

It was to the headlines rather than the reports that the government responded, issuing rebuttals and insults of increasing ferocity and absurdity, and showing that despite our careful briefings of officials and ministers before each report was published they had less interest in what those reports said than in protecting the government from political fallout or media scorn by attacking us.

The process reached its sorry climax when far from welcoming the final report as a contribution to evidence and debate, ministers first grossly misrepresented and then summarily dismissed it. For this they were widely criticised:

> Some of the leading voices in education appealed to the government to face up to the criticisms in the report and move on its recommendations.

DOI: 10.4324/9781315169378-7

Headteachers' leaders said any attempt to ignore it would be an 'act of weakness' on their part . . . Mick Brookes, general secretary of the National Association of Head Teachers, said: 'This comprehensive study of primary education must be taken seriously by government. The fact the work in progress has been completely ignored by the government is a sign of weakness. This report is truly independent, unlike work commissioned and controlled by the DCSF which largely says what it wants to hear. . .' Christine Blower, general secretary of the National Union of Teachers, said: 'It is absolutely extraordinary that the government has decided to ignore the Cambridge Review recommendations. Any government worth its salt, particularly in front of an impending general election, would have embraced this immensely rich report as a source of policy ideas. It is not too late for the government to recognise that not all good ideas emanate from the minds of civil servants.' Nansi Ellis, head of education policy and research at the Association of Teachers and Lecturers, said: 'Primary education must not become a battlefield in the forthcoming election – children and their learning will be the first casualties.'[2]

And

Growing anger in schools and teacher groups about the government's dismissal of the review . . . comes after a tumultuous week in which Balls was accused of being a 'bit of a bully' by Barry Sheerman, the Chair of the Commons Committee for Children, Schools and Families.[3]

And this, from distinguished educationist Peter Mortimore, who himself had directed a landmark study of primary schooling and had been a member of an earlier national enquiry:[4]

The final report of the Cambridge primary review (CPR) posed a significant test for political parties. Would their spokespeople appreciate its scope, study its research findings and rationally debate its ideas? Liberal Democrat education spokesperson David Laws was probably the most positive, noting 'anybody interested in improving primary education should take notice of this report'. Conservative shadow schools secretary Michael Gove saw it as 'thought-provoking and provocative' . . . Schools minister Vernon Coaker, however, brusquely dismissed three years of intensive work – including detailed consultations with practitioners, evidential reviews and international comparisons undertaken by some of the most knowledgeable university researchers in the country. Weep, Cambridge team. Your efforts to produce clear analyses and innovative ideas in the interest of fostering something better than political point-scoring, repetitive myths and ideological rigidity have been strangled at birth.[5]

When we met Secretary of State Ed Balls and Schools Minister Vernon Coaker at DfE just before the 2010 election they acknowledged they had been wrong to dismiss the report, though their admission was recorded only by ourselves and it came too late. But taking the longer view on which the work of the Cambridge Primary Review and Trust are predicated, Peter Mortimore continued:

> Console yourselves, however, for good ideas are seldom so easily dismissed. Twice I have seen work I have been involved with rejected, only for much of it eventually to be incorporated into official policy. The pity is that politicians, who pollsters tell us are only trusted by 13% of the population, can so easily make such fools of themselves by endeavouring to close down all thinking outside their own. How much wiser to welcome new ideas and give civil society, including teachers – who are trusted by 82% of the population – the chance to debate how best to improve the education of our youngest learners.[6]

Or, in the closing words of the final report:

> The Cambridge Primary Review . . . is not just for the transient architects and agents of policy. It is for all who invest daily, deeply and for life in this vital phase of education, especially children, parents and teachers.[7]

So here we are, education professionals all, soldiering on, investing in children's education daily, deeply and for life. There goes our one-time nemesis, former Secretary of State Ed Balls: out of office, out of Parliament and into Strictly Come Dancing; and in come Michael Gove and Nicky Morgan, dancing not the tango but the Brexit.[8] It was on the basis of the contrast between here today gone tomorrow politicians and those who are in it for the long haul, that we argued in 2009 that people who judged the Review solely by how much notice government took of it were missing the point. True, we made policy recommendations and some of them were even heeded; but much of what we reported was for teachers, not policymakers.

So it is the teachers who have heeded this message that the Cambridge Primary Review Trust celebrates. Their insistence on professional autonomy underpinned by reflection, evidence and vision underlines the force of another often-repeated quote from the final report: 'Children will not learn to think for themselves if their teachers are expected merely to do as they are told.'[9]

Taking the Review's 2009 recommendations and 2010 election priorities as starting points but responding to what by 2013 – the mid-point of the 2010–15 coalition government – were rather different circumstances, the Trust identified the eight priorities on which I shall shortly reflect: *equity*, *voice*, *community* and *sustainability* as guiding principles, and *aims*, *curriculum*, *pedagogy* and *assessment* as practical imperatives. These derived from the Review and the dissemination events that followed it, and have engendered policy engagement, new research

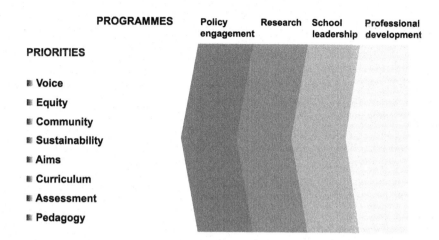

Figure 6.1 The Cambridge Primary Review Trust: priorities and programmes

and, through CPRT's regional networks, a CPD partnership with Pearson, and a Schools Alliance of forward-looking primary heads and teachers[10] (Figure 6.1).

The most widely visible aspect of CPRT's work has been the succession of research reports and briefings that we commissioned to update and extend those produced by the Review.[11] But there is more. Our regional networks have organised an impressive array of events and initiatives, often working closely with local members of the Trust's Schools Alliance.[12] We have contributed to numerous official consultations. We have joined forces with other organisations on campaigns such as Better Without Baseline, More Than a Score, and Bacc for the Future. Our (almost) weekly blogs have commented on issues and developments both transient and fundamental, and they have been contributed by heads, teachers, student teachers and journalists as well as academics.[13]

★★★

'What is and what might be' – the theme of this conference – is of course the title of HMI Edmond Holmes's classic critique of English elementary education in 1911.[14] It reminds us of a shared objective of the Cambridge Primary Review and the Trust: to combine reliable evidence about children, their world and their primary education with a valid vision for the future. As to the title of this session, 'what works' is a necessary test of every pedagogical proposition or decision but it has also become the mantra of those who cut to what they see as the only educational question worth asking, and it may signal a fixation on outcomes at the expense of purposes and processes. Is what works what matters?

Clear learning goals are essential; so too is the need to know to what extent goals have been achieved. But while some outcomes may well be laudable and appropriate, others may not, and in a democracy all should surely be subject to debate rather than decree. As to what matters, is it really essential, as one historically-challenged ministerial convert to E.D. Hirsch insisted to me, that every Year 6 pupil should know who shot England's King William II, especially when this is a question that no historian can answer? Or that every 16-year-old should be able to list the three causes of the English civil war – to which, before I could stop myself, I'm afraid I responded, 'Only three, minister?'

Too exclusive an emphasis on outcomes, even those that are sensible, may neglect not only questions about purposes and values but also the truth that for the child the experience of learning is no less important. Primary teachers were rightly incensed a few years ago when another minister announced that the most important outcome of primary education is making children 'secondary-ready', as if children's experiences during their intensely formative primary years have no value in themselves.[15] Anyway, given that in 2015 Ofsted published a report with the telling title *Key Stage 3: the wasted years?* the idea of 'secondary-ready' is problematic, to say the least.[16]

Further, from the broad range of possible outcomes of learning – academic, social, emotional, behavioural, aesthetic, moral, physical – only a small proportion are amenable to measurement, and in our data-driven education system this intrinsic weakness is almost certain to distort the curriculum. So, as my title invites, we must ask whether what works in education is what really matters.

What is and what might be. Evidence with vision. What works and what matters. To these I add a metatheme: policy. Since the 1988 Education Reform Act began to transfer hitherto devolved powers from local authorities and schools to Westminster, policy has become ever more inescapable, intrusive and impervious to criticism, and some believe that in terms of quality as well as quantity it may even be counterproductive. This was the view of those four eminent educationists who in 2008, at the height of New Labour's standards drive, sent an open letter to a national newspaper:

> Despite significant additional investment in education since 1997 and many welcome measures in all phases of education . . . policy is now working against the Government's own intentions. The current frenetic pace of change must slow down to what is possible . . . We have become increasingly dismayed by ministers who are intent on permanent revolution in every aspect of the education system from structures to qualifications. In so acting, they demonstrate a deep lack of trust in the professional education community.[17]

In his introduction to *What Is and What Might Be*, Edmond Holmes wrote in terms which seem to speak as directly to our situation now as to his in 1911:

> My aim . . . is to show that . . . the prevalent tendency to pay undue regard to outward and visible 'results' and to neglect what is inward and vital, is the source of most of the defects that vitiate education in this country.[18]

Having anticipated behaviourist psychology – 'undue regard to [the] outward and visible' – and the tyranny of SATs – 'undue regard to results' – Holmes continued:

> There is at least a breath of healthy discontent stirring in the field of elementary education, a breath which sometimes blows the mist away and gives us sudden gleams of sunshine, whereas over the higher levels of the educational world there hangs the heavy stupor of profound self-satisfaction. I am not exaggerating when I say that at this moment there are elementary schools in England in which the life of the children is emancipative and educative to an extent which is unsurpassed, and perhaps unequalled, in any other type . . . of school.[19]

★★★

Let us turn now to those eight priorities that have guided the Trust's efforts since 2013. In relation to each of them, what can we say about what is and what might be? About what policy has achieved and what policy has frustrated? And about what works and what matters?

Voice

We can begin on a positive note: *Advance children's voice and rights in school and classroom in accordance with the UN Convention on the Rights of the Child.* Carol Robinson's research update on voice[20] has stimulated initiatives in several of our regional networks, for it speaks to a wider interest in children's voice and rights that has taken the movement far beyond the formal procedures such as school councils that we documented in the Cambridge Review final report. So, for example, there are now 4000 UK schools working towards the UNICEF Rights Respecting Schools Award,[21] while many more that are not part of this scheme have signed up to the idea.

It is to be hoped that all of them understand that the real test of a school's commitment to voice lies not so much in national schemes and school structures, helpful though these may be, as in what happens in the classroom; and that if a commitment to voice does not translate into a pedagogy that empowers children's talk, respects their ideas and thereby gives them ownership of their learning – which is what the UN Convention on the Rights of the Child explicitly requires – it has barely scratched the surface of what 'voice' should mean.[22]

'Voice' and 'vote' have different Latin roots – vox/voice and votum/vow – but in a democracy the vote is the citizen's ultimate voice and in today's febrile political climate how people vocalise their views and use their votes has implications for voice in the classroom. On the one hand, an EPPI research review at the University of Bristol has shown that children's path to active and discerning citizenship starts not with lessons that preach 'British' values or the virtues of British parliamentary democracy but with classroom talk that encourages children to question, argue, reason, challenge the opinions of others and justify their own[23] – what I call dialogic teaching. On the other hand, and as far removed from this as it is possible to imagine, we have the divisive demagoguery and populist tribalism of Trump, Farage and some of the tabloids, the verbal and physical violence that they encourage – let us never forget Jo Cox[24] – and the replacement of evidence and reasoned argument by claims, lies and accusations that appeal to humanity's worst rather than its best. Voice is both the opportunity to talk and how that opportunity is exercised.

Another angle again. It would be facile to claim a connection between the growing abusiveness of political discourse and the rise of cyber-bullying, but for today's children social networking is routine and pervasive and it's therefore a dimension of voice that demands our attention, and urgently. Here I would commend another CPRT report, Cathy Burnett's *The Digital Age and its Implications for Learning and Teaching in the Primary School.*[25]

Equity

If we ask whether the voices of all children have an equal chance of being heard, then we see how voice relates to the next CPRT priority, equity: *Tackle the continuing challenge of social and educational disadvantage, and find practical ways to help schools to close the overlapping gaps in educational attainment.*

In recent years, governments of all persuasions have told us that they are committed to reducing social and educational inequalities. Building on a legacy of positive discrimination going back to Plowden and the 1960s Educational Priority Areas, significant public money now goes to the Pupil Premium and the 'what works' strategies evaluated by the Education Endowment Foundation. One of these is the joint CPRT/University of York project on dialogic teaching and social disadvantage.[26]

Meanwhile, we have a level of child poverty – currently 28 per cent – that is matched by few other rich countries, a growing gulf between rich and poor, and gross and stubbornly persistent inequalities of gender, race, culture and opportunity. And of course, and critically, the demographics of social and educational inequality closely coincide.

All this is well documented in not one but three CPRT reports. Together with Laura Vanderbloemen, Kate Pickett, co-author of the brilliant 2009 book *The Spirit Level*, has produced for us *Mind the Gap: tackling social and educational inequality.*[27] Here she revisits and extends her central thesis that unequal societies have unequal educational systems and that you cannot eliminate educational inequality without tackling social inequality. Next, Mel Ainscow and his Manchester colleagues have given us *Primary Schools Responding to Diversity: barriers and possibilities,*[28] and from Michael Jopling and Sharon Vincent we have *Vulnerable Children: needs and provision in the primary phase.*[29] Jopling and Vincent focus on what local authorities and agencies do, and what they might do better. The other two reports have more to say about national policy, and while both Kate Pickett and Mel Ainscow acknowledge the welcome boost to school income that the Pupil Premium provides, they highlight its limitations. Worryingly, Ainscow and his colleagues argue that the Premium may narrow rather than widen the vocabulary of social diversity:

> Teachers now commonly refer to 'Pupil Premium pupils' as though such a group can be defined meaningfully, when in fact it consists of no more than a highly diverse aggregation of individuals whose only common feature is that they have free school meals.[30]

And the government's response? On the one hand, thanks to the coalition government's Liberal Democrat partners, the Pupil Premium. On the other, and somewhat disregarding 1960s evidence about the damage to the self-esteem and life chances of those who were not deemed worthy of a grammar school education, we have Theresa May's proposal to reintroduce grammar schools.[31] To have two initiatives from the same government pulling in opposite directions, both in the name of narrowing the gap, is bizarre.

In any case, as Mel Ainscow warns, the definition of the gap to be narrowed has itself become narrower. Here we might recall that Labour's Narrowing the Gap programme focused on a much wider spectrum of disadvantage than income, including looked-after children, children with disabilities, children with special needs, those excluded from school, those with records of poor or patchy attendance, young offenders, young carers, children at risk, children living with vulnerable adults, children not fluent in English, children of asylum seekers and refugees, children with mental health problems and children from marginalised groups such as travellers.[32]

Community

Which leads to CPRT's next priority, community: *Promote community engagement and cohesion through school-community links and a community curriculum that supplements and enriches the national curriculum, and by developing communal values in school and classroom.* Drawing on evidence including its 'community soundings' – 87 focus group meetings in nine regional locations – Cambridge Primary Review argued that primary schools are not only pivotal to their local communities, but also, at their best, they model what community is about. As the final report said, joining those who take liberties with W.B. Yeats: 'Primary schools may be the one point of stability and positive values in a world where everything else is changing and uncertain. For many, schools are the centre that holds when things fall apart.'[33]

Like voice, community is a priority that is not subject to DfE policy requirements and where schools can make their own way. But, as also with voice, policy can make community harder to achieve. For while teachers and school leaders strive to create communal relationships and patterns of behaviour, communities outside the school that are fractured have a habit of intruding, and this fracturing is economic as well as social and cultural. Meanwhile, the stripping away of local educational governance and accountability diminishes community investment in neighbourhood schools, while performance tables, enforced academisation and the drive to an American-style marketised system are about division rather than solidarity. Here you should read Warwick Mansell's CPRT report on academies.[34] Mansell is particularly concerned about the dangers of unaccountable admissions policies, financial discretion and governance, and in the spirit of community argues: 'In the absence of good evidence showing why they should be dispensed with, local democracy, accountability and support should be maintained for all state-funded schools' and 'there should be maximum transparency at all levels of decision making about the future of schools. Users of services, and citizens generally, need to be involved in these decisions.'

Sustainability

The last in the cluster of CPRT priorities relating to children and their world is sustainability: *Embed sustainability and global citizenship in educational policy and practice, linking to the UN agenda for global education after 2015.*

David Cameron, the prime minister who announced that he would head 'the greenest government ever', later told his ministers to 'cut the green crap'.[35] His successor Theresa May duly obliged by abolishing the Department of Energy and Climate Change. And this despite the United Nations 2015 Sustainable Development Goals, the 2015 Paris Cop 21 Climate Change Agreement and its 2016 ratification.

Meanwhile, although education for sustainable development was a cross-curriculum requirement from 2000 to 2013, it was excluded from the national curriculum introduced in 2014. Meanwhile too, the nationalism, xenophobia and racism unleashed by Brexit dealt a body blow to the idea that learning and citizenship in our interdependent and fragile world must be global rather than merely national; and all over Europe right-wing nationalist leaders, emboldened first by Brexit and then by Trump, have been following suit.

As with voice, community and equity, the priority of sustainability carries forward the agenda of the Cambridge Primary Review which in turn reflects concerns expressed by parents, teachers, community leaders and children themselves. It is the children who have most to gain or lose from our decisions, so there's nothing remotely maverick about our pressing for education for sustainability and global citizenship. And as with voice, community and equity, the achievement of this priority is partly in teachers' hands, policy notwithstanding. To help them we have the CPRT report from Doug Bourn and his colleagues at the UCL Institute of Education, *Primary Education for Global Learning and Sustainability*.[36]

Aims

This takes us to the central question of what primary education is for. Once again policy fails us. Every version of the national curriculum since 1988 has been prefaced by a brace of goals that are not only platitudinous but also bear little relation to the content they precede. They are also habitually ungrammatical. Thus the current national curriculum, like its predecessors, says that the curriculum should promote 'the spiritual, moral, cultural, mental and physical development of pupils at the school and of society'. I can see how it is valid to speak of the spiritual, moral and cultural development of society, but what on earth is meant by the 'mental and physical development . . . of society'? Do societies have arms and legs? Anyway, Margaret Thatcher, on whose watch this crass phrase was invented, decreed that there's no such thing as society – though she presumably accepted the existence of legs.

It's not so much that the national curriculum doesn't have aims, for notwithstanding DfE's silly statement about the mental and physical needs of society, aims are all too clearly expressed by the subjects that ministers include and exclude, what they define as core and non-core, and the extent and kind of content they require for each; and it all adds up to the familiar regime of hammer the 3Rs, don't worry about the rest. No, my objection is the sheer dishonesty of the government's approach, with its expressed aims, however illiterate, claiming a broad, balanced, liberal education that celebrates 'the best that has been thought and said' while the curriculum itself as specified in the current national curriculum framework heads in the opposite direction towards minimalism, narrow instrumentalism and a disdain for culture that would have Matthew Arnold spinning in his grave at the nerve of those ministers who use his words to paper over the poverty of their vision.

In 2015, and underlining the government's failure both to come clean on aims and to engage in a proper debate on the matter – for the aims of public education are for all of us, not just ministers – the House of Commons Education Committee launched its own enquiry into the quality and purpose of education in England. In some irritation I penned a CPRT blog entitled 'What's the point?' and asked:

> When the mother of parliaments asks 'What's the point of education?' we might retort, descending to even greater depths of cynicism than usual, 'What's the point of telling you? What's the point of contributing to yet another consultation when on past form nobody takes any notice?' and indeed, 'You ask about educational purposes now? After hundreds of so-called reforms? Are you telling us that these reforms have all been, in the strictest sense of the word, pointless?'[37]

But then I remembered my duties as citizen, academic, educator and chair of this Trust, and submitted, on behalf of the Trust, a copy of the Cambridge Primary Review aims for primary education together with a commentary.[38] Those aims were grounded in an extensive enquiry that trawled the views of thousands of witnesses from all walks of life as well as official statements from many other countries. From this exercise we crystallised the 12 aims, placing them in three groups – children, their world, their education. Many schools have now adopted them and believe them to be wholly apposite.[39] Indeed, when you look at the middle four about 'self, others and the wider world' – encouraging respect and reciprocity; promoting interdependence and sustainability; empowering local, national and global citizenship; and celebrating culture and community – you may agree that these are if anything more urgent now than they were then.

But the crucial procedural point about aims is that they should mean what they say. They are not the icing on the curriculum cake but its raw ingredients. They should drive what is taught and how, and they should shape and inform the values and life of the school as a whole. If a school claims to foster children's engagement and autonomy, or sustainability and global citizenship, or to excite their imaginations, we are entitled to ask where and how. In the words of CPRT's aims priority: *Develop and apply a coherent vision for twenty-first-century primary education; enact [it] through curriculum, pedagogy and the wider life of the school.*

Curriculum

And what of curriculum? CPRT's priority is to *develop a broad, balanced and rich entitlement curriculum which responds to both national and local need, eliminates the damaging division of status and quality between core and non-core, and teaches every subject, domain or aspect to the highest possible standard.* We add that in the world's fifth richest nation this is surely a minimal requirement for public education, not an unattainable ideal.

After a protracted national curriculum review starting with Govian fanfares in 2011, the government invited but largely ignored the advice of its 'expert group' and thousands of equally expert submissions, bent the international evidence to suit its purposes, and proposed what it had decided before its review was launched. Subsequent consultations achieved some trimming at the margins – and I count the reinstatement of a programme of study for spoken language as a modest victory, for a Freedom of Information request[40] has shown that it was in direct response to the evidence I presented.[41] But otherwise, the September 2013 framework says it all: 88 pages for English, 52 pages for maths, 44 pages for science and just 35 pages for the remaining nine subjects, or two or three pages for each of the latter that are so brief and generalised as to be almost useless.[42]

So the old, deeply damaging two-tier curriculum continues to reign supreme, notwithstanding concerns expressed by chief inspectors as well as teachers and researchers. Meanwhile, drama is no more than implicit and what the framework *does* say, for example about literacy, has attracted as much dismay as what it doesn't. In any case, after all the fanfares and frustrations, it turns out that this national curriculum is not national at all, because it applies only to some schools. Indeed, it is neither national nor, in the sense that most people understand the word, a curriculum. Rather it is a list of subjects that starts in massive prescriptive detail before tailing off into oh-please-yourself insignificance, thus giving the lie to all that talk of 'breadth and balance', let alone 'the best that has been thought and said'. There is of course an alternative: the Cambridge Primary Review primary curriculum framework of aims and domains, which balanced national entitlement and consistency with, through its community curriculum, local responsiveness.[43]

What this sorry tale illustrates is disdain or evidence as well as poverty of vision. In the national curriculum, as in the proposed EBacc (from which the arts are excluded altogether) the arts fall victim to all three. Yet we know that the arts are not only essential in themselves for both individual development and national culture, but they also meet the most instrumental criteria of utility. In 2016 the arts industries contributed £84 billion to the UK economy,[44] and a US research review reported that properly conceived and rigorously taught the arts can enhance: pupil motivation and engagement, including attendance, persistence, attention, aspiration and risk-taking; pupil achievement in tests of reading and mathematics; skill transfer from the arts to other subjects, including, again, reading and mathematics; habits of mind across all areas of learning, including problem-solving, critical and creative thinking, and the capacity to deal with ambiguity and complexity; and social competencies including collaboration, teamwork, tolerance and self-confidence.[45]

Assessment

This priority is stated in terms which ought not to be problematic but for ministers apparently is: *Encourage approaches to assessment that enhance learning as well as test it, that support rather than distort the curriculum and that pursue standards and quality in all areas of learning, not just the core subjects.* What could be more obvious and desirable than this? Instead we have policies that distort the curriculum, treat tests in literacy and numeracy as proxies for children's learning across the curriculum as a whole, and generate unacceptable levels of stress among both children and teachers. Key Stage 2 tests remain the elephant in the curriculum.

Meanwhile, assessment enquiries are set up, they report, they recommend, they are followed by more reviews, and very little changes. Who now remembers the Secretary of State's Expert Group on Assessment in 2009? Or DfE's Testing and Accountability proposals in 2013? Or the 2015 Commission on Assessment Without Levels? Or Lord Bew's Key Stage 2 Testing and Accountability Review in 2011?

Now it is the Select Committee's turn. On 23 September 2016 it launched yet another primary assessment enquiry. We are told that it will 'scrutinise reforms to primary assessment and their impact on teaching and learning in primary schools . . . and cover the wider effects of assessment on primary schools, as well as possible next steps for Government policy'.[46]

If the Select Committee were only half aware of the evidence already assembled and cogently presented by teachers, researchers, professional associations, organisations like the Assessment Reform Group, campaigns like Better

Without Baseline and More Than a Score, and of course the Cambridge Primary Review and Trust; if, ignorant of all that, the Committee had read only Wynne Harlen's report for the Trust grounded in a lifetime of distinguished work in the field and entitled *Assessment, Standards and Quality of Learning in Primary Education*,[47] then it wouldn't need to launch yet another enquiry. The unfathomable question is why, when the case for genuine and radical assessment reform has been so strenuously and repeatedly made, and sound and workable alternatives have been proposed, successive governments take no notice.

Pedagogy

And so we come to the Trust's final priority and perhaps the heart of the matter: *Develop a pedagogy of repertoire, rigour, evidence and principle, rather than mere compliance, with a particular emphasis on fostering the high quality classroom talk which children's development, learning and attainment require.*

It is through pedagogy that aims become reality and a paper curriculum is translated into those classroom relationships, decisions, actions, interactions and experiences that produce learning. The Cambridge Review final report said 'Good teaching makes a difference. Excellent teaching can transform lives.'[48] The opportunities are high. So are the stakes.

Here the policy rubicon was crossed not with the current government's obsession with phonics but in 1998 by New Labour's literacy and numeracy strategies. Then, for the first time, ministers told teachers not just what to teach but how. Of course they have banged on since time immemorial about the advantage of so-called 'traditional' over so-called 'progressive' methods and have heaped insults on proponents of the latter. Yet until 1998 they held to the line drawn by then Secretary of State Kenneth Clarke in 1992, that 'questions about how to teach are not for government to determine'.[49]

For a while the coalition government appeared to revert to this position, claiming to banish New Labour's control freakery and give teaching back to teachers. But there are other ways of exerting influence on classroom life. Michael Gove did it by divisive rhetoric – 'enemies of promise/Marxists hell bent on destroying our schools' and all that. Nick Gibb has done it through phonics, which is essentially a matter of pedagogy but which he defined as curriculum so as to make it compulsory. The other ploy is less direct. Through a raft of so-called 'expert groups' whose generous complement of policy-compliant members produce supposedly 'independent' reports, government ensures that the agenda of a profession that ministers claim to want to liberate remains firmly on message. I exempt from this criticism three of the four members of the national curriculum expert group.

One such 'expert group' has just produced, with DfE support, a report on 'effective primary teaching practice' for the Teaching Schools Council.[50] I was consulted while this work was in progress and presented the group with all the relevant material from the Cambridge Review and Trust, including the Review's several reports on aspects of pedagogy and Usha Goswami's authoritative update for the Trust on the implications for teaching of what we know from neuroscience and psychology about children's learning.[51] But when the TSC report was published it ignored not only all this but also the even vaster body of evidence from Britain's biggest and most comprehensive programme of research into pedagogy, the ESRC Teaching and Learning and Research Programme – TLRP – that Andrew Pollard directed and to which I had also pointed.[52]

Making politically-vetted 'expert groups' the gatekeepers of good practice does not give teaching back to teachers. Teachers themselves, like other higher-order professionals, must have the autonomous command of the professional knowledge and evidence that their job requires. As the Cambridge Review said:

> We need now to move to a position where research-grounded teaching repertoires and principles are introduced through initial training and refined and extended through experience and CPD, and teachers acquire as much command of the evidence and principles which underpin the repertoires as they do of the skills needed in their use. The test of this alternative view of professionalism is that teachers should be able to give a coherent justification for their practices citing (i) evidence, (ii) pedagogical principle and (iii) educational aim, rather than offering the unsafe defence of compliance with what others expect. Anything less is educationally unsound.[53]

This, in fact, is in line with the government's professed intention to make teaching a self-improving profession and with the remit of the newly-established Chartered College of Teaching,[54] so although in 2009 some found it daunting it anticipated the current direction of travel. But if this seems to place too big a burden on individual teachers – why, you may ask, should each of us have to reinvent the wheel, and when do we have the time? – I stress, as the Chartered College stresses, that professional development and expertise are about partnership, networking and knowledge exchange, within schools, between schools, between teachers and researchers. The dialogic teaching principles of collectivity, reciprocity, mutual support and cumulative learning apply in the staffroom no less than the classroom. That's the approach that the Trust's networks have adopted through their reading groups, the South West Research Schools Network and the Research Active Schools Roadshows in Leeds, Canterbury and Exeter.

★★★

Conclusion

The penultimate chapter of the Cambridge Review final report classified New Labour's education policies by the responses that, according to our submission and soundings data, they provoked. At one extreme there was general approval, albeit with reservations, for Labour's childhood agenda – the Children's Plan,

Sure Start, Narrowing the Gap and the expansion of early childhood care and education. Most people felt that here the government had been right to intervene and its intervention had made a positive difference. At the other end were national targets and testing, performance tables, the naming and shaming of schools, and Ofsted inspection as it then was, all of which provoked widespread concern. Policies like EYFS and the national curriculum were seen as sound in principle but unsatisfactory in practice, while the national literacy, numeracy and primary strategies produced mixed reactions but veered more towards hostility than support.

Romping through CPRT's last four priorities – aims, curriculum, pedagogy and assessment – I suggest that the situation now is even worse than it was then. Aims remain a yawning gap between perfunctory rhetoric and impoverished political reality. The new national curriculum is considerably less enlightened than the one it replaced and indeed being no longer national it's hard to understand why it's there at all; national assessment remains contentious and is now even more confused and confusing than it was; and most government forays into pedagogy are naive, ill-founded and doctrinaire. In these matters, then, I submit – in the words of those distinguished figures who wrote to the press in 2008 - that policy remains the problem rather than the solution.

And when we observe ministers' dogged insistence, in the face of the growing crisis in teacher recruitment and retention, which itself speaks volumes about the culture that policy has created, that ministers are right and everybody else is an enemy of promise, we might again recall Edmond Holmes's judgement in 1911 that 'over the higher levels of the educational world there hangs the heavy stupor of profound self-satisfaction'.[55]

So it's clear that to our list of eight priorities we must add a ninth: as a precondition for any further attempts to reform English education, reform of the policy process itself.

Notes

1   On the cover of *Teaching Times 1:3* (2009) two sumo wrestlers slugged it out under the title 'Clash of the titans: Rose vs Alexander.' The small print read: 'Beyond the headlines the Rose Review . . . offers no change at all, argues Sue Lyle. Instead it's the independent Cambridge Primary Review that should shape future policy.'

2   Quotations collated by Polly Curtis in *The Guardian*, 16 October 2009.

3   Polly Curtis in *The Guardian*, 24 October 2009.

4   Mortimore *et al* 1988. Peter Mortimore, formerly Director of the University of London Institute of Education, also served as Associate Commissioner and member of the Research Committee for the 1991–33 Paul Hamlyn Foundation National Commission on Education.

5   Peter Mortimore in *The Guardian*, 3 November 2009.

6   Peter Mortimore in *The Guardian*, 3 November 2009.

7   Alexander 2010a, 514.

8   Ed Balls, Secretary of State at the Department for Children, Schools and Families (DCSF) from 2007–10, lost his Parliamentary seat at the 2015 general election. He was replaced as Secretary of State at the renamed Department for Education (DfE) by Conservative Michael Gove, who was followed by Nicky Morgan (2014). Gove and

Morgan were on opposite sides of the Brexit debate – he for, she against – until after the 2016 referendum. Meanwhile, Balls went into show business, competing in *Strictly Come Dancing*, *Would I Lie to You* and *Celebrity Best Home Cook*. Gove remained in government as a prominent member of the post 2019 Johnson cabinet. Morgan was elevated to the House of Lords.

9 Alexander 2010a, 496.
10 https://cprtrust.org.uk/about_cprt/priorities/ (accessed May 2021).
11 Listed and available for download at https://cprtrust.org.uk/about_cprt/cprt-publica tions/ (accessed May 2021).
12 https://cprtrust.org.uk/networks/ (accessed May 2021).
13 The CPRT blogs are archived at https://cprtrust.org.uk/cprt-blog/ (accessed May 2021).
14 Holmes 2011.
15 Clegg and Laws 2013.
16 Ofsted 2015a.
17 Coffield *et al* 2008.
18 Holmes 1911, v.
19 Holmes 1911, v–vi.
20 Robinson (2014).
21 www.unicef.org.uk/rights-respecting-schools/ (accessed May 2021).
22 For a discussion of voice in teaching, see Alexander 2020, 53–60, and Chapter 18 in this volume.
23 Deakin Crick *et al* (2005).
24 Jo Cox, Labour MP for Batley and Spen, was murdered by a far-right nationalist in June 2016.
25 Burnett 2016. By 2021 these anxieties were even more pronounced, and Ofsted published alarming findings on the role of social media in the rising tide of sexual abuse in schools and colleges (Ofsted 2021b).
26 https://cprtrust.org.uk/research/classroom-talk/ (accessed May 2020). See this book, Chapters 15–18, and Alexander 2020.
27 Wilkinson and Pickett 2010 (first published in 2009); Pickett and Vanderbloemen 2015.
28 Ainscow *et al* 2016.
29 Jopling and Vincent 2016.
30 Ainscow *et al* 2016.
31 Conservative Prime Minister Theresa May in 2016.
32 DCSF 2008.
33 Alexander 2010a, 488.
34 Mansell 2016.
35 Later disputed by Downing Street but at the time (November 2013) this was reported in the right-leaning *Sun* and *Daily Mail*, as well as the left-leaning *Guardian*.
36 Bourn *et al* 2016.
37 https://cprtrust.org.uk/cprt-blog/whats-the-point/ (accessed May 2021).
38 CPRT 2016. Reprinted as Alexander 2016a.
39 Alexander 2010a, 197–9. See also chapter 8.
40 DfE 2013a.
41 Alexander 2012a; DfE 2013a.
42 DfE 2013b.
43 Alexander 2010a, 237–78.
44 www.gov.uk/government/news/creative-industries-worth-almost-10-million-an-hour-to-economy (accessed May 2021 – press release from the Department of Culture, Media and Sport, 26 January 2016). By 2018 the figure was £92.5 billion (Cebr 2020).
45 PCAH 2011.
46 https://publications.parliament.uk/pa/cm201617/cmselect/cmeduc/682/68202.htm (accessed May 2021).

47 Harlen 2014.
48 Alexander 2010a, 279.
49 Quoted in Alexander *et al* 1992, 5.
50 Keeble 2016.
51 Goswami 2015.
52 James and Pollard 2008, 2011.
53 Alexander 2010a, 496.
54 https://chartered.college/aboutus/ (accessed May 2021).
55 Holmes 1911, vi.

7 Evidence, mediation and narrative

Edited version of the 2014 Godfrey Thomson Trust Lecture at the University of Edinburgh. Published under its original title – 'Evidence, policy and the reform of primary education: a cautionary tale' – in *Forum* 56(3), 349–75 (2014).

The 'pestilential calm of despotism'?

In 2008, at the peak of the Labour government's drive for educational transformation, four prominent academics wrote to *The Independent*:

> We are specialists with considerable experience of the different phases of education who have come independently to the same conclusion: that government policy is no longer the solution to the difficulties we face but our greatest problem. . . . It is not only the torrent of new policy that rains down on each sector, the constant changes in direction and the automatic rubbishing of any discomforting evidence. . . . It is also the failure of successive ministers to appreciate that reform has to be accompanied by continuity if the stability of our educational institutions and the quality of their courses are to be preserved.[1]

Since under Labour's coalition successors neither the torrent nor the attendant 'rubbishing' have abated, this complaint from Professors Ball, Coffield, Scott and Taylor deserves to be revisited.

Behind their letter lay a deeper unease: the centralisation of educational decision-making and control that England has experienced since 1988. This unease is now widespread, except perhaps among those who have benefited from ministerial patronage and preferment and the inducements and honours through which the coalition government's free school, academy and teaching school schemes have been promoted.[2]

For what cannot be denied is the extent to which ministerial power has increased. In 1950, Atlee's Minister of Education, Lancastrian George Tomlinson, famously said, 'Minister knows nowt about curriculum'.[3] This was a statement of legal fact, not a confession of ignorance. Government provided the administrative framework; local authorities and schools decided what and

DOI: 10.4324/9781315169378-8

how to teach. Even the inspectors stayed clear. When I started teaching in primary schools in 1964 I armed myself with the curriculum handbook produced for the Ministry of Education (as DfE was then known) by Her Majesty's Inspectorate (HMI). It was entitled, cautiously, *Suggestions for the consideration of teachers and others concerned with the work of primary schools.*[4] Education Minister Tony Crosland, who introduced sweeping changes to other aspects of English education, nevertheless respected this compact: 'I didn't regard either myself or my officials,' he said in 1967, 'as competent to interfere with the curriculum.'[5]

Fast forward to 2013 and Secretary of State Michael Gove. No polite 'suggestions for the consideration of teachers' in *his* curriculum prospectus, and certainly no disavowal of omniscience. Here he is, laying it on the line and lobbing one of his trademark insults while he is about it: 'We have stripped out the . . . piously vapid happy-talk and instead laid out the knowledge that every child is entitled to expect they be taught.'[6]

There has been a similar shift, in substance if not tone, in other areas of education, including pedagogy, the final frontier of professional autonomy. In 1991, echoing Crosland, Education Secretary Kenneth Clarke said: 'Questions about how to teach are not for government to determine.'[7] Just six years Tony Blair entered government with the slogan 'Education, education, education' and imposed closely-prescribed daily literacy and numeracy lessons on every primary school in England. These told teachers not just what to teach but when and how.[8]

Nor is the phrase 'rains down' in that letter to *The Independent* – 'the torrent of new policies that rains down' – mere hyperbole. Between 1996 and 2004 England's primary schools received 459 official documents on literacy alone.[9] That's over one a week, even before we start counting the many directives on numeracy and other matters in which government also believed it necessary to intervene. More recently, Stephen Ball takes a period of eight months between June 2017 and February 2018 and lists 18 major DfE initiatives to which schools – secondary and primary – were expected to respond, and comments:

> Despite the deregulation of provision and greater institutional freedoms offered to some schools, all schools are subject to targeted, systemic and partial, disparate and uncoordinated, and repetitive interventions from government . . . Schools are being expected to be both innovative and conservative, to deliver social mobility and social cohesion, to improve cognitive and noncognitive skills, to be collaborative and entrepreneurial. There is centralisation and fragmentation at the same time; there is deregulation, deconcentration, and intervention at the same time. The state acts as both gardener and gamekeeper – that is, it employs both direct and indirect forms of control, both prescription and direction, and contracting out and performance management – another kind of incoherence. In the midst of this hyperactivity, policy begets policy as new 'solutions' are generated to respond to the failures, inadequacies, and inefficacies of previous fixes.[10]

Staying in the same metaphorical territory as that *Independent* letter, it is generally accepted that the watershed in this process was the Thatcher government's 1987 Education Reform Bill, enacted as law in 1988. Of this the then Labour opposition education shadow Jack Straw said: 'Under the disguise of fine phrases like "parental choice" and "decentralisation", [it] will deny choice and instead centralise power and control over schools, colleges and universities in the hands of the secretary of state in a manner without parallel in the western world.'[11] Rousing words indeed, worthy of that other Jack Straw who in 1381 was one of the leaders of the Peasants' Revolt. But in view of Labour's reforms a decade later, Straw Junior might have added, 'You ain't seen nothing yet.'

As might Michael Gove. He continued but also far exceeded what had been initiated by the Conservatives in 1987 and Labour in 1997, further weakening local authority control, greatly expanding directly-funded academies along American charter school lines and encouraging parents, charities and business to set up government-funded free schools, all in the name of standards, choice and freedom. Meanwhile he tightened the government's grip on curriculum, assessment and inspection, while with local authorities in steep decline he removed the remaining checks and balances on absolute ministerial power, ensuring that nothing obstructed the line of command between his office and the schools.

It's therefore pertinent rather than fanciful to recall the warning of Chartist leader William Lovett in 1840:

> While we are anxious to see a general system of education adopted, we have no doubt of the impropriety of yielding such an important duty as the education of our children to any government . . . If ever knavery and hypocrisy succeed in establishing the centralising, state-moulding and knowledge-forcing scheme in England, so assuredly will the people degenerate into passive submission to injustice, and the spirit sink into the pestilential calm of despotism.[12]

Strong words, but then he was writing from Warwick Gaol having been imprisoned for posting placards condemning the Birmingham police for their heavy-handed response to a peaceful demonstration: not entirely unfamiliar territory. But Lovett's warning that some policies are too important for government, or that they trespass too far on individual liberties, is worth pondering; for state-moulding and knowledge-forcing are what, in some countries, education is very much about.

Yet undiscriminating opposition to centralisation is unhelpful and unrealistic. Governments are elected to govern, and even in authoritarian regimes some aspects of education are less centralised than others. Dale, for example, distinguishes *funding, regulation* and *delivery*; while OECD differentiates *organisation of instruction, personnel management, planning and structures* and *resources*.[13] The Cambridge Primary Review grouped 19 strands of educational policy into six broad areas before assessing their impact: children and families; curriculum; pedagogy;

assessment, standards and accountability; teachers, teacher education and work-force reform; national and local infrastructure, finance and governance.[14]

From these I select three examples: children and childhood, curriculum, and educational standards. I might also be expected to comment on the current rumblings about free schools and academies. These are central to Michael Gove's liberationist theology and are already provoking accusations of zealotry, perjury, incompetence and financial malpractice comparable to those roused by charter schools in the United States.[15] But the issue is too current and heated for considered assessment, and hard evidence is as yet too sparse.

About the paper's stance and focus I enter an important caveat. Complaints about 'the torrent of new policy that rains down on each sector, the constant changes in direction and the automatic rubbishing of any discomforting evidence' may challenge the way policy is created but do not necessarily prove that a policy is misguided in intention or ineffective in outcome. Such complaints prompt a necessary distinction between policy as promulgated, the policy process, and the way policy is enacted. In what follows I shall comment on all three dimensions and shall return to the distinction at the end. For the moment, we need to be alert to the danger of treating policy as monolithic.

Case 1: children and childhood

Following several appalling cases of child neglect and abuse which exposed a lack of co-ordination and liaison within and between the various local authority services concerned with children's education and welfare, Labour launched its 2003 'Every Child Matters' initiative. This required local authorities to provide 'joined-up' multi-agency services in education and care, and to give all children entitlement to support in respect of their health, safety, educational achievement and economic wellbeing. A Children's Commissioner was appointed. The remit of Ofsted (England's equivalent of Scotland's HMIE) was expanded to cover children's services as well as schools. Local authority directors of education became directors of children's services. The Department for Education and Skills became the Department for Children, Schools and Families. Michael Gove renamed it the Department for Education, though he did retain a Minister for Children and Families.

Then, encompassing inequality as well as protection, the Sure Start scheme was expanded to take in the 20 per cent of areas in England where social and economic disadvantage were most concentrated. These initiatives were followed by the 2004 Children Act, the 2006 Childcare Act, the 2007 Children's Plan and the 2007 Narrowing the Gap initiative which sought to reduce the gulf in social, educational and other outcomes between vulnerable children and the rest. Simultaneously, attempts were made to rationalise the complex mix of early years education and provision by requiring all providers, public and private, to adhere to the care and learning requirements of an Early Years Foundation Stage (EYFS).

Much of this work was taken forward by the government elected in 2010. Labour's child protection structures were retained, as, initially, was the EYFS.

Narrowing the Gap was upgraded to the Pupil Premium scheme, which in 2014 provided schools with an additional £1,300 for every pupil eligible for free school meals to help them raise the attainment of disadvantaged pupils. The cost of the Pupil Premium was substantial: £2.5 billion in 2014.[16]

Although questions have been raised about the implementation of some of these initiatives,[17] their rationale has been broadly accepted. There's a consensus, then, that in addressing gross inequalities and inadequacies in protection, support and provision for young children, and in attempting to close the attainment gap between disadvantaged children and the rest, not only is it right and necessary for government to intervene but government is perhaps the only body with the necessary power and resources to do so effectively. This indeed was the conclusion of the Cambridge Primary Review.[18]

Yet even here support shades into opposition. The Cambridge Review reported unease about the tendency for the developmental goals of the EYFS to be undercut by pressure to get children reading and writing as soon as possible. This transmuted into resistance when in 2014 the government made the EYFS non-statutory, replaced it with statutory baseline assessment and reintroduced tests of 7-year-olds. And when in 2007 the Review published research evidence identifying the increasing 'scholarisation' of early childhood through formal learning backed by increasing quantities of homework[19] – both of them starting at a much younger age in England than in many other countries – we triggered widespread support. Except of course from ministers: they accused us of being more interested in play than standards. That dichotomy, as every early years expert will testify, is untenable.

What government failed to understand – and regrettably this goes for some schools too – was that young children learn at least as much outside school as within it and that some of this learning is of a kind that schools can't replicate. Researchers calculate that school effects count for only about 30 per cent of pupil attainment.[20] This statistic is rightly cited to justify interventions of a compensatory kind with families that are vulnerable, disadvantaged or marginalised. But it's also an argument for respecting children's out-of-school learning and allowing parents the same autonomy that teachers constantly demand.

For behind anxieties about the increasing intrusion of the state into children's lives there's a debate about childhood itself. Protecting young children is one thing; prescribing the character of their lives is quite another. To secure balance in this debate, here's what the Cambridge Primary Review concluded from the many written submissions it received on this subject and from its conversations with parents, teachers, community leaders and children themselves in 87 'community soundings' in regional locations ranging from Cornwall to Northumberland and Lancashire to Kent, and including conurbations like Birmingham and London:[21]

> There are legitimate concerns about the quality of children's lives, but the 'crisis' of contemporary childhood may have been overstated, and children themselves were the Review's most upbeat witnesses. The real

and urgent crisis concerns those children whose lives are blighted by poverty, disadvantage, risk and discrimination, and in such matters governments are right to intervene. Meanwhile, among the many positives of modern childhood our report celebrates the evidence on just how much young children know, understand and can do, and argues for a primary education which heeds their voices and empowers them as both learners and citizens. But the report also argues that the unique character and potential of childhood should be protected from a system apparently bent on pressing children into a uniform mould at an ever-younger age.[22]

Case 2: curriculum

In the arena of curriculum, policies have proved even more contentious. The story starts in 1986 when, following ten years of ministerial muttering, Education Secretary Keith Joseph insisted there would be no national curriculum in England. One year later, as is the way with ministerial denials, a national curriculum was announced by his successor, Kenneth Baker. A year after that it was enshrined in law as the 1988 Education Reform Act.

Initial resistance to this paradigm of Lovett's 'centralising, state-moulding and knowledge-forcing scheme' was eventually replaced by acceptance that its content was benign rather than threatening – though there was an awful lot of it – and that it had secured children's entitlement to the broad basic education that in too many primary schools they had not previously received. Thus, ten years earlier, HMI had found that whether children encountered science, history, geography or music in their primary schools depended largely on what their teachers felt inclined to teach.[23]

The exceptions were literacy and numeracy, which have been constants in English primary schools since 'payment by results' in the 1860s, together usually occupying about half of each day. 'Do literacy and numeracy in the morning when the children are fresh' was the stock advice to new teachers, signalling that art, music and other trivia should be 'done' in the afternoon when the freshness has worn off. Despite this, the refrain from the political and media right has always been the claimed neglect of literacy and numeracy rather than the actual neglect of the arts and humanities.

Hence, in the list of education policy milestones in the third chapter of the final report of the Cambridge Primary Review you will find 'Back to basics' in 1969, 'Back to basics again' in 1992, and 'Back to basics yet again' in 1998.[24] The year 1969 refers to the now infamous Black Papers; 1992 was John Major's pre-election diatribe against progressive education – 'We will take no lectures from those who led the long march of mediocrity through our schools . . . My belief is a return to basics in education. The progressive theorists have had their say and . . . they've had their day.'[25] The year 1998 marked Labour's 'disapplication' of the non-core national curriculum so that schools would concentrate all their time and energy on implementing the government's literacy and numeracy strategies, targets would be met, and the Secretary of State would not have to honour his promise to resign.

Yet these earlier 'back to basics' flurries seem almost muted by comparison with events after Michael Gove launched the latest national curriculum review in 2011. Actually, this episode starts in 2007, under Labour. That was the point at which, having welcomed the Cambridge Primary Review when it was launched a year earlier, ministers became uneasy about the first of its interim reports and the anti-government spin the media attached to them. According to Mick Waters, the then head of curriculum at QCA, ministers saw which way the media wind was blowing and, aware that we were about to publish proposals on the primary curriculum, launched a pre-emptive strike in the form of their own primary curriculum review, commissioned from former primary chief inspector Jim Rose.[26] He and I had been friends and colleagues since the 1980s (and indeed had been joint members of an earlier government enquiry)[27] so this was frustrating to both of us and we attempted to pool our ideas. But ministers wanted none of this, and presented the two reviews as implacably opposed, as of course did the press.

The Rose curriculum report was published in 2009[28] and Labour immediately set in train the legislative process leading to its implementation. But they were too late. The Conservatives didn't like Rose, it fell victim to the pre-election legislative 'wash-up' when Parliament decided which bills to push through and which to dump, and one of the first acts of Michael Gove as incoming Secretary of State was to order a new national curriculum review with a very different remit. Primary schools, which had started preparing to implement Rose and were broadly in sympathy with its proposals, were not at all pleased.

The Rose report was unacceptable to Gove partly because he judged it to be tainted by 1960s progressivism (which it was not) but more simply because it was Labour's creation. For another constant in education policymaking in England is the lack of incrementalism in highly contested areas like curriculum and the refusal to respect and build on earlier achievements. Each new government rejects as a matter of course what has gone before and, in what is now a predictable display of ministerial machismo, replaces it with a 'tough new' initiative designed to bring schools back to the path from which they have strayed. In Gove's case, the neglected path was 'essential knowledge' in the 'basics' – as if Labour's daily literacy and numeracy lessons were about something else. Tough perhaps, but hardly new.

What Gove also did was to maximise the prospects for securing a national curriculum true to his personal beliefs by abolishing QCA, the body statutorily responsible for curriculum and assessment, and taking the entire process in-house at the Department for Education. He set up an 'expert panel' with a compliant chair but then rejected its report[29] because the panel's other members were off message.[30] The message in question came from two sources: first, E.D. Hirsch's critique of the knowledge deficit in the United States and his cataloguing of the 'core knowledge' that every American child should acquire;[31]

second, from a belief that the way to raise standards was to emulate the prescribed curricula of PISA high performers like Singapore, Hong Kong, South Korea and Japan[32] – though, significantly, not Finland, for Finland's PISA success was the product of a system that ideologically was as far removed as possible from the regimes of performativity and marketisation which Gove intended to impose.[33]

The Gove curriculum review was more than usually selective in its use of evidence about what was wrong with the existing national curriculum and what might be done to improve it. Thus, for example, instead of reducing the corrosive split between the core and non-core subjects, which had long been criticised by the inspectorate as well as by the Cambridge Review,[34] the government deepened it still further. This 'two-tier' curriculum (as former chief inspector David Bell called it[35]) not only undermined breadth, balance, quality and opportunities for learning transfer between subjects. It was also counterproductive, for inspection evidence had consistently shown that the primary schools whose pupils performed best in the national tests at age 11 were those that provided a broad, rich and well-managed curriculum aiming for high standards in all subjects, not just in the basics.[36] This finding was too counter-intuitive or inconvenient for the present government, just as it had been for Labour. Yet as far back as 1985 a Thatcher government White Paper had criticised the 'mistaken belief . . . that a concentration on basic skills is of itself enough to improve achievement in literacy and numeracy',[37] so in this matter recent governments have moved decisively backwards, failing even to heed the advice of their political kith and kin.

Then there's the perplexing case of spoken language in the new national curriculum, and here the story takes a more personal turn.

The long-standing evidence on the formative relationship between spoken language, cognition and learning, especially in the early and primary years, is widely accepted, as is the more recent evidence on the link between cognitively-challenging classroom talk and effective teaching.[38] In 2011, I contributed to an international conference in Pittsburgh under the auspices of the American Educational Research Association, which reviewed this evidence and concluded that we now have a critical mass of data showing not only that such talk advances children's engagement, learning and understanding but that it also raises their test scores in literacy, numeracy and science.[39] The Pittsburgh conference coincided with the launch of the current government's national curriculum review, which was in part impelled by concern about standards, so I took the matter straight to Michael Gove and proposed a high level seminar of ministers, officials and researchers to consider its implications for the new national curriculum. He agreed, and the seminar took place in February 2012, with keynotes from myself[40] and, by videolink from Pittsburgh, Lauren Resnick, a leading US researcher in this field.

At the seminar the case for raising and sharpening the profile of what at that time was called 'speaking and listening' was rehearsed and accepted. But afterwards, a minister who must remain nameless told me: 'I understand the arguments and evidence, but I daren't raise the profile of spoken language in the new national curriculum because it will distract teachers from their task of raising standards in literacy. And it will encourage idle chatter in class.'

'Idle chatter in class': the phrase is redolent of an era when children were seen but not heard, and lofty schoolmasterly disdain dismissed as inconsequential any talk other than 'correct' answers to closed questions. In the subsequent drafts of the new national curriculum, and notwithstanding the weight of evidence with which ministers had been presented, spoken language was given an even lower profile than previously.

Clearly, the minister just didn't get it. What others fully understood was that talk is an essential concomitant of learning to read and write, not a distraction from it, so literacy and oracy must go hand in hand. Self-evidently, talk is also vital in its own right. Further, the kind of classroom talk we were advocating is anything but 'idle'. It is purposeful, focused, structured, extended and cognitively challenging. But the minister stuck to his guns, and it was only after sustained pressure over the next 12 months that the government at last agreed to include a programme of study for spoken language in the final draft of its new national curriculum. However, though I count this a victory,[41] the published requirements remain too brief and generalised, so the fallout of misguided ministerial intervention in this vital matter will be with us for some time.

Here, then, we have a three-way tussle between peer-reviewed evidence, political ideology and personal prejudice, and evidence as always is the loser, so this episode really does raise the question of whether curriculum is one of those areas where policy is the problem rather than the solution. All the more so when, in September 2013, the government presented the final version of England's new national curriculum, with its deeper than ever divide between 'the basics' and the rest, its cursory treatment of the arts and humanities and its abbreviated inclusion of spoken language,[42] and did so under the banner of 'the best that has been thought and said'.[43] The phrase[44] was not attributed: perhaps it was hoped that an ignorant populace would credit *Culture and Anarchy* to the Secretary of State himself.

Case 3: standards

My third example, educational standards, is the catch-22 of centralisation. The more policymakers micromanage, the more they risk blame when things go wrong, and the more they then strive to deflect the blame back onto those who, having lost their autonomy, are no longer culpable. Thus it was with the Blair government's standards drive, and thus it may prove to be for the present government, which cites the need to raise standards to justify policies on the national curriculum, assessment, inspection, free schools, academies, teaching schools and much else. National tests are high stakes for teachers but for centralising governments they are no less so.

Labour's standards initiatives included: national literacy and numeracy strategies with prescribed daily literacy and numeracy lessons; the extension of the previous government's test regime to include targets for the percentage of 11-year-olds who must achieve given levels; the publication of school and local authority test results and league tables; beefed-up inspections resulting in the naming and shaming of underperforming schools; competencies and standards for teachers' initial training and continuing development; ring-fenced funding for relevant CPD; and the appointment of local authority school improvement partners charged with checking schools' measured outcomes and ensuring compliance with the national strategies.

This was the stick, and a fearsome one it was too. Small wonder that one of the Cambridge Review's research teams concluded that together these initiatives amounted to a 'state theory of learning'[45] – a post-Soviet echo of William Lovett's 'state-moulding and knowledge-forcing scheme'. Without doubt, thousands of teachers, as predicted by Lovett, sank into 'passive submission'. The carrot was a substantial increase in school funding, teacher pay and staff appointments: 35,000 additional primary teachers and 172,000 teaching assistants appointed between 1997 and 2009.

As is well known, David Blunkett, Labour's first Secretary of State, promised to resign if the government's 2002 target for literacy and numeracy standards was not met. It wasn't, but Blunkett moved to another ministry and his successor resigned instead. Labour then commissioned an evaluation of its literacy and numeracy strategies from the University of Toronto.[46] This offered a decidedly mixed conclusion, though that didn't stop government from claiming that the strategies were an unqualified success. Then came the Cambridge Primary Review. Mindful of the heat of this particular potato we commissioned no fewer than six independent reviews of national and international evidence on primary school standards from teams at Bath, Bristol, Durham, Cambridge and Manchester Metropolitan universities and the National Foundation for Educational Research.[47]

Then began the war of words. We published our six interim reports, together with briefings and press releases, in two instalments. As might be expected, our research teams exposed the complexity of the data and the difficulty of making hard and fast judgements, especially about trends over time. We identified evidence of initial success but also problems. Acting on the well-known journalistic maxim 'First simplify, then exaggerate',[48] the press ignored the positives in our reports and amplified the negatives with baleful headlines like: 'Primary tests blasted by experts' . . . 'Too much testing harms primary school pupils' . . . 'Literacy drive has almost no impact' . . . 'Millions wasted on teaching reading' . . . 'An oppressive system that is failing our children' . . . 'School system test-obsessed' . . . 'England's children among the most tested' . . . 'Our children are tested to destruction' . . . 'Primary pupils let down by Labour' . . . 'Primary schools have got worse' and 'A shattering failure for our masters'.[49]

Labour's response was bullish: 'There have never been so many outstanding primary schools' . . . 'The government does not accept that children are over-tested' . . . 'There have been unambiguous rises in results using standardised tests' . . . 'Primary standards are at their highest ever levels. This is not opinion: it is fact.'[50] Then Labour went for the jugular: 'These reports use tunnel vision to look at education' . . . 'Professor Alexander is entitled to his opinions but once again we fundamentally disagree with his views, as will parents across the country.'[51] (*His* views? These were the considered conclusions of six independent research teams). 'I am not going to apologise,' said the Secretary of State, 'for what parents want even if these researchers – on the basis of old research – don't like it.'[52]

In truth, our reviews of the evidence on standards led to something that neither politicians nor sub-editors can readily handle: a mixed message. The findings were both positive and negative. This was inevitable, because we tracked trends over time and uncovered methodological problems such as shifting test criteria and inconsistent data as well as the collateral curriculum damage[53] and increases in pupil and teacher stress that the press reported.

We also refuted[54] a number of the claims by which government defended its standards policy: testing of itself drives up standards; parents support testing; tests are the only way to hold schools to account; the pursuit of standards in 'the basics' is incompatible with a broad and balanced curriculum; literacy and numeracy test scores are valid proxies for standards across the entire curriculum; and – the most transparently unprovable claim of all – England has the highest standards ever. Ever? Since when? 1997? 1066? And who was present at the big bang to start measuring?

And so the slanging match over standards goes on, generating ever more heat than light. Before the 2010 election Labour cited PISA 2009 to prove the success of its drive to raise standards in England's schools. After the election the new government used PISA 2009 to show that, far from rising, student performance had 'plummeted' under Labour from 12th to 23rd in the world, and Michael Gove's doom-laden verdict to Parliament barely concealed his political delight: 'Literacy, down; numeracy, down; science, down: fail, fail, fail.'[55] However, after re-analysing the data, John Jerrim of London University's Institute of Education concluded that PISA 2009 neither justified such alarmist claims nor provided a safe basis for the sweeping changes which, in the name of standards, Gove's government had introduced.[56] Then, in an added twist, after Gove had hailed PISA boss Andreas Schleicher as 'the man who knows more about education than anyone on the globe' for handing him what he thought was such devastating political ammunition, Gove's erstwhile ministerial deputy Nick Gibb[57] criticised Schleicher for 'pushing a . . . progressive approach to education' because instead of signing up to Gove's 'essential knowledge' he talked about skills and competencies.[58]

Meanwhile, others have questioned PISA's validity and reliability and the way it has been elevated into a measure of the performance not just of samples of 15-year-olds in limited aspects of their learning, which it is, but of entire education systems.[59] An increasing number of governments have succumbed to PISA panic in a scramble to cherry-pick the policies of those jurisdictions that for the moment occupy the winners' podium. Never mind differences in history, culture, demography and politics: if Singapore's 15-year-olds score higher in maths than England's they must have superior policies and we should copy them. If Shanghai's students outperform England's in PISA, let's invite their teachers over to show ours how it's done. These, I hasten to add, are real examples.

As thus conceived, the PISA-fuelled global educational race is in danger of spiralling out of control. It certainly prompts bizarre policy responses. In presenting the 2012 draft of England's revised national curriculum the Secretary of State said, 'We must ensure that our children master the essential core knowledge which *other nations* pass on to their pupils.'[60] Other nations? Granted globalisation and the absolute imperative of an international outlook, this is a pretty rum definition of 'the best that has been thought and said'. And if, as Denis Lawton argues, curriculum is a selection from culture,[61] the Singapore mathematics syllabus is an odd place for England's cultural selection to start.

Recurrent themes: evidence, mediation and narrative

Childhood, curriculum and standards: three policy cases from the many more I could have provided. I want next to cross cut these cases with three themes relating to the policy process as a whole. They are *evidence, mediation* and *narrative*. After considering these I shall add one more dimension – the relationship between policy as prescribed and enacted and the challenge of judging impact – before offering a verdict on the quoted claim about educational policy in England with which I started.

Theme 1: evidence

Evidence-informed policy, the wags tell us, is really policy-informed evidence, because governments first devise their policies then look around for evidence to justify them, ignoring what doesn't fit. On the strength of the Cambridge Primary Review's experience I can confirm that the relationship between evidence and policy is at the very least uneasy. If not as brutally cynical as 'policy-informed evidence' implies, the process is certainly selective. Three kinds of selectivity seem to be at work: *electoral, ideological* and *methodological*.

Electoral selectivity is illustrated by the Labour government's blunt rejection of any evidence that challenged the efficacy of its standards drive because to acknowledge such evidence would have been, for a government committed to 'education, education, education', political suicide. Similarly, Conservative ministers' suspicion of spoken language, the educational power of which is amply demonstrated in research, in part reflected the fear that it would compromise the government's 'back to basics' pitch on reading, writing and school discipline.

Ideological selectivity is illustrated by the Conservative government's refusal to accommodate research and inspection evidence on the true problems of the primary curriculum – problems such as the backwash into entitlement, quality and standards of the two-tier curriculum and the distortions produced by high-stakes testing – because these conflict with ministerial preference for a narrow spectrum of supposedly essential and largely propositional knowledge. For that reason, against the evidence that standards and breadth are interdependent, governments continue to insist that literacy and numeracy must override all else.

Methodological selectivity is marked by both governments' preference for what the US National Research Council called 'Type 1' and 'Type 2' educational research, that is large-scale quantitative studies, and McKinsey-style extrapolations from these for the purposes of identifying cause, effect and solution. Conspicuously absent from this evidential bank are 'type 3' studies that engage with teaching and learning to the depth that improving them requires.[62] So the top-down character of policy is reinforced by evidence which is as detached from school and classroom realities as are the policymakers themselves, and this detachment inflates ministerial perception of what interventions dreamed up in Westminster can achieve in classrooms. School improvement is then reduced to tautological banalities such as 'The quality of an education system cannot exceed the quality of its teachers', and 'High performance requires every child to succeed', both of which are from Michael Barber, Labour's one-time chief adviser on standards.[63]

Theme 2: mediation

Policy reaches the public through the media, over which policymakers exercise as much control as they can through the apparatus of communication strategies, press officers, leak, spin, briefings on and off the record, attributed interviews, unattributed quotes and so on. The relationship is one of mutual dependence and is fraught with risks on both sides.

Those such as academics who seek to convey evidence to policymakers are similarly circumscribed. They can write journal articles that few people read, or they can engage directly, entering the same arena as the policymakers themselves. Knowing how much hung on successful media exposure for an enquiry that government had initially welcomed but hadn't commissioned, the Cambridge Primary Review recruited an experienced director of communications. Each report was accompanied by a four-page briefing plus a one-page press release, so it was available in full, in summary and as highlights. Each publication event was preceded by a press conference, telephone briefings of key journalists and, where possible, strategically placed articles or interviews by Review members.

In one sense the strategy was highly successful: on five of the ten occasions between 2007 and 2009 when the Review published its reports, independent media analysis showed that it was top UK news story overall.[64] What we could not control, of course, was the nature of that media coverage. In this, it was the sub-editors rather than reporters who most ruthlessly enacted that maxim, 'first simplify, then exaggerate'. Broadsheet reports that were perceptive and balanced were frequently undermined by their headlines.

Yet it was to the headlines, not the accompanying pieces and certainly not the Cambridge Review reports themselves, that ministers felt obliged to respond. In our print and electronic archives we have records of all media coverage of the Review and all published government responses.[65] There is a clear and direct relation between them. Government responded less to what we reported than to what the media said we had reported. When the media attacked the government, the government attacked us.

But there is another level of mediation, and it is rarely discussed. Behind the scenes, ministers who were too busy to read our reports and briefings relied on their officials and advisers to relay and explain their contents. Such government mediators were as adept at spinning to their ministers as their press officers were at spinning to the media. In 2008, *Guardian* journalist Jenni Russell lifted the lid on this hidden layer of research mediation:

> Since 2003, every education secretary and minister has been distinguished by an almost wilful determination to ignore the mass of research that does not suit their agenda. Politically, that is the easiest choice. They are encouraged in this by their senior civil servants, whose careers have been built around delivering a particular agenda, and who have nothing to gain by seeing it change course. What is truly alarming is that ministers rarely even glimpse the reports they dismiss. Last year I mentioned a particularly critical Ofsted report to one minister. 'Oh, my people tell me there's nothing new in that,' he said, breezily. In fact, it had a great deal that was new and important, and the individuals who put thousands of man-hours into preparing it were probably writing it for an audience of three – of which the minister who never read it was the most important one. It seems that the Cambridge Primary Review is meeting the same fate. This extensive, diligent review of published evidence and new research was dismissed in 10 seconds by another minister in a private conversation: 'My people say it's rehashed.' Publicly, the Department for Children, Schools and Families has written off the latest reports as 'recycled, partial and out-of-date'.[66]

The role of senior civil servants and advisers, and the extent to which they mediate incoming evidence in order to protect their backs, is certainly worthy of investigation, because such mediation compromises not only evidence, but also the very policy process these people are employed to serve. As it happens, it also flouts the UK Civil Service Code:

> You must: provide information and advice, including advice to ministers, on the basis of the evidence, and accurately present the options and facts; take due account of expert and professional advice.
>
> You must not: ignore inconvenient facts or relevant considerations when providing advice or making decisions; be influenced by the prospect of personal gain.[67]

There's a footnote to this. Just before the 2010 general election I had a meeting with the then Secretary of State and the Schools Minister about the need to give more serious consideration to the implications of our final report for post-election government policy. This time the minders didn't get there first, for the ministers both had their own well-thumbed copies of our report. Brandishing his copy the Secretary of State said, 'I've read this now. It's rather good. There's a great deal here that we can use.' A few weeks later he was out of government. His officials kept their jobs.

Theme 3: narrative

Evidence and policy require narratives. Evidence has to be interpreted, and politicians need to offer a simple and convincing tale if they are to persuade people not just to vote for them but also to accept the pain that policy can cause.

Each of the headed paragraphs in the briefing on the Cambridge Primary Review final report tells its own story: 'Primary schools: how well are they doing?' . . . 'What is primary education for?' . . . 'A world fit to grow up in' . . . 'Standards: beyond the rhetoric' . . . 'Children's needs: equalising provision in an unequal society' . . . 'The curriculum: not there yet' . . . 'Assessment: reform, not tinkering' . . . 'A pedagogy of evidence and principle, not prescription' . . . 'Expertise for entitlement: re-thinking school staffing' . . . 'From novice to expert: reforming teacher education' . . . 'Decentralising control, redirecting funds, raising standards' . . . and even 'Policy: solution or problem'.[68] *Our* problem was that for each of these stories the government had written its own, and the versions didn't necessarily agree. Indeed it's frequently the case that evidential and political narratives find themselves in conflict, for seeking truth and retaining power are rather different pursuits. So I want to end by mentioning two of the most persistent and problematic narratives in the world of primary education policy in England.

First, there's the narrative of *progress*. This is essential to political survival. Although Labour were foolishly profligate with their 'best ever' claims, progress also needs a baseline, for policymakers must tell convincing stories not just about what they have achieved but also about how bad things were when they arrived. Remember George Orwell: 'Who controls the past controls the future.'[69] So the current government habitually talks up 'the economic mess we inherited from Labour' but rarely mentions the bankers and speculators who were the true culprits. And here's Labour's own narrative of what it found in 1997 and what by 2007 it had achieved. The storytellers are Downing Street Director of Delivery Michael Barber and Schools Minister Andrew Adonis, as they then were.

> Until the mid-1980s what happened in schools and classrooms was left almost entirely to teachers to decide . . . but, through no fault of their own the profession was uninformed . . . Under Thatcher, the system moved from uninformed professional judgement to uninformed prescription. The 1997–2001 Blair government inherited a system of uninformed prescription and replaced it with one of informed prescription . . . The White Paper signals the next shift: from informed prescription to informed professional judgement. The era of informed professional judgement could be the most successful so far in our educational history. It could be the era in which our education system becomes not just good but great.[70]

Anyone teaching before 1997 would be understandably offended by Barber's charge that their professional judgements were uninformed, and of course the truth is very different. Before 1997 teachers were thoroughly trained, and they had opportunities for continuing professional development (CPD) considerably more generous and sustained than are available today. Local authorities were visible and indeed persistent in giving advice and support, providing CPD, checking on standards and indeed testing pupil attainment. From 1964 the Schools Council produced an impressive selection of curriculum materials for schools in a wide range of subjects. From 1988 a succession of agencies – NCC, SCAA, QCA, QCDA – provided statutory and non-statutory guidance and materials on the national curriculum. The unions attended not only to their members' pay and conditions of service but also to their professional development. From time to time, major independent reports appeared and were eagerly scanned for insight and ideas: Plowden of course, but also Bullock on language and literacy (1975), Warnock on children with special educational needs (1978), Cockcroft on mathematics (1982), Gulbenkian on the arts (1982), and several others. And even if every teacher did not sustain the professional reading begun in their initial training, most if not all school staffrooms offered them digests of news and research via the ubiquitous *Times Educational Supplement*. The entire system was subject to rigorous oversight by Her Majesty's Inspectorate of Schools (HMI) who not only inspected schools but also produced valuable surveys and discussion papers of their own on a wide range of topics.

The real difference before the 1997 Blair watershed was that this immense and diverse array of information was not owned, mediated or force-fed by government. In that deathless but telling Downing Street phrase, it was 'not invented here', so notwithstanding their training, the depth and range of their reading, their many staffroom discussions, the numerous courses they attended, the advanced diplomas and higher degrees they acquired, teachers before New Labour's new dawn were 'uninformed'.

Barber's claim that pre-Labour autonomy equated with ignorance allows him to assert that government needed to step smartly in and take control. Adonis picks up the tale, peppering it with claims that, again, the evidence does not support:

> We know that in the post-war period improvements in reading were static. It was precisely this analysis that led us in 1997 to seek a step-change in literacy through the introduction of the national strategies and daily literacy hour, an emphasis on phonics, and training for every teacher in literacy. This has worked. In recent years there have been unambiguous rises in results . . . We make no apologies for policies which are delivering the highest standards ever.[71]

There they go again: 'the highest standards ever'. But then along comes cheery Michael Gove. New voice, new story: 'Literacy, down; numeracy, down; science, down: fail, fail, fail.'[72]

The other recurrent narrative in English primary education, the habitual spur and accompaniment to 'back to basics', abandons all pretence at either rationality or veracity. It's the fable of an actual or planned take-over of English primary schools by left-wing, child-centred progressives. Named by some as 'the educational establishment', and by Toby Young as 'the Blob',[73] this motley gang is set on undermining the standards for which right-thinking and right-leaning ministers, newspapers and think tanks have so strenuously fought.

This McCarthyite nonsense has been around since soon after the 1967 Plowden report,[74] on which such follies are mostly blamed, even though during Plowden's most influential decade, the 1970s, the inspectorate reported that only 5 per cent of primary schools exhibited 'exploratory' Plowdenite characteristics and chalk-and-talk were the norm in three-quarters of them.[75] Hence, from one typically nasty bout of progressive-bashing in the early 1990s, 'Look on your works, Lady Plowden, and despair' . . . 'The education of millions of children has been blighted in the name of an anarchic ideology' . . . 'Children spend more time with paint pots than mastering the three Rs' . . . 'Happiness but little learning' . . . 'Trendies in class who harm pupils' . . . and much more, some of it barely repeatable.[76]

But repeat it we must, for in 2014 this narrative is alive and kicking; and it is nurtured by no less than England's Secretary of State for Education.[77] Those who during a period of invited consultation and feedback proposed an alternative national curriculum vision to his were denounced as 'enemies of promise' and 'Marxists hell-bent on destroying our schools';[78] while early childhood experts who raised legitimate questions about the kind of early years experience that will help children to thrive educationally were accused of 'bleating bogus pop-psychology', dumbing down and lowering expectations.[79]

It is narrative such as these that are the real enemies of promise, for they imprison political thinking and action within the same stock of endlessly repeated myths and reinvented wheels. So while the research narrative layers evidence upon evidence and takes our understanding forward, the political narrative pulls us back. Back to basics, back to basics again, back to basics yet again. Meanwhile, ministerial minders see to it that the evidence is ambushed and disposed of.

Towards a verdict: from prescription to enactment

If we now return to my initial question of whether in English primary education policy has become the problem rather than the solution, the answer may seem clear enough. If important evidence is ignored, distorted or traduced – whether from fear of tabloid headlines, the self-serving interventions of ministerial officials, because it is politically inconvenient or for other reasons – then the quality of policy as promulgated must suffer; and if the sheer quantity of initiatives generates policy fatigue, fear or resistance, then their effectiveness is likely to be diminished. These conditions have obtained in two of the three cases I have exemplified (curriculum and standards) and in others that I could have cited, while in the third example (childhood) acquiescence and support tipped into unease and even hostility when government appeared to be trespassing too far into children's formative development and their lives outside school.

Yet it will also be clear that we are discussing policies in the plural rather than policy as a monolithic entity, so the final verdict is likely to be mixed. Having weighed its evidence on the period up to 2009 the Cambridge Primary Review offered this assessment:

> It would . . . be wrong to infer that government intervention is never justified. Since 1997, funding for primary education has increased massively. The policy prospectus has included ambitious initiatives relating to children and families, early childhood, curriculum, pedagogy, standards and accountability, teachers and workforce reform, and national and local infrastructure. In the policy balance sheet the case for a national curriculum is generally accepted; the government's childhood agenda is warmly applauded; its obligation to step in to protect vulnerable children is understood; the move to integrated services for education and care . . . is welcomed.
>
> However, opinion is divided on workforce reform and the national strategies, and such division escalates into deep and widespread hostility when we move into the remainder of the government's 'standards' agenda – national targets, testing, performance tables and the current practices of external inspection (as opposed to the principle, which is generally supported). Here we emphasise that the debate is not about the pursuit of standards as such . . . but about the way they have been defined and

measured, and the strategies through which government has attempted to improve them . . . The issue is not whether children should be assessed or schools should be accountable, but how.[80]

Of course, the popularity of a policy – the main focus of the reactions summarised here – does not necessarily prove it to be right, any more than a policy constructed mainly with an eye for electoral gain is wrong. In the empirically and professionally contested area of educational standards, for instance, no political party can afford to appear soft in a public arena dominated by those tabloid headlines I've illustrated, so offending teachers and ignoring researchers may be the safer course, however contemptible we may judge such political calculations to be.

Further, though governments themselves talk of 'implementation' or 'delivery', such words are misleadingly clinical (or postal) because policies are enacted, sometimes untidily, rather than implemented as they stand, and enactment entails varying interpretations and practical responses.[81] The current government has naively judged that lifting features from Singapore's prescribed maths curriculum will raise standards, when Singapore's own evidence – and common sense – show that it's the *enacted* curriculum that makes the difference.[82] In approaching a verdict on the UK government's curriculum policies we must not make the same mistake, for a paper curriculum has limited meaning or force until it is given life by what teachers decide and pupils experience in the classroom; and between government directive and that experience are stages of translation, transposition and transformation by advisers, publishers, head teachers and teachers before the final enactment, so what is intended and prescribed by Westminster and experienced by children in schools even only a couple of miles away can be very different.[83] As I noted at the launch of the Cambridge Primary Review's successor, the Cambridge Primary Review Trust:

> Those who judge the Cambridge Review by the number of its recommendations that have been adopted exactly as they stand, or who presume that policy is the sole determinant of what schools do in areas to which policy applies, don't understand how either policy or classroom practice work or the complex array of factors to which each is subject. And policies have little meaning until they are enacted by schools, and to enact is to domesticate, reinvent or even subvert, not merely to comply. Domestication – adapting generalised policy to unique school circumstances – is perhaps the most common response.[84]

In relation to the particular case of curriculum reform, then, the key is pedagogy. That's why pedagogy has always been understood to be the final frontier of professional autonomy and it's why Labour's literacy and numeracy strategies marked the tipping point in the process of educational centralisation initiated by the 1988 Education Reform Act. The architects of those strategies knew exactly what they were doing when they judged that it was only by taking control of pedagogy that they would achieve their goal of raising literacy and numeracy standards. Others saw the strategies as an egregious and dangerous intrusion by the state into a domain where in a democracy the state has no business. Hence the properly understood overtones of a 'state theory of learning.'

So in this matter, much hangs on the extent of prescription and control. The Labour government's literacy and numeracy strategies were specified in the greatest possible detail, leaving little room for manoeuvre. They were then tightly policed through tests, inspection and local authority school improvement partners. In this case the line between prescription and enactment was short and direct, so both credit and culpability rested with government and political credibility dictated that evidential challenges of the kind offered by the Cambridge Primary Review must be neutralised by whatever means possible, fair or foul.

In this case, too, the impact of the standards drive could be fairly judged by the very tests of student attainment through which compliance was secured, not merely on the basis of teacher and parental response. Interestingly, the other tool for securing compliance, Ofsted inspections, offered a more positive judgement on the literacy and numeracy strategies than the tests, which suggests either an interesting comparison of subjective and objective evaluation or that Ofsted was not as independent as it claimed.[85] The Ofsted reports on the strategies also appeared to presume that compliance and outcome were synonymous – 'Not all teachers are using the strategies' assessment materials . . . some do not know about them . . .'[86] – as if the policy as promulgated was beyond reproach and the only obstacle to their success was the tiresome tendency of some teachers not to do as they are told.

Yet Ofsted's finger-wagging reminds us that even in such extreme cases of policy enforcement teachers are not wholly powerless and this indeed is one the most important messages that the Cambridge Primary Review has attempted to convey to a profession which has long complained of prescription but in which compliance is not always unwilling and which historically has tended towards dependency. For every teacher that saw in the Cambridge Primary Review a passport to liberation there were at least as many others that spoke of their need for 'permission' to do other than treat official directives as non-negotiable, and at least as many others again who were frankly more comfortable being told what to do and how to think. The centralisation of curriculum, pedagogy and standards in English primary education may be a classic case of Gramscian hegemony, a relationship between rulers and ruled that moves beyond the polarities of domination and subordination to degrees of consent.[87]

These qualifications about the variegated and reflexive nature of the policy process, even in centralised regimes, are important. However, for as long as evidence counts for so little, political narratives peddle fiction rather than fact, and considered critique is met by ministerial abuse, the balance of judgement may tend to support the four eminent academics with whose letter to *The Independent* I started. Moreover, their concerns are consistent with the findings of the Rowntree Foundation Power enquiry into the condition of British democracy, whose disturbing final report was published in 2006.[88] What we are dealing with here, therefore, are conditions in British political life that reach well beyond policy specifics like the national curriculum:

> The questionable evidence on which key educational policies have been based; the disenfranchising of local voice; the rise of unelected and unaccountable groups taking key decisions behind closed doors; the empty rituals of 'consultation'; the authoritarian mindset; and the use of myth and derision to underwrite exaggerated accounts of progress and discredit alternative views. . .[89]

By the same token, such conditions transcend personalities, offering little comfort to those who hoped that the July 2014 ministerial reshuffle and Gove's replacement as Education Secretary by Nicky Morgan might represent something more substantial than a cosmetic adjustment of tone. And so, as ministers and their leaders rehearse those stock postures, narratives and myths for which no rehearsal is necessary since we've heard them all before, all *we* can do is repeat a truth no less familiar:

> Deep and lasting improvements in England's education system will be secured only when, in their discourse and their handling of evidence, policymakers exemplify the educated mind rather than demean it, and practise the best that has been thought and said rather than preach it.[90]

Notes

1 Coffield *et al* 2008.
2 After the announcement of the 2014 New Year Honours, Warwick Mansell (2014a) noted that six of the seven new school dames and knights were or had been heads or sponsors of academies, while only one of them was working in the mainstream sector; and a further 17 people from academies gained other honours, compared with 15 from non-academy schools. Yet at that time only one in six of England's 21,000 state-funded schools were academies. Mansell (2014b) subsequently reported that the government had earmarked Primary Academy Chain Development Grants from public funds to encourage schools to convert to academies.
3 Widely quoted, but here from Lawton 1980.
4 Ministry of Education 1958.
5 Quoted in Kogan 1971.
6 Gove 2013a.
7 Quoted in Alexander *et al* 1992, 5.
8 DfEE 1998a, 1999.
9 Moss 2009.
10 Ball 2018, 230–1.
11 Straw 1987.
12 Lovett 1840.
13 Dale 1997; OECD 1998a. For discussion of centralisation/decentralisation in an international context, see 'Primary education and the state' in Alexander 2001a, 154–72.

14 Alexander 2010a, 469–70.
15 As recorded, for example, by Berliner and Glass 2014; Ravitch 2013.
16 DfE 2014.
17 Ainscow *et al* 2016; Mansell 2016; Pickett and Vanderbloemen 2015.
18 Alexander 2010a, 508–9, paras 144–6.
19 Mayall 2010.
20 For example, Berliner 2012.
21 Alexander and Hargreaves 2007.
22 Cambridge Primary Review 2009.
23 DES 1978.
24 Alexander 2010a, 40–3.
25 Major 1992.
26 Waters's testimony is quoted in Bangs *et al* 2010, 157.
27 Alexander *et al* 1992.
28 Rose 2009b.
29 DfE 2011d.
30 Pollard 2012.
31 Hirsch 1987.
32 Oates 2010.
33 Sahlberg 2011.
34 Alexander 2010a, 241–5.
35 Ofsted 2004.
36 DES 1978; Ofsted 1997, 2002a, 2004, 2009.
37 DES 1985.
38 Alexander 2020; Resnick *et al* 2015; Mercer *et al* 2020.
39 Papers arising from this conference are in Resnick *et al* 2014.
40 Alexander 2012a.
41 A PhD student's Freedom of Information request to DfE has revealed the influence of
    this author's 2012 DfE paper in persuading the government to change its mind: DfE
    2013a.
42 DfE 2013b. For a critique of the government's approach to the national curriculum, see
    Alexander 2012b.
43 DfE 2013b, 6, para 3.1: 'The national curriculum provides pupils with an introduction
    to the essential knowledge that they need to be educated citizens. It introduces pupils to
    the best that has been thought and said.'
44 Arnold 1869.
45 Balarin and Lauder 2010.
46 Earl *et al* 2003a, 2003b.
47 Tymms and Merrell 2007; Whetton *et al* 2007; Wyse *et al* 2007; Harlen 2007; Balarin
    and Lauder 2008; Cunningham and Raymont 2008. The first three re-evaluated the test
    data; the other three examined the test and inspection processes and other aspects of the
    standards drive.
48 Usually attributed to a 1950s editor of *The Economist*.
49 These headlines are referenced in Alexander 2011a. Most are also in the Cambridge Pri-
    mary Review media archive: http://www,primaryreview.org.uk/media/media archive
    2007.php
50 See note 49.
51 Ed Hawkesworth (DCSF press officer) 2007.
52 Ed Balls (Secretary of State for Children, Schools and Families) 2008.
53 This educational application of a phrase previously used by US four-star generals to
    explain away civilian casualties is from Nichols and Berliner 2007.
54 Alexander 2010a, 473–4.
55 Gove 2011.

56 Jerrim 2011.
57 Gibb is unusual in having held a ministerial position in education for so long: since 2010, in fact, apart from a short break. Meanwhile there have been five secretaries of state (Michael Gove, Nicky Morgan, Justine Greening, Damian Hinds, Gavin Williamson).
58 Craske 2021.
59 For instance: Alexander 2012e (see this volume, Chapter 21); Meyer and Benavot 2013.
60 Gove 2012 (my italics).
61 Lawton 1983.
62 NRC 2003.
63 Barber and Mourshed 2007.
64 Analysis undertaken for Richard Margrave, CPR Director of Communications, 2006–10.
65 Media coverage of Cambridge Primary Review: https://cprtrust.org.uk/cpr/cpr-media-coverage/. Media coverage of Cambridge Primary Review Trust: https://cprtrust.org.uk/about_cprt/media/media-coverage/. Many of these pieces quote government responses, but there is further material at the permanent paper and electronic archives of the Cambridge Primary Review held by the Borthwick Institute, University of York: https://borthcat.york.ac.uk/index.php/cpr
66 Russell 2008.
67 Civil Service (UK) 2010.
68 Cambridge Primary Review 2009. See this volume, Chapter 3.
69 Orwell 1946.
70 Barber 2001, 13–14.
71 Adonis 2007.
72 Gove 2011.
73 Young 2014; Craske 2021.
74 CACE 1967.
75 DES 1978.
76 These headlines were prompted by the 'three wise men' report of 1992, though they bore little relation to what it said. For an account of this episode and sourcing of the headlines in question, see Alexander 1997, 216–65.
77 In the July 2014 ministerial re-shuffle Gove was replaced as Secretary of State for Education by Nicky Morgan.
78 Gove 2013b.
79 Gove 2013c.
80 Alexander 2010a, 508–10.
81 Ball 2012.
82 Hogan *et al* 2012. See this volume, Chapter 9.
83 Alexander 2001a, 552–3.
84 Alexander 2014a, 158.
85 Ofsted 2002b, 2002c; Alexander 2004a.
86 Ofsted 2002c, para 9.3.
87 The exercise of power in the development of public education in England is explored in Green 1990; Alexander 2001a, chapters 6 and 7.
88 Joseph Rowntree Trust 2006.
89 Alexander 2010a, 481.
90 Alexander 2014a, 164. From keynote at the launch of the Cambridge Primary Review Trust in September 2013.

Part 2

Curriculum convolutions

8   Reform, retrench or recycle?

In May 2009 the Australian government set up a statutory authority to plan that country's first national curriculum, and in February 2010 the University of Melbourne convened a National Curriculum Symposium in the hope of feeding alternative perspectives and evidence into the reform process. *Reform, retrench or recycle? A curriculum cautionary tale*, slightly edited here, reflected on the situation in England as it was between the publication of the Cambridge Review's curriculum proposals in 2009 and the review of England's national curriculum initiated in 2011. With a general election in sight but not yet settled, it looked as if the version of the national curriculum in force since 2000 was about to be replaced by the secondary curriculum as reconfigured by QCA in 2005 and, for primary schools, the framework proposed in the 2009 Rose report. Indeed, although it must have known that this was electorally risky, the Labour government instructed schools to prepare to implement Rose, which they obediently did. In May 2010 the new government cancelled Labour's plans and ordered its own national curriculum review. Teachers were not impressed.

2010: the hybrid curriculum

The curriculum in England's state schools represents an uneasy accommodation, never fully resolved, between three traditions or legacies. First, the minimalism of the nineteenth-century elementary school curriculum, designed mainly for the children of the working poor in England's industrial cities, and concentrating on the three Rs, knowing one's place at the bottom of the social and economic heap, and little else. Second, also going back to the nineteenth century, a belief in the central and civilising role of subjects, especially the humanities and later science; a belief which derives from the so-called public – that is to say private – schools attended by those at the very top of the same social and economic heap, and by the grammar schools which imported public school customs and costumes and repackaged them for the middle classes. Third, occasional inroads into both of these two traditions made by so-called 'progressive' thinking of various hues, notably during the 1930s and 1970s, and generally defining itself as pro-child and anti-subject (which of course is a false dichotomy, one of many which bedevil curriculum discourse).

Progressivism is more transient than the other two traditions. Typically, it has flowered briefly before being scapegoated for Britain's educational, economic, social, moral and sporting decline. In the Cambridge Primary Review final report we charted three such episodes since the 1960s, under the headings 'back to basics' (1969), 'back to basics again' (1992), and 'back to basics yet

DOI: 10.4324/9781315169378-10

again' (1998).[1] Typically, too, these episodes may be connected to party political fortunes. In England, when political parties are in trouble or preparing to fight an election they talk tough on standards, and standards mean the 3Rs, no less and certainly no more.

Until 1988, England's education system was decentralised. Religious education was a legal obligation, but the rest of the curriculum was up to schools and to the local education authorities (LEAs) to which most of the funding for schools was devolved. In practice, and perhaps counter-intuitively, this was a recipe not for anarchy but for remarkable curriculum homogeneity: in secondary schools because of the constraints of public examinations, in primary schools from force of habit.

The 1988 Education Reform Act of Margaret Thatcher's Conservative government brought in England's first national curriculum. It was unapologetically cast in the grammar/public school mould of the conventional disciplines, though it also preserved the Victorian elementary school legacy of a sharp divide between the 3Rs and the rest. Science joined the 3Rs within a three subject core – English, mathematics and science – and primary science was one of the success stories of the first national curriculum. But after 1997 primary science was increasingly squeezed by the Blair government's insistence that only literacy and numeracy really mattered and – in the repeated words of Blair's first education Secretary of State – the job of primary schools was to teach children 'to read, write and add up' (but not, apparently, to subtract, multiply or divide, let alone to speak).

This neo-elementary view of the curriculum has been reinforced by high-stakes tests, narrowly-focused school inspection, published school league tables, commensurate requirements for teacher training, and targeted funding for teachers' continuing professional development. Politicians' advocacy of the wider curriculum has tended to be tokenistic rather than genuine. Thus, in 2003, the government launched a new national primary education strategy under the title 'Excellence and Enjoyment'.[2] It turned out that excellence was to be confined to literacy and numeracy while the rest of the curriculum was to provide the enjoyment, time permitting, thus signalling that literacy and numeracy are too serious to be enjoyable and that the arts and humanities may be fun but that's because they are not intellectually demanding.

That is not the cheap jibe it may seem: in England, the two-tier curriculum, and the profound lack of understanding which it displays about the cognitive power of the arts and humanities as well as their intrinsic educational value, is one of the biggest and historically most persistent obstacles to genuine curriculum reform.

Yet on paper the English national curriculum, as it stands in 2010, seems broad and liberal enough. At the primary stage, or what are called Key Stages (KS) 1 and 2 (that is, for children ages 5–7 and 7–11), it comprises three core subjects – English, mathematics and science – and up to ten others: art and design; citizenship (non-statutory at KS1 and 2); design and technology; geography; history; information and communications technology (ICT); modern foreign languages (statutory at KS2); music; physical education; personal, social and health education (PSHE) (non-statutory at KS1 and 2); and, statutory but with a non-statutory programme of study, religious education. Schools are also required to provide sex education.

There's a second axis, more about aspiration than formal requirement, comprising elements of 'learning across the national curriculum': spiritual, moral, social and cultural development; so-called 'key skills' such as communication, application of number, IT and problem-solving; 'thinking skills' like information-processing, reasoning, enquiry, creative thinking, and evaluation, together with financial capability, enterprise education and education for sustainable development.[3]

How these are to be realised through the specified subjects isn't made clear, and indeed there's a conceptual question about calling everything that isn't a subject a 'skill'. I shall return to this later.

Curriculum reform in England: a brief excursion

What has happened to the national curriculum which became law in 1988? In 1997, nine years after its introduction, it was up for review by the Qualifications and Curriculum Authority (QCA). By then, Labour's Tony Blair had replaced Conservative Prime Minister John Major, riding high on the slogan 'education, education, education' and determined to raise standards in literacy and numeracy. In pursuit of this agenda Blair introduced daily literacy and numeracy lessons to be taught to a tightly-prescribed formula in every classroom in every one of England's 17,300 primary schools, thus decisively breaking with the post 1988 understanding that governments may tell schools what to teach but not how; and he raised the public profile of national tests as measures not just of student progress but also of the performance of individual schools and the system as a whole.

So much was invested politically in these initiatives that the government could not allow a free rein to the planned 1997 review of the national curriculum. QCA – of whose governing board I was then a member – was told that it should confine itself to tidying up the curriculum at the margins, and that it should under no circumstances touch literacy and numeracy. When a group of us from QCA met the Secretary of State to protest about this, his chief standards adviser swiftly and smoothly intervened before the Secretary of State could answer. 'Minister,' he said, 'literacy and numeracy are standards, not curriculum. QCA may be responsible for the curriculum but you are responsible for standards.' Similarly, when Jim Rose was asked to redesign the national curriculum for primary schools, he was told that assessment was off-limits.[4]

So there you have the neo-elementary curriculum in a nutshell: literacy and numeracy are not part of the curriculum at all and therefore not up for discussion, while the notion of standards does not apply to the rest of children's education.

Fast forward another ten years, to 2007 and the next scheduled national curriculum review. As required, QCA started with the secondary curriculum, revising it for implementation in September 2008. It then turned its attention to the primary curriculum.

At that point the process encountered an unexpected obstacle. An independently-funded enquiry into the whole of primary education, the biggest since the Plowden report of 1967, had been launched in 2006 and had begun to publish interim reports which were supportive of some aspects of recent policy but not of all of them. Faced with the risk that this independent enquiry – it was of course the Cambridge Primary Review – might come up with a radically different model of the curriculum, and that this might command popular support, the government launched a pre-emptive strike. In 2008 it took the scheduled official primary curriculum review away from the supposedly arm's-length QCA, appointed its own review team instead, placed it in a government office at the within easy reach of ministers, and – just as in 1997 – instructed it to do what had to be done without in any way questioning existing policies and priorities. Indeed, contingent matters like the national tests and the literacy and numeracy strategies were explicitly excluded from the official review's remit. With impressive brazenness the government named its enquiry 'the independent primary curriculum review'.[5]

I will not dwell here on the messy politics of the two reviews except to suggest that this degree of overt politicisation of England's curriculum debate has compromised its credibility and outcomes, and there's a lesson in this for governments with interventionist inclinations everywhere. Rather, we need to keep in view the larger questions about curriculum purposes, values, structure and content.

On these, as might be expected, the two reviews pursued diverging paths in respect of three vital matters: the problems of England's national curriculum which needed to be addressed, the purposes and values which a revised national curriculum should pursue, and the structure and content of whatever might replace current arrangements. I shall now say something about each of these.

The curriculum problem: alternative diagnoses

The government's own primary curriculum review – the Rose Review – identified just one problem to be fixed: not aims, values, relevance or balance, let alone vision, but *manageability*. In the words of the review's leader: 'How can we best help primary class teachers solve the "quarts into pint pots problem" of teaching 13 subjects, plus religious education, to sufficient depth, in the time available?'[6] I hope you can get your heads round the pre-metrication metaphor of pints and quarts. Many younger teachers in England were baffled by it, assuming that a quart was a quarter of a pint and that consequently there was no problem. Choose your metaphors with care.

Actually, the perception of an overcrowded curriculum was widely shared. However, three separate studies by the national inspectorate, in 1978, 1997 and

2002, had shown that England's best primary schools, as judged by inspections and the national tests, succeeded not just in teaching the national curriculum as specified but also in achieving high standards in literacy and numeracy. This evidence, that breadth supports standards in the basics rather than undermines them, is crucial.[7]

Further, the government review's casual reference to 'primary class teachers'— that is, generalists who teach the entire curriculum to their classes, another Victorian legacy – ignored the possibility that part of the problem might be the way that primary schools are staffed; and that this pattern of staffing, which the ever-prudent Victorians adopted because it was cheap, might not be up to the demands of a curriculum vastly more complex than that of the 1870s, or to a pedagogy which claims to be about more than filling empty vessels with facts.

In contrast, and drawing both on its extensive evidence and on its freedom to roam across all aspects of education on which curriculum decisions are contingent, the Cambridge Primary Review judged that there was not one curriculum problem to be fixed, but several. For example, quoting from our final report:

- The detachment of curriculum from aims.
- The supplanting of long-term educational goals by short-term targets of attainment.
- The loss of the principle of children's entitlement to a broad, balanced and rich curriculum, and the marginalisation, in particular, of the arts, the humanities and, latterly, science.
- The test-induced regression to a valuing of memorisation and recall over understanding and enquiry, and to a pedagogy which rates transmission more important than the pursuit of knowledge in its wider sense.
- The dislocation and politicisation of both the whole curriculum and two major elements within it – English and mathematics – by the national literacy and numeracy strategies (the former much more than the latter) and the accompanying rhetoric of 'standards'.
- The use of a narrow spectrum of the curriculum (literacy and numeracy again) as a proxy for the quality of the whole, and the loss of breadth and balance across and within subjects as a result of the pressures of testing, especially at the upper end of the primary school.
- The parallel pressure, at the start of the primary phase, on the developmental early years curriculum introduced by the same government and widely supported by teachers and parents.
- Excessive central government prescription and micro-management, and the resulting loss of professional flexibility, creativity and autonomy.
- The historic split between 'the basics' and the rest of the curriculum, in which differential time allocations legitimately set in pursuit of curriculum priorities are compounded by unacceptable differences in the quality of provision.

- The continuing and demonstrably mistaken assumption that high standards in 'the basics' can be achieved only by marginalising the rest of the curriculum.
- A muddled discourse about subjects, knowledge and skills which infects the entire debate about curriculum, needlessly polarises discussion of how it might be organised, parodies knowledge and undervalues its place in education, and inflates the undeniably important notion of skill to a point where it, too, becomes meaningless.[8]

What we were saying in presenting this somewhat depressing list is that solving the 'quarts into pint pots' problem will achieve very little if the political, conceptual and ethical problems are not attended to.

Take the historic split between 'the basics' and the rest, which produces a curriculum which more often than not is two-tier in terms of quality as well as time. While many of today's political leaders in Britain believe that you can improve standards in the basics by concentrating on the basics alone, and find counter-intuitive the notion that basics and breadth are intimately related, it was not always so. In 1862 (sic) Matthew Arnold noted from his school inspections that progress in reading was fastest in classrooms where lessons were 'of a more varied cast' than the 3Rs alone,[9] though he was swimming against the elementary curriculum tide. A White Paper presented 123 years later by a Conservative government to the British Parliament said this:

> The mistaken belief, once widely held, that a concentration on basic skills is by itself enough to improve achievement in literacy and numeracy has left its mark; many children are still given too little opportunity for work in the practical, scientific and aesthetic areas of the curriculum which increases not only their understanding in these areas but also their literacy and numeracy . . . Over-concentration on the practice of basic skills in literacy and numeracy unrelated to a context in which they are needed means that those skills are insufficiently extended and applied.[10]

Although this hints that the relationship between basics and breadth works both ways, the point perhaps needs underlining. Children need the wider curriculum not just because it is educationally essential in itself, but also because it enhances and accelerates understanding in the so-called basics. And the fast-growing field of neuroscience supports this. Only this week, a paper at the conference of the American Association for the Advancement of Science reported that playing a musical instrument significantly enhances the brain's sensitivity to speech and shapes the brain's development so that it more effectively engages with basic tasks like reading and listening.[11] In the arts in particular, there's now a substantial research literature on the cognitive impact of activities which, in the political and public arena, tend to be judged on narrowly utilitarian grounds. With little difficulty we can make a much more persuasive case if we choose (see Chapter 12). On the other hand, if we end up arguing that the wider curriculum is needed only because it enhances the basics we shall be no further forward, so there are dangers in this updating of the old notion of the transfer of skill.

Aims

Then there's the matter of aims. The Cambridge Review criticised the very British tendency to detach curriculum from aims, or rather to devise a curriculum and then invent aims with which to legitimate it, so you'd expect us to have taken this part of the enterprise seriously. In contrast, the government's own review was about tidying up the existing curriculum rather than rocking the boat by asking what it was for, so it took the line of least resistance. The secondary curriculum review undertaken some years earlier by QCA had come up with a list of aims for secondary schooling. The government's primary curriculum review decided that these would do nicely for primary as well, rationalising its decision by arguing that the entire school system needed a single set of aims.

Actually, that argument has much to commend it, but it doesn't preclude a reassessment of the aims of each stage of schooling, or the possibility that the needs of 5-year-olds and 16-year-olds may not be identical and therefore that we may need both overall school aims and more specific aims for each stage. But of course the real objection to the government's approach was its continuing pursuit of what I have called the Mrs Beeton recipe for curriculum planning: first catch your curriculum, then garnish with aims.

Yet it is with some trepidation that I reveal the educational aims first adopted in 2008 for the revised secondary national curriculum in England and then in 2009 proposed by for the primary curriculum. The aims of both primary and secondary education, said the British government, are to produce:

- successful learners, who enjoy learning, make progress and achieve;
- confident individuals, who are able to live safe, healthy and fulfilling lives;
- responsible citizens, who make a positive contribution to society.[12]

The trepidation arises because you may possibly have seen these before. Was it perhaps in Scotland?

- successful learners
- confident individuals
- responsible citizens
- effective contributors.[13]

Or maybe, give or take the odd adjective, Singapore?

- self-directed learners
- confident persons

- concerned citizens
- active contributors.[14]

Or perhaps even Australia?

- successful learners
- confidential and creative individuals
- active and informed citizens.[15]

Is this a coincidence? Is it the case that great minds separated by geography, history and culture really do think alike? Or is this where globalisation has taken us, and do educational planners everywhere, regardless of geography, history and culture, now shop at the same curriculum supermarket?

But taking the *English* curriculum aims as they stand, and remaining diplomatically silent about those *Educational Goals for Young Australians*, my substantive concern is that they are perhaps too exclusively concerned with terminal outcomes – though that's probably why they secure such ready agreement, because of course we all want schools to produce people who are successful, confident and responsible, don't we? But such generalised aims don't get close enough to the educational action to tell us what schools should actually *do*, and on what a curriculum should try to concentrate. Successful learners in relation to what? Science? Safe-cracking? We need, then, aims with a more proximal focus and an ethical intent. Aims are about ends but they need to say something about means and values.

How did the Cambridge Primary Review approach the same task? The Review had an exceptionally broad remit. Defining aims was one of its themes, curriculum another, but so too were assessment, teacher training, school leadership, staff deployment, learning, teaching, governance, funding and much else. Overriding the education-specific themes were larger questions about childhood today and children's development, learning and needs, about parenting and family life, and about the condition of the society and world in which today's children are growing up. On all these matters the Review assembled evidence from its four principal sources: invited written submissions, commissioned surveys of published research, face-to-face regional and national soundings or focus group sessions, and re-assessments of official data, both national and international.[16]

It is out of all this data that the proposed aims for primary education have been constructed. They reflect concerns expressed in our evidence about, for example:

- the importance of a broad, rich curriculum at the primary stage as a proper foundation for subsequent choice and lifelong learning;
- the need for a modern understanding of childhood as being about agency, capability, voice and rights rather than passive learning and fixed developmental ages and stages;

- balancing education as preparation for what follows with education for its own sake, here and now (the official aims are all about what emerges at the very end of the process and see one stage of schooling essentially as preparation for the next);
- recovering the community cohesion and vitality which are felt to be in sharp decline in England as in many other countries;
- placing culture in all its senses – anthropological, artistic, Arnoldean – at the heart of the curriculum);
- responding to adult witnesses' anxieties about childhood wellbeing, social cohesion, international tension and global sustainability;
- advancing the cause of a genuinely participatory and critical democracy (the official aim of 'responsible citizens' can too easily mean merely doing as one is told);
- making the acts of exploring, knowing, understanding, creating, imagining, engaging, questioning and arguing central to life in classrooms, because aims are about *process* as well as content and outcomes.

The proposed aims are in three interlocking groups (Figure 8.1). The first group identifies those individual qualities and capacities which schools should strive to foster and build upon in each child, in whatever they do, and the individual needs to which they should attend:

- wellbeing
- engagement
- empowerment
- autonomy.

THE INDIVIDUAL
- Well-being
- Engagement
- Empowerment
- Autonomy

SELF, OTHERS AND THE WIDER WORLD
- Encouraging respect & reciprocity
- Promoting interdependence & sustainability
- Empowering local, national & global citizenship
- Celebrating culture & community

LEARNING, KNOWING AND DOING
- Exploring, knowing, understanding, making sense
- Fostering skill
- Exciting the imagination
- Enacting dialogue

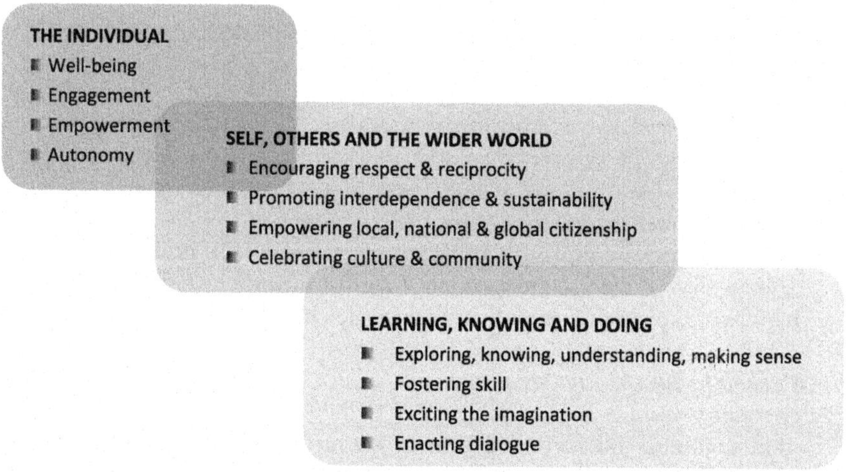

Figure 8.1 Aims for education from the Cambridge Primary Review

The second group includes four critically important orientations to people and the wider world:

- encouraging respect and reciprocity
- promoting interdependence and sustainability
- empowering local, national and global citizenship
- celebrating culture and community.

The third group focuses on the content, processes and outcomes of learning, or the central experiences and encounters which primary schools should provide:

- exploring, knowing, understanding and making sense
- fostering skill
- exciting the imagination
- enacting dialogue.[17]

As they stand, the headings may convey little. Each is elaborated and explained in our final report, which is where I'm afraid you'll need to go if you want the full picture. But, to give a flavour, here are three examples, one from each group. Again, I quote from the report:

Autonomy. To foster children's autonomy and sense of self through a growing understanding of the world present and past, and through productive relationships with others. Autonomy enables individuals to establish who they are and to what they might aspire; it enables the child to translate knowledge into meaning; it encourages that critical independence of thought which is essential both to the growth of knowledge and to citizenship; it enables children to discriminate in their choice of activities and relationships; and it helps them to see beyond the surface appeal of appearance, fashion and celebrity to what is of abiding value.

Empowering local, national and global citizenship. To help children to become active citizens by encouraging their full participation in decision-making within the classroom and school, especially where their own learning is concerned, and to advance their understanding of human rights, democratic engagement, diversity, conflict resolution and social justice. To develop a sense that human interdependence and the fragility of the world order require a concept of citizenship which is global is well as local and national.

Exploring, knowing, understanding and making sense. To enable children to encounter and begin to explore the wealth of human experience through induction into, and active engagement in, the different ways through which humans make sense of their world and act upon it: intellectual, moral, spiritual, aesthetic, social, emotional and physical; through language, mathematics, science, the humanities, the arts, religion and other ways of knowing and understanding. *Induction* acknowledges and respects our membership of a culture with its own deeply-embedded ways of thinking and acting which can make sense of complexity and through which human understanding constantly changes and advances. Education is necessarily a process of acculturation. *Exploration* is grounded in that distinctive mixture of amazement, perplexity and curiosity which constitutes childhood wonder; a commitment to discovery, invention, experiment, speculation, fantasy, play and growing linguistic agility which are the essence of childhood.[18]

The last of these, though offered merely by way of example, anticipates the stance taken by the Cambridge Primary Review on the content of the curriculum, for it insists on the centrality of knowledge, and of knowledge conceived as balancing the predictable and the open-ended, induction and exploration, familiarity and novelty, the public and the private, acculturation and self-actualisation.

Curriculum structure and content

The Rose Review of the primary national curriculum, as I've noted, tidied up existing arrangements. It did so by collapsing the current 13 subjects into six 'areas of learning' and by reducing and simplifying the content of each so as to make it more likely that quarts would indeed be able to fit into pint pots.[19] The risk, of course, was that because the problems identified by the Cambridge Review had not been admitted, let alone attended to, they would be transferred from the old framework to the new one.

So it's with the larger list of problems and challenges that the Cambridge Primary Review's alternative approach starts and you won't be surprised that we make curriculum reform conditional on the reform of assessment and on a reduction in political intervention, on neither of which was Rose permitted to comment.

But the Cambridge curriculum framework goes further still. Thus:

- It is driven and constantly informed by the 12 educational aims that I have outlined.
- It has regard to an explicit set of procedural principles, incumbent on schools and policymakers alike, which highlight entitlement, quality, equity, breadth, balance, local engagement, and guidance rather than prescription.
- It respects and builds on the best of early years provision that is now available in England, while at the end of the primary phase it seeks as seamless as possible a transition to the secondary curriculum.
- It dispenses with the notion of the curriculum core as three protected subjects, which itself perpetuates an increasingly questionable view of what

is 'basic' to a modern education, and places all curriculum areas within a unitary curriculum framework.

- It does so on the principle that although teaching time will continue to be differentially allocated, all areas are essential to young children's education, none is dispensable, and all must be taught to the highest possible standards.
- The hierarchy of 'the basics' and 'the rest' is – at last and not before time – abolished.
- To prevent the two-tier curriculum returning in disguise, the Cambridge framework requires that educational 'standards' should no longer be defined, by proxy, as performance in a narrow range of competencies in literacy and numeracy, but must be about the quality of the entire curriculum to which children are entitled; this, of course, has implications for assessment as well as the specification of curriculum and educational standards.
- At the same time, the Cambridge framework insists on the centrality of language, oracy and literacy not as a self-contained 'basic' but as enabling learning across a curriculum in which breadth and standards go hand in hand.
- Structurally, it is conceived as a matrix of 12 educational aims and eight domains of knowledge, skill, enquiry and disposition, with the aims locked firmly into the framework from the outset.
- It provides for a strong local component, differentiates the *national* and *community* curriculum, and divides time between them on the basis of 70/30 per cent of the yearly teaching total.

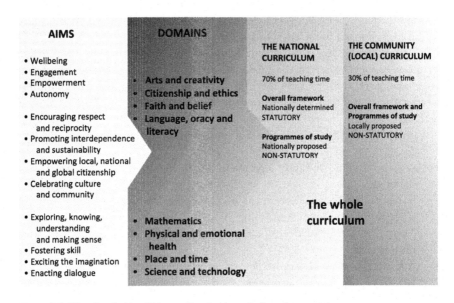

Figure 8.2 The Cambridge Primary Review curriculum framework

Why 'domains'?

The Cambridge Primary Review received many and various representations on what the curriculum should include, and it considered several different starting points. Some argued for the traditional subjects. Others insisted that subjects have had their day, that *how* children learn is more important than *what*, and that the curriculum should be reconfigured as generic processes or skills. Thus, the submission we received from one major organisation argued that we need:

> a skills-based curriculum, focused on the physical skills, the communication, interpersonal and intrapersonal skills and the thinking and learning skills as well as the academic skills which will be essential components of the educated person who is able to think and act effectively in the 21st century.[20]

The Rose Review also took this line, itemising 'literacy skills', 'numeracy skills', 'ICT capability', 'learning and thinking skills', 'personal and emotional skills', and 'social skills'.[21]

Others argued that the IT revolution had changed the curriculum debate, and the curriculum, for ever. In the words of one witness who was representative of many:

> Children do not need to know lots of dates. They can look up information on Google and store it on their mobile phones . . . The days of teachers barking out facts are long gone. Our job as teachers is to prepare children so that they can access information and knowledge in the modern world.[22]

Historians were understandably incensed at this parody of their discipline, but parody is what this kind of thinking depends on. The central problem here – so depressingly illustrated by that assertion that all children need today by way of a curriculum is Google and a mobile phone – is the equating of knowledge with facts or information, and the failure to grasp the vital place of pedagogy in mediating what the student encounters, learns, knows, understands and is able to do, and in translating the dead letter of specified content into something which engages, excites and inspires.

The Cambridge Review, then, argues against the reductionism which in England so often downgrades knowledge while elevating 'skill' or 'process' far beyond what these terms can sustain. Skill, at the level that educators conceive it, should always be grounded in knowledge, understanding and disposition, so that the skill is applied with discrimination and judgement; and 'process' in isolation is meaningless. A 'process of enquiry'? About what? 'Academic skills'? In relation to what? And what, if you pause to think about it, is an 'emotional skill'?

Knowledge vs skill, content vs process: these are two more of the dichotomies that frustrate curriculum debate. Further, the advancement of a process or skills-based curriculum, in which knowledge is reduced to the incidental or redundant, denies both culture and history. For the curriculum, as Denis Lawton pointed out years ago, is always and inevitably 'a selection from culture'[23]; and central to culture, in Clifford Geertz's famous definition, are the 'stories we tell ourselves about ourselves'[24] – mythical, religious, scientific, artistic, philosophical, mathematical, historical . . . and many others.

It is out of this discussion that the Cambridge Primary Review argues, first, that English curriculum discourse stands in urgent need of some conceptual ground-clearing about key terms like 'subjects', 'disciplines', 'knowledge', 'skill' and 'curriculum' itself; second, that a curriculum somehow has to combine both initiation into the existing culture and the building of capacities to challenge, extend and transform our thinking so that culture does not become moribund; and so that we stand a chance of tackling the problems which human ingenuity has put in the way of human dignity and survival, and of advancing rather than stifling the best that humankind has thought and said, and indeed, written, acted, painted, played, sung and danced. Hence, in that key twelfth aim about 'exploring, knowing, understanding and making sense', the distinction between *induction* and *exploration*. (For further discussion of this matter see Chapter 9.)

As we stipulatively define it, a curriculum domain has:

- epistemological or thematic coherence;
- an identifiable core of knowledge, skill, disposition and enquiry drawn from both established disciplines and other sources;
- the capacity to contribute to the pursuit of one or more of the 12 proposed aims;
- and, especially, that critical balance of induction and exploration.

The eight domains we identify as reconciling the various aims, claims, needs, imperatives and possibilities identified in the Cambridge Review's evidence and discussions are:

- arts and creativity
- citizenship and ethics
- faith and belief
- language, oracy and literacy (including ICT and a modern foreign language)
- mathematics
- physical and emotional health
- place and time (geography and history)
- science and technology.[25]

Most are familiar – that, given our stance on knowledge and culture, is not surprising – but, for reasons I have rehearsed, the domains are not necessarily what some advocates of 'traditional subjects' would like to see: that is to say, closely-prescribed bodies of propositional knowledge, transmitted and received but never questioned. So a domain inevitably incorporates a pedagogy, not just a content syllabus: a pedagogy of both induction and exploration. Like the 12 aims, each of the eight domains is carefully defined, and in the process some tricky categorical decisions are explained.

For example, in the descriptor for 'arts and creativity' we warn against too exclusive a concept of the latter:

> Creativity, of course, is not confined to the arts, but also entails what the Robinson enquiry called the 'democratic definition' of creativity, which 'is equally fundamental to advances in the sciences, in mathematics, technology, politics, business and in all areas of everyday life' and which has four features: the pursuit of purpose, the use of the imagination, originality, and the exercise of discriminating judgements of value.[26] The arts are indelibly creative, and properly pursued they achieve the aim of 'exciting the imagination' which features in our list of twelve. But we have also stressed that both creativity and imaginative activity can and must inform teaching and learning across the wider curriculum.[27]

We also argue – contentiously for some – that in a multi-faith and increasingly secular society, faith and belief have an essential place in the Cambridge primary curriculum because they are fundamental to England's history, culture and language as well as being central to the lives of so many of its people. But the treatment of faith and belief, as we propose it, does not extend beyond teaching about religion to the inculcation of particular religious beliefs – except of course in schools which have an explicit religious foundation and character that parents consciously choose for their children – for that would both deny pluralism and infringe the rights of those who have other or no religious beliefs. In any case, we do not define 'faith and belief' in exclusively religious terms, suggesting that 'other beliefs, including those about the validity of religion itself, should also be explored'.[28] This accommodates the concerns of both humanists and secularists that religious belief should not be privileged. But it's a difficult balance to strike.

Further, moral education and the treatment of ethical questions are handled within the domain 'citizenship and ethics' because although all religions have a moral component which must therefore be respectfully considered, they do not have a moral monopoly. Instead, the handling of ethical questions is seen as part of citizenship, which in turn gives life to several of the aims in the central group – respect and reciprocity, interdependence and sustainability, culture and community – and, through pedagogy, to the vital twelfth aim, enacting dialogue.

The grouping 'physical and emotional health' raised some eyebrows, but we argued:

> This deals with the handling of human emotions and relationships and with the human body, its development and health, together with the skills of agility, co-ordination and teamwork acquired through sport and PE as conventionally conceived. It is important that the significance of this

reconfiguration be properly understood and that neither emotional/relational understanding nor health be treated as a mere PE add-on. We believe that it makes medical as well as educational sense to group together physical and emotional health, and indeed for health as such to be named as a mandatory component of the child's curriculum for the first time. However, unlike the government's review, we do not go so far as to place well-being as a whole in the physical domain, for, as defined in our list of aims, well-being has aspects other than the physical, and although attending to children's physical and emotional well-being and welfare is an essential task for primary schools, well-being is no less about educational engagement, the raising of aspirations and the maximising of children's potential across the board. As with several other domains, we wish to stress that what is required here is a complete reconceptualisation.[29]

Then, again, what looks like the familiar territory of language and literacy is extended not just by the inclusion of ICT and a modern foreign language. It also gives oracy, at last, the pride of place it has rarely had in English education, ever since the Victorians said that children must learn to read and write to a functional level but feared to take literacy further, still less to unleash the subversive possibilities of talk. Given what we now from psychology, neuroscience and classroom research about the conditions for thinking, learning and effective teaching – including the effective teaching of literacy itself – the spoken word can no longer be viewed as a mere appendage to 'the basics', and certainly not as mere 'communication skills'.

Similarly, our report argues that information technology cannot be viewed, as it is in the government's specification, as a mere content-free 'essential skill'. We say (and again I quote):

> The task is to help children develop the capacity to approach electronic and other non-print media (including television and film as well as the internet) with the degree of discrimination and critical awareness that should attend reading, writing, talking and communicating of any kind. This, we believe, is an argument for treating ICT both as the cross-curricular informational tool which it obviously is, and as an aspect of the language curriculum which demands a rigour no less than should apply to the handling of the written and spoken word, and to traditionally-conceived text, information and evidence.[30]

These examples hint at debates about the domains, separately and in combination, with which our report engages and which we believe are central to proper curriculum discourse anywhere. There's much more to it than that, of course.

Where next?

The Labour government has accepted the recommendations of its Rose Review of the primary curriculum. Since this adhered faithfully to its narrow remit, refrained from questioning existing policy and for good measure was managed by DCSF staff, its adoption was a foregone conclusion. The proposals have now been incorporated into a parliamentary bill which the government hopes will very soon become law.

However, also very soon there will be a general election. The main opposition party, which is ahead in the opinion polls, has warned that it does not like the Rose framework and is under no obligation to implement it. So in England, despite the current government's best efforts to close it down, the debate about the purposes, content and quality of the foundational curriculum remains wide open, and the Cambridge Primary Review is far from alone in arguing this. It is clear from the extensive media coverage of our 31 interim reports and our final report, from our dissemination conferences and from the pronouncements of some pretty significant organisations and illustrious individuals, that the government's pre-emptive strike is widely deplored, and that alternative frameworks such as the one I've outlined have many supporters. These include a fast-expanding network of schools which have announced their intention to take forward the Cambridge Review's ideas, regardless of central directives. More fundamentally, there's a growing consensus across the spectrum of professional, parental, religious and public opinion that the neo-elementary curriculum has had its day, and that we need a richer and more humane educational vision for today's children and tomorrow's world.

Afterword

As noted elsewhere, the Rose Review was seen by some as a deliberate attempt to neutralise the extensive work on the curriculum being undertaken by the Cambridge Primary Review. Jim Rose himself did not acquiesce in such political manipulation and his final report referred to our work pointedly, frequently and constructively, seeking synthesis on matters such as educational aims and the balance of local and national curriculum requirements.[31] But all this became irrelevant when in May 2010 Labour lost the election and the incoming government cancelled the Rose implementation programme and announced its own national curriculum review. This provides our focus for the next few chapters.

Notes

1 Alexander 2010a, 39–47.
2 DFES 2003.
3 DFES 2003, 208.
4 Baker 2009.
5 The so-called 'Independent review of the primary curriculum' issued its interim report in December 2008 and its final report in April 2009. Rose 2008a, 2009b.
6 Sir Jim Rose, leader of the government primary curriculum review, on that review's website: www.dcsf.gov.uk/primarycurriculumreview/ (accessed 28 April 2009). The reference to 'quarts into pint pots' was later removed, almost certainly in response to our report's criticism.

7 DES 1978; Ofsted 1996, 1997, 2002a.

8 Alexander 2010a, 251–2.

9 From Arnold's *The Twice Revised Code*.

10 DES 1985.

11 Youde 2010. Her article reports on a paper by Nina Kraus for the American Association for the Advancement of Science.

12 http://curriculum.qcda.gov.uk/key-stages-1-and-2/aims-values-and-purposes/index/aspx (accessed February 2010).

13   www.ltscotland.org.uk/curriculumforexcellence/whatiscfe/purposes.asp   (accessed February 2010).

14 www.moe.gov.sg/education/desire-outcomes/ (accessed February 2010).

15 Ministerial Council on Education, Employment, Training and Youth Affairs (2008).

16 For details of the methodology of the Cambridge Primary Review, see Alexander 2010a, 15–20 and 515–43.

17 For the descriptors, see Alexander 2010a 197–9. For a full account of the genesis and justifications of the chosen aims, see Alexander 2010a, 175–97.

18 Alexander 2010a, 197–9.

19 Rose 2009a.

20 Alexander 2010a, 249.

21 Rose 2009b.

22 Alexander 2010a, 247.

23 Lawton 1983.

24 Geertz 1973.

25 The domains are discussed in Alexander 2010a, 265–72.

26 National Advisory Committee on Creative and Cultural Education 1999.

27 Alexander 2010a, 267.

28 Alexander 2010a, 268.

29 Alexander 2010a, 271.

30 Alexander 2010a, 270.

31 For example, Rose 2009b, executive summary paras 3, 10, 24; report paras 1.21, 1.22, 2.2, 6.13, the tabulated comparison of Rose and CPR on p 34, and endnotes on pp 136–41.

9   Epistemic imbroglio

'The primary curriculum: victim of a muddled discourse', *Children, Their World, Their Education*, 245–51 (2010).

It is essential to get the structure, balance and content of the curriculum right. It is no less essential to ensure that schools have the time and expertise to ensure that it is coherently planned and well taught. Neither of these things will happen until we sort out three terms in curriculum discourse that are familiar and essential yet too often are carelessly deployed. They are *subjects*, *knowledge* and *skill*. To these we add the contingent terms *discipline*, *curriculum* and *timetable*.

Subjects

The furore which greeted the interim report of the Rose Review in December 2008[1] illustrates the problem. Opinion split sharply into two camps: those who cheered the departure of subjects and those who condemned it. One side piled up the anti-subject insults – 'traditional', 'old-fashioned', 'artificial', 'irrelevant' and, for good measure, 'Victorian'. The other side defended subjects in the name of 'culture', 'continuity', 'standards', and of course the genuinely Victorian 'best that has been thought and said'. They also deplored Rose's 'areas of learning' as recipes for ignorance, or a return to the bad old days of the ubiquitous topic or project (even though Rose emphasised the place of subjects, however the curriculum was organised).

Older readers will recall that during the 1960s and 1970s subjects were similarly demonised and defended. At that time they were seen by many primary teachers, teacher trainers and LEA advisers as the antithesis of that seamless curriculum which children's nature and development were said to require. Subjects, it was claimed, fragmented and compartmentalised learning into 'little boxes'. 'It is important', said a memorandum in one school at this time, 'that the natural flow of activity, language and thought be uninterrupted by artificial breaks such as subject matter', and to reinforce the message that subjects were outmoded there were frequent references to the 'rigid timetables, clanging bells, silent cloakrooms, cramping desks and absurd rules' of the dark days of elementary schools,[2] though it was never clear what silent cloakrooms had to do with the curriculum.

DOI: 10.4324/9781315169378-11

The contributors to the Black Papers responded in no less baleful terms.[3] The folk memory of this discourse remains powerful, even though a large and growing proportion of primary teachers have known no educational world – their own or their pupils' – other than the national curriculum.

Apart from its residual 1970s colouring, what has happened here is that discussion of subjects has become entangled in a distinctly ill-informed discourse about the nature of knowledge. A subject is merely a named conceptual or organisational component of the curriculum. It can mean anything we want it to mean. It is, or ought to be, a wholly neutral term, available to support the efforts of those who strive to work out how, in terms of organisation, timetabling and professional expertise, the goals of a curriculum – any curriculum, ancient, modern or post-modern – can be achieved. Time may be seamless but children's attention is not; nor is their teacher's expertise. The different aspects of the curriculum need to be named, otherwise how else can we talk about them to children, parents or each other? The day and week need to be divided into periods of time that sensibly and appropriately enable these different aspects to be taught.

A subject's relevance, or lack of relevance, resides not in its name but, under whatever name is chosen, in exactly what is taught and how. A subject is not of itself 'old-fashioned' just because subjects have been used as an organising device for over a century. If, as enacted in the classroom, a subject is irrelevant, it is the teacher who makes it so.

This problem, we have to note, is very much a primary school one. Universities woo applicants with long and expanding lists of subjects, and no academic would countenance the accusation that his or her subject remains static or moribund in the way presumed by those who label subjects, *ipso facto*, 'old-fashioned'. For pushing at the boundaries of knowledge, understanding and enquiry is what academics do. For them, though many of the labels have a kind of permanence, the subjects themselves are constantly on the move. Indeed – and this perhaps is the ultimate irony – knowledge does not become outdated because it is framed by subjects; it does so because of the efforts of the very people who work within the boundaries of those subjects. In this sense, knowledge obsolescence and change are marks not of a subject's decline but of its vitality.

Throughout this chapter we use the word 'subject'. We would not wish any readers to assume that the usage is other than neutral. Because some people object to 'subjects' we could talk of 'components', 'elements' or 'parts' of the curriculum, but this would be an exercise in mere political correctness.

So when critics of the Rose Review's interim report complained of the 'death of subjects' there is a sense in which they were quite wrong, for one set of names, or subjects, was merely replaced by another, and what matters above all else is what, in terms of knowledge, understanding and skill, such new names denote. What the critics were really worried about was the exclusion from primary education of *disciplinary-based knowledge and enquiry*, and this exclusion in no way automatically follows from the re-naming of subjects as 'areas of learning'. It is possible that within Rose's 'areas of learning' what critics of his model associate with subjects (that is, disciplines) is not only alive and well but may even be strengthened. Equally, it is possible that the new labels reflect that very dilution or exclusion of discipline-based knowledge and enquiry which critics most fear and deplore.

In any case, subjects, disciplines and knowledge, still less subjects and a particular view of knowledge, are not synonymous. A *subject*, as we have said, is an organisational segment of the curriculum. It may or may not be coterminous with a particular *discipline* such as mathematics, science, art or geography. *Knowledge* is central to every discipline, but its precise place and character in school subjects as diverse as mathematics and PSHE are highly variable. The three terms should be used much more discriminatingly, and the word 'subjects', in particular, should be divested of its inherited ideological charge.

A different though related point was made by Norman Thomas, former chief inspector of primary education, in a post-Rose comment to the Cambridge Review. He was pleased that the Rose Review interim report acknowledged that there is a place on the timetable for both specific subject lessons and for thematic work. He argued, however, 'it should be made very clear that the sub-headings used in describing the curriculum do not prescribe the headings for the periods into which the timetable is divided. Indeed, whatever the title of the lesson, whether a subject or a theme, it is bound to include aspects of learning referred to within a number of different sections of the curriculum definition'.[4] Thus, while subjects divide the curriculum conceptually or organisationally, the timetable divides it temporally into lessons, and the two forms of division are not necessarily synonymous.

Knowledge

> Children do not need to know lots of dates. They can look up information on Google and store it on their mobile phones . . . The days of teachers barking out facts are long gone. Our job is to prepare children so that they can access information and knowledge in the modern world.[5]

Lest readers imagine that we quote with approval this testimonial to Rose's 'areas of learning', we say immediately that it puts in a nutshell much that is wrong with the way knowledge is talked about in primary education. Consider the assumptions here:

- knowledge is mere facts or information;
- such facts and information are there to be 'looked up' and 'stored', but never engaged with or questioned;
- knowledge is ineradicably associated with old-fashioned quasi-Gradgrindian teaching ('Teach these boys and girls nothing but Facts. Facts alone are wanted in life. . .'[6]);
- children may 'access' knowledge but it is no longer necessary for them, or their teachers, to know anything;

and, as a gratuitous swipe at one subject among several:

- history is about the learning of dates.

The most serious problem here is the equating of knowledge with facts or information. Propositional knowledge is but one kind of knowledge, and it is the essence of the mature disciplines that propositions must be tested, whether through that assembling and examination of evidence which marks out the methodology of the physical and human sciences, or by tests of technical mastery, experiential authenticity and aesthetic connoisseurship which may be applied in the arts; or simply against honestly-assessed experience. In any case, propositional knowledge need not be as sterile as 'the learning of dates' portrays it, and for many people the acquisition of information both excites and liberates. To tell children, at the start of lives in which they will be assailed by information which they fail to evaluate at their peril, and in which they will need and want to know and discover a great deal, that Google and a mobile phone will do the trick, is a travesty of what knowing and understanding ought to be about. Educationally, it is also highly irresponsible.

What is doubly disturbing about the point of view illustrated here is that England's national curriculum was initially credited with breaking away from such perceptions and encouraging greater attention to modes of enquiry and the assessing of evidence. But then, our witnesses have reported that one consequence of curriculum overcrowding in the past decade has been to force teachers more and more into transmission mode.

If the various domains of knowledge are viewed not as collections of inert or obsolete information but as distinct ways of knowing, understanding, enquiring and making sense which include processes of enquiry, modes of explanation and criteria for verification which are generic to all content in the domain, then, far from being redundant or irrelevant, knowledge provides the means to tackle future problems and needs as well as offering windows of unparalleled richness on past and present. Knowledge in this sense also provides the pupil with essential tools for testing the truth and value of all that information which pours from the internet, television, radio and newspapers, and the teacher's task becomes one of initiation into this critically-armed frame of mind rather than the mere transmission that is the stock-in-trade of the teacher 'barking out facts'. We cannot at the same time hope that science will enable us to cure the hitherto incurable disease, or offer the world a route to sustainability and survival, while asserting that subjects – including of course science – are educational old hat and need to be replaced by skills or themes. If teachers confine themselves to 'barking out facts', then they understand neither knowledge nor pedagogy.

Rejection of a knowledge-based curriculum, therefore, reflects in part a simple misapprehension about the nature of knowledge itself, and the partisan bodies of information with which mere transmission pedagogy and its totalitarian variant, indoctrination, are associated. But in the processual sense advocated earlier, mathematics, the sciences, arts and humanities will be no less relevant and useful in the twenty-first century than they were in the twentieth. For they develop rather than stand still, proceeding on the basis of cumulation, verification and/or falsification. Thus, Matthew Arnold's view of culture as 'the best that has been known and said in the world' needs to submit neither to relativist sneers nor to post-modernist nihilism. For by its sheer intellectual and imaginative power, and by its dogged integrity in the face of ignorance, scepticism or autocracy, the best of past thinking always tells us something new about ourselves and our world. Knowledge may be cumulative, but certain knowledge transformations and acts of artistic creation or scientific discovery are so fundamental that they never lose their power and should be visited afresh by each generation.

No less fundamentally, knowledge looks forward as well as back. Scientific research is permanently on the move and its truths are no sooner accepted than superseded, the arts are constantly pushing at the boundaries of form and expression, and for every conventional history there is a radical alternative. As for that traditional core of all curricula, literacy, it is right to ask whether what counted as literacy for the pen-pushing Victorian clerks of the British Empire can serve also as literacy for the global information age, even though some would continue to confine the debate to endless arguments about phonics. As Luke and Carrington argue, we may now need a pluralist vocabulary of 'literacies' which can accommodate, in a convincing and coherent way, text both print and virtual, literature both canonical and popular, and narratives both local and international.[7] The Rose Review's interim report commends the broadening of the concept of literacy to include 'scientific, technological, mathematical and economic "literacy"'.[8] On the other hand, we may also need to be alert to the possibility that the proliferation of 'literacies' carries the same danger as the proliferation of 'skills': the force and discipline of the word as originally used, and of the practice undertaken in its name, is weakened or lost.

All this is before we have begun to talk about public and private knowledge; about the way, within and outside the public forms of knowing and understanding, individuals make their own sense of knowledge 'out there' and accommodate it to their personal worlds. This, too, is an important area for educational debate, especially in the context of the movement towards constructivist pedagogy. So too is an understanding of the relationship between knowledge, social structure and power, for without that understanding we may not perceive how the elevation of certain kinds of knowledge represses others, and how a curriculum's 'selection from culture' may be interested only in the culture of a society's upper layers, thereby fuelling the sense of marginalisation or exclusion among those whose culture appears not to be valued. In our culturally plural, divided and unequal society, this apparently theoretical issue has very direct relevance to the work of teachers in some of the country's most challenging educational environments.

All these matters should be the stock-in-trade of the teachers who select, mediate and pronounce upon the knowledge which children encounter. The one thing needful here, apart from a very different discourse about knowledge from the one with which we are all too familiar, is that the study of knowledge itself should secure a central place in the training of teachers. At the moment, it is rarely seen.

Skills

A rather different kind of reductionism attends discussion of skills, currently the fashionable educational antidote to knowledge. At the same time as knowledge is downgraded to obsolescent information, everything else is elevated to a skill. So, for example, the Association of Teachers and Lecturers' submission to the Review claimed that today's children need

> a skills based curriculum, focused on the physical skills, the communication, interpersonal and intrapersonal skills and the thinking and learning skills as well as the academic skills which will be essential components of the educated person who is able to think and act effectively in the 21st century.

The belief here is that skills combine contemporary relevance, future flexibility and hands-on experience: that is, those attributes which knowledge is presumed to lack. The modes of knowing, understanding and enquiring embodied in the established disciplines are themselves reduced to 'academic skills' from which, presumably, knowledge is excluded. Skills, it is believed, transcend both knowledge and time.

In similar vein, the Rose Review's interim report proposes replacing the knowledge-rich core of the current national curriculum – English, mathematics and science – by a new core of four 'skills for learning and life' – literacy, numeracy, ICT and personal development;[9] while the QCA's 'big picture of the curriculum' highlights 'literacy, numeracy, ICT, personal, learning and thinking skills' but defines 'knowledge and understanding' merely as 'big ideas that shape the world'.[10]

In all such cases, the concomitant to the elevation of skill – in itself a necessary development – is the downgrading of knowledge, understanding, enquiry and exploration. But to set them in opposition is foolish, unnecessary and epistemologically unsound, for all but the most elemental skills – and certainly those that in educational circles are defined as 'basic skills' – require knowledge, and knowledge itself is far more than 'big ideas that have shaped the world'. Or indeed, far less, for is it proposed that ideas that have not 'shaped the world' should be excluded from the curriculum, that eminence matters more than destiny obscure? Whose world are we talking about anyway? Is there an applied judgement here that to 'shape' is to shape for the better? Does the definition encompass the casualties of world-shaping ambition as well as the usual list of heroes? And who decides on all these matters? The Secretary of State?

Further, in terms of our earlier argument that primary education should balance preparation for future needs and circumstances with attention to the needs and capabilities of children here and now, this shift is clearly driven by the former. Thus the Royal Society of Arts, Manufacture and Commerce (RSA) reworks the entire curriculum in terms of five areas of 'competence': for learning, citizenship, relating to people, managing situations, and managing information,[11] and the government identifies three broad domains of 'skill': vocational skills which are specific to particular work settings; job-specific skills distinctive to particular positions within a given occupation; and generic skills, transferable across different work and life settings.[12]

Clearly, the first two groups – vocational and job-specific skills – may provoke the same objection on the grounds of built-in obsolescence as knowledge-as-information. For this reason many advocates of this approach prefer to transfer them to the category of training/retraining in the more specific domain of vocational education, and place greatest emphasis during general schooling on the lifelong learning potential of the third group, generic skills. Here is a typical list:

- managing one's own learning
- problem-solving
- thinking
- research, enquiry and investigation
- invention, enterprise and entrepreneurship
- communication
- social and interpersonal skills
- teamwork
- leadership.[13]

We note immediately that David Hargreaves' list is no mere exercise in curriculum re-naming in pursuit of a spurious notion of 'relevance'. Everything here can make a strong claim to the status of skill as properly defined: the 'ability to do something (especially manual or physical) well; proficiency, expertness, dexterity . . . acquired through practice or learning'.[14] During the last few decades, 'skill' has lost its embedding in 'manual or physical' activity, possibly as these have lost their dominance in the world of work. What has not been lost is the sense of skill as the capacity to *do* something: a capacity which is in the broadest sense practical and which is honed through concentration and practice. This is why skill is so important in education, why it must complement knowing and understanding rather than supplant them, and why as a concept it must not be debased through inappropriate use.

It is therefore useful to note that Hargreaves' list includes capacities which are needed to advance knowledge and understanding (problem-solving, research, enquiry and investigation) and those which do not necessarily lie within the boundaries of a knowledge-based curriculum (invention, enterprise and entrepreneurship, social and interpersonal skills, teamwork, leadership). In this formulation, and unlike the re-naming instances we have given, skills extend the scope of the curriculum in a convincing and wholly necessary way.

Even so, if skills are *all* that a curriculum offers, as some of our witnesses have advocated, then we have a problem. Even when one hives off the explicitly vocational skills, most such models tend to be more strongly influenced by the needs of the workplace than by other contexts for life after school, let alone the needs of children here and now. And though the generic skills approach purports to address the claims of lifelong learning, it actually sells such learning short, for it elevates being able to do something over knowing, understanding, reflecting, speculating, analysing and evaluating, which arguably are no less essential to the fulfilled, successful and useful life. Indeed, without these capacities the exercise of skill becomes in a very real sense meaningless.

Skills are vital. We cannot survive without them. But, once again, educators should use the term more discriminatingly, otherwise we shall carelessly lose not only knowledge and understanding, but also skill itself.

Definitional footnote

We end up, then, with six basic curriculum terms in need of differentiation:

- *Curriculum*: what is intended to be taught and learned (the planned curriculum); what is actually taught (the curriculum as enacted); what is learned (the curriculum as experienced).
- *Subject*: an organisational or conceptual segment of the planned curriculum; it may be disciplinary, cross-disciplinary or thematic.
- *Timetable*: the way the planned curriculum is divided temporally into lessons or sessions as opposed to being divided conceptually into subjects.
- *Knowledge*: the process and outcome of coming to know, or the combination of what is known and how such knowledge is acquired. It encompasses knowledge both propositional and procedural, and both public and personal, and it allows for reservation and scepticism as well as certainty. It is neither synonymous with subjects nor all that a curriculum contains, though it is nevertheless a central goal of all education.
- *Discipline*: a branch of knowledge as systematised into distinct ways of enquiring, knowing, exploring, creating, explaining and making sense, each with its own key foci, preoccupations, concepts, procedures and products.
- *Skill*: the ability to make or do something, especially of a practical kind; requires knowledge but is distinct from it.

Notes

1 Rose 2008a.
2 Both quoted in Alexander 1984, 18.
3 Cox and Dyson 1971.
4 Thomas 2007.
5 A 'leading primary school head teacher' applauding the Rose Review's interim report for what he took to its view of knowledge: quoted in *The Times*, 9 December 2008 (Aaronovitch 2008). *The Economist* was less sanguine about this view of knowledge, preferring the Cambridge Primary Review account quoted above: 'They [Cambridge Primary Review] take this contention as their starting point for a passionate defence of knowledge as more than facts or information, to be stored or downloaded but not absorbed, questioned or created. Obvious enough, but is anybody listening?'

6 Charles Dickens, *Hard Times*, chapter 1.
7 Luke and Carrington 2002.
8 Rose 2008a, 2.25.
9 Rose 2008a, 2.23.
10 QCA 2007, 31.
11 Bayliss 1999.
12 DfEE 1998b.
13 Hargreaves 2004.
14 OED definition.

10 Entitlement, freedom and minimalism

The national curriculum review launched by Education Secretary Michael Gove in January 2011 was advised by an 'Expert Panel' chaired by Tim Oates, whose enthusiasm for E.D. Hirsch and the need to model the national curricula of PISA high performers strongly appealed to Gove. Other members of the panel were less convinced, and two of them – Mary James and Andrew Pollard – later distanced themselves from Oates and disowned Gove's framework for the national curriculum in England.[1] As originally presented, this paper was a keynote for the CPPS Westminster Seminar 'How can we build maximum benefit from the new national curriculum?' in April 2012. It responded to the Expert Panel's proposals published in December 2011.[2]

There has been much talk lately of professional freedom, curriculum minimalism, and the need to remove the accumulated curriculum 'baggage' of the past 25 years, concentrating instead on 'essential knowledge in key subjects'. This, we were told, is what they do in 'high performing jurisdictions', that is to say those countries, states and provinces whose students come top in the PISA reading, mathematics and science tests at age 15.[3]

I am struck by the fact that advocates of this course of action do not mention the principle that has prominently underpinned England's national curriculum since 1988: the entitlement of all children educated in state-maintained schools to a curriculum that is broad, balanced and relevant, and which promotes – I quote from the 1988 Education Reform Act – their 'spiritual, moral, cultural, mental and physical development and prepares [them] for the opportunities, responsibilities and experiences of adult life'.[4] Cumbersomely worded this may be, but if each of the identified aspects of children's development is given due thought and weight, they add up to a not ungenerous account of what a national curriculum can offer. My anxiety that this hard-won vision of educational entitlement might be sacrificed to the surface appeal of freedom and minimalism has prompted this paper's title.[5]

Entitlement, we should remember, was partly a response to 1970s inspection evidence that in many of England's primary schools children's access to subjects outside the 3Rs largely depended on what their teachers happened to be interested in or know something about. As a result, HMI reported, young children's encounters with, say, science, history, music or drama were a matter of chance.[6] The 1988 Education Reform Act ended this curriculum lottery, and primary

DOI: 10.4324/9781315169378-12

science was one of its success stories. Twenty-one years on, the Cambridge Primary Review (CPR) found that entitlement to breadth and balance had been progressively eroded by a succession of government initiatives and that it urgently needed re-affirming: partly as a basic educational right, partly because children deserve a proper foundation for later choice, but also because research and inspection had demonstrated that in our best primary schools high standards in literacy and numeracy are associated with a curriculum that is broad, balanced and well managed.[7] This is no coincidence, for we know that learning in one area can enhance learning in others.

Alongside their silence on entitlement, policymakers have become so fixated on those 'high performing jurisdictions', chiefly Singapore, Hong Kong and Finland, that they have failed to ask questions about society, childhood and education here in Britain. The word 'jurisdiction' tacitly sanctions this neglect, for it strips a country of the complexities of culture, values, social structure, politics and demography and reduces it to tidy legalities. But it is with the complexities that we must engage if we are to understand education elsewhere, explain why one country outperforms others, and devise a curriculum which is the best sense national.[8]

I wonder, too, whether 'jurisdiction' is chosen because it permits comparison at sub-national level to be smuggled into such discussions. This is taken to extremes in the third McKinsey report, whose high performers ('systems', admittedly, rather than 'jurisdictions') include Japan (a country with a population of 127 million), Alberta (a Canadian province with 3.7 million) and Aspire (a charter school 'system' in the state of California with just 40 schools).[9] On this basis, can we anticipate the one-school 'jurisdiction', much admired by Michael Gove and scaled up to provide a template for England's 24,604 other schools?[10]

So am I as worried now that we have the Expert Panel (EP) report on the new national curriculum as I was last year? Well, although ministers initially appeared to favour what I call 'minimalism 1' – detailed prescription for English, maths and science, with the rest of the curriculum left to chance – entitlement to breadth may be back in favour. Indeed, the DfE's own international trawl produced two reports that effectively turned the tables on 'minimalism 1' by showing that countries that do well in PISA and TIMSS require their pupils to study a broad range of subjects, and to pursue breadth within those subjects, up to age 16.[11]

So far so good – perhaps. However, over half of England's secondary schools and an increasing number of primary schools have become academies, and although they are obliged to teach English, mathematics and science in some form and secure 'breadth and balance' (which as usual are not defined), they do not need to follow the national curriculum. Thus, curriculum entitlement as a principle for the state sector as a whole, at least as it has been understood since 1988, appears to have been abandoned. Indeed, with so many schools able to opt out, we must ask in what sense the new national curriculum will be a national curriculum at all.

But this is not Expert Panel territory. They at least have endorsed breadth. They have made other positive proposals: on the centrality of knowledge; on relating such knowledge to children's development; on the importance of aims; on making space for local curriculum variation; on subdividing the four years of Key Stage 2 so that primary schools can more realistically secure progression and give each key stage a distinctive character; on the critical importance of oracy to children's learning across the curriculum and to the raising of educational standards.[12] But I do have reservations.

Let us start, as all curriculum planning should start, with aims. The EP confirms that aims are essential – it could hardly do otherwise – and proposes five broad 'aims and purposes of the curriculum'.[13] In some of these we even catch faint echoes of the principles and aims proposed by the CPR,[14] which indeed the EP acknowledges. Like CPR, the EP argues that such aims will apply with different force and in different ways as children move through their schooling, and that they should inform all aspects of school life, not just the curriculum.

There are two problems with the EP aims, however. First, if they are to be valid and useful, aims for a national curriculum need to arise from a searching analysis of the condition of British culture, economy and society: the challenges to be addressed, the individual and collective needs to be met, the values and principles to be advanced.[15] The EP report provides no such analysis or rationale, and in contrast to CPR – which having posed its questions about aims then sought answers from national and international research surveys, written submissions and focus groups all over the country[16] – DfE's call for evidence did not invite consideration of these matters. Instead, it launched straight into questions about the content of subjects whose candidacy for inclusion and places in the pecking order had already been agreed, treating aims as given. On the other hand, and my second concern, DfE did collect evidence on aims in high performing jurisdictions which the EP report duly summarised and took as its point of reference.[17] Such statements are definitely worthy of study, in relation not only to PISA but also to the fact of globalisation and the imperative of human interdependence – the CPR itself has a strong global dimension in the aims and the curriculum domains it proposes and the evidence on a wide range of issues on which it draws – but they should contribute to the national analysis for which I have argued, not replace it.

Regrettably, therefore, the EP report and the DfE's call for evidence combine to convey the clear message that the structure and content of the curriculum have been determined independently of the formulation of aims, and that the latter are cosmetic.[18]

What of the much-vaunted 'essential knowledge'? Like the EP, CPR has argued that knowledge is fundamental to all education.[19] In doing so, it has challenged those who claim that knowledge is redundant, subjects are old hat, and a modern curriculum should deal instead with 'skills and creativity'. Now skills and creativity are supremely important. But what kind of curriculum denies children access to some of humankind's principal collective ways of making sense? Or what skills can be exercised without knowledge? Or is it really possible to be creative yet ignorant? Or if subjects are old hat, how are they able to provide the frameworks within which the world's leading minds push forward the frontiers of scientific, medical and technical knowledge, and raise creative, artistic and literary endeavour to new heights? So let us dispense with such pointless polarities: children need knowledge *and* skill *and* creative capacities (and much more), not one to the exclusion of the others. And if subjects are old hat, it's the way they are taught that makes them so.

Yet although I agree with the Expert Panel over the importance of knowledge as such, I detect fudge over what knowledge matters most and indeed what 'knowledge' actually means. In the EP report, 'essential knowledge' is treated as synonymous with 'socially valued knowledge' and 'subject knowledge'.[20] But these are not the same. Subject knowledge may be socially valued but there's much socially valued and indeed essential knowledge that is not discipline or subject bound. Elsewhere the EP tries 'powerful knowledge'. But some of the world's most powerful knowledge has arisen from defiance of what is socially valued rather than from agreement with it, from swimming against rather than with the epistemic tide, so how does the conventionally 'essential' sit with the subversive possibilities of 'powerful'?

Anyway, who defines what knowledge is 'socially valued', 'powerful' or 'essential'? A so-called 'expert panel' whose expertise may or may not be superior to that of the thousands of others who have a view on such matters? The Secretary of State? E.D. Hirsch?[21] Not the 5,763 respondents to the DfE's call for evidence, that's for sure, because – to take just one example among many – 78 per cent of those who responded to the question on Design and Technology wanted it to be in the National Curriculum[22] yet the four members of the EP relegated it to the 'basic curriculum'.

Moreover, the EP report draws the boundaries of 'essential knowledge' somewhat tightly. 'The National Curriculum', it says, 'should set out only the essential knowledge (facts, concepts, principles and fundamental operations) that all children should acquire. . .'[23] 'Facts, concepts, principles and fundamental operations' works reasonably well for mathematics, up to a point for science, but not at all well for English or many other subjects, unless one presumes that (i) knowledge in the national curriculum is to be reduced to propositions and (ii) such propositions are to be transmitted but not investigated or tested in the way that true understanding demands. The verb 'acquire' after the EP's definition of essential knowledge seems to confirm this, and adds a ghostly Victorian echo of children as empty vessels.

What of curriculum scope and structure? In a key diagram, printed twice for good measure, the EP present the curriculum as a five-division league table.[24] Subjects in division one, the premier league, have 'detailed programmes of study and attainment targets'; those in division two have 'refined and condensed programmes of study and minimal or no attainment targets'; for those in division three there are no national requirements and subject content is determined by schools. Division four, oddly, includes two subjects that are specified yet 'not required'. In division five, at the bottom of the heap, are four subjects or areas of learning beyond the EP's remit, including that nettle that no national curriculum review has been prepared to grasp – though the Cambridge Primary Review did – religious education.

Into these five divisions are placed 17 subjects or areas of learning. But far from providing an argued reassessment of essential knowledge for the twenty-first century, the EP have in two senses merely confirmed the status quo. First, only those subjects that are in the current national curriculum are included in the new one, so earlier errors of both commission and omission are perpetuated. Second, we have yet again a high-status and protected core pursued at the expense of a low status and unprotected residue, except that in place of two divisions – what former HMCI and Permanent Secretary David Bell called the 'two tier curriculum'[25] – we now have five. There are minor adjustments in the lower divisions but overall the hierarchy remains exactly as it has been since the nineteenth century.[26]

It's as well to remind ourselves of the consequences of a hierarchy which is so strenuously reinforced, as in England it is, by tests, initial teacher training, CPD, school inspection and resources (what later in its report the EP approvingly calls 'control factors'[27]). It's a recipe for ensuring that those subjects that are least regarded are least well taught, thus confirming their lowly status, especially with pupils. Teachers who buck this trend do so – to their immense and lasting credit, especially among the children they inspire – against considerable odds. This structural double whammy is a far cry from the CPR's insistence that 'children have a right to a curriculum which is consistently well taught regardless of the perceived significance of its various elements or the amount of time devoted to them'.[28] Entitlement is meaningful only when it is about quality in the classroom as well as breadth on paper, and quality requires proper resourcing and close attention in teacher training, school staffing and CPD.

The EP may argue that they are offering the non-core subjects not relegation but freedom. But history and the CPR's evidence show that while our best schools maintain both breadth and quality, elsewhere the curriculum diminishes to what is tested and inspected, if not in nominal breadth then certainly in actual quality.[29] After evaluating its evidence on KS2 tests and Ofsted inspections the CPR recommended wholesale reform but stressed, lest its criticism of current arrangements be interpreted as rejection of testing and accountability in any form: 'The issue is not whether children should be assessed or schools should be accountable – they should – but *how* and in relation to *what*.'[30]

It is against this background that we should view the EP's decisive break with the 1988 Education Reform Act's version of entitlement. The 1988 Act envisaged a national curriculum in which not only the constituent subjects were specified but also, in relation to each of them, the 'knowledge, skills and understanding [and] the matters, skills and processes' required by the end of each key stage.[31] Breadth, in other words, amounted to considerably more than the checklist of subject labels to which, in the lower divisions of the EP's league table, it has now been reduced. Since the EP have said that 'the National Curriculum should set out only the essential knowledge . . . that all children should acquire',[32] it is hard to resist the conclusion that their naming of lower division subjects amounts to little more than tokenism, since nothing that these subjects entail is deemed sufficiently 'essential' to be specified.

It is in this somewhat unpromising light, too, that we should view prospects for the EP's proposed 'local curriculum' (division four in their framework), an idea the EP credits in part to the CPR[33] but which, as they have presented it, I don't recognise. The CPR proposed a 'community curriculum' which, with 30 per cent of the overall time, would encourage schools to forge local partnerships, address local needs and opportunities and give each curriculum domain local as well as national relevance.[34] But in the EP report the local curriculum becomes a repository for those subjects that haven't made the grade. One of them, up to age 11, is citizenship, which in relation to Prime Minister Cameron's promise to fix 'broken Britain'[35] seems pretty shortsighted.

The EP justifies re-arranging the current subjects, rather than reassessing both them and other claimants to a place in England's national curriculum, on the grounds that the government wishes to work within the current legislative framework.[36] Perhaps, mindful of 2010 and the Conservatives' last-minute scuppering of the Labour government's attempt to bring the Rose curriculum framework into law, ministers preferred not to take the risk.

At the CPPS seminar, Tim Oates said that my league table reading of the EP's subject framework was incorrect and the EP intended parity of commitment if not of classroom time. In the interests of fairness to the EP, I record his objection. But if he is right then the EP has managed to mislead not only myself but many other commentators too, as well as those subject associations with a particular interest in the subjects or areas that have apparently been relegated.[37] The issue, of course, is not so much the EP's claimed intention, for its overt commitment to breadth is clear enough, but the classroom consequences of the model through which the intention is enacted.

My reading is further confirmed by the EP's approach to curriculum coherence. The EP lists 'control factors' such as testing, inspection and professional standards which they say will ensure that a revised national curriculum is taught as specified.[38] Elaborating this recently to the House of Commons Education Committee, Tim Oates said: 'A system is regarded as "coherent" when the national curriculum content, textbooks, teaching content, pedagogy, assessment, drivers and incentives all are aligned and reinforce one another.'[39]

Apart from its excessive faith in the now somewhat tarnished nostrums of systems theory, and its striking detachment from the messier realities and relationships of educational policy and practice, the Oates maxim raises three more immediate points about the curriculum. First, by 'curriculum coherence' the EP signals not coherence across the curriculum as a whole (as the phrase implies) but consistency of message and approach within a subject. Second, coherence in this narrower sense applies only to the first division subjects – English, maths and science. This tends to confirm the league table because there's an unavoidable implication that quality and standards in the other subjects don't matter, and to these subjects few if any control factors are applied.

(In conversation, senior Ofsted staff have told me that school inspection checks for 'breadth and balance' may amount to no more than asking heads whether given subjects are listed in the school's paper curriculum, and what happens in the classroom is neither here nor there.) In other words, the EP's 'curriculum coherence' portends consistency in three subjects at the expense of the quality of other subjects and coherence of the curriculum as a whole.

Third, far from being novel, hasn't this been tried before, and recently? In Labour's drive to raise standards through national literacy and numeracy strategies, the control factors – content, pedagogy, testing, inspection, teacher training, CPD, resources, support – were aligned exactly as Tim Oates proposes, producing what one of the CPR's witnesses called a 'state theory of learning'.[40] Yet was Labour successful in its bid to use multiple control factors to secure curricular and pedagogical compliance and hence raise standards? As the Cambridge Primary Review has shown, the evidence on this was decidedly mixed and certainly not of a kind to warrant the pre-election claims about 'the highest standards ever'; but the collateral damage was undeniable.[41] And doesn't all this talk of 'control factors' sit rather uneasily with the coalition's assurances about respecting teachers' expertise and judgement? Only connect, Expert Panel, only connect.

This brings me back to those 'high performing jurisdictions'. The lemming-like rush of some governments to jettison what is distinctive about their national education systems in favour of what can be imported from PISA high performers – what I call 'PISA panic' – raises urgent concerns about the uses and abuses of international educational comparison.[42] Here, to close, are a few of them.

First, we must ask whether in relation to England's performance the panic is really justified. When the results of PISA 2009 were published, the government and the media immediately claimed that far from achieving 'the highest standards ever' under Labour, the performance of England's 15-year-olds in literacy, mathematics and science had 'plummeted' while educational expenditure had rocketed.[43] This interpretation of PISA 2009 informed both the 2010 White Paper and the 2010–12 national curriculum review. Tim Oates's high-performing jurisdictions/essential knowledge/control factors thesis[44] was enthusiastically endorsed as the basis for this – possibly (we can only speculate) because it played both to traditionalist educational sentiment and the teaching profession's desire for greater freedom while keeping government firmly in control. However, expert commentators such as John Jerrim of IoE have comprehensively re-analysed England's performance in PISA 2009 and have concluded that neither PISA nor TIMSS justifies such alarmist claims or provides a safe basis for major policy changes.[45] Studies commissioned by the CPR from researchers at Durham University and the National Foundation for Educational Research came to a comparable conclusion about Labour's very optimistic spin on the international and national test data.[46] It works both ways: it would seem that in the matter of educational standards in England over time, neither New Labour hyperbole nor Coalition alarmism is justified. It would be unfortunate, to say the least, if the EP were to find themselves implicated in the orchestration of PISA panic.

Second, those who use international data to argue or imply a simple cause-effect relationship between a prescribed curriculum focusing on 'essential knowledge in key subjects' and the capacity to outperform other countries in TIMSS and PISA risk false correlation, or the philosophers' 'fallacy of division'. X may well be a common feature of high-performing education systems a, b, c, d and e, but that doesn't demonstrate a cause-effect relationship between feature and performance. And if x is also a common feature of *low*-performing systems g, h, i, j and k, then the claimed relationship is clearly inadmissible. In fact, a curriculum constructed in terms of 'essential knowledge in the key subjects' is the basis of most of the world's national curriculum specifications, PISA successes and failures alike,[47] though of course they may differ in their view of which subjects are 'key' and what knowledge is 'essential'. But − and here's what matters − countries certainly differ, often dramatically, in the conditions and practices through which the prescribed curriculum is enacted.

Third, as David Hogan's extensive research in high-performing Singapore reminds us, the prescribed curriculum is a relatively blunt instrument for raising standards. What matters, again, is the curriculum as enacted by teachers, and the gulf between what governments prescribe on paper and what teachers do in their classrooms can be very wide.[48] The most effective way to raise and maintain standards − this is stating the obvious − is to improve teaching and learning.

Fourth, it's true that control factors like standardised textbooks (or national literacy strategies, or approved phonics schemes) can be used to narrow the gap between the prescribed and enacted curriculum and make teachers toe the line, though that's a pretty rum definition of professional freedom. However, as Hogan's Singapore research also shows, while such devices may raise the floor of teaching quality and educational attainment, they may also lower the ceiling, frustrating the creativity and idiosyncrasy that characterise outstanding teachers, and confining pupil performance to what is required. In so doing, they may also limit the capacity of the system to innovate and improve.[49]

Fifth, although much is made of Finland, politically inconvenient truths about Finland's success are often ignored. Finland's own experts argue that its TIMMS and PISA performance comes from a culture which has an exceptionally high regard for literacy, a highly qualified, well respected, trusted and autonomous teaching profession, an unshakeable commitment to social and educational equity, a successful comprehensive school system, and close alignment not of curriculum prescription, testing, textbooks and inspection but of public policy in education, the economy, employment and social welfare.[50] This echoes Wilkinson's and Pickett's finding that reducing inequality is the key to raising national standards in education, health and other areas,[51] while OECD's own commentary on the 2009 PISA results underlines equity as a major factor in the success of PISA high performers.[52] For Britain and the United States, which are among the most unequal of all the OECD nations and where the gap between rich and poor continues to widen, this is a hard lesson for governments to accept, let alone apply.[53]

Sixth, Tim Oates argues that it's important to look back to how Finland reached its current PISA supremacy rather than focus exclusively on what the country does now. That makes sense. But Oates then claims that Finland's success 'can be traced to highly centralised control in previous decades, including control of textbooks'.[54] In contrast, Pasi Sahlberg, Director General in Finland's Ministry of Education and Culture and one of Finland's leading researchers, argues that Finland got where it is now not by adopting such policies but by abandoning them.[55] Whose version of Finland's educational history is correct?

Finally, while they praise Finland some governments prefer to copy the United States, hence high-stakes testing, punitive inspection, supercharged superheads and the marketisation of schooling – strategies which the Finns reject and which, as Diane Ravitch, Sharon Nichols, David Berliner[56] and other leading American researchers show, don't necessarily deliver on standards. In the matter of learning from other cultures, or even jurisdictions, could it be the case that ideology counts for more than evidence? (For further discussion of the uses and misuses of international educational comparison, see Chapters 20 and 21.)

Conclusion

In 2011, I wrote in *The Guardian*:

> At the start of the latest national curriculum review two versions of 'minimal entitlement' appear to be on offer. Minimalism 1 reduces entitlement to a handful of subjects deemed uniquely essential on the grounds of utility and international competitiveness. The first criterion is too narrowly defined and the second falls foul of the hazards of international comparison. Minimalism 2. . . strives to balance the different ways of knowing, understanding, investigating and making sense that are central to the needs of young children and to our culture – and hence, surely, to an entitlement curriculum – and achieves the required parsimony by stripping back the specified content of each subject to its essential core. This is a very different core curriculum to the winner-takes-all version with which we are more familiar. Rather than a small number of core *subjects*, we have core *learnings across a broad curriculum*, every subject or domain of which, by reference to a well argued set of aims, is deemed essential to a basic education.[57]

It will be evident that if the centrally-prescribed curriculum is to be slimmed down, then I favour minimalism 2. Indeed, the idea of 'core learnings across a broad curriculum' informed the CPR's 2009 proposals for a domain-based curriculum.[58] However, while the EP report endorses breadth in the prescribed curriculum, its framework retains features of minimalism 1 and as enacted it could compound those problems of the divided curriculum which have diminished the education of generations of children and frustrated the cause of raising standards.

At the same time, the EP's stated rationale for its approach to 'essential knowledge' – the need to emulate the curricula of 'high-performing jurisdictions' – collides head-on with the hazards of international comparison. Further, its advocacy of control factors is so preoccupied with education elsewhere that it ignores recent lessons much closer to home, for between 1997 and 2010 such control factors were systematically and vigorously applied in England's schools, but to debatable and arguably damaging effect.

Notes

1 British Educational Research Association (BERA) 2012; James 2012.
2 DfE 2011d.
3 Oates 2010.
4 Education Reform Act 1988, 1.
5 Alexander 2012b, 2011c.
6 DES 1978.
7 Alexander 2010a, chapter 14; DES 1978; Ofsted 1997, 2002a, 2008, 2009, 2010b.
8 On the importance and proper assessment of the place of culture in international educational comparison, see Alexander 2001a.
9 Barber *et al* 2011.
10 24,605 was the figure on the DfE website in April 2012.
11 DfE 2011a, 2011b.
12 DfE 2011d.
13 DfE 2011d, chapter 2.
14 Alexander 2010a, chapter 12.
15 From the CPR final report (Alexander 2010a, 174): 'Prominent among the questions which the Cambridge Primary Review posed for itself and its witnesses in 2006 were these: What is primary education for? To what needs and purposes should it be chiefly directed over the coming decades? What core values and principles should it uphold and advance? Taking account of the country and the world in which our children are growing up, to what individual, social, cultural, economic and other circumstances and needs should it principally attend? Hinting that the task of defining the aims of primary education was not entirely straightforward, we also asked: How far can a national system reflect and respect the values and aspirations of the many different communities – cultural, ethnic, religious, political, economic, regional, local – for which it purportedly caters? In envisaging the future purposes and shape of this phase of education how far ahead is it possible or sensible to look?'
16 Alexander *et al* 2010, chapters 10–13, 241–340; Alexander and Hargreaves 2007.
17 DfE 2011d, Annexes 1 and 2.
18 This sequence was later confirmed by a member of the Expert Panel, Mary James (2012).
19 DfE 2011d, chapter 1; Alexander 2010a, chapter 14, especially 245–51.
20 DfE 2011d, chapter 1.
21 Hirsch's work was warmly commended by both the Secretary of State and Tim Oates, chair of the 'expert panel'. Hirsch 1987, 2007.
22 DfE 2011c, 31.
23 DfE 2011d, 6.
24 DfE 2011d, 29 and 71.

25 'We cannot afford, and our children do not deserve, a two-tier curriculum' (Ofsted 2004). For further discussion of the divided curriculum and its educational consequences, see Alexander 2010a, chapter 14.

26 See the striking juxtaposition of subject requirements and hierarchies, from the 1904 Board of Education Regulations, the 1967 Plowden Report and the current National Curriculum, in Alexander 2010a, 211.

27 DfE 2011d, 55–6.

28 Alexander 2010a, 505.

29 Alexander 2010a, chapters 13, 14, 16 and 17.

30 Alexander 2010a, 500.

31 Education Reform Act 1988, 2.

32 DfE 2011d, 6.

33 DfE 2011d, 21.

34 Alexander 2010a, 262–3 and 273–5.

35 Prime Minister Cameron in speeches in April 2010. The fixative was to be 'the big society'.

36 DfE 2011d, 20.

37 See, for example, Richards 2012.

38 DfE 2011d, 55–6.

39 Oates 2012.

40 'A state theory of learning . . . based on the idea that a combination of repeated high stakes testing, a national curriculum and mandated pedagogy in literacy and numeracy will raise standards', Maria Balarin and Hugh Lauder, in their research survey for the CPR. Balarin and Lauder 2008.

41 The evidence on Labour's 1997–2009 standards drive is assessed in the CPR final report, Alexander 2010a, 469–74, and in greater detail in six of its commissioned research surveys: Tymms and Merrell 2007; Whetton *et al* 2007; Harlen 2007; Balarin and Lauder 2008; Cunningham and Raymont 2008; Wyse *et al* 2007. See also this volume, Chapter 4.

42 For a discussion of these issues, see Alexander 2012e and this volume, Chapter 21.

43 Toby Young in the *Daily Telegraph*, 7 December 2010. In the House of Commons the Secretary of State said 'Literacy, down; numeracy, down; science, down: fail, fail, fail.'

44 Oates 2010.

45 Jerrim 2011.

46 Tymms and Merrell 2007; Whetton *et al* 2007.

47 Benavot 2008.

48 Hogan *et al* 2012.

49 Hogan *et al* 2012. However, we might also note Margaret Brown's observation that Labour's National Numeracy Strategy 'had the effect of increasing the range of attainment although it was designed to reduce it' (Brown and White 2012). Either way, Oates's notion of 'control factors' is problematic.

50 Lyytinen 2002; Fredriksson 2006; Sahlberg 2011.

51 Wilkinson and Pickett 2010.

52 OECD 2010c.

53 Alexander 2010b. See this volume, Chapter 20.

54 Oates 2010, 2012.

55 Sahlberg 2011.

56 Ravitch 2010; Nichols and Berliner 2007.

57 Alexander 2011c.

58 Alexander 2010a, chapter 14 and recommendations 46–53, 494–5.

11 Neither national nor a curriculum

A few months after the Expert Panel report discussed in the previous chapter, the Secretary of State published his draft proposals for the national curriculum in primary schools. What follows is an extract from the author's response to these on behalf of the Cambridge Primary Review, as reprinted in *Forum* 54(3), 369–84 (2012). The final requirements for the revised national curriculum were published in 2013, implementation began in September 2014, and at the time of writing this version still applies to England's schools.

Introduction

On 11 June 2012, Secretary of State for Education Michael Gove published draft programmes of study (PoS) for English, mathematics and science in the primary phase of England's national curriculum, the review of which he initiated in January 2011 with the appointment of an 'Expert Panel' chaired by Tim Oates.

The Secretary of State's 2012 proposals are accompanied by a letter to the Expert Panel chair.[1] Others have responded in detail to the draft programmes of study and the view of primary school English, mathematics and science that they reflect. This chapter concentrates on the Secretary of State's letter because it is the closest the government comes to providing an account of the character of the national curriculum as a whole. Such an account ought to be a requirement of any national curriculum review worthy of the name, for three subject syllabuses hardly constitute a curriculum, so what the Secretary of State says on the matter requires scrutiny.

The use of international evidence

The injunction to emulate the policies and successes of 'high performing jurisdictions' appears several times in the Secretary of State's letter and the quoted phrase has become something of a policy mantra, rather affectedly peppering the discourse of this entire national curriculum review. However, despite the confidence and frequency of claims about what 'high-performing jurisdictions' are up to, the government seems unaware of (or uninterested in) the spectrum of relevant evidence from international comparison outside what the US National Research Council calls Type 1 and Type 2 studies,[2] or of the tendency

DOI: 10.4324/9781315169378-13

of policymakers everywhere to over-interpret the PISA and TIMSS international student achievement data, or of the hazards of naive, mono-factorial and otherwise unsustainable attributions of cause and effect in accounting for other countries' success.[3]

The Department for Education (DfE) has certainly been made aware of reservations about its use of international data. For example, I submitted a paper on such matters in November 2011[4] and have regularly copied officials into other relevant material.[5] I have also put the DfE in touch with authoritative sources in other countries whose expert knowledge of those countries may well exceed that on which ministers have chosen to rely.[6]

It is not just that international evidence has been cited selectively and tendentiously in support of the line taken by the current national curriculum review, essential though such evidence undoubtedly is. It is also clear from the Secretary of State's letter that the limited range of international evidence of which ministers have been made aware has been allowed to supplant or become a proxy for the independent analysis of those circumstances and needs – cultural, social, demographic and economic – that are unique to this country and no less important a determinant its national curriculum.

There are several points at which the Secretary of State's letter illustrates this distortion, perhaps most strikingly when it says that we must 'ensure that our children master the essential core knowledge which *other nations* pass on to their pupils' (his words, my italics).[7] Clearly, in an interdependent and competitive world it is useful to know what other nations define as 'essential core knowledge' in the school curriculum, but it is surely taking matters too far to ordain that because a sample of their 15-year-olds outperforms a sample of our 15-year-olds in the PISA tests those nations' accounts of 'essential core knowledge' should replace our own.

This edict is so blinkered in its take on what a national curriculum is about, anthropologically so naive in its detaching of knowledge from the culture that creates it, and logically so bizarre – because of course it is not the content that generates test success in the content but the way it is taught – that it should be repeated lest in scanning the Secretary of State's letter we overlook it. We must, he says, 'ensure that our children master the essential core knowledge which other nations pass on to their pupils'.

So the Secretary of State has failed to grasp both the pitfalls and true value of international comparison. We study education elsewhere to learn from it, not to copy it. Even granted the fact of globalisation and the imperative of economic competitiveness, there is much more to shaping a national curriculum than mimicking the curricula of PISA high performers; and it has yet to be shown that such mimicry raises standards. In any case, risking a pun, in this matter double standards all too often apply. Thus British governments voice admiration for high-performing Finland but then, finding Finnish education policies politically unpalatable, they copy the United States, whose schooling system performs relatively modestly in PISA and by some accounts verges on the dysfunctional. Meanwhile, the true lessons from Finland go unheeded.[8]

Aims

In both its final report and its evidence to the government's national curriculum review, the Cambridge Primary Review devoted much attention to the aims of our national education system, and the imperatives and values that might shape it over the next few decades.[9] This work was informed by widespread stakeholder consultation across the country as well as by commissioned searches of published national and international evidence.[10] The Review also deplored the typically British tendency to determine aims after the event, so that they decorate school prospectuses and entrance halls rather than shape the curriculum in action.

The Expert Panel referred to this work but did not use it, and proposed instead five aims with no obvious evidential provenance. These in turn were ignored by government, which fell squarely into the trap against which we had warned. Having determined the precise structure of the curriculum and much of its content, the Secretary of State now invites us to enter into discussion about the aims which his non-negotiable curriculum specification can be claimed, *post hoc*, to pursue, thus guaranteeing that yet again the aims will be no more than cosmetic.

Further, although the intended consultation on aims seems somewhat pointless, the Secretary of State says in his letter that in this matter he will privilege the views of teachers. This is wrong. In a pluralist democracy the aims and values underpinning the state's maintained education system concern every citizen, not just those who happen to be teachers. Where teachers' views should have supremacy is in deciding how within schools and classrooms the agreed national aims should be implemented. In this and other ways the Secretary of State's stance on aims is a long way from what the Cambridge Primary Review took to be a matter of basic common sense:

> Aims should be grounded in a clear framework of values – for education is at heart a moral matter – and in properly argued positions on childhood, society, the wider world and the nature and advancement of knowledge and understanding. And aims should *shape* curriculum, pedagogy, assessment and the wider life of the school, not be added as mere decoration.[11]

Standards and accountability: the core and the rest

Like the government, Cambridge Primary Review stands firmly for high educational standards and the public accountability of schools and their teachers. However, it differs from government and the Secretary of State in the matter of how standards should be defined and how accountability should be exercised. In his letter, the Secretary of State defines standards as how well pupils perform in English, mathematics and science, and accountability as how such performance is publicly demonstrated. He also urges high expectations for other subjects even though these will not be tested nationally. The latter sentiment is welcome, but we should remind ourselves of the familiar and well-documented tendency for schools to concentrate on what is tested to the detriment if not the exclusion of the rest.[12] Further, for the subjects outside the core – that is, those subjects whose content is to be determined by each school individually – it is hard to know how accountability can be meaningfully demonstrated in other than a highly localised and non-transferable sense.

In contrast, Cambridge Primary Review maintains that educational standards deriving from a national curriculum should encompass all aspects of that curriculum, not just testable aspects of three of its subjects. Schools should in turn be accountable for the quality of the whole curriculum, not merely part of it; and such accountability should be demonstrated by a variety of indicators, measures and procedures, not just through national tests. Or as the Review expressed the matter in its list of policy priorities presented to the incoming government in 2010:

> Stop treating testing and assessment as synonymous. Stop making Year 6 tests bear the triple burden of assessing pupils, evaluating schools and monitoring national performance. Abandon the naive belief that testing of itself drives up standards. It does not: good teaching does. Initiate wholesale assessment reform drawing on the wealth of alternative models now available, so that we can at last have systems of formative and summative assessment – in which tests certainly have a place – which do their jobs validly, reliably and without causing collateral damage . . . The issue is not *whether* children should be assessed or schools should be accountable – they should – but *how* and in relation to *what*.[13]

It is a source of considerable disappointment to us that the government's Bew review of testing did little more than scratch the surface of these issues,[14] and that ministers continue to treat tests, assessment and accountability as synonymous. It is also clear that for accountability and quality to be guaranteed beyond the three core subjects, there need to be agreed national frameworks of some kind for those subjects whose content schools are invited to determine for themselves.

Spoken English

The Secretary of State, and the draft programmes of study, announce that 'the importance of spoken language should be a priority throughout the new national curriculum'. What is proposed in the draft programmes of study starkly contradicts this, and the letter itself reveals an extraordinarily restricted view of spoken language and its place in children's development and education, confining its purposes to 'supporting the development of reading and writing' and the teacher's task to ensuring that pupils 'master formal English through poetry recitation, debate and presentation'.[15]

Indeed, there is deep concern in many quarters about what is seen as a severe weakening of the profile of spoken language in the draft programmes of study compared with previous versions of the national curriculum, and this despite the considerable array of evidence with which ministers and DfE have been presented. That evidence makes talk that is cognitively challenging and rigorously orchestrated absolutely essential to children's thinking, learning and understanding both within each subject and across the curriculum as a whole. It is also a vital tool for effective communication and a lifeline for those children who are disadvantaged socially and linguistically. And we now have a critical mass of international evidence demonstrating that high quality talk raises tested standards in the core subjects.[16]

Of all this, as of alternative evidence on international comparisons, ministers and DfE officials are fully aware. Indeed, in February 2012, at my request, the Department organised a seminar on spoken language in the national curriculum attended by lead NC review officials, national and (by videolink) international experts, and the Schools Minister. The event was preceded by extensive correspondence and meetings with both ministers and officials, including the Secretary of State himself.[17]

I and several others who participated in the DfE seminar are particularly concerned that the statements on spoken language that head each of the three draft programmes of study are so brief and bland as to be almost pointless; that they are further weakened by not being followed through within each PoS; and especially that spoken language is no longer to be a distinctive strand of the teaching of English.

Although the partial attempt to implement the DfE seminar's recommendation of 'talk across the curriculum' is a small step forward, it is not convincingly pursued in the mathematics and science drafts, or even in the reading and writing components of the English draft, where the relationship between spoken and written language is of critical importance. As to the removal of the spoken language strand from English, this is an error which in my judgement cannot be allowed to stand. It appears to be informed by the wholly mistaken belief that in the teaching of English there is no more to spoken language development than what can be subsumed in reading and writing.

In fact, children's acquisition of the knowledge, understanding and skill that enable them to use spoken language with the fluency and flexibility necessary for learning, employment and life requires attention to talk in its own terms *as well as* in the contexts of reading and writing. This is emphatically not an either/or issue, for such a focus draws on knowledge about the dynamics, registers and grammars of spoken language, and of language in use in a wide variety of real-life contexts, a pursuit which is distinct from the teaching of reading and writing. This is something employers and university admissions tutors readily understand when they complain about school leavers' restricted powers of oral communication and their limited ability to shift from informal and colloquial talk to the more precise and formal registers required for presenting and defending a case, explaining ideas, probing others' reasoning or participating in discussion.

Far from prioritising talk as claimed in the Secretary of State's letter of 11 June, the decision to remove it as a distinct strand of the English PoS represents a backward step – one, indeed, which may well frustrate two of the government's key intentions: to raise educational standards and to close the gap between disadvantaged children and the rest. Incidentally, the Expert Panel's suggestion that spoken language can be enhanced by highlighting it in curriculum aims is a non-starter and should be disregarded. It is what is required by the programmes of study that makes the difference. Spoken language must remain as an explicit strand of the English programme of study.

I have to say that I am also somewhat baffled by this turn of events, for at the DfE seminar on 20 February the Schools Minister signalled his acceptance of the arguments I have summarised. However, he also expressed the fear that raising the profile of spoken language could 'encourage idle chatter in class'. I say again here, as I said then, that those of us working in this field have long advanced something which is neither idle not mere chatter: an approach to spoken language that is rigorously planned and implemented; that engages and sustains children's attention to the task in hand; that challenges and stretches their thinking; that probes their understanding and misunderstanding, building on the one and rectifying the other; that demands as much of the teacher's expertise as it does of the child's developing linguistic skills. In any case, one child's idle chatter may be another's exploratory talk, especially where early years teaching and learning are concerned.

It would surely be a matter of deep concern to every parent and teacher if the ministerial perception I have quoted were to triumph over a body of international evidence which is as conclusive as it is vast, and if as a consequence children were to be denied access to the full cognitive, social and pedagogical potential of classroom talk properly managed.

We urge ministers to reverse their ill-advised decision on spoken English. We also remind them of the evidence we reviewed with them at the February 2012 DfE seminar on Oracy, the National Curriculum and Educational Standards.[18] Not to act on that evidence would be irresponsible. It is true that the evidence also shows that in too many classrooms the quality of talk is not what it should be, but that is precisely why the government needs to give a clear lead; and it is why raising the profile of spoken English in the curriculum needs to be accompanied by action in initial teacher training (ITT) and continuing professional development (CPD). On this front, ministers should be encouraged by the considerable strides that some schools and ITT/CPD providers have made, even though the national picture remains uneven.

Perpetuating the divided curriculum?

It is good to see that the Secretary of State endorses the principle of curriculum breadth for which the Cambridge Primary Review has so strenuously argued. However, what is proposed is breadth in a severely qualified form.

Schools will be required to teach, alongside the three core subjects, 'art and design, design and technology, geography, history, ICT, music and physical education across all the primary years'.[19] However, that formula guarantees breadth on paper only, for the programmes of study in these subjects will be very brief, and what is taught will be largely determined by schools.

This may seem not unlike what Cambridge Primary Review commended in its own curriculum framework.[20] But whereas the Review's framework proposed a measure of local discretion and variation for *every* subject, though within clear agreed national parameters, the Secretary of State offers such freedom only for those subjects he deems relatively unimportant. In contrast, for English, mathematics and science he proposes to specify in exhaustive detail 'the content that each child should be expected to master . . . every year'.[21] Since this contrast is reinforced by assessment requirements, with English, mathematics and science subject to national tests and 'some form of grading of pupil attainment', we can be reasonably sure on the basis of past experience that in a significant proportion of schools teachers will teach to the test and have scant regard for the rest of the curriculum.

As Cambridge Primary Review argued in its final report and its evidence to the national curriculum review, the only meaningful notion of a broad curriculum is one in which breadth is allied to quality, and where all children encounter a curriculum in which every subject is taught to the highest possible standard regardless of how much or how little time is allocated to it.

Here, history is once again a sobering guide to where the government's proposed approach could take us. For during the 1970s and 1980s inspection evidence showed that while literacy and numeracy were always taught in primary schools, the fate of the rest of the curriculum depended on the inclinations and expertise of each school's teaching staff.[22] In our best primary schools this autonomy yielded a curriculum of vision, vitality and rigour. At worst it meant that during their seven critical years of primary education many children encountered little or no science, history, music or drama (for example), and when they did so those encounters were fleeting and undemanding. In these schools, teachers' freedom to choose what subjects to teach, and with what degree of conviction, effectively denied their pupils the later freedom of choice for which a balanced and well-taught foundational curriculum, grounded in much more than functional literacy, is the minimum prerequisite. Especially hard hit, as always, were those children whose families lacked the resources to make good the deficit out of school.

This is the warning from recent educational history that the government's national curriculum review must not ignore. Freedom for teachers – a necessary corrective to 13 years of government micro-management – cannot be pursued at the expense of young children's need for a proper foundation for later learning and choice.

What former HM Chief Inspector and DfE Permanent Secretary David Bell called the 'two tier curriculum' (the 'basics' and the rest), and what the Cambridge Primary Review evidence has shown to be a hierarchy of teaching quality as well as allocated time, is one of the problems of English primary education most urgently in need of attention.[23] Not only has it not received such attention in these proposals: it has been reinforced.

Looking forward or harking back?

There are three further difficulties with the proposed approach to shaping the whole curriculum. First, just as the *lessons* of history in respect of the two-tier curriculum have been ignored (indeed the lessons of Britain's educational history overall appear to have been overtaken by the obsession with the contemporary activities of 'high-performing jurisdictions'), so the *habits* of history have been allowed to persist unchallenged. The start and end points of this review have been the same hierarchy of subjects that frames the current national curriculum. Neither the government nor the Expert Panel appears to have asked whether this hierarchy, which goes back to the 1988 Education Reform Act (and indeed to a century before that) remains appropriate for the next generation of children. The omission is as curious as it is serious, given how much we have heard about modernisation, globalisation, the changing international situation and the need to plan for the future; and it seems decidedly odd to look forward by harking back. This retrospective tendency is underlined by the fact that the one subject in the current national curriculum which the Secretary of State does *not* prescribe is one of its most recent and welcome arrivals: citizenship.

Second, the anomalies of the current national curriculum – notably, perhaps, the handling of faith – are allowed to persist, presumably on the grounds that attending to such anomalies would require legislation, and legislation is what the whole curriculum package seeks to avoid. I should add – and the Cambridge Primary Review curriculum proposals underline this – that what we object to here is not religious education but the persistence of the 1944 Butler Act's separation of the 'religious' and the 'secular' curriculum, a separation that makes it difficult to approach the treatment of faith in contemporary education and society in a manner that is properly in tune with the cultural, religious and moral condition of Britain 70 years after Butler.[24]

Third, the entire framework is informed by a view of 'essential knowledge' which is frequently hinted at but never explicated or justified, though enough has been said about the influence on these proposals (including by ministers themselves) of the ideas of E.D. Hirsch[25] for the rationale to be pretty clear, and that rationale is undoubtedly illustrated in the three proposed programmes of study.

However, just as we challenged the idea that the future of spoken language in young children's education can depend on one minister's misguided musings about 'idle chatter in class', so we would wish to challenge the assumptions that it is for ministers in a culturally diverse democracy to determine exactly what knowledge is essential for every child and what knowledge is not, and that they are competent to do so. These constitute a clear and dangerous breach with arrangements enshrined in the 1988 Education Reform Act which have held until now: namely that the political and educational risks of ceding such powers to a politically partisan Secretary of State are such that national curriculum planning should be delegated to an 'arm's-length' non-departmental public body (NDPB); that this body should be required to consult widely and without fear or favour, and draw on a generous and appropriate range of expertise; and that the resulting national curriculum proposals should be placed before Parliament for a full debate rather than be imposed from Sanctuary Buildings.[26]

Neither national nor a curriculum?

This takes us to our final concerns about what the Secretary of State has proposed. We have to ask whether what we have here represents a national curriculum that is worthy of the name. We believe that there are four senses in which it does not.

First, the proposed 'national' curriculum will be required for some children in the nation's maintained schools but not for all of them. Academies and free schools may opt out. If there is to be a national curriculum at all, then it should be both an entitlement for all children in maintained schools and an obligation on all those who teach in those schools.

Second, there is little evidence in the Expert Panel report, and even less in the Secretary of State's proposals, of the kind of close and careful weighing of national culture, national needs and England's unique and hugely complex mix of commonality and diversity that should precede and inform any attempt to devise a national curriculum that has a reasonable chance of speaking to the condition of more than a minority of the nation's children and families. The Cambridge Primary Review undertook this task, working both from published evidence and an extensive programme of discussions with stakeholders – including children, parents, teachers, community representatives, business leaders, faith leaders, local and national politicians from all parties, and many others in different parts of the country. In this programme CPR also made a point of meeting and hearing from children and families who in our society tend to be marginalised, disadvantaged and vulnerable. It is regrettable that DfE, and indeed the Expert Panel, have ignored this extensive and vital work.

Third, although the responsibility for initiating a review of the national curriculum rests with government, government has an equal responsibility to ensure that what emerges is able to unite the majority of the electorate behind a view of the curriculum for state-maintained schools to which most can subscribe. Indeed on pragmatic grounds alone this makes sense, for a policy which teachers and parents support is more likely to be successful in practice than one with which they unwillingly comply. The contrary evidence from the period 1997–2010 is very clear on this score.

Equally, the national curriculum is surely one area of public policy where a government has an obligation to try to achieve political consensus and where the debate ought to rise above party politics. Instead, this venture has been pursued in an aggressively party political manner and both evidence and expertise have been viewed through an unashamedly ideological lens. Alternative views and evidence on curriculum scope and balance, or on the nature and structure of knowledge, have been dismissed out of hand as leftist or 'progressive', which for those of us who believe in an inclusive, rational, principled and evidentially-grounded approach to curriculum thinking is as inaccurate as it is insulting.

Fourth, what we have here are proposals not for a curriculum but for just three subjects. The attempts by the Expert Panel, the Cambridge Primary Review, the Rose Review and others to conceive of the curriculum as a whole, addressing questions of scope and balance in relation to individual, cultural and economic need, have been rejected in favour of the assumption that if the inherited 'core' subjects are prescribed in detail the rest can sort itself out. Past evidence shows that in relation to what happens in many schools this assumption is optimistic.

So in four decisive senses what is proposed is neither national nor a curriculum: it is for some of the nation's children in state-maintained schools but not all of them; it offers no account of the national culture and circumstances to which a national curriculum ought to relate, being influenced more by dubious extrapolations from what other countries do; it makes no attempt to reach a consensus on values and rationale, presuming instead that it is entirely proper in a democracy for a national curriculum to serve as a vehicle for imposing upon the majority the values, beliefs and prejudices of an ideological minority; and it represents not so much a curriculum as a syllabus for three subjects.

Implementation issues

Genuine curriculum reform cannot be achieved merely by redefining what is required, for the curriculum as enacted in schools and classrooms is a much more powerful determinant of educational quality and progress than the curriculum as prescribed on paper.

DfE has been advised that if it aligns with the prescribed curriculum various 'control factors' like testing, inspection, teacher training and approved textbooks it will have a better chance of ensuring that teachers teach what is required and of reducing the gap between prescription and enactment.[27] However, far from being the novel insight its proponents claim, this is precisely what was attempted with Labour's national literacy, numeracy and primary strategies between 1998 and 2010. Not only did this approach work only up to a point; it also caused considerable collateral curriculum damage, alienated much of the teaching profession and replaced the autonomous judgement which is essential to intelligent and effective teaching by dependence and unthinking compliance. This is yet another historical lesson that has been ignored.

The precedent is doubly important, for the new national curriculum requirements will be implemented in a context where established forms of professional support – notably from QCDA and local authorities – are no longer available.

This situation makes it all the more urgent that government addresses the problem of curriculum capacity about which it was warned in the Cambridge Primary Review final report and in numerous subsequent exchanges. The Review argued that children are entitled to a curriculum which is taught to the highest possible standard in all its aspects, yet HMI and Ofsted have consistently revealed considerable variation in the quality of subject teaching across the primary sector, especially in relation to the non-core subjects, and it is clear that this relates to schools' access to appropriate levels of subject and pedagogical content knowledge.

In 2011, the Secretary of State accepted the Review's recommendation on this matter[28] and initiated an enquiry into the capacity of primary schools to plan and teach a broad curriculum to a consistently high standard. The enquiry was undertaken internally, and for reasons that were not explained the resulting report was not made publicly available.[29] However, the Review remained closely involved and the DfE report supported the published conclusions of both itself and Ofsted, namely that curriculum capacity is indeed insufficiently comprehensive in many primary schools; and the curriculum has expanded in scope and complexity beyond what the inherited and funded pattern of generalist class teaching can sustain.

The solution is not as simple as replacing generalists by specialists, though nurturing and more effectively deploying specialist expertise is certainly an essential element. I have proposed a range of strategic options for tackling the problem, ranging from the diversification of models of initial teacher training (as opposed to routes into teaching, which are already diverse) to more flexible ways of deploying staff both within and between schools.[30] As yet, the options have not been properly discussed. The matter cannot be postponed much longer.

We stress, however, that in the coming discussion curriculum capacity must not be equated solely with subject knowledge, essential though subject and subject-specific pedagogical content knowledge[31] certainly are:

> The term 'curriculum capacity' refers to the human and other resources that a school is able to command in two areas, relating to (i) the aims, scope, structure, balance and content of the curriculum as a whole, and (ii) the detailed planning and teaching of individual curriculum subjects, domains or aspects. A school is regarded as having appropriate curriculum capacity if it is able to conceive and plan a broad, balanced and coherent curriculum in pursuit of relevant and properly argued educational aims; and if each subject, domain or aspect of that curriculum is planned and taught to a consistently high standard, regardless of how much or little time is allocated to it.[32]

Capacity in the first sense is even more important when, as under the Secretary of State's proposals, a national curriculum review offers schools no meaningful perspective on the curriculum as a whole.

Notes

1 Gove 2012.
2 National Research Council 2003. This matter is pursued later in this volume (chapters 20–22).
3 Alexander 2012e. See this volume, Chapters 20 and 21.
4 Alexander 2011e.
5 For example, Alexander 2012a, 2012c.
6 For example, Pasi Sahlberg in Finland and David Hogan in Singapore.
7 Gove 2012, 2.
8 Sahlberg 2011; Alexander 2012c.
9 Alexander 2010a, 174–202.
10 Chawla-Duggan and Lowe 2010; Shuayb and O'Donnell 2010; Machin and McNally 2010; White 2010.
11 Cambridge Primary Review 2010 (my italics).
12 Mansell 2007; Mansell and James 2009; Harlen 2007, 2014.
13 Cambridge Primary Review 2010.
14 DfE 2011e.
15 Gove 2012, 3.
16 The evidence later published in Resnick, Asterhan and Clarke 2015 was already in the public domain and had been brought to the attention of the Secretary of State by this author. See Chapter 15, footnotes 31 and 32.
17 The correspondence and meetings in questions are listed in full in Alexander 2012a.
18 Alexander 2012a.
19 Gove 2012, 4.
20 Alexander 2010a, 261–77.
21 Gove 2012, 3.
22 DES 1978; House of Commons 1986.
23 First noted by this author in his distinction between 'curriculum 1' and 'curriculum 2' in Alexander 1984, and discussed yet again in Alexander 2010a, 241–5. HMCI David Bell's warning – 'We cannot afford, and our children do not deserve, a two-tier curriculum' – is in Ofsted 2004.
24 Alexander 2010a, 232–5 and 268.
25 Hirsch 1987, 2007.
26 Sanctuary Buildings, Westminster, is the home of the Department for Education. The non-departmental public bodies (NDPBs) in question were the National Curriculum Council (NCC, 1988–93), the School Curriculum and Assessment Authority (SCAA, 1993–7), the Qualifications and Curriculum Authority (QCA, 1997–2007), and the Qualifications and Curriculum Development Agency (2007–12). In 2011 the government set up a Standards and Testing Agency but placed national curriculum planning under direct ministerial control. See Baker 2013.
27 Oates 2010; DfE 2011b, 2011d.
28 '[We recommend] a full national primary staffing review of the relationship between (i) the curricular and other tasks of primary schools as they are now conceived, (ii) the roles and numbers of teachers and other professionals required, (iii) the expertise and training/retraining which this analysis dictates . . . The potential to tackle the problem through clustering, federation, resource-sharing, teacher exchange and all-through schools should also be examined' (Alexander 2010a, 506).
29 See Chapter 14.
30 Alexander 2012f, 2013. See this volume, Chapter 14.
31 The distinction between subject knowledge and pedagogical content knowledge is Lee Shulman's. Shulman 1987.
32 Alexander 2013. See Chapter 14.

12 Beyond the reach of art

'The Arts in Schools: making the case, heeding the evidence': keynote at the Curious Minds/RECAP Conference on Intercultural Dimensions of Cultural Education, Chester, July 2017. An earlier and less Anglocentric version was given at the Copenhagen Cultural Children's Summit, organised by Barn-drømmen at the Royal Danish Theatre in October 2016.

We know that at their best the arts excite, amaze, inspire and move us; that they illuminate and enrich our lives; that they deepen our awareness of who and what we are; that they enable us to step out of the here and now into the realm of the possible and barely apprehended; that they nurture essential and transfer-able skills; that they confront conventional wisdom and speak truth to power; that they encourage us to think and feel more deeply; that they are unique and powerful ways of making sense of ourselves and our world; that they embody much of what it means to be civilised. In short, we know that the arts are truly and profoundly educative. These things being so, there surely can be no ques-tion that immersion in the arts is the right of every child and the obligation of every school.

Policy tells a very different story. In 2013 the UK government issued to England's schools a new national curriculum with a very old message.[1] For primary schools the published requirements ran to 88 pages for English, 51 pages for mathematics but just two for visual arts, two for music and none at all for drama or dance, apart from passing mentions under English and PE – a staggeringly cursory treatment whose stern criticism by the Henley report on cultural education ministers cheerfully ignored.[2] Then, for secondary students, the EBacc, introduced in 2010 by Michael Gove, purported to make GCSEs more 'rigorous' by excluding creative and artistic subjects altogether.[3] Predict-ably, the effect of this decision on student choice, school provision and teacher training in the visual and performing arts has become increasingly acute in sec-ondary schools and higher education.[4] Meanwhile, national tests reinforce the stockade between the so-called core subjects and the rest, and school inspec-tions police it.

No amount of DfE or Ofsted rhetoric about a 'broad and balanced curriculum' can reverse the damaging consequences of such policies. Ofqual figures show EBacc subject entries up, but non-EBacc subject entries down,

DOI: 10.4324/9781315169378-14

yet again.[5] A House of Lords debate deplored the fact that for two years in a row there was an 8 per cent drop in creative GCSEs, and Kenneth Baker, ministerial architect of England's first National Curriculum in 1988, called the decline in technical and creative GCSEs 'a disgrace'.[6] By 2017, the proportion of school students taking arts subjects was the lowest for a decade.[7] Arts courses in universities, and in some cases whole departments, were closing or under threat because of funding cuts,[8] and ministers were actively encouraging this process by calling arts subjects 'dead-end' (Secretary of State Gavin Williamson) and warning that students who take them would be 'held back' (Secretary of State Nicky Morgan).[9]

Ministers might assure Lord Baker that it is for schools to decide the place of creative subjects in the curriculum and that students should be free to choose from what is available, and in a strict sense they would be right. Yet policy sets the boundaries of opportunity and accountability within which schools must work. It signals to teachers, parents, employers, the public – and of course children themselves – what kinds of learning matter most and least, what it means to be educated, and by what fundamental values a national culture is shaped and defined. Hence the current paradox: a curriculum that we are told is informed by so-called 'British' cultural values but which pushes to the margins culture as many understand it.

Naturally, I'm aware that this begs the question of whether we define 'culture' in its anthropological or artistic sense, or indeed as both of these and more, though such questions appear not to have troubled those who have decreed that democracy, the rule of law, individual liberty and inter-faith tolerance are the only so-called British values that matter.[10] By way of contrast we might note that the Henley report included in its generous definition of cultural education 'archaeology, architecture and the built environment, archives, craft, dance, design, digital arts, drama and theatre, film and cinemas, galleries, heritage, libraries, literature, live performance, museums, music, poetry and the visual arts'.[11] These, equally, are the stuff of democracy, liberty and tolerance. Only connect. . .

But the government's recurrent bouts of PISA panic leave little time for culture however it is defined. So here's the question: how can we persuade policy-makers and educational leaders that exercises like PISA should *serve* education, not drive it, and that while STEM subjects – science, technology, engineering and mathematics – are indeed vital foundations for learning, employment and economic competitiveness, the arts and humanities (now fighting their considerable corner under the banner of SHAPE[12]) have educational, economic and social claims which, properly examined, are equally strong?

I want to suggest two responses. First, we should publicise the evidence. Second, we should expose the myths by which, for some people, even the strongest evidence is outweighed. We may not be wholly successful in our efforts to change entrenched ways of thinking, but we can try.

★★★

An evidence-based case for arts education was made as long ago as 1982 in the Gulbenkian report, *The Arts in Schools*.[13] Yet while bringing good cheer to believers, Gulbenkian had limited impact elsewhere. Then in 1999 the government enquiry chaired by Ken Robinson produced a report[14] that set the arts in the broader context of culture and creativity, thus enabling it to appeal to others than the already convinced. Robinson argued that creative capacities are needed in all walks of life, including business, industry, science and technology – a proposition which, of course, our best scientists and business leaders have always understood.

As well as mainstreaming the idea of creativity, Robinson brought businesses on side and encouraged partnerships between artists, performers and teachers of a kind that across the UK are now commonplace. However, one thing did *not* change as a result of Robinson: the national curriculum. Here the message was clear: by all means do exciting things outside the classroom, but inside the classroom the old subject hierarchy remains fixed and immutable.

After Robinson came a major report from the United States. In 2011, President Obama's Committee on the Arts and Humanities published *Reinvesting in Arts Education: winning America's future through creative schools*.[15] Like Robinson, the President's Committee argued that economic success requires creative capacities, though it placed greater emphasis on the arts as such than Robinson, whose report tended to lose them in its quest to popularise the idea of generic creativity. Like Robinson, the US report saw the future less in traditional teaching than in partnerships between artists and teachers, arts organisations and schools. However, its main value was the way it pulled together research evidence showing how the arts in schools can have a positive impact on educational outcomes. Of these it highlighted five:

- *Student motivation and engagement*, including attendance, persistence, attention, aspiration and risk-taking.
- *Student achievement* in tests of reading and mathematics.
- *Skill transfer* from the arts to other subjects, including, again, reading and mathematics.
- *Habits of mind* across all areas of learning, including problem-solving, critical and creative thinking, and the capacity to deal with ambiguity and complexity.
- *Social competencies* including collaboration, teamwork, tolerance and self-confidence.

(The use here of reading and mathematics performance to justify arts education should be noted but for the moment parked, as I shall return to it later.) The US report also cited a study by James Catterall that followed students from school into adulthood, and showed that such outcomes can have a lasting effect on students' lives. And of disadvantaged students Catterall said: 'Arts-engaged low-income students are more likely than their non-arts-engaged peers to have attended and done well in college, obtained employment with a future, volunteered in their communities, and participated in the political process by voting.'[16]

A further body of evidence comes from neuroscience, which though still in its relative infancy indicates links, for example, between music training, phonological awareness and early reading skills (something the Hungarian composer Kodály spotted back in the 1930s); between the disciplined practice required for learning to play an instrument and improvement in other cognitive domains; between musical training and the ability to manipulate information; between arts training and the development of executive attention, 'especially the abilities to control emotions and to focus thoughts, which are critical aspects of . . . general cognition . . . and . . . social and academic success';[17] though in relation to arts partnership schemes we should also note that what makes the difference is not brief exposure, however stimulating and enjoyable at the time, but sustained engagement.

What was the impact of that illuminating report from the President's Committee on the Arts and Humanities? Sadly but symptomatically, my American colleagues shrug and tell me that few American educators have even heard of it. They tell me that no evidence, however conclusive, can resist the pressure of high-stakes testing and the Common Core Curriculum Standards.

Then, in 2012, we had the Henley report on cultural education, which was more about mission than evidence but maintained the push towards an outward-looking approach involving not only partnerships and hubs but also national awards and ambassadors to raise the profile of cultural education and cultural achievement.[18] The government response was ostensibly supportive, though more supportive of Henley's recommendations on partnerships than of what he said about the place of the arts in the national curriculum. There, as I've noted, change was not permitted.[19]

By now it's clear that in this area, as in so many others, governments are selective in their use of evidence. We must not be. It is therefore right that I should balance the four enthusiastic reports I've mentioned with a more guarded account. The Endowment Foundation (EEF) uses DfE funding to commission randomised control trials of initiatives that look likely to improve the educational performance of disadvantaged children. Responding to pressure from those who complained that most EEF trials are limited to outcomes in English, maths and science, the Foundation commissioned a review of 200 research studies in arts education.

Although the resulting EEF report[20] confirmed some of the findings reported elsewhere, for example the non-musical benefits of learning to play a musical instrument, it could find no proof of the impact of the visual arts on educational attainment and very little positive evidence relating to drama, dance, poetry or creative writing. Disappointingly, the report concluded: 'Though there are promising leads, at the moment there is not enough robust evidence to be able to demonstrate a causal link between arts education and academic achievement.'[21]

However, I have four reservations about the EEF review. First, it did precisely what its critics had complained about (and what I also noted in relation
to the US report): it confined its interest in educational 'outcomes' to test
scores in English and mathematics. Second, most of the studies it reviewed
were of primary school pupils taught by non-specialists, where we know that
lack of subject and pedagogical content knowledge can diminish both teacher
expectations and pupil learning. That is hardly a fair basis for assessing what
the arts can do for such learning if well taught. Third, it judged all the studies it reviewed against the so-called 'gold standard' of the randomised control
trial (RCT), with its use of matched control and experimental groups. No
methodology other than the experimental or quasi-experimental was deemed
sufficiently robust. However, not only is considerable insight available from
some of those many other research studies that the EEF review chose to ignore,
but transferring to the complexities of teaching a model devised for clinical
drug trials is highly contested,[22] and to accept it without question was unwise.
Fourth, having concluded that its evidence showed few causal links between
arts education and what it chose to define as academic achievement, the EEF
report said: 'Almost all of the studies in this review were rated as providing
weak evidence because of serious design flaws.'[23] This, I'm afraid, is the point
where the Education Endowment Foundation report scuppers itself. If the
research studies in question are methodologically so weak, then they don't
prove anything either way, negative or positive.

So where does this leave us? Setting the Education Endowment Foundation's
somewhat self-defeating report alongside findings from other sources, I submit
that we do in fact have a growing body of evidence in addition to the research
studies listed in the President's Committee report, some of it striking. Here are
some examples.

In Leeds, Opera North's *In Harmony* programme aims 'to inspire and transform the lives of children in deprived communities, using the power and disciplines of community-based orchestral music-making'. The Leeds project is
one of six, with others in Gateshead, Lambeth, Liverpool, Nottingham and
Telford. In Leeds every child spends up to three hours each week on musical
activity and some also attend Opera North's after-school sessions. Most children learn to play an instrument and all of them sing. For the Hull children,
singing is if anything even more important. Children in both schools give
public performances, joining forces with Opera North's professional musicians.
For the Leeds children these may take place in the high Victorian surroundings
of Leeds Town Hall.

In 2016 the programme's evaluation reported dramatically improved test
results in – what else? - language and mathematics.[24] Methodological caution
requires us to warn that the test gains in question reflect an apparent association
between musical engagement and standards of literacy and numeracy rather
than the proven causal relationship that would be tested by a randomised control trial. But the gains are sufficiently striking, and the circumstantial evidence
sufficiently rich, to persuade us that the relationship is more likely to be causal

than not, especially when we witness how palpably this activity inspires and sustains the enthusiasm and effort of the children involved. Engagement here is the key: without it there can be no learning.

It's a message with which for many years arts organisations and activists have been entirely familiar, and which they have put into impressive practice. To many members of Britain's principal orchestras, choirs, art galleries, theatres and dance companies, working with children and schools is now as routine as the shows they mount, while Creative Partnerships and its successor Creativity, Culture and Education (CCE) have pursued on an even larger scale the objective of immersing children in the arts by enabling them to work with leading arts practitioners.[25] Creative Partnerships was established by the Labour government in 2002 in the wake of the Robinson report. Under the leadership of first Peter Jenkinson and then Paul Collard it prospered until it was axed by the Conservative-led coalition government in 2011. But by then a succession of evaluation reports had yielded positive findings[26] on which CCE and Paul Collard were able to build. Similar work, focusing particularly on children scoring high on indices of economic and social disadvantage, and those in hospices for terminal care, has been undertaken by Children and the Arts, successor to the Prince's Foundation for Children and the Arts and an organisation of which I am proud to have served as a trustee.

In Germany, Deutsche Kammerphilharmonie Bremen moved its headquarters and rehearsal space into an inner-city secondary school. This created first unease, then a dawning sense of opportunity and finally an extraordinary fusion of students and musicians, with daily interactions between the two groups, students sitting alongside orchestra members at lunch and during rehearsals, a wealth of structured musical projects and dramatic improvements in student motivation, engagement and behaviour. As a result, the school was transformed from one to be avoided to one to which parents from other parts of Bremen eagerly competed to send their children.[27] Building on these successes, the school became home to a concert hall and the award-winning Future Lab, which uses music to unlock the potential of disadvantaged children. The project then went nation-wide and in 2017 established a Future Lab in Tunisia.[28]

Perhaps the most celebrated example is Venezuela's El Sistema, which since 1975 has promoted 'intensive ensemble participation from the earliest stages, group learning, peer teaching and a commitment to keeping the joy of musical learning and music making ever-present' through participation in orchestral ensembles, choral singing, folk music and jazz. El Sistema provides the model for In Harmony, the English programme whose work through Opera North led to those improvements in test results in Leeds; and for Sistema Scotland, which has projects involving nearly 2000 children in Stirling, Glasgow and Aberdeen. The official evaluation of In Harmony cites 'positive effects on children's self-esteem, resilience, enjoyment of school, attitudes towards learning, concentration and perseverance' with, as a bonus, 'some perceived impact on parents and families including raised aspirations for their children, increased enjoyment of music and confidence in visiting cultural venues, and increased engagement with school'.[29] Similar findings are reported from Sistema Scotland.[30]

There are many more examples like these. But here we return to our caveat about the 2011 US report. It is tempting to try to persuade sceptics of the value of arts education by using those outcome measures to which they give highest priority. Hence the number of research studies that assess impact not in terms of outcomes specific to the arts themselves but by reference to reading and mathematics. The danger of presenting the case in this way, necessary in the current policy climate though it may be, is that it reduces the arts to the status of servant of other subjects, a means to someone else's end rather than an end in itself. ('Why study music?' 'To improve performance in maths'.) It also blurs the vital differences that exist between the various arts in terms of their form, language, concepts, practice and modes of expression. Literature, creative writing, the visual arts, music, drama and dance may have elements in common – form, for example, is fundamental to all of them – but each is also in obvious ways distinct. Each art has its own language, engages specific senses, requires specific skills and evokes distinct responses.

Until schools have the courage to champion art for art's sake, and to make the case for each art in its own terms, then arts education will continue to be relegated to the margins of the curriculum.

★★★

I said earlier that in order to persuade we should not only argue from the evidence but also expose the myths to which people have recourse either because they know no better or because they find the evidence inconvenient. Let us now consider three of these myths.

First and most familiar is the view that the arts are about feeling and doing rather than thinking, and that they are therefore intellectually undemanding. We find this view reflected in the exclusion of the arts from typical lists of 'academic' subjects and of course from the EBacc; and their demeaning labelling as 'soft'. We find it in the traditional relegation of arts subjects to the late afternoon, on Friday as often as not (a tendency that Benjamin Britten upended in his *Friday Afternoons* songs for children). We find it in the EEF report that concluded that there is no evidence that the arts have a positive impact on academic achievement, which was defined as achievement not in the supposedly non-academic arts but in English and mathematics. We find it in New Labour's 2003 manifesto on curriculum and educational standards entitled *Excellence and Enjoyment*.[31] This rightly argued that teachers should strive for both excellence and enjoyment in learning, but then made it clear that excellence comes from literacy and numeracy, and enjoyment from the other subjects – implying, conversely, that the arts are not about excellence while reading and maths are much too puritanical in their pursuit of excellence to be enjoyed. As, sadly, many test-driven Year 6 pupils would agree.

And so, not surprisingly, we continue to hear children themselves saying, 'It's only art.' Only? Talk to any writer, artist, musician, actor, dancer or film-maker and you'll learn something of the knowledge, skill, intellectual effort and even pain that go into creative activity of any kind. Yet interestingly, Howard Gardner reports that 'there has been almost a conspiracy of silence among artists concerning the arduous training and the keen mental efforts involved in artistic practice . . . artists have hesitated to acknowledge the cognitive dimensions and demands of their chosen field'.[32] So artists themselves could to help us puncture the myth that the arts are intellectually undemanding.

Here's an example, admittedly from a somewhat specialised corner of musical performance. Anyone who has studied Bach's trio sonatas for organ will know how keenly they stretch the mind and body as well as elevate the spirit. Right hand, left hand, fingers, legs, heels, toes: each of them tracing melodic lines which are independent as to their journeys around the three keyboards – two manuals and pedals – yet are also parts of a complex but coherent contrapuntal and harmonic creation. This music is not just technically demanding. Eyes, hands and feet must be co-ordinated while the mind simultaneously sustains three independent yet interwoven musical lines and the architecture of the whole. When John Ruskin wrote that 'art is that in which the hand, the head, and the heart . . . go together',[33] he probably had painters in mind, not organists.

Then there's the myth that schools can either pursue high standards in so-called core subjects like language, maths and science, or they can offer children a broad and rich curriculum, but that it is not possible to do both of these equally well. This myth, peddled by most recent UK governments, has been debunked not just by research but also by Ofsted. Inspection evidence consistently shows that the primary schools that achieve best results in the national literacy and numeracy tests are those that provide a curriculum that is broad, rich and well-managed, and in which all subjects, not just those that are tested, are treated seriously. The inspectors reckon that the connection between curriculum breadth and standards in literacy and numeracy is causal rather than merely a matter of statistical association, and their findings reinforce research evidence on learning transfer between subjects.[34] That apart, children surely have a right to a curriculum that treats every subject with equal seriousness, regardless of how much time it is allocated, and educational standards are about the quality of learning in all subjects, not just those that are tested.[35] If a subject is worth teaching at all, it should be taught well.

Linked to the myths that the arts are intellectually undemanding and that they are incompatible with high standards in literacy and numeracy is the myth that the arts are not useful socially or economically. This one has been demolished by government itself. In 2016 the government reported that what are called the 'creative industries' contributed £84 billion every year to the UK economy. The then Minister for Culture, Ed Vaizey, said:

> The creative industries are one of the UK's greatest success stories, with British musicians, artists, fashion brands and films immediately recognisable

in nations across the globe. Growing at almost twice the rate of the wider economy our creative industries are well and truly thriving.[36]

Yet even as Vaizey was celebrating that £84 billion bonus and its spectacular growth rate, his colleagues at DfE continued to exclude arts subjects from the EBacc in the teeth of objections from the great and good and a 100,000-signature petition organised by Bacc for the Future,[37] with the lamentably predictable result that the number of students taking arts subjects at GCSE fell steeply.[38] Tightening the screws, the last remaining A level examination in art history was set to be scrapped in direct response to the government's education policy,[39] and was saved at the last minute only after a high-profile campaign led by the likes of the Tate, the Courtauld Institute and the National Gallery, not to mention celebrity historian Simon Schama, who talked of a 'big dull axe wielded by cultural pygmies'.[40] Seeing which way the wind was blowing, ex-Education Secretary Michael Gove, whose curriculum policies had undoubtedly earned him Schama's insult, strategically converted to the cause and tweeted that the arts 'stretch minds and expand sympathies'.[41] By 2018, the annual income generated by the creative industries had risen to £111 billion, accounting for 9 per cent of jobs and 5 per cent of the UK economy – bigger than the automotive, life sciences, aerospace, oil and gas sectors combined.[42]

Thus, evidence from one government department exposes the folly of another – £111 billion from the creative industries on the one hand, the forced decline of the arts in schools on the other – and once again we witness an absence of joined-up political thinking in Downing Street, which one might have expected to have some kind of strategic oversight of the work of DCMS and DfE. In any case, to judge the value of the arts in terms of national economic impact may be persuasive but it is far from sufficient; just as it is not sufficient to deduce the impact of the arts on individual children from their test scores in literacy and numeracy. We have seen that when children engage meaningfully in the arts they gain in terms of motivation, attendance, engagement, aspiration, risk-taking, achievement across the curriculum, skill transfer to other subjects, habits of mind such as problem-solving and creative and critical thinking, and social competencies such as collaboration, tolerance and self-confidence. These outcomes are not only invaluable for the individual; they also contribute to the common good. They must be celebrated for what they are.

Interestingly, Andreas Schleicher of OECD and PISA now argues that the vocabulary of 'hard' and 'soft' subjects (usually equated respectively with STEM and SHAPE) may need to be inverted. Giving evidence to the House of Commons Education Committee in 2019 he said:

We talk about 'soft skills' often as social and emotional skills, and hard skills [as] . . . science and maths, but it might be the opposite. The science and the maths might become a lot softer in the future when [the need for such knowledge] evaporates . . . whereas the hard skills might [turn out to be qualities such as] curiosity, leadership, persistence, resilience.[43]

★★★

I end by noting three problems whose persistence reinforces myths of the kind I have outlined. First, there's the problem, alluded to by Schleicher, of the habitually dualist or dichotomous mindset: thinking versus feeling, cognitive versus affective, academic versus practical, theory versus practice, 'hard' sciences versus 'soft' arts, knowledge versus skill, excellence versus enjoyment, depth versus breadth, subjective versus objective, and of course as the ancestor of them all, mind versus body. We don't need a philosopher to remind us that all of these are unnecessary and untenable. But they are also hard to shift, for they are rooted not just in today's educational thinking but also, hence my allusion to Descartes, in the history of western culture.[44] So we can counter this tendency by making inclusivity our cardinal curriculum principle, confirmed by Courtney Cazden: 'Not either/or but both/and'.[45] We can and must pursue thinking *and* feeling, the academic *and* the practical, sciences *and* arts, depth *and* breadth, knowledge *and* skill, and so on. Far from being mutually exclusive these are both complementary and interlocking. For the arts, as Howard Gardner and John Ruskin remind us, are incontrovertibly a matter of mind as well as hand, eye, ear or body.[46]

Second, there's the problem of how the arts are perceived when the available paradigm for assessing their impact allows only metrics. Many research studies, as we have seen, use standardised tests in reading or mathematics as proxies for attainment in the arts. But if *outcomes* specific to the arts are marginalised because they don't fit the measurement paradigm, then *aims* specific to the arts will be marginalised too. As the great American arts educator Elliot Eisner warned in the 1960s, there's an inherent problem in the way we define both aims and outcomes in the arts, and a naive dichotomy of 'subjective' and 'objective' is part of the problem.[47] Arts outcomes *can* be assessed, but the task requires a more subtle and flexible approach. Eisner tried to capture this in his distinction between instructional and expressive objectives and his efforts to extend the vocabulary of arts assessment beyond the limited array of outcomes that can be quantified into the more elusive realm of educational connoisseurship and criticism.[48]

Finally, there's the problem of understanding. Myths of the kind I have exposed stem in large part from simple ignorance of what the arts are about and the capacities that creative endeavour requires. And I'm afraid this isn't just a matter of political or public perception: we must also accept that the considerable level of understanding and skill that good arts teaching requires is not as widely available in our schools as it should be, and Ofsted evidence confirms this.[49]

For what we don't fully understand we won't teach well, and probably won't value either, and the resulting combination of inadequate professional knowledge, low esteem, low expectations, uninspiring teaching and limited outcomes will reinforce and perpetuate the myths and misunderstandings about the arts and arts education that I've mentioned. Not least among children, who in their turn may become parents, teachers and even national decision makers. Thus does the cycle repeat itself.

But as teachers like Andria Zafirakou have triumphantly demonstrated, when the arts are taught well, and teachers have the knowledge, skill and imagination to teach them with flair and enthusiasm, their impact can be spectacular.[50] We know it, children know it, their parents know it, even economists know it – and the evidence proves it. We can and must break the cycle. Certainly we should strive, albeit against the odds, to educate our policymakers. But we may also need to re-educate ourselves.

Notes

1 DfE 2013b.
2 DCMS/DfE 2012a, 58.
3 www.gov.uk/government/publications/english-baccalaureate-ebacc/english-baccalaureate-ebacc (accessed May 2021).
4 https://baccforthefuture.com/news/2019/the-bacc-for-the-future-campaign-launches-manifesto-ahead-of-general-election-2019 (accessed May 2021).
5 Staufenberg 2017.
6 www.baccforthefuture.com (accessed May 2021).
7 Adams 2017.
8 Bakare and Adams 2021.
9 Paton 2014; Hinsliff 2021
10 Ofsted 2015b.
11 DCMS/DfE 2012a, 3.
12 SHAPE: Social Sciences, Humanities and the Arts for People and the Economy. A campaign launched in 2020 by the British Academy with UK Research and Innovation (UKRI). Morgan Jones *et al* 2020.
13 Gulbenkian 1982.
14 NACCCE 1999.
15 PCAH 2011.
16 PCAH 2011, 18.
17 Posner and Patoine 2009; Goswami 2015.
18 DCMS/DfE 2012a.
19 DCMS/DfE 2012b.
20 See and Kokotsaki 2015.
21 See and Kokotsaki 2015, 3.
22 Ginsburg and Smith 2016.
23 Ginsburg and Smith 2016, 4.
24 www.operanorth.co.uk/news/dramatic-sats-results-increase-at-schools-working-with-opera-north (accessed May 2017).
25 https://en.wikipedia.org/wiki/Creative_Partnerships; www.creativitycultureeducation.org/our-story/ (accessed April 2021).
26 For example: Ofsted 2006; Sharp *et al* 2007; McLellan *et al* 2012.
27 Pickles 2015.
28 www.kammerphilharmonie.com/zukunft-gestalten/zukunftsabor/ (accessed May 2021).
29 Lord *et al* 2015.

30 Moore and Harkins 2017.
31 DfES 2003.
32 Gardner 2006, 97.
33 Ruskin 1986.
34 Alexander 2013.
35 Alexander 2010a, recommendation 125.
36 DCMS 2016.
37 www.baccforthefuture.com/sign-the-petition.html
38 www.baccforthefuture.com/
39 www.artlyst.com/articles/association-of-art-historians-condemns-scrapping-of-alevel-art-history
40 Weale 2016.
41 Weale 2016.
42 DCMS 2020.
43 George 2019.
44 Explored more fully in Alexander 2008b, chapter 4.
45 Cazden 2001, 56.
46 Gardner 2006, 97–101; Ruskin 1986.
47 Eisner 1969.
48 Eisner 2005, chapters 2–5. Eisner, E.W. (2005) *Reinventing Schools: The Selected Works of Elliot W. Eisner*. London: Routledge, chapters 2–5.
49 For example: Ofsted 2012a, 2012b, 2013, 2015a, 2017.
50 Andria Zafirakou teaches the arts to disadvantaged and marginalised children at Alperton Academy in Brent, west London. In 2018 she won the Varkey Foundation Global Teacher Prize.

13 True grit

Extracts from Cambridge Primary Review Trust blogs 26, 53 and 30 (2015).[1] Here we have just two examples from those bids for school attention and curriculum time that punctuate the period between one national curriculum review and the next.

True grit

Those who thought that the departure of Education Secretary Michael Gove might give schools a breather before the 2015 election, liberating them from the weekly explosion of initiatives and insults, reckoned without the ambition of his successor. These days, few education secretaries of state are content to do a good job, deeming it more important to leave an indelible mark in the name of 'reform'. To this lamppost tendency Nicky Morgan appears not to be immune.

Having told children not to bother with the arts, her wheeze, and it's a biggish one, is to make Britain 'a global leader in teaching character and resilience . . . ensuring that young people not only grow academically, but also build character, resilience and grit'. To that end, DfE has invited bids for projects showing how 'character' can be built, and on 16 March there will be a grand ceremony at which 'character awards' of £15,000 each will be presented to 27 schools, with a £20,000 prize for the best of the best. Morgan modestly defines her chosen legacy as 'a landmark step for our education system'.

In the same way that Labour claimed, witheringly but inaccurately, that before the imposition of its national literacy and numeracy strategies England's primary teachers were 'professionally uninformed', so Nicky Morgan's happy discovery of something called 'character' implies that schools have hitherto ignored everything except children's academic development; and that creativity, PSHE, moral education, religious education and citizenship, not to mention those values that loom large in school prospectuses, websites and assemblies and above all in teachers' daily dealings with their pupils, were to do with something else entirely. Remember the not-so-hidden 'hidden curriculum'? If there is a 'landmark step' then, it is not character education but its political appropriation and repackaging.

So what, in Morgan's book, constitutes 'character'? Its main ingredients, as listed in the guidance to applicants for the DfE grants and character awards, are

DOI: 10.4324/9781315169378-15

'perseverance, resilience and grit, confidence and optimism, motivation, drive and ambition'. (Readers will recognise 'resilience' as one of the most overused words of recent years.) Well down the list come 'neighbourliness', 'community spirit', 'tolerance' and 'respect'.

Like so much in recent English education policy, this account of character is imported from the United States. The Morgan character attributes are almost identical to those in the eponymous Paul Tough's book *How Children Succeed: grit, curiosity and the hidden power of character*,[2] and in Dave Levin's evangelising Knowledge is Power Program (KIPP).[3] Here, then, we have a melding of the no-holds-barred values of corporate America with that fabled frontier spirit portrayed by John Wayne. 'Grit' anchors the education of character in both worlds.

But there's a third element. In a speech in Birmingham last November prefiguring the DfE announcement, Morgan said pupils should 'leave school with the perseverance to strive to win . . . to revel in the achievement of victory but honour the principles of fair play, to win with grace and to learn the lessons of defeat with acceptance and humility'.[4] No prizes for spotting the source of that little homily. These are unambiguously the values of England's nineteenth-century public schools: values directed not to the nurturing of mind or empathy but to physical prowess on the games field, an education veritably conceived as no more and no less than a game of rugby or cricket. And not just education: life and death too, as immortalised in the New-bolt poem in which the playing field morphs into the trenches of 1914–18: 'There's a breathless hush in the close tonight/Ten to make and the match to win/The Gatling's jammed and the colonel dead/Play up, play up and play the game.'

If character is important, which it surely is, is such an idiosyncratic and unreconstructedly male account of it good enough, and is it for government to impose this or any other notion of character on every child in the land, of whatever inclination, personality, gender or culture? In one of two excellent blogs on this subject that I urge prospective applicants for the DfE awards to read, John White thinks not. He says: 'Nicky Morgan is not wrong to focus on personal qualities, only about the set she advocates. This is tied to an ideology of winners and losers.' (As indeed is Morgan's scheme itself: did it need to be a competition?) White reminds us of the considerably more rounded values framework appended to the version of the national curriculum that was introduced in 2000 and superseded in September 2014, and he argues that 'no politician has the right to steer a whole education system in this or any other partisan direction'.[5] For White, Morgan's foray into character education is further confirmation of the need for curriculum decisions to be taken out of the hands of politicians and given to a body which is more representative, more knowledgeable and culturally more sensitive.[6]

The other recent must-read blog on character education is by Jeffrey Snyder in the United States. He cites evidence that 'character' is more likely to be determined by genetically-determined personality traits than the efforts of teachers, and indeed he argues that anyway nobody really knows how to teach it. In this context it's worth asking what those pupils subjected to 1850s/1950s character-building really learned, and whether there is indeed a correspondence between success on the playing field, in work and in adult life. And since you ask, did fagging and flogging really make for manliness (whatever that is) or were they merely perversions by another name?

Snyder argues, too, that the 'perseverance, resilience and grit' account of character 'promotes an amoral and careerist "looking out for number one" point of view' adding, tellingly: 'Never has character education been so completely untethered from morals, values and ethics.' As a result, 'character' is as likely to be harnessed to the pursuit of ends that are evil as to those that are good. 'Gone,' adds Snyder, 'is the impetus to bring youngsters into a fold of community that is larger than themselves . . . When character education fails to distinguish doctors and terrorists, heroes and villains, it would appear to have a basic flaw.'[7]

Snyder's third objection, and it applies both to the Morgan view of character and the Gove account of essential knowledge, is the sheer narrowness of the underlying educational vision. In this context, it's worth asking how the Cambridge Primary Review's 12 educational aims might be classified. Are 'wellbeing', 'engagement', 'empowerment' and 'autonomy' about character or something else? Do such responsive and responsible CPR aims as 'encouraging respect and reciprocity', 'promoting interdependence and sustainability', 'empowering local, national and global citizenship' and 'celebrating culture and community' have anything to with resilience and grit?

Actually they do, for it takes considerable grit and resilience to live the values of reciprocity, interdependence and community in a culture of winner-takes-all individualism; or to champion sustainability when the prevailing ethic is rampant materialism and unfettered economic growth; or, as so many educationists have learned to their cost, to hold firm to a principled vision of children's education in the teeth of government atavism and disdain. Captains of industry and sports personalities do not, as Morgan appears to believe, have a monopoly of courage and determination. In any event, the imperative here is to tie perseverance, grit and resilience to socially defensible aims and values, for, as Snyder notes, that for which we teach children to strive must be educationally worthwhile.

It will be interesting to see what accounts of character, and what strategies for promoting it, DfE rewards when it distributes its grants and prizes for character education. With the national strategies Labour gave us what one CPR witness called a 'state theory of learning'. Will the coalition government's bequest be a state theory of character? Let's hope that Morgan's judges put vision, ethics, social responsibility and plurality back into the frame.

We can presumably trust that proposals to reintroduce fagging and flogging are unlikely to be shortlisted, though these days one never knows.

True grit – the sequel

Having now seen the list of awards[8] I must eat some though certainly not all of my words, for among the winners are some undoubtedly impressive and indeed moving initiatives, including several schools striving to raise disadvantaged children's self-esteem, and these are reassuringly remote from the headline-grabbing crudity of the Nicky Morgan paradigm.

Yet even before the results were announced there were rumblings about the competition procedure, which required interested schools to nominate themselves and then justify their claims to a prize by briefly answering six questions. One of these asked for evidence of the impact of their character-forming strategies on their students, but critics of the scheme claimed that such evidence counted for less than the eloquence of schools' answers, that these were not independently checked for accuracy, and that the provision of genuinely verifiable evidence was optional.[9]

We have not been told how many of England's schools entered this somewhat bizarre competition, but we can safely assume that the overwhelming majority did not. Most, quite simply, will have been too busy to do so. Some will have been unwilling to have their names linked to what looked suspiciously like a pre-election political stunt. Others will have been justly offended by the implication that schools don't attend to their students' personal and interpersonal development unless DfE instructs them to, and that even then they require a £15,000 incentive. Others again will have objected to being told to replace their carefully conceived and sensitively nurtured efforts in this direction by a recipe from which ethics, communality, plurality, social responsibility and global understanding are apparently to be excluded. And, for that matter, the Cambridge Primary Review aims of respect, reciprocity, interdependence, sustainability, culture and community – ingredients, in fact, of citizenship. But then, Ms Morgan's government has made citizenship optional at Key Stages 1 and 2. So, following the criticisms of White and Snyder quoted earlier, does individual 'character' now matter more than the common good?

Which is not to say, as I've already stressed, that the winners did not deserve to be recognised for the work they do. But equally deserving of recognition, surely, are the thousands of schools whose teachers value and nurture 'character' with no less commitment and success, and perhaps more consistently manifest that character by not competing with others to advertise the fact.

All of which raises a troubling question about the government's cynical view of professional motivation. Not only are there many more awards for teaching now than there were, say, 30 years ago – in itself no bad thing in a country that has tended to take this most essential of professions for granted – but the award industry has become increasingly and dangerously politicised, with what Warwick Mansell has calculated as a disproportionate showering of gongs on academy heads.[10]

Fortunately, most teachers are motivated by something more profound and less self-serving than the hope or expectation of such baubles. Indeed, in the matter of leading our children by example, we might argue that it's the unsung thousands of teachers who disdain ministerial threats and bribes who most truly manifest grit and resilience.

Ms Morgan modestly lauded her character-building wheeze as 'a landmark step for our education system'. If we add together all the landmark steps announced by recent education ministers we'll have a veritable staircase. Does it, I wonder, lead up or down?

Mindful or mindless?

I have been invited to attend a conference on the educational and economic importance of 'non-cognitive skills'. The invitation is accompanied by a glossy booklet in which various notables expatiate on the 'development of character, non-cognitive skills, mindfulness and well-being'.

The invitation arrived while I was checking the final draft of the new CPRT report on children's cognitive development and learning, commissioned from leading cognitive neuroscientist Usha Goswami.[11] The two documents couldn't be more different. In Goswami's report, cognition – the ways, following Bruner, that humans 'achieve, categorise, remember, organise and use their knowledge of the world' – is at the heart of the educational enterprise. But the conference booklet castigates this focus on cognition, re-labelled 'cognitive skills', for neglecting much of what education should be about.

What is going on here? And does it matter?

Let's take the second question first. Well yes, how we think about thinking, learning and knowing matters a great deal, and to no group of professionals should it matter more than to teachers, for exciting and advancing these processes in pursuit of an educational vision is their job. Indeed, one of the strengths of the professional world of primary education used to be its belief in the need for classroom relationships and decisions to be grounded in evidence about how young children develop, think and learn. Reflecting this, seven chapters of the final report of the Cambridge Primary Review are devoted to children and childhood.[12]

Such evidence doesn't stand still, which is why CPR commissioned the research reviews that CPRT is now revisiting and updating.[13] Nor is child developmental evidence on its own a sufficient basis for teaching, though there was a time during the 1960s and 1970s that some believed this and constructed teacher training courses accordingly, thereby offering trainees knowledge of children but not of how to teach them. Now, thankfully, our take on pedagogy is more comprehensive.

So when someone says 'I've seen the future and it's non-cognitive', is this the latest stage in the refinement of our account of teachers' core business or merely the latest educational fashion? What, to return to my earlier question, is going on here?

My unsolicited conference booklet answers thus: today's schools are failing to equip tomorrow's citizens and employees with what they will need in order to cope, work and prosper in a fast-changing world, so something different is needed. Nothing new here of course: during the past few decades pundit after pundit and report after report have levelled this same charge at established patterns of schooling in the UK. The current iteration focuses, with some justice in view of the UK's poor showing in international studies, on the importance of wellbeing and children's capacities to manage their lives positively and productively. This was the claimed impetus for the Secretary of State's recent intervention on character, grit and resilience. But what is worrying about the current packaging of character, grit and resilience under the apparently novel banner of 'non-cognitive skills' is the way that far from offering something new it recycles and perpetuates some of the oldest, most damaging and least tenable dichotomies in the book, re-launching them with a brace of terminological contradictions.

One such is the conference title's stunning paradox of non-cognitive mindfulness. Another is the very concept of a 'non-cognitive skill'. Is this possible? The authoritative Foresight Report on mental capital and wellbeing[14] thinks not. Though in execution some skills become so habitual that we stop thinking about them, few if any skills are genuinely mindless. Acquired and honed through training and practice, skills also require knowledge and reflection, especially when – as with the skills with which education is particularly concerned – skills are infinitely perfectible. But then the problem here is in part linguistic, for these days every conceivable educational goal is tagged a 'skill' and knowledge is nowhere: basic skills, numeracy skills, literacy skills, creative skills, emotional skills, interpersonal skills, hard skills, soft skills, thinking skills, cognitive skills, non-cognitive skills. . .

Then, recycling that ancient dichotomy, my conference glossy continues:

> Schools need to teach students not only academic knowledge and cognitive skills, but also the knowledge and non-cognitive skills they will need to promote their mental and physical health and successfully contribute to the economy and society . . . to counter the idea that promoting cognitive development and academic attainment is all that matters for the economy.

Here, not only are 'cognitive' and 'academic' equated; they are also seen as neither conducive to children's mental health nor economically relevant. So much for maths, science, design and technology and, oh yes, literacy.

Or take this definition, from a companion source: 'Non-cognitive skills are those academically and occupationally relevant skills and traits that are *not* specifically intellectual or analytical in nature.' Academic but non-cognitive? Academically relevant but not intellectual?

Or this: 'Non-cognitive skills include persistence, communication skills and other "soft" skills that are not objectively measured . . . unlike cognitive skills, which educators can measure objectively with tests.' So communication, that most basic and demanding of basics, is 'soft', non-cognitive and unable to be assessed. How and about what do we communicate if communication excludes cognition? And what touching faith in the objective measurability of the rest of the mainstream curriculum.

Or again, pursuing the same eccentric process of re-classification, the conference glossy helpfully includes in its list of 'non-cognitive skills' not just familiar items like 'perseverance' and 'self-control' but also 'meta-cognitive strategies' and 'creativity'. Apart from the mind-boggling idea that something can at the same time be meta-cognitive and non-cognitive, it's the assertion that creativity excludes cognition – in the face of centuries of artistic and scientific endeavour – that most brutally nails this nonsense.

Knowledge versus skill, hard subjects versus soft, cognitive versus creative, cognition versus meta-cognition, thinking versus feeling, mind versus body. Here, sartorially updated for 2015, is that same 'muddled and reductive discourse about subjects, knowledge and skills' of which the Cambridge Primary Review final report complained, a discourse in which 'discussion of the place of subjects is needlessly polarised, knowledge is grossly parodied as grubbing for obsolete facts, and the undeniably important notion of skill is inflated to cover aspects of learning for which it is not appropriate'.[15] Which is why, of course, supposedly 'non-cognitive' creativity is relegated to the non-core and Friday afternoons – something that in the interests of a more rounded education the apostles of non-cognitive skills rightly want to change, but for the wrong reasons. What a muddle.

So it was with relief that I turned back to Usha Goswami's report for Cambridge Primary Review Trust. For here in place of fads, fancies, cod psychology and epistemological car crashes we have evidence carefully accumulated, searchingly sifted and expertly assessed; and, interestingly, a kind of resolution of the problem of how to define and place those wider attributes we all accept are necessary in today's world – for I stress that I'm as concerned as anyone else that schools should motivate and engage children, build their confidence, help them to manage their learning and their lives, and develop their social and communicative capacities. But, crucially, what the non-cognitive skills people see as separate from academic activity, Usha Goswami sees as intrinsic to it. Her stance is not the exclusivity of cognitive *versus* non-cognitive, but the inclusivity of cognitive *plus* meta-cognitive. In a key section on meta-cognition and executive functioning, she writes:

> Metacognition is knowledge about cognition, encompassing factors such as knowing about your own information-processing skills, monitoring your own cognitive performance, and knowing about the demands made by different kinds of cognitive tasks. Executive function refers to gaining strategic control over your own mental processes, inhibiting certain thoughts or actions, and developing conscious control over your thoughts, feelings and behaviour . . . As children gain metaknowledge about their mental processes, their strategic control also improves. Developments in metacognition and executive function tend to be associated with language development, the development of working memory (which enables multiple perspectives to be held in mind) and nonverbal ability.[16]

The report then goes on to document strategies through which in the classroom these capacities can be developed.

In other words, what the non-cognitive skills people present as a curriculum issue is in reality a pedagogical one. Of course, there are always questions to be asked about the relevance, scope and balance of the curriculum, but England's not-so-new national curriculum does not address them. But communication, motivation, engagement, perseverance and self-control do not require the addition of a battery of pseudo-skills to an overcrowded curriculum. They require us to think differently about how we teach what is already there. So, given that one of the non-cognitivists' main concerns is the contribution of education to the economy, I might just arm myself with an update of Bill Clinton's 1992 election slogan, turn up at that conference and shout, 'It's the pedagogy, stupid.'

Notes

1 https://cprtrust.org.uk/cprt-blog/true-grit/ (True grit) https://cprtrust.org.uk/cprt-blog/true-grit-the-sequel/ (True grit – the sequel) and https://cprtrust.org.uk/cprt-blog/mindful-or-mindless/ (Mindful or mindless?) (accessed May 2021).
2 Tough 2013.
3 www.kipp.org (accessed May 2021).
4 Morgan 2014.
5 White 2015.
6 See the discussion of curriculum control in chapter 11.
7 Snyder 2014.
8 www.gov.uk/government/news/winners-of-the-character-awards-announced (accessed May 2021).
9 Scott 2015.
10 Mansell 2014a, 2014b, 2015.
11 Goswami 2015.
12 Alexander 2010a, 51–156.
13 The 28 Cambridge Primary Review research surveys are listed and downloadable at https://cprtrust.org.uk/cpr/cpr-publications/. The 10 Cambridge Primary Review Trust research surveys are at https://cprtrust.org.uk/cpr/cpr-publications/ (accessed May 2021).
14 Government Office for Science 2008.
15 Alexander 2010a, 245–50 (see this volume, Chapter 9).
16 Goswami 2015, 15–16.

14 Curriculum capacity and leadership

Cambridge Primary Review identified a 'long-standing failure to resolve the mismatch between the curriculum to be taught, the focus of teacher training and the staffing of primary schools', and recommended a review of primary school staffing with particular reference to schools' capacity to teach every aspect of the curriculum to a high standard regardless of the time allocated.[1] The government accepted this recommendation and work started in January 2011, under the auspices of DfE but in partnership with the Review, which organised focus group meetings for the DfE team and provided source material. The resulting report, completed in 2012, confirmed much of the Cambridge Review's analysis but for reasons which he did not divulge, Secretary of State Gove declined to make it public.[2] In 2016 Cambridge Primary Review Trust attempted to persuade Gove's successor, Nicky Morgan, to revisit the matter but without success. Meanwhile, the DfE-supported National College for School Leadership commissioned *Curriculum Freedom, Capacity and Leadership in the Primary School* (2013), the 'Expert Perspective Thinkpiece' that appears, slightly edited, here.

Leadership for what?

Though style is a significant factor in a leader's success, what really matters is how far leadership achieves its purposes. So the validity of those purposes, the clarity with which they are defined and the arguments and evidence by which they are justified should concern us no less than the way they are pursued. Yet the current preoccupation with leadership 'style' – whether 'charismatic', 'inspirational', 'visionary', 'dynamic', 'democratic' or 'transformative' (or in Ofsted parlance 'ambitious', 'uncompromising' and 'relentless'[3]) – can all too readily push such matters into the background; and where style triumphs over substance, leaders may pursue purposes that not only escape the scrutiny they require but aren't able to withstand it. Just as charismatic politicians may persuade otherwise discerning voters to support dubious policies, so children may be efficiently taught nonsense and schools may be inspirationally (or relentlessly) led in the wrong direction. Outrageous? Yes indeed, for we know it happens.

Thus, leadership requires mastery of more than how to lead, and educational leadership requires both expertise of a generic kind in the art and skill of leading and specific expertise in the art and skill of educating. We might call these the *dynamic* and *substantive* aspects of leadership, or leadership's 'how' and 'what'. Extending our working definitions for the discussion that follows, we refer to the sum of the different kinds of expertise that a school as a whole is

DOI: 10.4324/9781315169378-16

able to command, for teaching and for leading teaching, as its *professional capacity*. As a subset of this, what a school has at its disposal for leading curriculum thinking and planning and for providing its pupils with an appropriate and well-taught curriculum in the classroom constitutes its *curriculum capacity*.

Note that pupils themselves contribute to a school's curriculum capacity, through the knowledge and understanding they bring from outside school into the classroom and the insights which perceptive teachers gain from watching and listening to them at work and play.[4] Effective pedagogy is in part about unlocking and building upon this prior pupil knowledge. In this thinkpiece, however, I concentrate on the curriculum capacity of teachers and school leaders.

These initial propositions about educational leadership have a further and perhaps less obvious implication. In the distinctive context of education – which is about values as well as efficiency, and where learning responds to example as well as precept – it can be argued that the leadership circle is squared only if leadership is pursued in a way which is true to the purposes for which it claims to stand. This is why the current trend of transferring leadership structures, strategies and hence values from – say – business to schools needs to be handled carefully; and it is why the Cambridge Primary Review (hereafter CPR) argued that if educational aims are to have any point at all then they must be pursued in the head's office and the staffroom no less assiduously than in the classroom.[5] If a school aims to open children's minds, advance their understanding, excite their imaginations, build their confidence and develop their sense of mutual obligation, it is unlikely to do so if its professional culture manifests fixed ideas, limited understanding, closed minds and rigidly hierarchical relationships. A school justifies its claim to be a 'learning community' when, in David Hargreaves's words, 'the learning of both staff and students is governed by a common set of principles'.[6]

These opening arguments point to a more discerning vocabulary of success in leadership than the question-begging terms in my second paragraph, let alone vague adjectives like good/bad, or strong/weak or the ubiquitous but meaningless 'great'. Thus educational leaders may be judged *effective* if their strategies achieve specific measurable objectives such as improved pupil attendance, test scores or GCSE results. They may be judged *principled* if at the same time they pursue a larger educational vision and do not allow this to be compromised by important but inevitably narrow measures of effectiveness and accountability. They may be judged *exemplary* if they themselves also model, in the ways they think, talk and act, the attributes of the educated person. They may be judged *outstanding* if, and only if, they are successful in all of the first three senses.

My use of 'outstanding' here is deliberate, for I am well aware that 'outstanding' is the top grade in the Ofsted inspection framework and that 'the quality of leadership and management in the school' is one of the 'four key judgements' which, since 2012, Ofsted inspectors have been required to make.[7] As hinted earlier, the 'outstanding' grade descriptor for school leadership makes much of a leader's 'ambitious', 'relentless' and 'uncompromising' pursuit of excellence,[8] as we might think it should. However, 'relentless' has unappealing as well as praiseworthy overtones, while if a leader is so uncompromising that he/she is not prepared to listen to others or admit the possibility of being wrong then a school is in deep trouble. (That applies to leaders everywhere, whether of schools or nations.)

Aspiring school leaders might therefore find it instructive to compare and try to reconcile the visions of curriculum capacity and leadership set out in the Ofsted inspection schedule and in this thinkpiece, starting with definitions of 'outstanding' and continuing the exercise with the two documents placed side by side. For example, can a leader be both 'exemplary' and 'relentlessly uncompromising'? In any event, we need to broaden our account of successful educational leadership beyond the narrow accounts of 'delivery' and 'effectiveness' that have dominated policy discourse in recent years, and we should keep in mind the need for 'fit' between educational ends and professional means as we consider some of the imperatives of educational leadership in the specific domain of curriculum.

Elsewhere, I have advocated the reform of classroom learning through dialogic teaching; but I also suggest that the dialogic principle, and its preferred characteristics – collective, supportive, reciprocal, deliberative, cumulative, purposeful – apply no less to professional learning and school self-improvement.[9] In this regard, what I find encouraging about those models of leadership that emphasise empowerment, partnership, mentoring, coaching and the building of social capital,[10] is that they align much more closely with our current understanding of children's learning and the more overtly interactive and reciprocal pedagogy that it requires than does traditional top-down leadership. Far from being an impossible ideal, therefore, in many schools what I define as 'exemplary' leadership is within reach.

Professional freedoms old and new

This thinkpiece is launched in the context of ministerial promises of a greater measure of professional freedom in curriculum and related matters than was permitted during the period 1997–2010. We have emerged from an era in which, in pursuit of 'standards', schools were subjected to a regime of top-down prescription, micro-management and enforced compliance. Critics agree that this probably went too far,[11] and the coalition government elected in 2010 promised to give teaching back to teachers, announcing that from 2014 they would leave many more aspects of the national curriculum to schools' discretion. Meanwhile, Labour's apparatus of professional support and/or scrutiny, from national strategies and QCDA to local authority SIPs, was to be reduced or dismantled.

To early and mid-career teachers this vision of professional freedom may look unprecedented, but it is not. During the four decades after the 1944 'Butler' Education Act, and especially after the phasing out of the 11-plus test during the mid-1960s, primary schools effectively created their own curricula. But that extent of freedom raised serious questions of curriculum consistency, quality and entitlement that the inspectorate deplored[12] and the national curriculum was partly designed to address. In any case, many local authorities, not to say school heads, had firm views on the curriculum and were happy to impose them. On these matters we should therefore take the long view.[13]

We might also wish to examine the reality of the freedoms on offer after 2014. Abolishing QCDA, SIPs and other bodies and roles does not herald a return to the 1970s so much as transfer control over curriculum matters from statutory agencies to ministers, while closing QCDA removes the last of the political checks and balances that have been in place since the 1988 Education Reform Act. Indeed, the language of 'controls' and 'control factors' was explicitly and approvingly used throughout the 2011–13 national curriculum review.[14] Further, the new curriculum 'freedoms' do not apply to the core subjects, which in the post-2014 national curriculum are specified in greater and more prescriptive detail than previously, so here teachers' room for manoeuvre is actually diminished; while restricting these freedoms to the non-core subjects may be another way of saying that they do not matter.

Old habits die hard: curriculum policy, leadership, structure and discourse

Assumptions and practices in contemporary primary curriculum leadership are shaped not just by recent policies and the burgeoning leadership industry but more fundamentally by two historically-embedded features of primary schools. First, such schools are staffed by teachers who may well have specialist curriculum interests and expertise but are usually deployed as generalists. Almost inevitably therefore, such teachers teach outside their curriculum strengths as well as within them. Second, compared with secondary schools and as a consequence partly of their generalist staffing and partly of their smaller size, the professional structure of all but the largest primary schools has tended to be relatively flat.

These features are connected. In a generalist culture, in which everyone does everything and is assumed to be competent to do so, there is no pressing need either for an elaborate professional hierarchy or for much by way of leadership of specifics. Conversely, although the larger size of most secondary schools of itself dictates a more elaborate staff hierarchy and managerial structure, the structural default, born of specialist subject teaching, is departmentalisation. So the primary school structure that dominated the first two-thirds of the twentieth century was the simplest imaginable: two zones of influence, the head and the rest, 'my school' and 'my class', with the deputy head available for covering in the head's absence but rarely having a significant role beyond that. If there was to be a curriculum leader it would be the head. He/she would shape the curriculum and determine its content, characteristically making rather more of 'my values'/'my beliefs' than of collective knowledge. Teachers would implement that vision, such as it was, enjoying the often limited freedoms that the head was prepared to sanction.

In the other zone of influence, the generalist class-teacher system that was devised for England's system of 'education of the poor, or primary education'[15] was instituted not for educational reasons but because it was cheap. In the nineteenth century the basic curriculum was narrower than now so the classteacher system was also tolerably efficient. However, once the primary curriculum expanded and the goals of primary education became more ambitious, as they did from the 1930s onwards,[16] so the system's limitations become ever more apparent. By 1978, HMI were reporting an alarming lack of consistency in the scope and quality of the curriculum across England's primary schools – which, it will be remembered, still made their own decisions on curriculum matters – and HMI showed a close relationship between these qualitative variations in curriculum provision and the extent and level of curriculum expertise which schools commanded.[17] They found it unacceptable, for example, that the scientific understanding of children in one school could be systematically and progressively fostered from age five onwards while elsewhere children could enter secondary school without having encountered anything remotely resembling science, and that such matters depended entirely on the interest or whim of a school's head and the profile of expertise across its staff.

HMI therefore recommended that all schools should appoint subject-specific curriculum co-ordinators who would combine generalist teaching of their own class with cross-school curriculum support, and many schools, though not all, began to implement this. HMI's survey evidence showed that such people, provided that they were properly trained and given appropriate time and resources, could raise expectations and improve a school's 'match' between curriculum provision and pupils' perceived capabilities.[18] HMI also signalled, as the curriculum debate heated up following Prime Minister Callaghan's Ruskin College speech of 1976, that the curriculum lottery exposed by their surveys should be replaced by statutory curriculum entitlement, and this was the key promise and achievement of England's first national curriculum in 1988.

Note that throughout this entire period, both before the arrival of curriculum co-ordinators/subject leaders and after it, there was an assumption that curriculum capacity was a matter for each school *on its own*, supported (or instructed) by local authority advisers. The possibility of partnership between schools, which is now a familiar feature of the landscape of educational reform, was rarely entertained. Indeed, since school partnership requires power to be shared rather than concentrated as in the 1960s-1980s model of primary headship, back then such a notion would have received short shrift.

During subsequent decades the post-1978 primary curriculum leadership model – generalist teachers also serving as cross-school specialist 'co-ordinators', 'consultants', 'advisers' or 'leaders' – was developed and embedded but could be refined only up to a point. So although a House of Commons enquiry and, later, Ofsted showed that the model was most successful when curriculum consultants/advisers were able to work with those teachers who needed support in their own classrooms, the primary funding formula was premised on the generalist model and rarely permitted this.[19] Nor did it allow a more adventurous deviation from the established staffing structure and culture apart from performance subjects such as music or PE where lack of expertise was most conspicuous. (Lack of expertise can more readily be concealed in non-performance subjects, but it may be just as serious.) After 1984, meanwhile, initial teacher training was required to give greater attention to the development of teachers' curriculum specialisms,[20] while with the arrival of the national curriculum in 1988 primary schools moved more rapidly from the simple two-tier structure to a greater degree of quasi-secondary departmentalism, with many classteachers doubling up as year/key stage/subject/SEN co-ordinators and the tide gradually turning towards distributed leadership. Paradoxically, the now-defunct national strategies required compliance but also encouraged networking. The process accelerated with the workforce reforms of the 1990s and was greatly facilitated by the dramatic increase in support staff from 75,000 in 1997 to 172,000 in 2008.

In other respects the professional culture of primary schools was less ready to shift. The 1992 'three wise men' report both recorded and provoked strong resistance in schools to the idea even of contemplating alternatives to the generalist classteacher system, let alone introducing them, and found few takers for its suggestion that primary schools might profitably explore a more flexible and targeted combination of generalists, consultants, semi-specialists and full specialists.[21] Thus a generalist class-teacher system that had been initiated purely on the grounds of cost had become a way of life with its own staunchly-defended professional rewards and claimed educational benefits.

Yet the evidence that this inherited structure and its attendant professional culture were no longer fully fit for educational purpose continued to stack up. From 1997 the apparatus of high-stakes tests, targets, national strategies, league tables, inspection and the rest put an inherently fragile system under markedly greater pressure.[22] Drawing together the evidence from research, inspection and thousands of witnesses, the Cambridge Primary Review showed that the primary curriculum 'problem' could not be explained simply in terms of the 'quarts-into-pint-pots' diagnosis of the 2008–10 Rose Review,[23] but was more complex and – for children – educationally much more damaging. For while there was indeed a common perception of curriculum overload, in the sense that many teachers believed that too much was prescribed for the time available, successive Ofsted studies showed that a significant proportion of primary schools successfully and convincingly taught the full national curriculum as prescribed.[24] Therefore the national curriculum could not be said to be inherently unmanageable. The real problem had to lie elsewhere, in the way schools managed, staffed and taught what was required. The Cambridge Review argued, citing evidence from both inspection and research, that the more fundamental and long-term curriculum problem in primary schools was one of curriculum capacity, expertise and leadership[25] – the focus of this thinkpiece.

Meanwhile, the principle, since 1988 enshrined in law, that all children are entitled to a 'balanced and broadly based' curriculum,[26] was being compromised by the overriding emphasis placed after 1997 on 'standards' in literacy and numeracy, defined rather narrowly as Year 6 test scores. To this tendency the arts, the humanities and even the core subject of science were becoming increasingly vulnerable, while across the curriculum – and even within the tested subjects of English and mathematics – memorisation and recall were being pursued at the expense of understanding and enquiry, and transmitting information was counted more important than the pursuit of knowledge in its proper sense.[27]

Thus, the post-1997 reforms had exacerbated the historic split between 'the basics' and the rest of the curriculum, reinforcing what Ofsted called a 'two-tier' curriculum[28] in which differential time allocations legitimately set in pursuit of curriculum priorities were compounded by unacceptable differences in the quality of provision as between these two segments. This drastic loss of curriculum balance and coherence was further fuelled by a policy-led belief that high standards in 'the basics' can be achieved only by marginalising much of the rest of the curriculum. In fact, and the point has been central to CPR's approach to curriculum reform, HMI and Ofsted evidence consistently shows the opposite. Far from being incompatible, 'the basics' and 'the rest' are vitally interdependent, and our best primary schools achieve high standards in both.[29] Yet policymakers continued to resist the argument, and the evidence, that standards in literacy and numeracy are raised not by neglecting the wider curriculum but by celebrating it. They were criticised for their obstinacy as long ago as 1985, in a Conservative Government White Paper, but this cut little ice, and anyway politicians have short memories.[30] It was therefore encouraging, initially at least, that the Cambridge Review's campaign on this matter received support from the 'expert panel' advising the government's 2010–12 national curriculum review.[31]

If there was a problem with the discourse of curriculum policy and reform, in some parts of the teaching profession there was also a problem with the discourse of curriculum itself. The Cambridge Review found, as had commentators since the 1960s, that all too often – though I stress not by any means universally – the debate about curriculum in primary schools was infected by reductionist claims and muddled thinking. Subjects, regardless of how they were conceived and organised, were dismissed as incompatible with children's development. Since at birth, it was argued, children 'don't think like that' then they should for ever more be denied the opportunity to do so – an argument which seemed to be about disempowering young minds rather than otherwise. 'Themes' were preferred not so much because when confronted by a school-devised thematic curriculum children happily confirmed that they do think like that (do they?) but more probably because they weren't subjects; indeed, when asked what makes a good teacher the Review's child witnesses said 'they know a lot about their subjects'.[32] Interestingly, research on multiple and variegated intelligence suggests that humans have a biological disposition to think in some of the distinct ways that over the millennia have developed into disciplines of enquiry, so subjects may be rather less 'artificial' than their detractors claim.[33]

Meanwhile, knowledge in its limitless variety, richness and transformative power was parodied as the mere transmission of outdated facts and hence rejected as irrelevant to a modern curriculum, thus at a stroke severing the learner from history, culture and some of humankind's principal ways of making sense and acting on the world. In its place 'skills' were inflated to the point of meaninglessness, encompassing everything that a child should encounter, learn and know (except that the child would not *know* but 'learn how to learn'). 'Creative' similarly ballooned far beyond its proper meaning, being for some teachers a serious intention pursued with the necessary rigour, but for others a mere shibboleth which invited not the discipline of the truly creative mind but the self-indulgence of doing one's own thing without bothering to argue a proper educational case. As with 'themes', calling such a curriculum 'creative' was believed to be justification enough. Far from elevating creativity this casual usage devalued it.[34]

Into the vacuum stepped the curriculum snake oil vendors, peddling for a few thousand pounds apiece their 'creative curriculum' and 'skills curriculum' packages to schools desperate for something to plug the gap and lacking the capacity to realise that they – and especially their pupils – were being taken for a ride.

Bizarrely, much of this was justified on the grounds of 'modernity': knowledge is old hat, we were told, themes and skills are what today's children and tomorrow's world need. But history shows that we had been there before, in the 1960s and 1970s. Here, recycled barely without modification, were the same slogans. Here was the same perplexing urge to disenfranchise the young mind while claiming to liberate it. But since history was one of the despised subjects, the 'modernisers' neither knew this nor realised that it was they who risked putting the clock back.

Stopping the rot: re-thinking curriculum capacity

The Cambridge Primary Review argued that all children in primary schools should be entitled to a curriculum which: enacts a coherent and properly argued set of educational aims; secures high standards in literacy and numeracy yet is also broad, balanced and rich; engages children's attention, excites and empowers their thinking, and advances their knowledge, understanding and skill; attends to children's present as well as their future needs, providing a proper foundation for later learning and choice; addresses the condition of society and the wider world; ensures progression from early years through primary to secondary without losing its developmental distinctiveness at any of these stages; and is taught to the highest possible standard in all its aspects, not just in 'the basics'.[35]

In its central three chapters the CPR final report presented the evidence on which this view is based and the 'coherent and properly argued' aims that drive it, and readers are encouraged to read these chapters in full and examine the framework for an aims–driven, domain–based curriculum to which its evidence and argument lead.[36] Yet in some respects what CPR proposed was quite modest, and it was presented not as a utopian vision but as the least that one of the world's richest nations should be prepared to offer its children – hence the emphasis on statutory entitlement. This, then, was the bottom line for CPR's evidence to the 2010–12 national curriculum review,[37] and the December 2011 report from the review's Expert Group acknowledged its force, especially in respect of the arguments about the centrality of knowledge, the imperative of curriculum breadth, the relationship between standards in literacy and numeracy and the quality of the wider curriculum, and CPR's idea of a 'community curriculum' to balance and extend what is required nationally.[38]

Note, however, that our definition of entitlement is about the scope and quality of the curriculum as experienced by pupils, rather than curriculum breadth on paper. A 'broad and balanced' curriculum in official documents or a school prospectus is meaningless without commitment to ensuring that schools have what it takes to pursue excellence in all aspects of such a curriculum. 'Entitlement' relates to the curriculum as enacted and experienced, not just as prescribed.

In parallel, therefore, CPR pursued its argument that if the government was serious about curriculum reform then the question of curriculum capacity and leadership in primary schools could no longer be kicked into touch as it had been on so many previous occasions since the 1970s:

> The long-standing failure to resolve the mismatch between the curriculum to be taught, the focus of teacher training and the staffing of primary schools must be resolved without delay. The principle to be applied as the one of entitlement adopted throughout this report: children have a right to a curriculum which is consistently well-taught regardless of the perceived significance of its various elements or the amount of time devoted to them.[39]

If schools were to take advantage of the new curriculum freedoms and to exercise informed discretion over those subjects where attainment targets were no longer to be specified or the content was for schools themselves to determine, the fundamental principle of children's curriculum entitlement required that schools should be able to demonstrate commensurate curriculum capacity, expertise and leadership – those very attributes about which successive HMI and Ofsted studies had generated such disturbing evidence. Accordingly, CPR recommended a full national primary staffing review which would investigate the relationship between primary schools' curricular responsibilities, the staff numbers, roles and expertise available to fulfil these, and the implications for initial teacher training and CPD.[40]

In 2011, following extensive discussions between CPR and DfE, this recommendation was acted on. DfE launched an enquiry into 'the capacity of the primary workforce to plan and teach all aspects of a broad curriculum to a high standard'. The enquiry was conducted in-house rather than as a public review along the lines of that initiated by the coalition government on the national curriculum, but its work fed into the latter, not least because the national curriculum review remit explicitly raised questions about implementation and hence schools' curriculum capacity and leadership.

The enquiry entailed desk reviews of evidence from research and inspection, focus group meetings with representatives from a range of professional organisations and constituencies, and visits to schools. The resulting report was completed early in 2012 but never published, although I was sent a copy in strict confidence and in response to a Freedom of Information request a *Times Educational Supplement* reporter managed to obtain a version that was so heavily (and inexplicably) redacted that it was unusable. For its part, the Schools Minister's cover letter with my unredacted copy said:

> As you are aware, this project was an internal review into existing evidence and an assessment of whether there are important gaps in our understanding that need to be filled. Therefore, it is not our intention to make it publicly available. I am sure that you will understand that I must ask you not to circulate the report any further. Any conclusions drawn from this analysis will be fed into the [national curriculum] review process.[41]

As word about the government's curriculum capacity enquiry spread, so did rumours about where it would lead. This was inevitable given that although conducted in-house the enquiry entailed several focus group meetings, including one with all the main subject associations, so it could hardly be kept under wraps. A typical newspaper headline was: 'Primary review could spark rise in specialist staff'.[42] But although ministers may have encouraged such rumours by publicly commending more specialist teaching in primary schools,[43] CPR insisted that this was only one of the options available and in that sense revisited the notion of a broader and more flexible generalist-consultant-semi-specialist-specialist staffing continuum of the kind that was first flagged in the 1992 'three wise men' report. Indeed CPR had explicitly warned that the debate about curriculum capacity should avoid 'the simple opposition of "generalists" and "specialists"'.[44] CPR also encouraged government and schools to explore the possibilities of sharing expertise and exchanging staff between schools, a strategy facilitated by the move to school clustering and partnership started under Labour and accelerated from 2010 under the banner of academies and teaching schools.

What, then, do we mean by 'curriculum capacity'? We have already emphasised that it both includes but is much more than specialist teaching expertise in individual subjects. As argued by CPR, a school's curriculum capacity includes, as a minimum, two main components:

- The knowledge of curriculum matters which is required if individual teachers and/or the staff of a school collectively are to engage in intelligent thinking and discussion about *the curriculum as a whole*, and are to move from such deliberation to defining educational aims and planning a curriculum that takes informed and principled advantage of such freedoms as DfE permits and 'engages children's attention, excites and empowers their thinking, and advances their knowledge, understanding and skill'.

- The knowledge of *specific subjects, domains or aspects of the curriculum* which is needed for translating a national curriculum or a school's own curriculum into viable classroom experiences that meet the CPR's entitlement criterion of being taught to a high standard regardless of their perceived priority or the amount of time allocated to them.

In so far as they have concerned themselves at all with such matters, policy-makers have concentrated almost exclusively on capacity in the subject-specific sense, and especially the expertise needed in the high-stakes domains of literacy and numeracy. Hence the focus of those successive reports from HMI and Ofsted, the 1998–2010 literacy and numeracy strategies, targeted initial teacher training, CPD and inspection, the Rose and Williams reviews of primary reading and mathematics teaching,[45] and latterly government hints about specialist teaching. The neglect of schools' capacity in non-core subjects and the curriculum as a whole no doubt reflects the view that when the whole effectively equates with what is prescribed, tested and inspected, such capacity is the preserve of government and its agencies (especially the now-defunct QCDA) rather than schools. Or, more cynically, if the 3Rs are secure the rest doesn't matter.[46] This was a shortsighted view even then, for a school curriculum is more than the sum of its parts, a curriculum in action is more than what appears on paper, and far from being mutually exclusive breadth and high standards in the 3Rs are interdependent. The view is even more ill-advised now that the task of achieving curriculum coherence has been explicitly handed over to schools.

Yet, subject to these important caveats the focus on expertise in my second sense is correct, for international evidence on what differentiates the best teachers from the rest clearly shows that 'the degree of challenge that the curriculum offers [and] the teacher's ability for deep representations of the subject matter' is pivotal to any teaching which aspires to more than the merely pedestrian.[47] This is curriculum capacity in the sense that American educationist Lee Shulman uses it, a combination of the teacher's own 'content knowledge' of the subject(s) taught and his/her 'pedagogical content knowledge' (PCK) of how the subject is best translated into curriculum experiences that are right for particular children and classroom circumstances.[48] The key word here is 'pedagogical', for pedagogy is what translates a prescribed or paper curriculum into an enacted and experienced one.

The distinction between subject knowledge and PCK is especially important now that policymakers themselves are talking so much about the former. I hope they understand that though 'knowing your subject' is clearly essential, 'knowing your subject in the way that is required for teaching it' entails much more.

Yet even this isn't enough. Specific subject knowledge and PCK are necessary but far from sufficient conditions for curriculum capacity, for this formula says nothing about the knowledge and skills with which PCK needs to be combined in order to generate viable and appropriate classroom experiences – relating, in particular, to children's development and learning, pedagogy, assessment and of course curriculum planning.

Nor or of course does PCK *per se* attend to the imperatives of thinking about the curriculum as a whole, a field where evidence and experience consistently show that schools often fall well short of the minimum quality of informed debate that is required. The sometimes ill-informed discourse about subjects, knowledge, skills, the 'creative' curriculum and so on, as examined in Chapter 9 and the final Cambridge Primary Review report, bears depressing witness to this.

The ingredient most commonly and conspicuously absent from many primary schools' curriculum capacity in this wider sense is epistemology: exploration of the nature and relationship of knowledge, belief and experience; of contingent fields such as reason, judgement and imagination; of how within cultures such as ours we make sense of, act on and communicate about our inner and outer worlds; and of the nature of the various distinctive modes of thinking, enquiring and doing through which such sense is made and action is taken – which some would call 'subjects', others 'disciplines' or 'domains'.

To some this may seem hopelessly abstruse. To them I would say that it is simply not possible to conceive a school curriculum without reference to questions such as these. Indeed, I'm prepared to stick my neck out – as I first did on this matter in a book published nearly in 1984[49] – and assert that much of the prevailing curriculum discourse that dismisses subjects as developmentally inappropriate and knowledge as intrinsically outmoded or irrelevant reflects not so much curriculum creativity or modernity as ignorance about matters which should surely be second nature to anyone involved in the business of educating.

I have illustrated rather than catalogued the wider aspects of curriculum capacity. Epistemology is central, but so too are cultural and pedagogical understanding, plus the direct, hands-on local knowledge of the children being taught and the families and communities from which they come. I have not listed the aspects in detail but I hope I have said enough to open up the possibility of conceiving of curriculum capacity much more broadly than in terms of subject-specific expertise alone, or needlessly polarised arguments about generalists *versus* specialists.

Conclusion: from capacity to leadership

I have argued that curriculum leadership – especially in a self-improving school system – is about building *capacity*, and I have defined that capacity in two broad senses: (i) relating to the aims, scope, structure, balance and content of the curriculum as a whole; (ii) relating to the detailed content, sequencing and teaching of specific subjects.

I have also identified three levels at which curriculum capacity is needed:

- school level: the capacity of school leaders to stimulate, inform and shape whole-school curriculum discussion, debate and planning;
- intermediate level: the capacity of subject leaders to plan, guide, monitor, support and where necessary teach their particular curriculum subjects or domains across the school;
- classroom level: the capacity of individual teachers to plan, teach and assess those specific aspects of the curriculum for which they are responsible – all of them in a generalist model, one or two of them in a specialist model, or a combination in the more flexible model of primary school staffing towards which some schools at last are tending.

I said at the outset that school leaders need generic expertise in the art and skill of leading, teachers need expertise in the art and skill of teaching, and schools collectively need both. Taking the educational subset of *curriculum* leadership we can now propose the following:

Curriculum leadership is not synonymous with school leadership, and in today's primary and secondary schools curriculum leadership is to a considerable degree distributed. Yet heads retain a vital role. Not all curriculum leaders are heads, but all heads are curriculum leaders.

A head's school-level curriculum leadership requires not just generic leadership skill but also curriculum capacity in sense (i) above – relating to the curriculum as a whole. A school-level whole curriculum leader must have a sufficient grasp of epistemological, developmental, cultural and pedagogical matters to promote intelligent, informed and purposeful debate about curriculum aims, values, structure and content across the school as a whole and to ensure that this feeds into meaningful and successful curriculum planning and teaching.

But bearing in mind that good teaching *at any educational level* is necessarily informed by a sound grasp of the content and pedagogical content knowledge of each specific subject/domain or aspect of the curriculum being taught, school-level curriculum leadership also requires strategies for auditing the school's pool of curriculum capacity in sense (ii) above (relating to individual subjects) and judging when and how to intervene if PCK falls short in any subject or classroom, in order that the school can meet the unarguable educational condition of children's entitlement to a curriculum of consistent *quality* as well as breadth. Developing such staffing strategies requires a completely open mind on the matter of how specialist curriculum expertise can be located and best deployed, and on the balance of generalists, consultants, co-ordinators, semi-specialists, specialists and other roles. It also requires honest acceptance of the limits to a school's ability to locate or generate the necessary capacity from within, and of the advantages of sharing curriculum resources and expertise between schools, even though this may mean a reduction in autonomy. Or, as David Hargreaves puts it:

> At the heart of partnership competence is social capital, which consists of two elements, trust and reciprocity . . . When social capital in an organisation is at a high level, people start to share their intellectual capital, that is, their knowledge, skills and experience . . . When people offer to share their knowledge and experience, reciprocity is enhanced along with trust. In other words, as intellectual and social capital gets shared, social capital rises, and a virtuous circle between intellectual and social capital is stimulated.[50]

For as long as primary schools choose or are forced by their funding to opt for the generalist staffing model, it can be argued that all class teachers need both whole-curriculum expertise in sense (i) above – because they are responsible for the totality of what children in their class encounter and learn – and the contingent pedagogical content expertise for such subjects as they teach unaided (sense (ii)). This combination, in any case, is arguably a condition of the democratised professional discourse that goes with distributed leadership. Moreover, good school-level curriculum leadership will encourage a climate in which teachers are able to admit the limitations of their PCK of specific subjects and will accept whatever alternative provision is deemed appropriate – a climate, again, which requires that combination of trust and reciprocity to which Hargreaves refers.

Finally, at the intermediate level, schools need to continue to build curriculum capacity in that sense of cross-school subject leadership on which most of the literature on these matters tends to concentrate.

What does all this imply for aspiring and newly-appointed primary heads? Referring back to the initial discussion of how we recognise successful leadership, a school leader will move from *effective* to *principled* in the specific domain of curriculum only if he/she combines viable strategies for leadership and support in specific curriculum subjects or domains with knowledgeable and rigorous leadership of thinking about the curriculum as a whole. With luck, the way he/she thinks and talks about curriculum and the extent to which he/she models sound educational values and principles on a day-to-day basis will also make that leadership *exemplary*.

Here, then, is the leadership challenge. CPR's final report says that the test of true professionalism, in teaching as in medicine, is that the practitioner is able to justify his or her actions by reference to evidence, aims and principles 'rather than by offering the unsafe defence of compliance with what others expect'.[51] This test applies no less to school leaders, especially in the context of self-sustainability. Freedom entails responsibility, and responsible freedom of action requires the freedom of mind that comes from seeking knowledge, learning from experience, and critically discussing and reflecting on both.

If the self-sustaining school is one that doesn't take the easy line of blaming others for its decisions – whether DfE, Ofsted, SATs, SIPs or parents – and feels no need to seek permission to innovate, then equally such a school has no truck with born-again sloganising about 'children not subjects' or the 'skills-based', 'thematic' or 'creative' curriculum. Compliance must not be replaced by nonsense. Evidence from research, inspection and shared experience, understanding of curriculum matters, rigour in curriculum discourse, preparedness to acknowledge that the generalist classteacher system isn't sacrosanct, a flexible approach to school staffing, a desire to share intellectual capital between schools as well as within them and hence enhance the capacity of schools collectively as well as individually, all informed by an unshakeable commitment to 'a curriculum which is consistently well taught regardless of the perceived significance of its various elements or the amount of time devoted to them':[52] these are the name of the new curriculum leadership game, and the shift from centralised direction to school self-improvement[53] gives our latest generation of school leaders the chance to break the mould.

Provided, that is, that the shift is more than ministerial rhetoric, and the 'freedom' promised by ministers is not control in disguise.

Notes

1 Alexander 2010a, recommendations 125–8.
2 Helen Ward of *The Times Educational Supplement* requested a copy of the report from DfE under Freedom of Information legislation and received one which had been heavily redacted. My own copy, of course, was complete but confidential. As puzzling as DfE's refusal to release the report in full was the fact that my name and the considerable investment in this initiative by the Cambridge Primary Review were among the content to be redacted. Well, not really puzzling.
3 Ofsted 2012c.
4 See the chapter 'Children's lives outside school' in Alexander 2010a, 63–72; Mayall 2010.
5 Alexander 2010a, 191–201 and 257–8.
6 In conversation about a draft of this thinkpiece. My thanks to David Hargreaves for this.
7 Ofsted 2012d, 2021a.
8 Ofsted 2012c, 18–21.
9 Alexander 2020, 131–3.
10 For example, as discussed in Hargreaves 2011. Note again that this offers a somewhat different take on leadership to that commended by the Ofsted inspection framework.
11 The evidence on the trajectory of government policy from 1997 to 2010, and its impact on primary education, is comprehensively reviewed in Alexander 2010a, chapters 8, 9, 11, 13, 15–17, 20–22 and, in summary form, on 469–83 and 508–10. For additional evidence see the research reviews of Balarin and Lauder (2008), Noden and West (2010), Cunningham and Raymont (2010), Wyse *et al* (2010), Tymms and Merrell (2007), Whetton *et al* (2010). See also this volume, Chapter 4.
12 DES 1978, 1979, 1982, 1983.
13 For a historical overview of post-war developments in English primary education, with particular reference to the post-Plowden period 1967–2010, see Alexander 2010a, chapter 3. The chapter also contains a timeline of 'policy milestones' from 1944 to 2010. For CPR's discussion of leadership see Alexander 2010a, chapter 22 and the CPR

research reviews of Stronach *et al* (2010), McNamara *et al* (2010), and Burgess (2010). For a potted history of English primary education going back to its furthest origins, see Alexander 2001a, chapter 6.

14 Oates 2010; DfE 2011d. See chapters 10 and 11.

15 This notorious but revealing definition is from Robert Lowe, architect of the 1862 Revised Code and 'payment by results'.

16 With strong encouragement from the Hadow and Plowden enquiries (Board of Education 1931; CACE 1967).

17 DES 1978.

18 DES 1978, 96–7 and 119, 124.

19 House of Commons 1986; Ofsted 1994, 1996, 1997. The 'three wise men' report was one of several which directly challenged the inherited primary funding formula (Alexander *et al* 1992, paras 4 and 149). Another was the CPR final report (Alexander 2010a, recommendation 150, p 509).

20 Following DES Circular 3/84 and the establishment of the Council for the Accreditation of Teacher Education (CATE), precursor to TTA and TDA.

21 Alexander *et al* 1992, paras 139–50.

22 Alexander 2010a, chapters 16, 17 and 23; Tymms and Merrell 2007; Harlen 2007; Wyse *et al* 2007.

23 Rose 2009b.

24 Ofsted 2008, 2009, 2010b.

25 Alexander 2010a, chapters 14 and 21, and especially 431–4.

26 Education Reform Act 1988, 1.

27 Alexander and Hargreaves 2007; Alexander 2010a, chapter 13; Wyse *et al* 2007.

28 The phrase was HMCI David Bell's, in Ofsted 2004.

29 DES 1978; Ofsted 1997, 2002a, 2008, 2009, 2010b.

30 DES 1985; See also Alexander 2010a, 243.

31 DfE 2011d, 23. But not for long.

32 Alexander and Hargreaves 2007, 14.

33 See, for example, the work of Howard Gardner and Robert Sternberg as discussed in Alexander 2008b, 144–6.

34 See 'The primary curriculum: victim of a muddled discourse' in Alexander 2010a, 245–51, and Chapter 13 in this volume. For a commentary on the causes and earlier manifestations of this 'muddled discourse' see Alexander 1984.

35 Alexander 2010a, 504–6.

36 Alexander 2010a, chapters 12 ('What is primary education for?'), 13 ('Curriculum past and present') and 14 ('Towards a new curriculum').

37 Cambridge Primary Review 2011.

38 Alexander 2010a, 273–5; DfE 2011d.

39 Alexander 2010a, recommendation 125.

40 Alexander 2010a, recommendation 127.

41 Letter from Schools Minister Nick Gibb to Robin Alexander, 20 January 2012.

42 *Times Educational Supplement*, 4 February 2011.

43 For example, in the Secretary of State's speech at the conference launching the government's Teaching Schools scheme in September 2011.

44 Alexander 2010a, recommendation 128.

45 Rose 2008b; Williams 2008.

46 The evidence in support of this claim of relative official neglect of the wider curriculum is summarised in the Cambridge Primary Review final report: Alexander 2010a, 240–5.

47 Berliner 2004, 24–5.

48 Shulman 1987.

49 Alexander 1984.

50 Hargreaves 2011, 3.

51 Alexander 2010a, 496, recommendation 60.
52 Alexander 2010a, 505, recommendation 125.
53 The National College uses the term 'self-sustainability' while David Hargreaves (2010, 2011, 2012) opts for 'self-improvement'. Though the difference may seem slight, I prefer the latter because 'self-sustainability' may invite a defiant self-sufficiency which sets its face against school-school partnership. 'Self-improvement' is less insular.

Part 3

Speaking but not listening

15 Promise and politics of talk

Evidence to the All-Party Parliamentary Group (APPG) on Oracy (2019). The author gave both written and oral evidence to this inquiry, which published its final report in April 2021.[1]

The APPG oracy initiative is the latest in a long line of attempts to raise the profile of spoken language in schools, so the 'growing consensus' claimed on the APPG website is neither as recent nor as steady as is implied. Crucially, however, that consensus has eluded policymakers, and herein lies one of the 'barriers' which the APPG inquiry invites us to expose. Another is the professional culture of schools themselves, even though most teachers are generally ahead of policymakers in their understanding of the developmental and educational importance of talk and their desire to act on that understanding in children's interests – as, professionally, they should be. But a third barrier is the legacy of the mindset that shaped state education in England in the 19th and early 20th centuries and yielded a curriculum in which what is deemed 'basic' to children's education is still perceived by some in pretty well the same terms as it was before the 1870 Education Act. Thus, for example:

(1861) The duty of the state in public education is . . . to obtain the greatest possible quantity of reading, writing and arithmetic for the greatest number.
(1993) The principal task of the teacher . . . is to ensure that pupils master the basic skills of reading, writing and number.[2]

That formula, notable as much for what it excludes as what it includes, has been trotted out by ministers at regular intervals since England's first national curriculum was introduced in 1988, and if the APPG inquiry is to make a difference it needs to understand this history and to learn from previous attempts to expand the vision, if vision it is. Having been professionally involved in education since 1964 I have witnessed many of these attempts and have been party to several of them. The most recent episodes are particularly relevant because they relate to the version of England's national curriculum that was introduced in 2014 and with which at the time of this inquiry schools are expected to conform, so I shall refer to them in greater detail.

DOI: 10.4324/9781315169378-18

Expanding the vision isn't only about making room for oracy. What also needs to be challenged is the assumption that the pursuit of excellence in the 3Rs is incompatible with a broad and rich curriculum that includes not only oracy but also the arts, sciences, humanities and more. As the Cambridge Primary Review records, it was a Conservative government White Paper that, as long ago as 1985, exposed the folly and evidential frailty of this belief, while since then HMI and Ofsted have consistently shown that primary schools that perform well in literacy and numeracy embed that work in a broad curriculum and can achieve excellence across the board.[3]

Over the past 25 years I have developed a theory and practice of what I call 'dialogic teaching', a pedagogy that prioritises oracy but also goes beyond its conventional definition. For although the quality of the student's talk must always be our central concern, classroom dynamics make such talk inescapably dependent upon that of the teacher, and in particular on whether the teacher limits the student's opportunities to giving required answers to closed questions – the traditional teaching default of 'recitation' – or opens up the student's talking and thinking through 'extending' moves and structured discussion. 'Oracy' focuses on the pupil; dialogic teaching attends to the talk of all parties.

As it progressed through projects in primary schools in Barking and Dagenham, Bolton and North Yorkshire, this approach was evaluated, refined and disseminated to secondary schools as well as primary, and between 2004 and 2018 sales of successive editions of the teachers' manual *Towards Dialogic Teaching: rethinking classroom talk* exceeded 21,000.[4]

Then, from 2014–17, the approach was subjected to randomised control trial by the Education Endowment Foundation (EEF) in a project directed by Frank Hardman and myself and involving nearly 5000 Year 5 students in socially disadvantaged areas of Birmingham, Bradford and Leeds.[5] The intervention deployed bespoke professional materials, brief but intensive training of the teachers involved, and the use of peer mentoring and video for their professional planning, development and support. The independent evaluation reported that after only 20 weeks students in the intervention group were up to two months ahead of their control group peers in standardised tests of English, mathematics and science.[6] This outcome prompted EEF to list *Dialogic Teaching* alongside *Philosophy for Children, Talk for Literacy* and *Thinking, Doing, Talking Science* as four particularly promising initiatives in this area.[7]

Dialogic teaching, as I have defined and developed it, is a pedagogy of the spoken word that harnesses the power of talk to stimulate and extend students' thinking, learning, knowing and understanding, and to enable them to discuss, reason and argue. Holding to the principle that while children and classrooms have much in common every educational setting and encounter is unique, the approach eschews the methodology of 'one size fits all'. Instead it presents repertoires of teacher and student talk on which the teacher draws according to circumstance and need while having regard to certain non-negotiable dialogic principles. It thus provides teachers with a flexible framework for action rather than a formula. It does, however, highlight specific key talk moves on which the quality of student's talking and associated thinking have been shown particularly to depend.[8]

Between 2006 and 2010, I directed the Cambridge Primary Review, the UK's most comprehensive enquiry into primary education since the 1960s. The Review's extensive evidence on this matter enabled it to recommend that spoken language should be given much higher priority in the curriculum, teaching and teacher training.[9] The Review's successor, the Cambridge Primary Review Trust, built on these recommendations by joining forces with the University of York and the Education Endowment Foundation in the dialogic teaching project and trial referred to previously.

On the strength of all this work the Cambridge Primary Review and I gave evidence to the coalition government's 2011–13 review of the National Curriculum. Separately, between 2011 and 2014, I entered into extended correspondence and had numerous meetings with DfE ministers and officials about the place of talk in the national curriculum and schools more generally. This protracted but only partly successful effort to get government to take the matter as seriously as the evidence by then dictated is recounted later in this chapter.

Oracy: justifications, definitions, problems

The term 'oracy' was coined in 1965 by Andrew Wilkinson in conscious counterpoint to 'literacy' and in an effort to give speaking and listening parity with reading and writing,[10] and the term was revived during the 1990s by the National Oracy Project. Meanwhile, pioneering work on talk in learning and teaching was being undertaken by Douglas Barnes, James Britton, Harold Rosen and Frankie Todd in the UK and by Courtney Cazden and Hugh Mehan in the US.[11] These researchers contrasted talk's formidable potential to advance children's learning and understanding with the actual character and quality of the talk offered and experienced in many classrooms, dominated as it then was by the three-move initiation-response-evaluation (IRE) exchange of recitation teaching: closed teacher question, required student answer, positive or negative teacher evaluation. Since then, researchers have recorded the dogged persistence of recitation while advocating and evaluating various alternatives, for while recitation teaching prompts and tests recall, and indeed the student's ability to spot the 'correct' answer, it does not meet the most important criterion of productive classroom talk, namely that it should 'require students to think, not just report someone else's thinking'.[12] There are various responses to this challenge,[13] and much of the underlying research has been brought together in two major collections of papers.[14]

The various approaches also have in common a vision of why high quality classroom talk is important, though the scope of that vision varies. My own list includes:

- *Talk for thinking*. Talking and thinking are intimately related. Language builds connections in the brain; during the early and pre-adolescent years pre-eminently so. As we talk and exchange thoughts with others, so do we learn to think for ourselves.

- *Talk for learning.* Learning is a social process, and talk helps to scaffold thinking from the given to the new. Within classrooms, talk also engages students' attention and motivation, increases their time on task and produces observable and measurable learning gains.
- *Talk for mastery.* Through talk, students continue to deepen their understanding within each curriculum domain, subject or area of learning, acquiring familiarity with its register, taking ownership of its language and concepts, and achieving epistemic fluency and mastery.
- *Talk for communicating.* We use language of all kinds to exchange and negotiate meaning and engage in everyday transactions; but it is principally through spoken language that we do so.
- *Talk for relating.* Talk builds and consolidates social relationships and gives us the confidence and competence to handle them. Reading and writing are largely solitary, and in some circumstances competitive too. Talk by its nature is interactive, collaborative and inclusive.
- *Talk for acculturation.* Talk expresses and helps us to engage with what we have in common with others in our community and culture. It locates the individual within society, and society within the individual.
- *Talk for democratic engagement.* Talk is vital for civic participation and engagement. Democracies, and institutions at every level within them, need people who can argue, challenge, question, present cases and evaluate them; and who can test the argument and rhetoric of others.
- *Talk for teaching.* Well-structured talk gives teachers access to students' thinking, and thereby helps them to diagnose needs, devise learning tasks, probe understanding, assess progress, provide meaningful feedback, and support students through the challenges they encounter; and hence teach more effectively.[15]

But here paths diverge, for while most advocates of dialogic teaching conceive of talk and its impact along these lines, *oracy* may be more narrowly conceived. So, for example, Voice 21 defines it as 'the ability to communicate effectively', asserting that 'one of the biggest barriers to young people getting on is a lack of eloquence. Employers put good oral communication at the top of their requirements for employees. Yet we rarely teach it systematically in schools.'[16] Oracy Cambridge expresses the task in similar terms: 'In the world of work, the value of effective spoken communication is almost universally recognised. Job adverts emphasise the importance of being a confident communicator, or a strong "team player".'[17]

In both specifications the function of oracy centres largely on communication, and on communication of one kind and for a single purpose. Though communication skills are undeniably important – witness my list – talk is about much more than this. Children's lives as adults will extend well beyond the workplace, and our world needs people who can do more with language than 'communicate effectively'. In fact, the two quoted definitions of oracy are more restricted than that of Andrew Wilkinson, the begetter of the term, and of the 1987–93 National Oracy Project. Wilkinson himself made a distinction between 'oracy as competence' (that is, 'communication skills' as listed earlier) and 'oracy for learning'; while in pursuit of the latter the National Oracy Project argued – adapting the words of Lev Vygotsky – that 'talking together, with adults and with peers, is the most important means by which children learn to think',[18] and the Project's publications ranged widely across the fields of cognition, learning, teaching and social development. Of course, the communication skills/workplace branding of Voice 21 and Oracy Cambridge may well be about *realpolitik* or funding, but the difference is stark, and I urge APPG to be alive to this and adopt a more comprehensive vision such as that set out here.

Actually, I would encourage APPG to go further still, and ask itself whether 'oracy' is the right term, for apart from its inescapably instrumental connotations, its relationship to literacy is implicitly and unhelpfully oppositional. Even if it is deemed necessary for campaigning purposes, positioning oracy in contradistinction to literacy, let alone confining its outcomes to communication, is to risk perpetuating what anthropologist Jack Goody called the 'grand dichotomy'. This presents the oral and the written as hierarchical and mutually exclusive and written proficiency as the true measure of education. Though we know that talk comes first both historically and for the developing individual, human language has evolved primarily for face-to-face interaction. The balance and function of the oral and written vary across cultures but both are profoundly important.[19] Lest this be regarded as a merely theoretical proposition it should be noted that when Ofsted inspectors check children's 'work', they mean their *written* work. Talk is an educational end in itself, not merely the servant of literacy.

Gordon Wells summarises the essential differences between spoken and written discourse in familiar terms (concrete/abstract, dynamic/synoptic, social/individual, action/reflection and so on) before commenting:

> What such an . . . account fails to capture . . . is the more dynamic manner in which talk and text can complement and enrich each other through an exploitation of the . . . relationships between them. For it is when participants move back and forth between text and talk, using each mode to contextualise the other, and both modes as tools to make sense of the activity in which they are engaged, that we see the most important form of complementarity between them. And it is here, in the interpenetration of talk, text, and action in relation to particular activities, that . . . students are best able to undertake . . . the[ir] . . . apprenticeship into the various ways of knowing.[20]

Talk, text and action: so, as Shirley Brice Heath has also argued, the oral and the written are best understood not as the dichotomy that Jack Goody deplores but as overlapping continua with structures, functions and registers that are both distinct and shared.[21] Further, as Wells shows, each form is immeasurably enriched if the teacher encourages them to interact in the way he/she plans and conducts lessons. The dialogic relationship that Wells posits is very different from the way that in many classrooms oral discussion precedes the inevitable 'Now write about it', as if talk is no more than prelude to something much more important and, especially, more worthy of assessment. This, I should add, is a very English approach and from my classroom research in other countries I have shown that that an approach closer to what Wells advocates is readily observable elsewhere.[22]

Oracy, policy and politics: milestones, warnings and lessons

To return to 1965 and all that. After Wilkinson's coining of 'oracy' and the seminal *Language, the Learner and the School* of Barnes, Britton and Rosen, the next milestone was the 1975 Bullock Report *a Language for Life*, one of several major reports that deserved much more attention than they received.[23] Its powerful chapter on oral language remains highly pertinent and many of its recommendations, notably on oracy and language across the curriculum, have yet to be implemented. A recent publication from the Education Endowment Foundation seems to echo Bullock in proposing 'disciplinary literacy across the curriculum'[24] though this welcome idea focuses more on subject-specific vocabularies and concepts than the way that language works within and across subjects and in both its oral and written forms, as proposed by Bullock and, earlier, by Harold Rosen.[25]

A decade or so later, in 1989, England's first national curriculum made 'speaking and listening' a formal requirement, both within the newly-designated 'core' of English, mathematics and science, and across the curriculum. The Kingman and Cox reports of 1988 and 1989 examined questions of content and implementation and concluded, among other matters, that a major bar to reform was teachers' inadequate knowledge about language, or KAL. Simultaneously, the National Oracy Project worked with and through teachers to monitor and advance the quality of classroom talk. Taken together, these various initiatives marked a high point in official recognition that the oral needed to be treated no less seriously than the read and written.[26]

The backlash was not long in coming. While the National Curriculum English Working Group had endorsed the principle that through talk children should explore ideas, develop genuine understanding and learn to think for themselves, others insisted that education is necessarily a transaction between the knowledgeable teacher and the ignorant pupil and that time should not be wasted on uninformed pupil opinion or aimless chatter. And while the Working Group argued that oracy was essential to democratic engagement and that in this process the understanding of the varieties, uses and misuses of language was essential, the same critics argued that the central linguistic task of schools was to inculcate Standard English. As a result, the extensive materials piloted by the National Oracy Project to support the Speaking and Listening component of the 1989 National Curriculum disappeared almost without trace, and the government's Language in the National Curriculum (LINC) project was closed before its work was complete. Oracy was, and remains, an intensely political matter.[27]

Nevertheless, the 1989 National Curriculum Speaking and Listening requirements remained in place, and they survived the 1997–8 review and re-emerged, slimmed down but intact, in the National Curriculum as revised for introduction in 2000 (I was on the Board of the Qualifications and Curriculum Authority – QCA, by then the responsible quango – during this period and witnessed the deliberations at first hand).

However, a different kind of broadside was fired by the government's 1998 National Literacy Strategy (NLS), which effectively overrode the revised national curriculum and sharply downplayed spoken language. Indeed, when in 2003 the literacy and numeracy strategies were merged within the Primary National Strategy (PNS), talk was not mentioned at all in its manifesto *Excellence and Enjoyment*.[28] In response to widespread criticism, talk was subsequently patched back in, though neither effectively nor enthusiastically.

Meanwhile, building on my own international classroom video and transcript data, QCA began from 2001 to develop multi-media materials to support a more rigorous approach to the handling of talk in primary classrooms. David Reedy, David Rosenthal and I filmed in classrooms in different parts of Britain, I drafted the handbook, and we waited for publication. In the end, the initiative fell foul of turf wars between QCA and the government-controlled PNS, and in a re-run of the LINC episode only a single clip from the dozens of videotaped lessons was ever released. But the handbook survived and from 2004 onwards, no longer subject to government control or permission, it was taken up by many schools.[29]

Spoken language featured prominently in the final reports of both the Rose Review of the primary curriculum and the Cambridge Primary Review,[30] but with the change of government in 2010 Rose was dropped and a new review of the entire National Curriculum was launched. Paradoxically, at a time when research was yielding more and more evidence on the importance of talk in learning and teaching, and teachers were increasingly and enthusiastically opting into the agendas of oracy, dialogic teaching, exploratory talk, accountable talk and other talk-rich approaches, spoken language was marginalised by ministers to an extent not witnessed since long before Bullock.

In September 2011, I attended an international conference in Pittsburgh at which leading researchers pooled their evidence on the educational impact of high quality classroom talk and concluded that there could no longer be any doubt that it made a significant difference in terms not only of students' oral capacities but also their engagement and tested learning outcomes. On my return I immediately wrote to the Secretary of State, summarising the evidence, urging that it be acted on, and requesting that DfE organise an in-house seminar to review the implications for the national curriculum review.[31]

He agreed, and the seminar took place in February 2012, with keynotes from myself and, by videolink from the US, Professor Lauren Resnick (organiser of the 2011 Pittsburgh conference). I also provided a paper reviewing progress since Bullock, current evidence, and future options.[32]

Attendees, including the Schools Minister, judged the evidence and arguments to be timely and convincing. Yet we were informed that the government would not act on them for fear of (i) distracting teachers from the task of raising literacy standards and (ii) encouraging 'idle chatter in class'. Both objections, which eerily echoed those of two decades earlier to Cox, LINC and the National Oracy Project, were as contrary to the evidence and our intentions as it is possible to imagine. Combining the oral with the written demonstrably enhances literacy, and the kind of talk we were advocating was purposeful and rigorous.

Nevertheless, after the seminar I logged three recommendations for the National Curriculum with the Secretary of State: a separate and greatly strengthened spoken language component in the English programme of study; a fuller articulation of the relationship between speaking, reading and writing; and a clear statement on the central role of spoken language in every other area of the curriculum, tailored to show the relationship between the kind of talk required and the distinctive register, vocabulary and conceptual framework of each subject.

Yet when the draft programmes of study for the revised National Curriculum appeared in June 2012, spoken language was no longer an explicit strand in the programme of study for English – as it had been since 1989 – and elsewhere it featured scarcely at all. The reasoning, apparently, was that talk is merely the medium of teaching and not a curriculum matter, so its use is for teachers to determine. On 14 August 2012, Neil Mercer, Jim Rose (of the Rose Review and Ofsted) and I wrote to the Secretary of State to protest, reminding him of the evidence and the February 2012 recommendations, and challenging the ministerial reservations of which we had been made aware: that raising the profile of spoken English would encourage not rigorous and high quality talk but 'idle chatter'; that it would deflect attention from reading and writing and hence frustrate efforts to raise literacy standards; that spoken English has no content other than what arises from reading and writing; that the advocacy of talk was merely an expression of a soft-centred 'educational establishment' agenda.[33]

DfE agreed that modifications were possible and invited us to join officials in drafting them. During the next few months we had several meetings at DfE and exchanged numerous drafts, but there was a pervasive tension between our desire to secure for spoken language the prominence we believed it deserved and the duty of officials – as they saw it – to respect ministers' desire to keep its profile as low as possible. Overly favouring the latter, the subsequent proposals still failed to recognise spoken English to the extent we advocated, and we again complained about this to the Secretary of State.[34] The compromise outcome, in the revised National Curriculum as published in September 2014, was the reinstatement of spoken language as a statutory requirement for English with a generalised programme of study that would apply to Years 1–6 and a strong prefatory statement applying to all four Key Stages. Similar statements were inserted into the requirements for mathematics and science. (A later Freedom of Information request to DfE from a PhD student at the University of York confirmed that what persuaded ministers to change their minds was my DfE paper of February 2012.)[35]

Yet although we ensured that spoken language had a statutory presence and the requirements, as far as they went, were sound, they remained minimal. Eighty-one pages of England's current National Curriculum Framework Document are devoted to reading and writing during the primary years. Spoken language has just two.[36]

In curriculum terms this brings us up to date, and the contrast between the view of oracy in schools and policy has rarely been this stark, notwithstanding the occasional emollient ministerial statement during the past year or two. Of course, it could be argued that if all teachers shared our view of spoken language in learning and teaching and had the professional knowledge and skill to enact it there would be no problem, and spoken language would achieve its required prominence and impact without ministerial intervention. But in matters of curriculum and assessment England's system of public education is highly centralised and many teachers feel compelled to concentrate on what is required and tested at the expense of what they may believe to be educationally desirable or even essential. Within this culture of compliance, reducing spoken language to two pages out of 83 delivers a pretty unambiguous message about what really matters, and Ofsted inspections reinforce it.

So policy must change and in this as in other matters it really should not require such strenuous and protracted efforts as are recorded here to get ministers to attend to evidence, especially when they make so much of 'evidence-based policy'. Yet there are other levers. For example, with the personal advocacy of its former CEO, Kevan Collins, the Education Endowment Foundation has devoted a significant part of its budget to 'what works' projects that foreground the power of high quality classroom talk with disadvantaged pupils, and – as we have seen – independent evaluations have shown this expenditure to be amply justified. And the research keeps mounting up. Evidentially, there is now no room for doubt that such talk, provided that it is genuinely and rigorously dialogic, really does make a difference to students' motivation, engagement and learning outcomes, as well as to their capacities of a specifically oral and generically cognitive kind.

We are also much clearer about what it is about such talk that makes this difference. Space does not allow me to go into detail, but it is clear from the ESRC project of Howe, Hennessy and Mercer,[37] the EEF project led by Frank Hardman and myself,[38] and the work of Michaels, O'Connor and others in the US,[39] (i) that high quality and genuinely reciprocal talk builds the meta-cognitive capacities that are essential to students' 'learning how to learn' and becoming autonomous thinkers and reasoners, and (ii) that, operationally, a great deal hangs on what discourse analysts call the 'third turn'. That is to say, on what, having asked a question and received an answer, teachers do with what their pupils say; and, in discussion, on how both teachers and pupils respond orally to each other's contribution. Do they ignore it? Do they receive it without comment? Do they comment briefly upon it but then move swiftly on (as in traditional classroom exchanges)? Or do they engage with it and thereby extend the dialogue, probe the reasoning, bring others into the discussion, and collectively deepen the understanding?[40] It is to the latter pattern of talk that our efforts should be chiefly directed, for the sake of our democracy as well as the education of our children.

We also know why it is that traditional, monologic IRE/recitation teaching persists. It persists partly because it most aptly expresses the traditional view that education is a process of transmission from those who know to those who don't; partly because it gives the teacher security, for who controls the talk controls both the behaviour and the direction of epistemic travel; and partly as a matter of professional socialisation and habit: this is how we have always taught and how we ourselves were taught, so why should we change? It is therefore heartening to note that there is no barrier to the transition to dialogic teaching. In our EEF project some of the most enthusiastic practitioners of dialogic teaching were the recently-qualified teachers, yet some of the most impressive were in their middle and later careers. The younger group had no deeply-rooted habits to unpick; the older group combined embedded mastery with the confidence to try something new.

Supplementary note: oracy, classroom layout and the Covid-19 pandemic

This additional note, written at the suggestion of Emma Hardy MP, the inquiry chair, deals with just one issue: the relationship between the physical layout of classrooms, the quality of talk for learning and teaching and the current requirement on schools to ensure that pupils and teachers maintain social distance.

In its *Guidance for Full Opening Schools* (7 September 2020) the Department for Education advises, among its many measures for reducing Covid transmission risk, that:

> Maintaining a distance between people whilst inside and reducing the amount of time they are in face to face contact lowers the risk of transmission. It is strong public health advice that staff in secondary schools maintain distance from their pupils, staying at the front of the class . . . Schools should make small adaptations to the classroom to support distancing where possible. That should include seating pupils side by side and facing forwards, rather than face to face or side on, and might include moving unnecessary furniture out of classrooms to make more space.[41]

This and other measures in the DfE guidance will seem eminently sensible. But in the particular context of the Oracy APPG enquiry, and given that it is taking place while DfE and schools are making strenuous efforts to recover the ground lost since March 2020, it may be useful for the APPG to add this question to those it has already posed: as schools return to a kind of normality after the Covid lockdown, how can they energise the character and quality of classroom talk on which the evidence shows that effective learning and teaching depend, while keeping their pupils and teachers safe?

Talk is shaped by many forces and factors. One of them is the physical setting in which it takes place, which in turn influences its dynamics. The bipartite layout of the House of Commons encourages and indeed legitimates the adversarial and often eristic exchanges and binary argument in which some MPs delight but others deplore. That would be more difficult if seating were in the round and/or MPs sat where they liked rather than with their own kind. In respect of the DfE guidance on classroom layout, it would seem that many schools are interpreting 'teachers . . . at the front of the class . . . pupils . . . facing forward' as requiring the once universal layout of desks or tables in rows, as opposed to the now more common arrangement, in pre-Covid primary schools at least, of tables pushed together to allow seating and working in groups. At present, clearly, the latter is out of the question.

The current advantage of the first of these two arrangements is that it maintains social distance. It may also be perceived to enable the teacher to cover curriculum ground more speedily and efficiently, at a time when there is much catching up to do, by using direct instruction. That claim, we know, is open to question, while the disadvantage of desks/tables in rows facing 'the front' (i.e. the teacher and the whiteboard or screen) is that it signals, and permits, only a limited range of talk, especially by the pupil. Given that the Oracy APPG is being advised by many of its witnesses to encourage pupil talk of the richest possible diversity and quality, this should be a matter of interest and perhaps concern; doubly so when children have been deprived by the pandemic not only of good quality pedagogical talk but also of the wider benefits of social and verbal interaction with their peers.

In fact, there are not two possibilities for classroom layout but three (at least). As I note elsewhere:

> There are three basic options: tables arranged separately in rows, tables arranged side by side in a squared-off horseshoe, with the teacher on the open fourth side, or tables pushed together to seat small groups in what conference organisers fancifully call 'cabaret style'. Each strongly signals a particular pattern of talk and who controls it: teacher-controlled recitation,[42] instruction or exposition (rows), student-student small group discussion (cabaret), whole class collective interaction (horseshoe).

I add:

> We have found that the horseshoe arrangement is the most flexible, for with minimal physical adjustment it allows whole class direct instruction,

whole class collective discussion, and paired talk, while by the simple and speedy expedient of switching chairs to the inside of the horseshoe it also facilitates small group discussion.[43]

The horseshoe arrangement is in common use in several other countries and as a consequence of projects like the 2014–17 Education Endowment Foundation dialogic teaching trial,[44] it can now sometimes be found in the UK. In fact it came into prominence here, and achieved success, during the 1990s in the London Borough of Barking and Dagenham, where it was adapted from high-achieving schools in Germany and Switzerland. Roger Luxton (then Chief Inspector for that local authority and later its Director of Children's Services) and his colleague Graham Last reported that:

> High quality talk and discussion involving the whole class predominates . . . There is less embarrassment about speaking aloud to the whole class than frequently found in English classrooms . . . The optimal room layout is the horseshoe arrangement of tables or desks, promoting as it does maximum but controllable interaction between pupils.[45]

Luxton, Last and their colleagues encouraged this layout as the necessary condition for what they called 'interactive whole-class teaching', with the emphasis at least as much on the quality of interaction, and the involvement in such interaction of all pupils, as on the whole-class organisation (an emphasis that was missed by those who welcomed or criticised it as a return to chalk-and-talk: it was more sophisticated than that). However, as the earlier quotation shows, the other virtue of the horseshoe is that of the three basic layouts it is the most flexible. And critically at this time, in the horseshoe arrangement – unlike the other two – all the pupils can see each other as well as their teacher, so it enables and encourages talk of a collective, reciprocal, mutually-supportive and dialogic kind, including the discussion that we know to be so important to pupil learning, alongside the classic routines of teacher-led Q and A, exposition and instruction.

But, in the context of Covid, how safe is it? Much depends, of course, on the size and shape of individual classrooms and the amount of furniture they contain, though note that the quoted DfE guidance advises removing unnecessary furniture to create space, and that this advice applies whatever layout is used. Having seen the horseshoe arrangement in productive use in classrooms in the UK and other countries, I suggest that in rooms of sufficient size it may be as safe as desks/tables in rows. Pupils sit side by side as required by DfE, and while they face each other and the teacher they do so not in unsafe proximity across their tables but at a distance across the width, length or diagonal of the room.

It may seem odd to devote so much attention to what some will view as the rather mundane matter of seating. But the quality of talk for learning and teaching cannot be understood, still less improved, in isolation from other essentials of classroom life. The physical layout of classrooms is just one of these. A weakness of much writing on oracy is that it may be persuasive on talk as such, but not so good on how talk relates to other aspects of pedagogy like space, time, pupil grouping, curriculum content, task, learning activity, assessment, and the rules, routines and rituals that bind all these together.[46]

Teachers are currently confronted by two imperatives: to keep their pupils and themselves safe, and to maximise the quality of the teaching and learning for which they are professionally responsible. In the modest matter of classroom layout there could well be more room for safe manoeuvre than the DfE advice may be *thought* to imply (for note that it does not actually instruct teachers to arrange desks/tables in rows).

In any event, we need to do everything we can to generate classroom talk of the kind and quality that the international evidence tells us is essential to children's thinking, learning and understanding. At a time when the pandemic has denied children so much, we cannot deny them this too.

Afterword

The All-Party Parliamentary Group (APPG) published its final report in April 2021.[47] In May, Emma Hardy MP, the inquiry chair, tabled a parliamentary question about action the government intended to take to ensure that schools were meeting the spoken language requirements of the national curriculum, for the APPG inquiry had revealed that many were not.[48] Rather than answer the question, Schools Minister Nick Gibb – he of 'idle chatter' memory – merely copied and pasted these requirements into a written answer, gratuitously signalling that they mattered less than that 'every young person should be able to use Standard English'.[49]

Emma Hardy tried again, this time asking about government action to 'tackle the language gap between the most and least advantaged pupils', a perennial challenge which teachers said had been greatly exacerbated by the Covid-19 pandemic.[50] Once more Schools Minister Gibb saw the question as an opportunity to parade his fixations, this time on phonics.[51]

By July 2021, three months after its publication, the APPG Oracy report had yet to receive the government's considered response. On the basis of the minister's parliamentary answers and the government's track record on spoken language as charted in this and earlier chapters, such a response looked unlikely.

Notes

1 Alexander 2019a; Oracy All-Party Parliamentary Group 2021.
2 From the 1861 Newcastle Commission Report on elementary education and the 1993 Dearing Report on the National Curriculum. Arnold 1960; Dearing 1993.
3 DES 1985; Ofsted 1994, 1996, 1997, 2002a, 2004, 2008, 2009; Alexander 2013.

4 Alexander 2017a, 2020.
5 https://cprtrust.org.uk/research/classroom-talk/ (accessed May 2021).
6 Jay *et al* 2017; Alexander 2018. See this volume, chapter 17.
7 https://educationendowmentfoundation.org.uk/tools/promising/ (accessed May 2021).
8 For the current iteration of this approach, together with a review of the contingent research and frameworks for teaching and professional development, see Alexander 2020.
9 Alexander 2010a, especially 268–71 and 305–7; Mercer and Howe 2010.
10 Wilkinson 1965.
11 Barnes *et al* 1969; Barnes and Todd 1995; Cazden 2001; Mehan 1979.
12 Nystrand *et al* 1997, 72.
13 Lefstein and Snell 2014; Kim and Wilkinson 2019.
14 Resnick *et al* 2014; Mercer *et al* 2020.
15 Alexander 2020, 130.
16 www.school21.org.uk/voice21 (accessed July 2019).
17 https://oracycambridge.org (accessed July 2019).
18 Norman 1992, ix.
19 Goody 1987.
20 Wells 1999, 146–7.
21 Heath 1999, 111.
22 Alexander 2001a, especially chapters 15 and 16.
23 DES 1975, chapter 10 and recommendations 108–20.
24 Education Endowment Foundation 2019.
25 DES 1975; Rosen 1971.
26 DES 1988, 1989; Norman 1992.
27 Barnes 1988; Edwards and Westgate 1994; Carter 1997.
28 DfES 2003.
29 Alexander 2017a. The first of the eventual five editions was published in 2004.
30 Rose 2009b; Alexander 2010a.
31 Letter from Professor Robin Alexander to Secretary of State Michael Gove, 30 September 2011.
32 Alexander 2012a.
33 Letter from Robin Alexander, Neil Mercer and Jim Rose to Secretary of State Michael Gove, 14 August 2012.
34 Letter from Robin Alexander, Neil Mercer and Jim Rose to Secretary of State Michael Gove, 14 April 2013.
35 DfE 2013a.
36 DfE 2013b.
37 Howe *et al* 2019.
38 Alexander 2018 (see this volume, Chapter 17).
39 Michaels *et al* 2008; Park *et al* 2017; Resnick *et al* 2015.
40 Alexander 2020, 106–233 (see this volume, Chapter 18).
41 www.gov.uk/government/publications/actions-for-schools-during-the-coronavirus-outbreak/guidance-for-full-opening-schools (accessed September 2020).
42 The US term for the classic initiation-response-evaluation (IRE) exchange of closed teacher question, single, 'correct' answer and minimal (right/wrong) teacher evaluative feedback. As Lauren Resnick noted in her presentation to the Oracy APPG on 9 September 2020, recitation, or teaching-as-transmission, is in teachers' DNA and is therefore hard to shift.
43 Alexander 2020, 140–1.
44 Alexander 2018 (see this volume, Chapter 17).
45 Luxton and Last 1997.
46 Alexander 2001a, 265–570, 2020, 124–68.

47 Oracy All-Party Parliamentary Group 2021.
48 As claimed in a policy note from the APPG to Members of Parliament.
49 UK Parliament 2021a. The national curriculum requirements 'pasted' into the minister's response were from DfE 2013b, 18.
50 Oracy All-Party Parliamentary group 2021, 13.
51 UK Parliament 2021b.

16 Evaluating dialogic teaching

Initially presented at the biennial EARLI conference in Tampere, Finland in 2017. The expanded version in *Research Papers in Education 33(5)* (2018) – 'Developing dialogic teaching: genesis, process, trial' – has been abridged for this chapter. Note that the dialogic teaching framework referred to here has been through several iterations and modifications since it was first proposed in 2002. The 2016 version is retained here because it was the one used in the randomised control trial that the chapter describes.[1] For the most recent framework see Alexander 2020, where it is presented in detail and with examples. A note at this chapter's end summarises differences between the two versions.

This chapter describes the Cambridge Primary Review Trust/University of York Dialogic Teaching Project and the thinking that informed it. Funded in 2014–17 by the UK Education Endowment Foundation (EEF), the project piloted and implemented a programme designed to energise classroom talk and thereby enhance students' engagement, thinking, learning and attainment in contexts of social and educational disadvantage. In line with the emphasis on 'what works' in the EEF funding criteria, the intervention was based on an existing approach – in this case a specific version of dialogic teaching[2] – for which there existed *prima facie* evidence of efficacy,[3] and it was subjected to randomised control trial (RCT) by an independent team.[4]

The intervention had two strands, pedagogical and professional. Being contingent, both are described here. The ensuing account of the intervention's implementation and impact draws partly on reports from the externally-led RCT, which focused chiefly on tested student learning outcomes;[5] and partly on the project's in-house evaluation, which used interviews and coded videodata to track the intervention's reception and progress, and its effect on the classroom talk that was the project's central concern.[6]

The first part of this chapter describes the intervention and the professional development programme through which it was realised. The second part outlines and reports on the evaluation. The third introduces the exploration in Chapter 17 of how and why dialogic teaching makes a difference.

DOI: 10.4324/9781315169378-19

Intervention

The intervention as pedagogy

Evidential basis and general character of the approach

There is no single and agreed definition of the term 'dialogic teaching'. Indeed, it would be somewhat paradoxical if having intimated the liberality of dialogue this were not the case. Yet the various shades of meaning intersect with a reasonable degree of coherence. So in this chapter the term will be used stipulatively to connote a pedagogy of the spoken word that is manifestly distinctive while being grounded in evidence, discourse and assumptions that have much in common.

The evidence has a number of strands – psycholinguistic, sociolinguistic, neuroscientific, philosophical, pedagogical – but in this context three are pre-eminent and should be briefly rehearsed. First, psychological research, increasingly supported by neuroscience, demonstrates the intimate and necessary relationship between language and thought, and the power of spoken language to enable, support and enhance children's cognitive development, especially during the early and primary years.[7]

Second, classroom research testifies to the way that the recitation or IRE (initiation-response-evaluation) exchange structure, which centres on closed questions, recall answers and minimal feedback, and in many schools remains the pedagogical default, resists change despite abundant evidence that it wastes much of talk's discursive, cognitive and educational potential.[8]

Third, various remedies have been mooted,[9] while broad trends in thinking and practice have been identified by Lefstein and Snell and systematically compared by Kim and Wilkinson.[10] However, though these share a commitment to elevating the profile and power of classroom talk, and though they are invariably defined by their advocates as 'dialogic', the approaches are far from identical, especially in respect of their scope. Some approaches advocate a specific practice or method,[11] while for others dialogue is situated less exclusively within a wider interactive spectrum. Some focus largely or exclusively on the talk of the teacher[12] or the student[13] while others, including the one under discussion here, aim to attend to both, arguing that although student talk must be our ultimate preoccupation because of its role in the shaping of thinking, learning and understanding, it is largely through the teacher's talk that the student's talk is facilitated, mediated, probed and extended – or not, as the case may be. Hence the effort, to which all interested in dialogic pedagogy subscribe, to move beyond the monologic dominance of recitation/IRE and develop patterns of classroom interaction that open up students' speaking and listening, and hence their thinking, and which strive to distribute the ownership of talk more equitably.

In differentiating the various pedagogical approaches, Lefstein and Snell show how they vary not only in respect of strategy but also in the way they reflect contrasting notions of dialogue's nature and purposes.[14] My own work draws on transnational and cross-cultural classroom research to show how classroom cultures, values and interactions are variously shaped by collective, communitarian and individualist emphases in accounts of social relations and by culturally-located stances on human development, the nature and acquisition of knowledge and the act of teaching itself. Eschewing the popular dichotomising of teacher-centred/child-centred or transmission/discovery, I differentiate these as 'transmission', 'initiation', 'negotiation', 'facilitation' and 'acceleration'.[15]

Given this diverse cultural and philosophical genealogy, it is inevitable that strategies for talk reform have equally different emphases. My own take on dialogic teaching owes most to the foundational works of Vygotsky, Bruner and Bakhtin,[16] while strategically it is closest to those of Nystrand, Resnick, and Michaels and O'Connor.[17] Yet it is also *sui generis*, for, as just noted, it devotes equal attention to the quality of teacher and student talk, and to the agency of others – fellow students as well as teachers – in the latter. It also rejects the view that there is one right way to maximise talk's quality and power (for example, through small-group discussion, or 'interactive whole-class teaching' as mandated in 1998 by the UK government's National Literacy Strategy) and instead advances the need for every teacher to develop a broad *repertoire* of talk-based pedagogical skills and strategies and to draw on these to expand and refine the talk repertoires and capacities of their students. Acknowledging the uniqueness of each classroom's personalities and circumstances it gives the teacher the responsibility for deciding how the repertoire should be applied. This responsibility is progressively shared with students, the development and autonomous deployment of whose own talk repertoires is the ultimate goal.

This commitment to repertoire combined with teacher and student agency is fundamental. It reaches back to the author's contribution to the UK government's enquiry 1991–2 into primary education, which made a similar case for repertoire-based teaching,[18] and to my long-standing antipathy to the either/or, them-and-us dichotomising tendency that characterises much of the wider educational and pedagogical discourse.[19]

The approach is no less distinctive for treating talk not in isolation but as part of a generic model of teaching in which interaction takes its place alongside, and is contingent on, the invariants of *frame* (space, student organisation, time, curriculum, rules and routines), *form* (the lesson) and *act* (task, activity, interaction and assessment). That model was devised to make sense, as far as possible in a non-ethnocentric manner, of observational, video and interview data from classrooms in England, France, India, Russia and the United States.[20] Practical examples of its application in the present project might include the attention given to the relationship between the character and quality of talk and the teacher's handling of time and pace, student grouping and classroom layout, to the balance and relationship of oral and written activity, and to the mutually reinforcing and overlapping processes of dialogic interaction and assessment for learning.[21]

A dialogic teaching framework

The dialogic teaching framework under discussion – which, as a note at the end of this chapter explains, has been revised and extended in light of the project described here and other recent evidence – has four main components: *justifications, principles, repertoires* and *indicators*. The repertoires are the heart of the operation. They are guided and refreshed by the principles and indicators, while the justifications provide their springboard.

JUSTIFICATIONS

Education is an ethical as well as instrumental endeavour, so teachers must consider why talk in general, and talk of the kind commended, are so important. Seven justifications are proposed, listed here as headings only, but elsewhere enunciated more fully[22]: *communicative, social, cultural, political/civic, psychological, neuroscientific*, and *pedagogical*.

The first four justifications take up ethical positions, admittedly sustained by pragmatism. They argue that children need to be able to communicate, build relationships, participate in their culture, value collective identity and cohesion, and become engaged and active citizens. Language in all its forms is viewed as vital for each of these. The last three justifications derive from research evidence, of the kind referred to earlier, concerning the relationship between spoken language, synaptogenesis and cognitive development, and the character, possibilities and pitfalls of classroom talk as observational research has charted it.

Generous though this justificatory catalogue may be, it requires further comment on how the intended pedagogy relates to the broader educational aims it purports to serve. Between 2006 and 2010, the author led the Cambridge Primary Review, the UK's most comprehensive enquiry into the condition and future of primary education for half a century.[23] One of the review's ten themes was educational aims for the twenty-first century: what they currently are, and what they might be. After consulting widely in the UK and trawling other educational systems, the enquiry drafted, and after consultation confirmed, 12 aims for public education grouped in fours under the headings of 'The Individual', 'Self, Others and the Wider World' and 'Learning, Knowing and Doing' (see Chapter 8). Several of these resonate with the notion of dialogic teaching. In relation to the citizenship aim, for example, Michaels *et al* point out:

> Dialogue and discussion have long been linked to theories of democratic education. From Socrates to Dewey and Habermas, educative dialogue has represented a forum for learners to develop understanding by listening, reflecting, proposing and incorporating alternative views. For many

philosophers, learning through discussion has also represented the promise of education as a foundation for democracy.[24]

The democratic claim for dialogic pedagogy has been furthered empirically by an extensive literature review on citizenship education,[25] though lest this looks altogether too neat and unproblematic, Michaels *et al* warn that with classroom discourse as with civic discourse, 'the gap between the idealised and realised is daunting'.[26]

One Cambridge Primary Review aim is more synoptic than the others, commanding attention to the idea that dialogue is much more than classroom talk and that education itself is dialogue:[27]

> *Enacting dialogue.* To help children grasp that learning is an interactive pro-cess and that understanding builds through joint activity between teacher and pupil and among pupils in collaboration, and thereby to develop pupils' increasing sense of responsibility for what and how they learn. To help children recognise that knowledge is not only transmitted but also negotiated and re-created; and that each of us in the end makes our own sense out of the meeting of knowledge both personal and collective. To advance a pedagogy in which dialogue is central: between self and oth-ers, between personal and collective knowledge, between present and past, between different ways of making sense.[28]

If one accepts the dialectical account of knowledge and its acquisition and growth intimated here,[29] a pedagogy hegemonised by recitation/IRE is unten-able not so much on the familiar grounds of efficiency – for by its own lights it can be very efficient – as because its account of efficiency is predicated on teaching as transmitting, learning as receiving and knowing as repeating. A dia-logic pedagogy doesn't necessarily presuppose a dialogic epistemology, but a dialogic epistemology cannot realistically be fostered by other than a dialogic pedagogy.

PRINCIPLES

The model's second element adumbrates five principles or tests of dialogic teaching: *collective* (the classroom is a site of joint learning and enquiry); *recipro-cal* (participants listen to each other, share ideas and consider alternative view-points); *supportive* (participants feel able to express ideas freely, without risk of embarrassment over 'wrong' answers, and they help each other to reach common understandings); *cumulative* (participants build on their own and each other's contributions and chain them into coherent lines of thinking and understanding); *purposeful* (classroom talk, though open and dialogic, is struc-tured with specific learning goals in view).

These again subdivide. Collectivity, reciprocity and supportiveness charac-terise the classroom culture and pattern of relationships within which dialogue is most likely to prosper, its learning potential has the best chance of being realised, and students will be most at ease in venturing and discussing ideas. These three principles are consistent with the epistemological stance encapsulated in the aim from the Cambridge Primary Review cited earlier. But as the final principle reminds us, classroom discussion, though valuable in itself, is also a means to an educational end, and it must therefore square the circle of a Bakhtinian commitment to dialogue as unending and a pedagogical commitment to the student's understanding and mastery of specific ideas. Similarly, attention to the principle of cumulation, which underpins enquiry and knowledge growth in academic communities as well as classrooms, ensures that discussion is genuinely dialectical yet builds on what has gone before, advances understanding and is not merely circular.

Cumulation, we have found, is the most difficult of the principles to enact, because while collectivity, reciprocity and support relate to the *dynamics* of talk, cumulation attends to its *meaning* and therefore simultaneously tests teachers' mastery of the epistemological terrain being explored, their insight into students' understandings within that terrain, and their interactive skill in taking those understandings forward.

As an example of the definitional minefield that is dialogic teaching we might note that Mercer and Littleton characterise talk as 'cumulative' when 'speakers build positively *but uncritically* on what others have said'.[30] While excluding critical interventions may meet our third criterion (supportiveness) it may also discourage argumentation and propel discussion towards premature or unfounded consensus, thereby foreclosing cumulation of the more exacting kind referred to in the previous paragraph. Within the dialogic teaching framework outlined here, cumulation is probably closer to 'accountable talk' as defined by Resnick, Michaels and O'Connor[31]: 'Speakers make an effort to get their facts right and make explicit their evidence behind their claims or explanations. They challenge each other when evidence is lacking or unavailable.'[32] Mercer and Littleton classify this kind of talk as 'exploratory' which suggests that their use of the term 'cumulative' deals more with the social relations of talk than its substance and trajectory.

The five principles are not confined to any one preferred pattern of organisation, and our interest in building a comprehensive pedagogical repertoire contrasts, say, with Mercer's initial preoccupation, following Barnes and Todd,[33] with the dynamics and benefits of small-group discussion,[34] which in the present model is just one of the several patterns of interactive organisation that dialogue can enrich, albeit an important one that should be fully exploited.

REPERTOIRES

The framework includes six repertoires: *interactive settings, everyday talk, learning talk, teaching talk, questioning* and *extending*.

REPERTOIRE 1 – INTERACTIVE SETTINGS

Classrooms allow three organisational settings or modalities for student–teacher and student–student interaction: whole class, group and individual. Given that the actors include both teachers and students, these expand to five: *whole-class teaching (teacher–student), group work (teacher–student, teacher-led), group work (student–student, student-led), one-to-one (teacher–student)* and *one-to-one (student–student pairs)*.

Being forms of organisation rather than kinds of talk, these in effect mark one axis of a grid, while the various kinds of talk outlined in repertoires 2–6 occupy the other axis. The resulting (virtual) grid immediately and vastly expands the possibilities captured by the framework, and reminds us that while group discussion, whole-class teaching and paired talk offer distinct social, communicative and affective payoffs, the cognitive leverage they exert depends more on the character and quality of the talk being pursued than on their organisation as such, even though each organisational form entails opportunities and constraints that are different from the others.

REPERTOIRE 2 – EVERYDAY TALK

The other axis starts with six broad kinds of talk which engender and sustain everyday interaction: *transactional, expository, interrogatory, exploratory, expressive* and *evaluative*.

This repertoire reminds us that whatever else schools do, they should equip children with the capacities to manage social encounters, tell and explain, ask different kinds of questions, explore ideas, articulate feelings and responses, and frame opinions and judgements. But in order to teach effectively, teachers themselves need to master, model and deploy this most basic range, remaining alive to the tendency of traditional teaching to omit the fourth and fifth above while restricting the scope of the others.

REPERTOIRE 3 – LEARNING TALK

In classrooms, the kinds of everyday talk listed can be expanded into 11 categories of student talk for learning: *narrate, explain, speculate, imagine, explore, analyse, evaluate, question, justify, discuss* and *argue*.

These are coupled with four conditions or capacities that students need to develop to allow such talk to happen and to take full advantage of its possibilities. They should: *listen, think about what they hear, give others time to think,* and *respect alternative viewpoints*.

The last four are in the manner of norms or ground rules for discussion as proposed by, among others, Michaels, O'Connor, Mercer and Littleton.[35] The norms elaborate and facilitate the dialogic teaching principles of collectivity, reciprocity and supportiveness.

It is axiomatic that teachers themselves need to command and preferably model the range of talk in repertoires 2 and 3. But while such repertoires are not unique to teachers, comparative classroom research has charted a narrower spectrum of talk strategies specific to teaching: *rote, recitation, instruction, exposition, discussion* and *dialogue*.

Although Philip Jackson was right to point out that unlike, say, 'doctors, lawyers, garage mechanics and astrophysicists' teachers lack an agreed technical vocabulary[36] – though if managerialist jargon and cliché count as technical vocabulary, the language of educational leadership, if not that of teaching, is changing fast – we know that in the classroom teachers do think and talk in professionally-specific ways,[37] and recitation is perhaps the most uniquely teacherly talk of all. Repertoire 4 arose from international classroom observation and video analysis,[38] and serves as an empirical as well as conceptual corrective to the familiar opposition of 'transmission' and 'discovery' – telling children *versus* letting them find out for themselves. Currently, dare I suggest, we might perhaps be wary of updating this, quasi-moralistically, to recitation (bad) *versus* dialogue (good). For as I note elsewhere:

> There is a danger . . . that we consign all but the last two of these forms of classroom talk to the despised archive of 'traditional' methods. In fact, exposition and recitation have an important role in teaching, for facts need to be imparted, information needs to be memorised, and explanations need to be provided, and even the deeply unfashionable rote has a place (memorising tables, rules, spellings and so on). However, the joint solving of problems through discussion, and the achievement of common understanding through dialogue, are undeniably more demanding of teacher skill than imparting information or testing recall through rote or recitation.[39]

Dialogic teaching, therefore, encompasses the full range of teaching talk listed at Repertoire 4 but privileges the last two and especially dialogue in the more specific sense of interaction that, at best, extends the spectrum of student learning talk as in Repertoire 3. In contrast, though it does indeed have its place, the closed/recall questions that typically initiate recitation allow students to tell/narrate and, at a pinch, to explain, but not to speculate, imagine, explore, analyse, argue or ask questions of their own. Recitation is rarely other than monologic. Yet, as Nystrand cogently concludes from his study of teaching in eighth and ninth grade literature classes:

> The results of our study suggest that authentic questions, discussion, small-group work, and interaction, though important, do not categorically produce learning; indeed we observed many classes where this was not the case. We also found that recitation is not categorically ineffective; rather, its effectiveness depends on how teachers expand IRE sequences. The

underlying epistemology of classroom interaction defines the bottom line for learning: what ultimately counts is *the extent to which instruction requires students to think, not just report someone else's thinking*.[40]

REPERTOIRE 5 – QUESTIONING

This repertoire encompasses the following dimensions of classroom questioning: its *character* (using Nystrand's distinction between 'test' and 'authentic' questions); *management of participation* – rotation (short question and answer exchanges round the class), or extension (longer exchanges confined to smaller number of students); the use and extent of wait time to encourage students to think before making a contribution and, more subliminally, to encourage teachers to ask questions that deserve such thought in place of a simple recall answer; *response cues* – the contrasting strategies of bidding (hands up to answer), and nomination (questions directed to specific students); *feedback* (formative, evaluative); *purpose* (for example elicit, recall, develop, probe, manage; and *structure* (closed, open, leading, narrow, discursive).

Incidentally, although 'wait time' is the term famously coined by Rowe[41] and since then used by many others, teachers in this project found 'thinking time' to be more useful because it eliminates any vestiges of Beckettian doubt about what or whom the questioner is waiting *for*.

Even allowing for progress since Flanders proposed his 'rule of two thirds', classrooms remain places where it is the teacher who asks most of the questions.[42] Yet a dialogically-informed questioning repertoire must allow for the possibility that students too will have questions to ask and should be encouraged and if necessary trained to do so. Repertoire 5 therefore starts with Nystrand's classic distinction between 'test' and 'authentic' questions,[43] which refers to the character and intention of questions that the teacher poses, and the latter's options for inviting and handling student responses, but ends with sub-repertoires of questioning purposes and structure that apply to *all* questions, regardless of who poses them.

REPERTOIRE 6 – EXTENDING

This final repertoire, developed by Michaels and O'Connor,[44] was not in the dialogic teaching framework as initially ventured, but with the authors' permission and following their own evaluation[45] it was incorporated into it for the EEF project, and to encouraging effect. 'Extending' proposes nine moves through which the teacher can help students to: *share, expand and clarify thinking* ('time to think', 'say more', 'revoice'); *listen carefully to one another* ('rephrase or repeat'); *deepen reasoning* ('ask for evidence of reasoning', 'challenge or seek counter-example'); and *think with others* ('agree/disagree and why', 'add on', 'explain what someone else means').

Michaels and O'Connor call these 'talk moves' but in relation to the comprehensive ambition of our dialogic teaching framework this label risks excluding talk whose agents, character and purposes go beyond what the authors list. I therefore prefer the more focused term 'extending', since in relation to students' contributions and hence their thinking that is what the Michaels and O'Connor moves aim to do.

This repertoire is the logical sequel to questioning, and it offers as prompts utterances that are at once readily memorable and epistemologically positioned, and through which teachers can take student responses and contributions and build them into discussion chains, thereby modelling as well as advancing the principle of cumulation as outlined. However, practically suggestive though these moves are, Michaels and O'Connor echo Nystrand (quoted earlier) in warning that 'the simple deployment of talk moves does not ensure coherence in classroom discussion or robust student learning'.[46]

INDICATORS

The framework is completed by a list of 61 indicators that specify in practical terms how dialogic teaching looks and sounds. These cover the contexts within which dialogic teaching is placed and the classroom conditions that optimally support it, and the properties of the talk itself. The list is preceded by a warning: 'What follows is intended to serve a heuristic purpose, not to be translated into a checklist to which teachers are required to conform. If that were to happen, its dialogic intention would be defeated.'[47]

If a 61–item list, heuristic or otherwise, appears daunting or unmanageable, the framework ends with a more succinct summation of the kind of talk we are hoping for:

- *interactions* which encourage students to think, and to think in different ways;
- *questions* which invite more than simple recall;
- *answers* which are justified, followed up and built upon rather than merely received;
- *feedback* which, as well as evaluating, leads thinking forward;
- *contributions* which are extended rather than fragmented or prematurely closed;
- *exchanges* which chain together into coherent and deepening lines of enquiry;
- *discussion and argumentation* which probe and challenge rather than unquestioningly accept;
- *scaffolding* which provides appropriate linguistic and/or conceptual tools to bridge the gap between present and intended understanding;
- *professional mastery of subject matter* which is of the depth necessary to liberate classroom talk from the safe and conventional;

- *time, space, organisation and relationships* which are so disposed and orchestrated as to make all this possible.

The ultimate test of genuinely dialogic teaching as defined here is captured in quotations from Nystrand and Bakhtin: 'What ultimately counts is the extent to which instruction requires students to think, not just report someone else's thinking'[48] and 'If an answer does not give rise to a new question from itself, it falls out of the dialogue.'[49]

In the first quotation, or maxim, Nystrand reminds us that supposedly 'dialogic' patterns of talk are not intrinsically productive, and that while classroom talk is in part directed to communicative facility and effectiveness, if its impact is not primarily *cognitive* then the prospects for learning – and indeed the value of what is communicated – are greatly diminished. Complementing that warning, and moving from the cognitive power of exchanges to their component moves, Bakhtin's sense of dialogue as an unending process or quest argues a shift in the centre of discursive gravity from what the teacher asks, instructs or tells – the main focus of traditional classroom observation instruments, perversely even those used by some committed dialogists[50] – to what the pupil says and, especially, what the teacher *does* with what the pupil says.

Prior evidence of the effectiveness of the approach

So: dialogic teaching is here expanded or reduced to specific justifications, principles, repertoires and indicators in pursuit of the aim of socially and cognitively empowering talk. Although it is correct for the EEF project evaluation team to assert, as they did, that before our project there had been no randomised control trial of this version of dialogic teaching in practice,[51] internal evaluations of its precursors in London and North Yorkshire, using different methods, had reported broadly positive outcomes.[52] Subsequently, Lefstein and Snell provided an external, ethnographically-forensic perspective on the London project, and investigated the resulting changes in classroom talk and the dilemmas these provoked in one of that project's schools.[53] Three years on from our initial intervention they found clear evidence of a well-embedded signature pedagogy,[54] and confirmed our initial findings on the ways that both teacher and pupil talk had changed:

more use of 'questions which probed and/or encouraged analysis and speculation'; greater use of 'paired talk to prepare for whole class discussion'; a 'more flexible mix of different kinds of talk – recitation, exposition, discussion, dialogue'; and 'an increase in pupil contributions of an expository, explanatory, justificatory or speculative kind.' These changes were apparent in our 2008–9 observations.[55]

Once this version of dialogic teaching is located within the extended family of talk reform approaches with which it has most in common, we find further evidence that dialogue makes a difference. Thus, Hattie's synthesis of 800 meta-analyses relating to student attainment shows that the biggest effect sizes available by the mid 2000s related to teaching strategies in which the quality of talk is paramount: reciprocal teaching, feedback and student self-verbalisation, for example.[56] Extending the nexus, Black, Harlen and others find essential affinities between dialogic teaching and assessment for learning.[57] Meanwhile, Galton compares the pedagogical talk of mainstream teachers and arts practitioners. For the latter, expressive and evaluative talk are as prominent as the other kinds of 'everyday talk' – transactional, expository, interrogatory, evaluative – listed in Repertoire 2, and one only has to listen for a few moments to actors or chamber musicians rehearsing to understand how cumulation depends on collectivity and reciprocity, and how all three are essential to the melding of acquired artistic skill, creative impulse and divergent viewpoints for the furtherance of a creative activity's purpose. But what is particularly striking about Galton's observations and interviews is how students felt about the talk encouraged by the visiting arts practitioners. Contrasting it with fear of boredom and making mistakes in mathematics lessons, they found these arts sessions engaging and stimulating, and the talk far less likely to be imbued with negative comment or dominated by procedural niceties and time-watching. Meanwhile Galton observed patterns of interaction that could have come straight from a dialogic teaching manual:

> Compared to teachers, creative practitioners . . . gave pupils more time to think when planning and designing activities . . . extended questioning sequences so that classroom discourse was dialogic rather than . . . the more usual 'cued elicitations' . . . offered more precise feedback . . . tended to extend rather than change pupils' initial ideas . . . built appropriate scaffolding into the task instead of using teacher dominated approaches such as *guided discovery* . . . were more consistent in their management of learning and behaviour.[58]

In the context of an intervention such as the one under discussion, where efficacy in the official evaluation is judged solely by student scores in standardised tests, the motivational power of this kind of talk can all too easily be missed. It should not be. Engagement, after all, is a prerequisite for learning, and engagement in contexts of social disadvantage may not be readily won. Nor should we puritanically sniff at what Galton's young interviewees called the 'fun' of creative activities, for why shouldn't learning be enjoyable?

In 2011, many workers in the field of classroom talk reform met in Pittsburgh USA under the auspices of the American Educational Research Association (AERA). The resulting research compendium summarised the conference's evidential baseline as follows:

> Students who had experienced this kind of structured dialogic teaching *performed better* on standardised tests (i.e. tests that the investigators did not

control) than similar students who did not have discussion experience. The data also showed that some students *retained* their learned knowledge for two or three years. More surprising, in some cases students even *transferred* their academic advantage to a different domain (e.g. from science instruction to an English literature exam).[59]

Later, having reviewed the conference papers, Lauren Resnick was able to confirm the premise that dialogic teaching 'can produce learning gains that go well beyond the topics actually discussed' and added that it is able to generate not only this extent of learning transfer but also 'a more general ability to learn, an ability that we often attribute to intelligence'.[60]

This seemingly bold claim, that talk not only advances learning as it is defined for educational purposes but also 'socialises' the intelligence that is held to condition such learning (hence the AERA book's telling title 'Socializing Intelligence. . .') in fact elides with current thinking about the malleability of human intelligence, the capacity of schooling to raise IQ scores,[61] and evidence that in modern societies measured intelligence appears to be growing.[62]

The intervention as professional development

We turn now to the professional development programme through which dialogic teaching as outlined was to be fostered.

Stages and schools

The intervention had three stages: pilot (2014–15), trial (2015–16) and follow-up (2016–17). The pilot took place in ten of the London primary schools that had been involved in the earlier project.[63] It was hoped that returning to these schools would facilitate a fruitful conversation with the teachers involved about the benefits and challenges of the chosen strategies.

The trial took place with 5000 students and 208 teachers in 78 schools in the cities of Birmingham, Bradford and Leeds. The target figure was 80 schools; 78 agreed to participate; being in federated pairs four schools were treated as two, so for analytical purposes the number was 76. By the start of the trial this had reduced to 72, but – questionably – although the pre-intervention withdrawals played no part in the programme they were included in the RCT's data analysis on the basis of 'intention to treat'.

The project's third stage enabled the in-house evaluation to be completed and the project team to honour its commitment to those schools which agreed to participate in the project in the expectation of developmental and pedagogical benefits but found themselves in the control group. This situation often prompts post-randomisation dropout, and to reduce the risk we offered these schools the opportunity to participate in a repeat of the programme as trialled, though without the same intensity of monitoring and support, or, of course, the tests.

The Education Endowment Foundation, which commissioned and funded the project, uses UK government funding to select and trial promising initiatives for closing the attainment gap between disadvantaged children and the rest. Accordingly, all schools in both pilot and trial met the official poverty criterion of a high proportion of children (at least 20 per cent) eligible for free school meals (FSM). In addition, English was the additional language (EAL) rather than the mother tongue of about half the students involved. Participating schools were also required to be large enough for there to be at least two parallel classes in each year. The students were all in their penultimate year of primary education, that is aged 9–10 or Y5 (year 5, or 4th grade in US terms).

Strategies

The intervention's professional development programme combined seven strategies: *induction and training; mentoring; video/audio; guided planning, target-setting and review; whole-school involvement; materials and professional study;* and *monitoring and support from the project team.*

STRATEGY 1: INDUCTION AND TRAINING

In July 2015, following randomisation by the evaluation team, mentors, Y5 teachers and headteachers in each intervention school were invited to attend full-day induction sessions in Birmingham (for Birmingham schools) or Leeds (for schools in Leeds and the neighbouring city of Bradford). Mornings were devoted to introducing dialogic teaching, afternoons to explaining the professional development programme. In September 2015, following the summer holiday/recess and immediately before the start of the scheduled programme, mentors returned for a full-day training and simulation session. Between these two sessions participants were asked to read and familiarise themselves with the project print material of which all were given copies at the induction, and to ensure that they knew how to operate the digital video camera and audio voice recorder with which, on the same occasion, each school was provided.

At the end of each of the intervention's two phases, that is in December 2015 and May 2016, participants met again in Birmingham and Leeds to share experiences, review progress and hear about the development team's in-house evaluation.

STRATEGY 2: MENTORING

The mentors – one in each school – were expected to be experienced teachers though not necessarily members of the school's senior management team. Indeed, a hierarchical or inspectorial view of mentoring was strongly discouraged and schools were asked instead to foster a relationship of peers embarking on a shared journey in which professional learning is mutual and discussion is open, advisory and non-judgemental. Such a relationship is particularly important in the arena of classroom talk, which is at the heart of every teacher's professional activity yet also raises questions which are as much personal as professional and need to be handled with sensitivity to the feelings of those involved.

In relation to each of the programme's fortnightly cycles, described at 'phases and cycles' later, mentors worked with their teacher mentees to foreground within the planned lessons those aspects of teacher and/or student talk on which the handbook invited them to focus. At the end of each cycle they jointly reviewed video examples of the resulting practice in accordance with protocols provided in a linked review booklet, noting strengths and areas for further development. Typically, this meeting then moved from review to planning for the next cycle.

It was for participants to choose whether the mentoring sessions should be one-to-one or joint – that is, with all of a school's project teachers coming together to share experiences and view and discuss each other's video extracts. Most opted for the latter arrangement and testified to its value.

STRATEGY 3: VIDEO/ AUDIO

Video and audio are not only ideal for capturing classroom interaction as both sound and behaviour, for talk is what is signalled by body language and gesture as well what we say and hear. They are also powerful tools for professional self-evaluation and development. In this project, video was used during the induction and training, but its principal purpose was to provide the material upon which teachers and mentors would jointly work. Recordings fixed teachers' entering pedagogy as baselines for tracking and assessing their progress; and when subjected to close analysis they enabled teacher and mentor to identify aspects of classroom talk on which it might be beneficial and, in some instances, necessary to work. Video fulfilled the secondary purpose of enabling the development team to assess the intervention's progress and impact, adding matched recordings from control schools.

As one who had used video and audio recording since the 1980s both for studying talk and supporting professional development,[64] I had noticed teachers' tendency when viewing classroom video clips to concentrate more frequently and critically on the actors' observable behaviours than on the words uttered or meanings exchanged. In order to alert teachers themselves to this viewer bias as well as to counter it, the training sessions worked in turn on three versions of the same lesson extract. First an audio recording directed attention to the form and meaning of talk, and to these alone. Then a transcript allowed more detailed study in which specific speech exchanges, moves or acts could be revisited as many times as necessary. Finally a video clip enabled participants to observe the interplay of talk's linguistic and paralinguistic features and place the talk heard, read and now viewed in its full pedagogical context.

Incidentally, though these days digitalised video is *de rigeur*, the power of audio alone to concentrate attention on the *language* of interaction should be emphasised, and of course it is less intrusive. Re-reading James Britton's pioneering discussion of lesson transcripts[65] gives one a sense of the investigative wonderment unleashed by the invention of reel-to-reel audiotape.[66]

STRATEGY 4: GUIDED PLANNING, TARGET-SETTING AND REVIEW

Each cycle in the post-training programme began with planning and target-setting and ended with review, and the video/audio recordings contributed to one or both of these. What was being planned for each cycle was not a deviation from the intended curriculum but a sharper and more self-conscious focus on the part within it that oral pedagogy might play. This required teachers to audit and map the talk in their classrooms, single out those aspects on which, within their planned lessons and the required focus of each of the intervention's cycles, they should work, and then do so in a systematic way. Baseline sessions in September initiated this process, but development came from repeating the planning/review sequence rather than waiting until the end of the programme to assess progress. Hence the 11 planning/review/refocusing cycles discussed in the next section.

STRATEGY 5: WHOLE SCHOOL INVOLVEMENT

Individual development and innovation are most successful when they are supported by the school's leadership and embedded in its everyday professional discourse. Although the trial was confined to teachers and students in Year 5, schools were encouraged to take ownership of both the pedagogy and the development strategy and to explore their application across the school.

STRATEGY 6: MATERIALS AND PROFESSIONAL STUDY

In this project it was axiomatic that teachers learn from examining the practice of both themselves and others, and that effective professional development requires understanding of the ideas and evidence on which the objectives of the development are based. To this end, all participants were provided with a suite of print materials and online access to these and other material. The print materials included: a 68-page handbook which set out the project's aims and processes and detailed the intervention programme in full and week by week, supporting this with brief accounts of dialogic teaching and mentoring, and exemplificatory transcripts of lesson extracts;[67] a booklet containing planning/review forms for each cycle, with appropriate prompts;[68] Alexander's *Towards Dialogic Teaching: rethinking classroom talk* (5th edition), this being the work on which the intervention was principally based; the *Talk Science Primer* of Michaels and O'Connor[69] which lists and provides the rationale for the nine 'extending' moves listed in Repertoire 6; and a laminated sheet entitled *Dialogic Teaching Repertoires* which reduced dialogic teaching, for easy and daily reference, to its barest essentials.

To these was added, to deepen mentors' understanding and sensitise them to the uses of video, Lefstein and Snell's book of case studies with its linked website with lesson video clips.[70] The project's own online resources included the handbook and planning/review forms together with two DVDs created by the project team: *Dialogic Teaching* and *Video Recording in Classrooms*. All these materials were distributed at the July 2015 induction sessions in the expectation that they would be studied before the programme started in September.

STRATEGY 7: MONITORING AND SUPPORT

During each of the programme's two phases every intervention school was visited at least once by a member or members of the project team. The visits entailed meetings with the Y5 teachers, their mentors and, where possible, school heads. Progress was reviewed, video clips were discussed, planning/review booklets were examined, and problems needing resolution were identified and, ideally, resolved. The problems were typically of a kind that teachers themselves were happy to articulate, but in some cases, for example where the relationship between mentor and teachers was not working or the planning/review sessions were skimped, it was necessary for the project team to intervene. If resolution was not possible in one visit, the project's school liaison officer would return to the school and then maintain contact by phone and/or email for as long as was necessary.

Alongside monitoring and trouble-shooting, the visits fulfilled the more formal purpose of acquiring interview data for the project's in-house evaluation. This aspect is dealt with more fully later in this chapter.

Phases and cycles

The programme comprised 11 planning/review/refocusing cycles. Each lasted for two weeks except the one-week opening and closing cycles. The programme was spread across two school terms or phases. Phase 1 (cycles 1–6) ran from 21 September to 18 December 2015, Phase 2 (cycles 7–11) from 4 January to 18 March 2016. The entire programme occupied 20 weeks.

In Phase 1, entitled *Expanding Repertoires*, teachers and mentors:

- Made video/audio lesson recordings to use as baselines for future development and comparison, and scheduled dates for subsequent recording and mentoring sessions (cycle 1).
- Discussed and agreed with students the conditions and norms for talk on which the success of this short but intensive programme would partly depend (cycle 2).
- Mapped and began to refine talk repertoires for whole-class teaching, focusing first on the teacher's questions, instructions and explanations (cycle 3), then on moves to extend the contributions of the student (cycle 4).

- Shifted the focus to repertoires for small-group and one-to one discussion, both teacher-led and student-led (cycle 5), consolidating the norms and generic talk repertoires from the previous cycles.
- With the building blocks in place, and mindful that successful learning and teaching depend on the student's engagement, identified and worked on those kinds of talk which are most likely to secure this engagement and make the talk truly inclusive (cycle 6).
- Pulled together material from the programme so far in preparation for the mentors' plenary (cycle 6).

In Phase 2, entitled Advancing Dialogue, teachers and mentors:

- Initiated and implemented an intensive six-week programme of teaching in the National Curriculum core subjects English, mathematics and science which consciously applied and sustained the full range of talk repertoires opened up during Phase 1 (cycles 7, 8 and 9).
- Explored dialogic teaching across the wider curriculum by focusing in addition on National Curriculum non-core foundation subjects (cycle 10).
- Pulled together evidence from Phases 1 and 2 for the final plenary for all project participants (cycle 11).

Directed and responsive foci

The piloted version of this programme had been relatively flexible, presenting in some detail the properties of dialogic teaching to be aimed for while leaving teachers and mentors free to devise their own routes to these. This produced variation between teachers, as to both focus and quality, which was greater than could be accommodated by the methodology of the randomised control trial, which required a high degree of implementation fidelity. The loose framework of the pilot was therefore replaced by the intensive programme, as outlined, in which the focus and tasks for each cycle were precisely specified. At the same time, there needed to be room for variation in each teacher's circumstances, capacities and needs, so a distinction was made between the programme's 'directed' and 'responsive' foci. To quote from the project handbook:

> The *directed focus* is what we ask all schools to follow during the cycle in question in order to ensure consistency and progression. Within each cycle lasting a fortnight (all but two of them), planning/target setting should be done early in the first week and review/refocussing at the end of the second. This will ensure that each such cycle includes at least 6–7 days for teaching to the cycle's aims and targets. The *responsive focus* is an aspect or aspects of classroom talk to which individual teachers and mentors decide they would like to attend in order to extend or add to the directed focus. This will reflect the unique circumstances and needs of each teacher and

his/her class. As a reminder of the need for the responsive focus and the discretion it offers, a blank 'responsive focus' column is included in the planning/review forms.[71]

Allowing for a responsive focus within each cycle alongside what the project itself directed seemed an appropriate compromise between the fidelity demanded by the trial and the flexibility necessary in all teaching. However, the shift from the latitude that teachers were given in the pilot to the closely-prescribed framework of the trial was of such an order of magnitude that the team feared that teachers might find it excessive. It was with some relief, therefore, that when we raised this at the plenary session at the end of Phase 1, mentors affirmed that they and their teaching colleagues not only found the framework helpful rather than overly prescriptive but that given the intervention's complexity and brevity, anything less would have left some of them floundering. But they also welcomed the deviation that the responsive focus allowed.

Planning and review protocols

For each cycle mentors were asked to refer to and complete with their mentees a planning/review form either in longhand in a special booklet or electronically on forms downloadable from the project website.[72] The forms reminded teachers and mentors of each cycle's directed focus and provided prompts for planning and review. The planning prompts included reference to relevant sections and pages in the print materials. The planning and review prompts appeared in the first column while the second and third columns, headed 'Directed focus – plan/review' and 'Responsive focus – issues to take forward', were mostly kept clear for the mentor's comments.

Evaluation

Evaluation design

Randomised control trial[73]

The trial organised independently by a separate team at another university (Sheffield Hallam) used a three-level clustered RCT design (pupils within classes with schools), with randomisation at school level and the classes divided equally into intervention and control groups. From the target number of 80 schools, as noted earlier, 78 were recruited (counted as 76 because two pairs of schools were federated) and were included in the trial on the basis of intention to treat, though the actual number participating in the intervention, after pre-intervention withdrawals, was 72. To be included in the trial, schools needed to have at least two parallel Y5 classes (US 4th grade) and at least 25 per cent of their students eligible for free school midday meals (FSM). The actual average FSM proportion, overall, was 35 per cent.

The evaluation team used as outcome measures GL Assessment Progress Tests in English, mathematics and science.[74] Students were randomised at classroom level to participate in one of these so that at the assessment point, in late May 2016, one third of each class took each test. The evaluation team argued that this reduced the testing burden on pupils and teachers without significantly reducing the statistical power of the analysis.

Tests were scored by GL Assessment, the company that published the tests. The scoring was blind and for each measure the raw, unstandardised score was used in the analysis. The primary analysis of the intervention's impact, based on intention to treat (38 intervention group schools) rather than actual participation in the intervention (31 schools), was a multilevel regression model of each outcome measure, using as covariates (i) membership of the intervention group, (ii) KS1 point score[75] and (iii) FSM eligibility.

The primary analysis included subgroup analyses for FSM students to assess whether the intervention had differential impact on these students, who, being economically the most disadvantaged, are the main target group for all EEF projects and trials.

Controversially, but in accordance with EEF RCT practice, there were no pre-tests. EEF argues that suitably rigorous sampling and randomisation enables intervention effect sizes to be reliably calculated from outcome measures alone.

School, student and teacher numbers at each stage of the trial process are shown in Table 16.1. The school and student attrition recorded in the table

Table 16.1 Schools, students and teachers in the dialogic teaching trial

Recruitment	Schools approached: 80
	Schools agreeing to participate: 78
	Counted in the RCT as: 76 (two pairs of schools were federated)
	Pre-intervention withdrawals: 6 schools
	Actual participation: 72 schools
Allocation, intention to treat	78 schools counted as 76
	Intervention group: 38 schools, 2,492 students, 118 teachers (a)
	Control group: 38 schools, 2,466 students, 90 teachers
Test data collected	Intervention group: 31 schools, 2,097 students (b)
	Control group: 38 schools, 2,466 students
Test data analysed	Intervention group: 31 schools, 1,832 students (c)
	Control group: 31 schools, 2,080 students

(a) 80 class teachers, 38 mentors.

(b) In addition to the six pre-intervention school withdrawals, one school failed to return test data. 395 students were therefore lost to the follow-up.

(c) Complete datasets were unavailable for 265 students in the intervention group and 386 in the control group either because of student absence or opt out, or because tested students could not be matched with available data on KS1 attainment or FSM eligibility.

allowed EEF to give it a security rating of 3 out of 5. EEF deemed this sufficient for concluding that attainment gains made by intervention group students over their control group peers were due to the intervention rather than other factors.

External process evaluation

Alongside the trial the Sheffield team organised a qualitative implementation and process evaluation. This included a postal survey intended to include all intervention group teachers, mentors and headteachers but which yielded a very low return rate, telephone interviews with six teachers, eight mentors and three headteachers, and classroom observation and interviews in three schools.[76]

In-house formative evaluation

The in-house evaluation by the York-based development team, which was entirely separate from the trial team's process evaluation, had two strands: an interview programme undertaken in intervention schools only; and a comparative analysis of videotaped lessons from both intervention and control schools.

INTERVIEWS

Two sets of interviews were conducted with teachers, mentors and headteachers in each intervention school. The first took place during the programme's Phase 1 (autumn 2015), the second towards the end of Phase 2 (spring 2016). The focus in each case was participants' adherence to and divergence from the specified programme, challenges encountered during its implementation, and its perceived impact on teaching, learning, student engagement and classroom talk. The interviewers, who were all members of the York team, worked to an agreed schedule of questions. Answers were recorded on a proforma for later analysis using the NVivo software for qualitative data. To the interview programme was added scrutiny of the cycle-specific planning/review forms completed by the mentors for each of the teachers they were supporting, to allow deeper insights into fidelity, feasibility and utility.

VIDEO DATA[77]

In order to assess the pedagogic impact of the intervention it was necessary to videotape lessons in sub-samples of both the intervention and control groups, and to do so twice so as to track development and progress over time. Video recordings of English, mathematics and science lessons were made (i) early in phase one (week beginning 21 September 2015) to provide a baseline, and (ii) towards the end of Phase 2 (fortnight beginning 22 February 2016).

Fifteen teachers from the intervention group and 11 from the control group agreed to be video-recorded. The intervention group teachers were self-selected in response to a request for volunteers at the July 2015 induction sessions. Self-selection was the only realistic possibility: to impose selection on top of the other demands of the project could have been counterproductive for retention. The control group teachers were selected on the basis of school-school matching.

Each teacher was recorded twice, in Phase 1 and again in Phase 2, yielding a theoretical total of 156 lessons (two English, two mathematics and two science in each case). In fact, because not all of the designated teachers taught science, the total number of lessons recorded was 134 (67 in each phase). The resulting recordings were subjected to both quantitative and qualitative analysis.

For the quantitative analysis, some of the key verbal indicators of typical classroom talk, both traditional and dialogic,[78] became the basis for a coding system that was piloted in the London schools before being finalised and applied to the trial stage video data. Coders were trained and checked to maximise coding consistency. The coding system was uploaded into the Noldus Observer XT 12.5 software in order to generate quantitative data from the coded exchanges. These were then statistically analysed using SPSS. The analysis was undertaken twice for the purpose of cross-validation, first internally at the University of York, then externally by Kirkdale Geometrics.[79]

The quantitative analysis undertaken to date covers:

Student and teacher talk (aspects of Repertoires 3, 4 and 5): change in the ratio of teacher talk to student talk over time, and intervention/control comparisons; change in the ratio of recitation to discussion/dialogue over time, and intervention/control comparisons.

Teacher talk (aspects of Repertoire 6): intervention/control differences in teacher extending moves; development in teacher extending moves over time (from Phase 1 to Phase 2) and intervention/control comparisons; teacher extending move differences between English, mathematics and science.

Student talk (aspects of Repertoires 3, 4 and 5): intervention/control differences in the ratio of brief to extended student contributions; change in the ratio of brief to extended student contributions over time (from Phase 1 to Phase 2) and intervention/control comparisons; brief/extended ratio differences between English, mathematics and science; frequency of sub-types of extended student contributions, derived from the project's categories of learning talk (Repertoire 3).

Evaluation outcomes

Although the headline findings of the RCT may be of greater public interest – and after the release of its report they did indeed provoke media attention[80] –

chronology and logic require that the findings from the in-house evaluation, which tracked the intervention's progress towards the point at which student attainment was tested, be presented first.

In-house evaluation: interview data[81]

PROGRAMME IMPACT

Overall, participating teachers claimed direct positive gains from the programme for classroom talk, student engagement and student learning, and for their own professional understanding and skill. Specifically:

- Norms for student talk were fairly quickly established and embedded.
- Teachers learned to extend their basic talk repertoires and their skill in using them.
- Specific teaching strategies such as questioning, discussion and feedback became more systematic and effective.
- Exchanges were lengthened, sustained and deepened.
- Students' preparedness to listen to each other improved.
- Interaction became more inclusive, with fewer students isolated, silent or reluctant to participate, while previously dominant students became less inclined or able to monopolise the talk and teachers' attention.
- With an increased emphasis on a supportive, reciprocal talk culture, students gained in confidence and became more patient and better attuned to each others' situations and keen to provide mutual support in both talking and learning.
- There were also subject-specific gains. In English, teachers reported improved student vocabulary, better discussion, and evidence of transfer of verbal gains from oral to written work. In mathematics, students became more adept at explaining the reasoning behind their solutions and thus providing teachers with a firm basis for both feedback ad further extension. In science, the democratisation of questioning that is a feature of dialogic teaching fed into a more genuinely scientific stance in students' investigations and discussions.

PROGRAMME IMPLEMENTATION

Overall, checks on mentors' entries in the planning/review forms confirmed interview claims that the programme was implemented with a reasonable degree of fidelity and that it was both useful and feasible. Specifically:

- By the end of the intervention, every school had completed all 11 cycles of the programme.
- 57 per cent of schools reported that they had followed the programme exactly as specified in the handbook while 43 per cent had made modifications, though still within the specified framework.

- The main challenges faced were: insufficient time for teachers and mentors to plan and review (33 per cent of schools in both phases 1 and 2); national curriculum and assessment changes; staff changes (including among those immediately involved); pupil changes (high student turnover affected many project schools); and unanticipated events such as staff illness, especially in Phase 2.
- However, most of the challenges that teachers faced were intrinsic to school life rather than generated by the project. No innovation would have escaped them.
- For the critical role of mentor, which requires time for preparation and follow up as well as face-to-face meetings, time pressures were less of an issue for those mentors who held senior positions allowing administrative release.[82]

The more limited process evaluation undertaken by the external team in conjunction with the RCT arrived at similar conclusions to these, so it is not necessary to list them separately. However, one frequently-voiced opinion from the external team's survey and interviews should be noted here. When interviewed before the results of the trial were announced, teachers believed that the intervention was too short to achieve a discernible impact on student learning – even though they also asserted that its positive effect on students' engagement and patterns of talk, the prerequisites for the hoped-for learning gains, was speedily apparent – and that a period of at least a full school year would be more effective. In the event, teachers' pessimism about learning outcomes was misplaced, for the intervention's impact on student test scores was no less discernible than on student engagement and talk, as we shall see next. But the point is well made – and the project team itself had already registered it with EEF, the funding body whose evaluation paradigm had been responsible for the intervention's brevity.

In-house evaluation: video data[83]

Comparison of coded talk acts and exchanges in intervention and control classrooms showed significant differences emerging between the two groups over the two terms of the intervention. These differences were striking in both teacher and student talk. For example:

CLOSED AND OPEN TEACHER QUESTIONS

In all three core subjects, the ratio of closed to open teacher questions was fairly evenly balanced in Phase 1 but by Phase 2 intervention teachers were making greater use of open questions than their control group peers. The argument here is that while closed or 'what?' questions require largely pre-ordained responses dependent on recall or at best instant calculation, open and ideally authentic questions launched by 'how?' or 'why?' or 'what if?'

encourage reasoning, speculation and more active cognitive and indeed social engagement – provided, of course, that the teacher allows appropriate wait/thinking time.

TEACHER EXTENDING MOVES

Intervention teachers were trained to deploy a variety of moves to probe, extend and follow up student contributions (Repertoire 6) on the principle that these would both increase students' interest and engagement and enhance their cognitive gains. Differences between the two groups in respect of these were most marked in mathematics and science, where by Phase 2 the intervention teachers were making significantly greater use of wait/thinking time, revoicing, rephrasing, seeking evidence of reasoning, challenging, requesting justification and so on.

BALANCE OF RECITATION AND DISCUSSION/DIALOGUE

In English and mathematics, comparable ratios of recitation to discussion and dialogue in the intervention and control groups were transformed into significant differences by Phase 2, with intervention teachers making much greater use of discussion and dialogue. In this matter, science was again somewhat different in that in Phase 1 the intervention group was already making greater use of discussion and dialogue than the control group. This lead was sustained into Phase 2 and increased as the intervention progressed.

BALANCE OF BRIEF AND EXTENDED STUDENT CONTRIBUTIONS

In English and mathematics, the ratio of brief to extended student contributions in Phase 1 was the same in intervention and control classrooms. By Phase 2, there were statistically significant differences between the groups in respect of an increase in extended student contributions and a decrease in brief contributions. In science, the intervention group started the programme with a higher ratio of extended to brief student contributions than the control group. (Given that this happened after the induction and training it may suggest that the programme's messages in this regard were more readily implemented in science than the other two subjects, or even that primary science teaching is more instinctively dialogic.) This difference was sustained into Phase 2.

THE REPERTOIRE OF STUDENT TALK

As emphasised earlier, the present version of dialogic teaching attends as closely to the talk of the teacher as to that of the student, because it is through the teacher's talk that the student's talk is either confined within the tightly controlled boundaries of recitation or encouraged through discussion and dialogue to enlarge its discursive and semantic repertoire and hence its cognitive power. Hence the focus on the balance of closed and open questions, recitation and dialogue, and on brief and extended student contributions. For while dialogic teaching as conceived here accepts the need in certain circumstances for closed questions, recitation and brief student contributions, it also affirms that unless the quantity and quality of student talk is extended well beyond these traditional patterns of exchange into a more extensive interactive repertoire, the full communicative and cognitive potential of classroom talk will remain largely unrealised. In the end, therefore, it is the student's talk that matters most, and it is to the teacher's agency in securing the enhancement of student talk that dialogic teaching is directed.

To judge student talk merely by the length of utterances, as in the analysis of brief/extended contributions referred to, is useful only as a preliminary or general indicator of quality. What matters is the form of student talk that opportunities for its temporal extension allow, for extended talk may be − in terms of the most demanding of the five criteria of successful dialogic teaching − cumulative, or it may be merely circular, and this is a particular risk in classroom discussion. (Compare with the observation of Michaels and O'Connor that 'the simple deployment of talk moves does not ensure coherence in classroom discussions or robust student learning'.)[84]

Here, the 11 categories of learning talk in Repertoire 3 (narrate, explain, speculate, imagine, explore, analyse, evaluate, question, justify, discuss, argue) provided the necessary analytical indicators. These were modified for coding purposes as 12 sub-types of extended student contributions which also included student responses to some of the key extending moves in Repertoire 6. The modified coding categories for student learning talk were: expand/add, connect, explain/analyse, rephrase, narrate, evaluate, argue, justify, speculate, challenge, imagine, shift position. These were applied to video transcript samples from both the intervention and the control groups in weeks 1 and 18–19.

The differences by the latter stage of the intervention were striking. By then, intervention group students had become markedly more expansive in their contributions and exhibited higher levels of explanation, analysis, argumentation, challenge and justification. Their talk, then, was without doubt more dialogic than that of their control group peers. Though there were between–subject differences, the overall pattern of intervention/control contrast obtained across all three subjects tested for the RCT.

Randomised control trial

Thus the in-house evaluation undertaken by the project team demonstrated that the professional development programme, though brief, produced changes in teachers' thinking and practice which led to the widening and intensification of the students' own talk repertoires, and the Sheffield team's external process evaluation confirmed these trends, though without the benefit of the video data which would have enabled it to compare talk in the intervention and control groups and to do so systematically.

To those who believe in the value of dialogue as an educational end in itself, as considered earlier in this paper, this finding could have been sufficient, but EEF exists to trial and disseminate interventions that reduce the attainment gap among disadvantaged children, so for them the test scores mattered above all else. The evaluation's overall conclusions, which added findings from the independent process evaluation to the effect sizes, recalculated by EEF as months of progress, were as follows and are quoted verbatim from the Sheffield team's report:

1. Children in dialogic teaching schools made two additional months' progress in English and science, and one additional month's progress in mathematics, compared to children in control schools, on average.
2. Children eligible for free school meals (FSM) made two additional months' progress in English, science and mathematics compared to FSM children in control schools.
3. The intervention was highly regarded by headteachers, mentors and teachers, who thought that the dialogic teaching approach had positive effects on pupil confidence and engagement.
4. The majority of participating teachers felt that it would take longer than two terms to fully embed a dialogic teaching approach in their classrooms. It could therefore be valuable to test the impact of the intervention over a longer period.
5. The intervention requires teachers to change classroom talk across the curriculum, supported by training, handbooks, video and regular review meetings with mentors. Future research could aim to differentiate the effects of these different elements.[85]

The cost of the intervention was calculated as GBP52 per student per year, which made this intervention one of the cheapest trialled by EEF. About its main findings and conclusions the EEF evaluation report also observed:

*   At 20 weeks/two terms the intervention was too short to achieve its maximum impact, and a longer intervention could well have produced even larger differences in attainment between the two groups.
*   Given that it can take two or three years for a complex intervention to be fully implemented the RCT was undertaken too soon.
*   The findings may have been affected by unobserved differences between schools that withdrew from the trial and those that remained.
*   The intervention was unusual among those trialled for EEF in that it sought to improve attainment across the curriculum, and succeeded in doing so. Most EEF projects deal with one subject only.[86]

The evaluation team added this significant admission:

> Limitations to the methodological approach taken here mean that there may be positive effects of the intervention that could not be detected, or that effects observed may be underestimated.[87]

Converting effect sizes to months of progress in order to give teachers and policymakers a more meaningful basis for their decisions is of course far from straightforward. EEF explains its conversion procedure, assumptions and caveats in a technical paper[88] which remains on the Foundation's website even though I understand that EEF no longer accepts its rigid low/medium/high banding of effect sizes because these take no account of an intervention's character or – crucially – its length. (Additional progress of two months after 20 weeks is clearly more noteworthy than it would be after 60 weeks.)

Conclusion

To summarise. The intervention had two strands, pedagogical and developmental. Grounded in a specific but established approach to dialogic teaching, steered by print materials, in-school mentoring and video/audio analysis, and supported by externally-provided training and monitoring, it used a 20-week cyclic programme of planning, target-setting and review to encourage teachers to expand their and their students' repertoires of classroom talk in the direction of dialogue and argumentation. The required changes were argued on evidential and ethical grounds as a necessary basis for increasing engagement, improving learning and enriching education among all children, but especially those from the poorest families, where educational underachievement is at its most marked.

Interviews conducted in parallel by the development and external evaluation teams found teachers highly supportive of the programme's aims and strategies though mindful of its challenges. The development team's analysis of video-recorded lesson episodes from both intervention and control group classrooms showed how talk in the intervention classrooms begin to shift in the intended direction early on, and continued to do so, with considerable divergence in patterns of both teacher and student talk evident by week 19. Similarly, and we believe consequently, after the 20-week programme the randomised control trial found that students in the intervention group were two months ahead of their control group peers in standardised tests of English, mathematics and science, despite the fact that problems such as school attrition and the required brevity of the intervention are thought to have caused its impact to be understated.

It has been objected that RCTs are not well suited to an arena as complex, idiosyncratic and ephemeral as teaching, and that their claim to represent the 'gold standard' in educational and social research is overstated, misguided and perhaps even imperialist.[89] This is not the place to assess such claims, but it is right briefly to note reservations about the RCT paradigm as it was applied in this particular case.[90]

The RCT used checked but nevertheless subjective Y2 teacher assessments as measures of prior attainment, instead of a proper pre-test of the target groups immediately before the Y5 trial. Further undermining the reliability of this procedure, the rapid student turnover that characterises inner-city schools with high proportions of disadvantaged/FSM/EAL students schools meant that the cohort tested in 2016 was appreciably and perhaps unsustainably different from that tested in 2013.

The RCT failed to deploy appropriate procedures to address the acknowledged problem of missing data at the school and classroom levels.

The RCT relied on standardised tests in English, mathematics and science as sole measures of the programme's educational outcomes, to the exclusion of measures of student engagement and spoken language which were actually agreed at the outset and would have allowed the programme's impact to have been evaluated in a manner more consistent with its aims. Fully consistent and valid measures would also most certainly have yielded a bigger effect size.

The decision to calculate effect sizes separately by subject, especially in view of the fact that only one third of the students took each test, further weakened the power of the analysis. A combined multivariate analysis would have reduced error and made the effect calculation more secure.

The external evaluation report did not comment on the EAL dimension, despite the fact that English was the second language of half of the students and that the intervention group had a larger proportion of EAL pupils than the control group (53 per cent compared with 47 per cent[91]). Talk reform is doubly challenging in the EAL context, and the weighting of this measure of disadvantage against the intervention group may have further reduced compromised effect size.

The report also said little or nothing about other obvious differences within the student population such as gender, ethnicity, cultural background and special needs. So, for example, combining several of these variables we note that a significant proportion of the students were girls of Muslim Asian heritage, and while the RCT may have been methodologically unsuited to tracking the qualitative impact of the intervention on sub-groups such as this, the external process evaluation arguably could and should have done. Similarly, 16 per cent of the students in each group (intervention and control) were classified as having special educational needs (SEN) but their progress was not separately investigated. The only subgroup to be separately analysed was FSM pupils. These accounted for 35 per cent of each group and, as noted, they did better than the intervention group as a whole in the mathematics test. But we are not told why.

Although the report acknowledged that 'limitations to the methodological approach taken here mean that there may be positive effects of the intervention that could not be detected, or that effects observed may be underestimated',[92] nothing was done to reduce the risk or address the problem. And since the effects are quantified it would have been helpful if the extent of their possible underestimation could also have been quantified.

And yet . . . A two-month student attainment advantage from a 4.5-month intervention might be rated pretty impressive; and if in the estimation of the independent evaluation team and EEF – neither of which had an interest in talking up the outcomes – the balance of the RCT's unreliability leans towards underestimation of the effect size rather than exaggeration, then we might as well accept the finding. Further, although we in the development team objected to aspects of the RCT as conceived, conducted and reported, we also embraced the advantage, in terms of its public credibility, of escaping the stricture that RCTs are too frequently compromised by association with the intervention's developer.[93] As EEF points out, all its evaluators are entirely independent of the teams developing the interventions they evaluate, and 'are appointed through a competitive tendering process and reviewed for any academic conflict of interest'.[94]

The evaluation report recommended that a follow-up project should disaggregate the elements of the professional development programme and implemented them with separate groups of teachers so that their effects might be individually tested. Though we certainly need to know what in this intervention made such a difference in so short a time, this recommendation seems to reflect both misunderstanding of the intervention's essentially holistic character and the extent to which education RCTs have been colonised by the dosage mindset of the drug trial industry from which they seem to have been imported, as if training = 1 dose, training + mentoring = 2 doses, training + mentoring + video = 3 doses, training + mentoring + handbook = 4 doses, and so on. We wonder what would constitute a dialogic teaching overdose.

This brief diversion into educational pharmacology aside, the external evaluation report offered little by way of explanation or diagnosis from the quantitative and qualitative evidence it assembled. Lacking the essential and agreed measure of spoken language it was unable to track the intervention through to the transformation of students' talk that was its object, and it was left to the development team to plug this critical gap with its own video data. Nor, crucially, could the RCT differentiate the relative impact of the intervention's pedagogical and developmental strands. Referring merely to 'the intervention', this RCT, for all its statistical wizardry, was a remarkably blunt instrument.

Frustratingly, in matters of cause and effect and the differential response to a talk-rich intervention from the various student sub-groups mentioned, we can draw little from the official evaluation and instead must extrapolate from other sources. This is our task in chapter 17.

Postscript: modifications to the dialogic teaching framework since the EEF trial[95]

The framework referred to, and trialled in the EEF project, had four segments: *justifications*, *principles*, *repertoires* and *indicators*. To these the latest version (2020) adds *definitions* and *stance*. The justifications are broadly the same, though there are now eight rather than six.[96] To the initial five principles, in line with the need for greater emphasis on argumentation, has been added a sixth, *deliberative* ('participants discuss and seek to resolve different points of view, they present and evaluate arguments, and they work towards reasoned positions and outcomes'). The repertoires have been substantially revised. Those featuring in the EEF trial included *interactive settings*, *everyday talk*, *learning talk*, *teaching talk*, *questioning* and *extending*. The current version expands these to *interactive culture*, *interactive settings, learning talk, teaching talk, questioning, extending, discussing* and *arguing*. The indicators are reduced in number to their essentials. Earlier versions were somewhat repetitious and the elaboration of the repertoires for the current version made many of them redundant.

Despite these changes, the essential core of the version as trialled remains intact, as does its epistemic and pedagogical stance. The changes constitute, as is surely right, development and refinement in light of experience and evidence rather than a radical change of direction.

Notes

1 Alexander 2015a.
2 Alexander 2017a, 2017b, 2020.
3 Alexander 2003, 2005a, 2005b; Lefstein and Snell 2011.
4 Details at https://educationendowmentfoundation.org.uk/our-work/projects/dialogic-teaching/ (accessed May 2020).
5 Jay *et al* 2017.
6 The development project was based at the University of York and the evaluation at Sheffield Hallam University.
7 Britton 1969; Bruner 1983, 1996; Bruner and Haste 1987; Tough 1979; Wood 1998; Goswami 2015.
8 Barnes *et al* 1969; Barnes and Todd 1977; Sinclair and Coulthard 1975; Mehan 1979; Cazden 2001; Mehan and Cazden 2015; Nystrand *et al* 1997; Alexander 2001a, 2008b; Mortimer and Scott 2003; Hardman *et al* 2003; Smith *et al* 2004; Galton *et al* 1999, 2008; Resnick *et al* 2015.
9 For example, Mercer and Hodgkinson 2008; Resnick *et al* 2015; Mercer *et al* 2020.
10 Lefstein and Snell 2014; Kim and Wilkinson 2019.
11 For example, Reznitskaya 2012, 2013.
12 Wragg and Brown 1993, 2001.
13 Norman 1992; Mercer 2000; Dawes *et al* 2004.
14 Lefstein and Snell 2014.
15 Alexander 2001a, 2008b, 2009c.
16 Vygotsky 1962, 1978; Bruner 1983, 1996; Bakhtin 1981, 1986.
17 Nystrand *et al* 1997; Resnick *et al* 2010; Michaels and O'Connor 2012, 2015.
18 Alexander *et al* 1992.
19 Alexander 1984, 2008b.
20 Alexander 2001a, 265–528; 2008b, 45–50 and 180–3. See chapter 19.
21 Black and Wiliam 1998; Black *et al* 2003.
22 Alexander 2017a, 2020.
23 Alexander 2010a; Alexander *et al* 2010.
24 Michaels *et al* 2008, 296.
25 Deakin Crick *et al* 2005.
26 Michaels *et al* 2008, 296.
27 I first advanced this theme in a public lecture in Hong Kong entitled 'Education as Dialogue' (Alexander 2006b). It was revised as 'Pedagogy for a runaway world' in Alexander 2008b, 121–53.
28 Alexander 2010a, 399.
29 Interestingly, though my approach to dialogic teaching has affinities with Lauren Resnick's idea of 'accountable talk', the paper by Michaels *et al* (2008) seems to tie its important principle of 'accountability to knowledge' to a somewhat more canonical account of knowledge than the one adopted here.

30 Mercer and Littleton 2007, 51 (my italics).
31 Michaels *et al* 2008; Resnick *et al* 2010.
32 Michaels *et al* 2008, 283.
33 Barnes and Todd 1977.
34 Mercer and Littleton 2007.
35 Michaels *et al* 2008; Michaels and O'Connor 2015; Mercer and Littleton 2007.
36 Jackson 1968, 143.
37 Schön 1983; Calderhead 1993.
38 Alexander 2001a.
39 Alexander 2001a, 526–7.
40 Nystrand *et al* 1997, 72 (their italics).
41 Rowe 1974, 1986.
42 Dillon 1988.
43 In Nystrand *et al* 1997, 38.
44 Michaels and O'Connor 2012.
45 Michaels and O'Connor 2015.
46 Michaels and O'Connor 2015, 358.
47 Alexander 2017a, 41.
48 Nystrand *et al* 1997, 72.
49 Bakhtin 1986, 168.
50 Just as IRE is dominated by the teacher's utterances, so traditional interaction analysis coding instruments tend to explicate the first move in the IRE sequence in greater detail than the other two. The landmark Flanders FIAC instrument from which so many later observation instruments derive (Flanders 1960) had seven kinds of teacher talk but only two for the student and a pretty basic and content-free twosome at that: 'Student talk – response' and 'Student talk – initiation'. We might be unconcerned about this on the grounds that it accurately reflected the way teaching was in the 1960s – if it invariably was, which I doubt – were it not for the fact, even in the context of the analysis of dialogue, that even today 'we still make teacher talk, and especially teachers' questions, the centre of observational and analytical gravity, providing many more categories of teacher talk than of student talk and therefore allowing ourselves a far less nuanced study of the latter' (Alexander 2015c, 433).
51 Jay *et al* 2017.
52 Alexander 2003, 2005a, 2005b.
53 Lefstein 2010; Lefstein and Snell 2011, 2014.
54 Lefstein and Snell 2014, 31.
55 Lefstein and Snell 2014, 36; quoting Alexander 2005b.
56 Hattie 2009.
57 Black *et al* 2003; Harlen 2014.
58 Galton 2008, x.
59 Resnick *et al* 2015, 1 (authors' italics).
60 Resnick 2015, 441.
61 Berliner and Biddle 1995, 50.
62 Flynn 1987; Neisser 1998, cited in Resnick *et al* 2015, 443–4.
63 Reported in Alexander 2005b and revisited in Lefstein and Snell 2014.
64 Alexander 1988, 2001a, 2003, 2005a, 2005b; Alexander and Willcocks 1995.
65 Britton 1969.
66 In the EEF project each school was given one Panasonic HC-W570EB-K Full HD Camcorder with Twin Camera, one Olympus VN-732PC 4Gb Digital Voice recorder, one Hama Star 61 Tripod, 1 Transcend 64 Gb Premium SDXC Class 10 Memory card, a camera case and batteries. The induction day included a video training session and participants were to able access online a specially-prepared training DVD.
67 Alexander 2015a.
68 Alexander 2015b.

69 Michaels and O'Connor 2012.
70 Lefstein and Snell 2014.
71 Alexander 2015c, 24.
72 Alexander 2015b.
73 The description in this section draws on the account provided in the evaluation report of Jay *et al* (2017).
74 Test details are at https://educationendowmentfoundation.org.uk/our-work/projects/dialogic-teaching/.
75 KS1 point score: students' scores in the tests at the end of Key Stage 1 (Y2, US 1st grade). These were used not to establish a baseline but to assess how far the intervention's impact depended on prior attainment.
76 A full account of the process evaluation, and copies of relevant protocols, appears in Jay *et al* 2017.
77 This section draws on Jan Hardman's contribution to Alexander *et al* 2017.
78 The dialogic teaching indicators were modified from Alexander 2017a, 40–4.
79 For coding frames and details of the analytical procedures and software used, see Hardman 2019, 2020.
80 See links to media stories at http://cprtrust.org.uk/about_cprt/media/media-coverage/.
81 This section draws on the contributions of Taha Rajab and Mark Longmore to analysis of the interview data and to its reporting in Alexander *et al* 2017.
82 Alexander *et al* 2017, 5–6.
83 This section again draws on Jan Hardman's contribution to the video analysis as reported in Alexander *et al* 2017; Hardman 2019, 2020.
84 Michaels and O'Connor 2015, 358.
85 Jay *et al* 2017, 4.
86 Jay *et al* 2017, 44–6.
87 Jay *et al* 2017, 44.
88 Higgins *et al* 2012.
89 Berliner 2002; Prideaux 2002; Norman 2003; Sullivan 2011; Ginsburg and Smith 2016; Pogrow 2017.
90 I am grateful to Frank Hardman and the late Harvey Goldstein for their technical comments on the dialogic teaching project's RCT.
91 Jay *et al* 2017, 24.
92 Jay *et al* 2017, 44.
93 Ginsburg and Smith 2016, ii.
94 Nevill 2016, 2.
95 Described in detail in Alexander 2020, 124–68.
96 They are listed in chapter 15.

17 The unquestioned answer

A Dialogic Teaching Companion, 106–23 (2020). The journal article adapted for Chapter 16 originally ended by positing explanations for the success of dialogic pedagogy, some grounded in evidence and others more speculative. That section has been replaced by this chapter, which takes advantage of research published since the EEF project and explores dialogic cause and learning consequence in greater depth.

We have known for some time that talk is essential to young children's cognitive development and learning. Now we have evidence that classroom talk that is configured reciprocally and dialogically is effective in relation to tested learning outcomes. But the research literature is less clear about which particular features of dialogic pedagogy exert the greatest leverage, or wherein lies dialogue's 'ingredient x'.

The parts and the whole

We start, however, with a caveat about the disaggregation that the quest for 'ingredient x' seems to invite. Take the 2014–17 Education Endowment Foundation (EEF) dialogic teaching project discussed in the previous chapter. Each of its two strands, pedagogical and professional, was designed holistically. So although it may have been statistically feasible to weigh the relative merits of, say, the teacher's 'questioning' moves and the 'extending' moves that then probe and build upon students' answers, such an exercise would have been logically untenable: for there can be no extending without questioning both before and after the student contribution that is to be extended. Questions before that contribution provoke a response which further questions can probe and build upon. Each repertoire relates to the others logically as well as in intent and practice. The same applies to the professional strand: while we exploited evidence showing that mentoring and video are effective tools of professional development, in our project these were interdependent, with mentors using the videos made by their teacher mentees as the primary focus of the mentoring sessions.

For the comprehensiveness of the project's conception of dialogic teaching was one of its defining features and strengths. In bearing simultaneously on talk's aspects and actors we believed it was more likely to generate an interactive

DOI: 10.4324/9781315169378-20

culture or stance that was *pervasively* dialogic than if we had tried to manipulate or train for, say, teacher questioning or feedback alone, or if we had concentrated only on small-group or whole-class discussion. What mattered, then, was the creation of a classroom ethos that became progressively and – we hoped instinctively – more dialogic in all its aspects.

Generic explanations

The project was comprehensive in another sense: it aimed to have application and purchase across the curriculum. That is why, in the trial, learning outcomes were assessed in three curriculum domains when in most EEF trials they are confined to one. This enabled EEF to venture, in its press release on the project evaluation report, its own ingredient x (the italics are mine):

> The consistent results *across subjects* suggest that the approach may improve children's overall thinking and learning skills rather than their subject knowledge alone. This is backed up by evidence summarised in the Sutton Trust/EEF Teaching and Learning Toolkit [constructed from findings from this and two other EEF projects, Philosophy for Children, and Thinking, Doing, Talking Science] that advises that *metacognition approaches – strategies that encourage pupils to plan, monitor and evaluate their learning* – are a particularly effective way of improving results.[1]

Here EEF extrapolates a shared feature from three projects that used different talk-based strategies to advance the same principle: giving students a stake in the planning and evaluating of what they learn, a strategy that echoes the studies of talk and text by McKeown and Beck, and Nystrand.[2] There can be, surely, no co-construction without co-ownership.

Lauren Resnick reviewed a much larger number of dialogic teaching studies before proposing three similarly generic explanations for the score gains achieved by the students involved.[3] First, there is what she calls the 'specific skills' explanation. Students in the projects reviewed by Resnick acquired 'knowledge or skills of performance that can be carried from one situation to another . . . With repeated opportunities for reasoning through dialogue, students imitate and refine skills that then . . . become available to them in other domains.' This explanation, in fact, is close to that offered by EEF. Dialogic teaching, then, includes pedagogical features that combine to advance students' learning in a range of curricular contexts. Perhaps 'generic' or 'transferable' would be a more exact epithet for these capacities than 'specific'.

Second, Resnick proposes an 'I can learn' explanation, a variation on the 'Pygmalion in the classroom' proposition that students rate themselves as they are rated,[4] so that the heavily judgemental ambience of traditional classrooms causes some to spiral triumphantly up in their views of themselves as learners while others spiral irredeemably down, with learning outcomes following the same trajectories. Dialogic teaching, however, proceeds on the basis that *all* students are capable thinkers and reasoners, and that (Resnick's words, my italics):

> *Students' ability to reason is implicit* when teachers ask them to reflect on their own thinking, to explain what led them to a particular conclusion, to put another student's idea in their own words, or to agree or disagree with an idea that has been presented.[5]

She adds, citing Resnick, Michaels and O'Connor:

> Moreover, these kinds of conversation can change *teachers'* views of their students' abilities by giving teachers greater access to their students' thinking processes. It is not unusual for teachers who have begun to use dialogic instruction to express surprise at how 'smart' their students are.[6]

So, this argument goes, if we believe in our students, make this clear in our dealings with them, and invite them to engage in the kind of reasoning that in IRF/IRE is closed off by the third turn (F/E), they will believe in themselves.

Resnick calls her third explanation the 'culture of argumentation'. This is about the power of the collective and what Mercer calls 'interthinking'.[7] It also provides a peer-peer variation on Vygotsky's zone of potential development (ZPD) and his maxim that 'what a child can do today with adult help he/she will be able to do independently tomorrow'.[8] Resnick writes (my italics and insertion):

> In a dialogic classroom, students engage [collectively] in a process of argumentation that has the potential to go beyond any *individual* student's power of reasoning. The students challenge one another, call for evidence, change their minds, and restate their claims, just as adults do . . . in the world outside school.[9]

I have added 'collectively' in parentheses to accentuate the counterpoint to 'individual'. The unvoiced final clause here is 'though *inside* school this is precisely what students are not normally expected to do'. 'Collective' heads the list of core principles or criteria of dialogic teaching.

Resnick adds that what matters is the argumentation as such rather than adherence to the rules of argument observed, or at least claimed, by logicians, and that 'the focus is on reasoning and knowledge rather than its forms of expression'.[10] This, again, aligns with EEF's meta-cognition conclusion, quoted earlier.

There is synergy between these three explanations, EEF's comment about student ownership and meta-cognition, and my approach to dialogic teaching. Meta-cognitive transfer across the curriculum was presumed in the EEF project's rationale and design, the randomised control trial appeared to confirm it and in its press release EEF, as we have seen, promoted it. Resnick's 'specific skills'/transfer explanation gives added point to the scope and diversity of the 'learning talk' repertoire that dialogic teaching aims to foster and exploit. This includes forms of student talk such as explaining, speculating, imagining, analysing, exploring, evaluating, justifying, questioning, discussing and arguing that are equally essential to literary, historical and scientific discussion and enquiry, while Galton's comparison of teachers and creative practitioners working with children shows how these forms are no less fundamental to artistic activity.[11] Similarly, Resnick's 'I can learn' hypothesis underlines the importance of dialogic teaching's principle of supportiveness, while her 'culture of argumentation' endorses the principles of collectivity and reciprocity.[12]

One further explanation suggests itself. Like EEF, Resnick properly concentrates on the transferability of dialogic habits of *student* talking and thinking across curriculum domains. But the 'culture of argumentation' embraces *teachers* no less than students, and 'I can learn' is most likely to convince the students when their teacher believes 'I can teach' (dialogically). After all, it takes two, at least, to dialogue. One reason why recitation persists is that it enables the teacher to retain control of the trajectories of both lesson content and student behaviour. Exposure to the consequences of publicly and perhaps incorrectly answering 'test' questions[13] is highly risky for students, and in the interest of maintaining their ascendancy some teachers prefer to keep things that way. Hence the well-documented student counter-culture of classroom risk-avoidance[14] and the tactics that students adopt in response to what they perceive as the prevailing view of 'communicative competence' – by, for example, bidding to answer questions in a way that 'balances the risks of not being noticed against the risks of being ignored as too enthusiastic'.[15]

In contrast, dialogic teaching is predicated on ceding to students a significant degree of control of both content and behaviour, and it therefore transfers some of the risk of public exposure back to the teacher, and not all teachers are happy with that. At the same time, the dialogic teaching principles of collectivity, reciprocity and supportiveness[16] aim in different ways to minimise students' sense of risk and their fear of its consequences, because only then will they talk as freely as true dialogue requires; while through the various teacher talk repertoires the teacher scaffolds exchanges that 'guide, prompt, reduce choice and expedite "handover" of concepts and principles'.[17]

Similarly, Galton's suggestive descriptions of creative practitioners working with children show – perhaps as much because they are not teachers as because they work in the creative domain – how they instinctively allow wait/thinking time and democratise control of exchanges: 'Creative practitioners seem more comfortable with silence. . . [and frequently] reverse roles so that the pupils and not the adult ask the questions.'[18] Compare this again with the EEF's deduction that the common feature in its trials of dialogic teaching, primary science and P4C was 'strategies that encourage pupils to plan, monitor and evaluate their learning'.

Resnick extrapolates one more important finding from the studies she reviews from the 2011 Pittsburgh conference: that most of them were able to achieve positive results, in terms of outcomes, retention and transfer, on the basis of relatively short but intensive spells of dialogue. That, too, chimes with the findings of our EEF project, in which an intervention of just 20 weeks accelerated attainment gains by two months; and with those for P4C, which concentrates broadly dialogic activities into one or two intensive sessions each week. We aim for a culture of argumentation, but can be reassured that a little dialogue appears to go a long way.

Specific explanations

In search of additional 'ingredients x' we turn next to two large-scale projects which have tried empirically to tease out the specific moves in dialogue that make the greatest difference. Earlier I warned of the dangers of attempting to disaggregate such moves in approaches that are conceived holistically as total pedagogies with interdependent elements. That warning should be kept in mind.

We start, inevitably, with the EEF project. As I have noted, the imposed methodology of an independently-executed randomised control trial concentrated on the impact of our dialogic teaching package *as a whole* on test score outcomes in English, mathematics and science. It did not look more discriminatingly at cause and effect. However, alongside the external RCT the project team undertook its own diagnostic study of classroom processes and teacher perceptions using interviews and coded lesson videos. The video analysis is particularly pertinent here because it compared lessons from matched intervention and control group classrooms and tracked changes in both groups over time, that is, at the start of the 20-week intervention to which just one of the groups was subject and close to its end.

The video dataset included 134 lessons in the three subjects tested in the RCT: English, mathematics and science. A report from the project team and two papers by Jan Hardman describe the methodology, including the video coding frame, in full.[19] Here it suffices to note the headline findings.

Lessons in the intervention group – the group whose students made significant test score gains by the end of the programme – showed a marked and increasing divergence from those in the control group in respect of the features listed next. (Note that the video analysis dealt only with teacher-student interaction in whole class settings: the project itself, in line with the imperative of repertoire, encouraged a wider range of interactive possibilities.)

- *The balance of closed and open questions.* Intervention group teachers made greater use of open questions than their control group peers.
- *Teacher talk moves.* Intervention group teachers made significantly greater use, especially in mathematics and science lessons, of wait time, revoicing (the teacher verifies his/her understanding of what the student has said), rephrasing of student contributions, seeking evidence of the student's reasoning, challenging students' responses and inviting justification of them.

- *Balance of recitation and discussion/dialogue.* Changing this balance in favour of the latter, while not excluding the former, was one of the intervention's chief aims, and with the intervention group teachers it was achieved.
- *Balance of brief and extended student contributions.* Again, the ratio of brief to extended student contributions shifted markedly towards the latter in the intervention group but remained constant in the control group.
- *The repertoire of student talk.* Perhaps most strikingly, students in the intervention group became markedly more expansive in their contributions and exhibited much higher levels of explanation, analysis, argumentation, challenge and justification. Their talk, then, was clearly more dialogic than that of their control group peers.'[20]

Taken together, these aspects of teacher and student talk can fairly be presumed to have contributed to the test score gains made by the intervention group students, and bearing in mind the concern I expressed earlier about disaggregating talk moves that are logically interdependent, the fact that our analysis was not able to differentiate the precise impact of the various dialogic features listed is not necessarily a failing.

However, one recent project has attempted to do just this. The 2015–17 ESRC-funded project 'Classroom dialogue: does it really make a difference for student learning?' was led by Christine Howe, Sara Hennessy and Neil Mercer. Bringing complex statistical techniques to bear on coded lesson videos from 78 classes in 48 schools featuring whole-class teaching rather than group work, they concluded that the most productive teacher talk moves in respect of student outcomes as measured in the Year 6 SATs (the tests in English and mathematics taken by 11-year-olds in English primary schools) were:

- 'Elaboration invitations', defined as 'invites building on, elaboration, evaluation, clarification of own or another's contribution.'
- 'Elaboration' (i.e. students' response to the first bullet point), defined as 'builds on, elaborates, evaluates, clarifies own or other's contribution'.
- 'Querying', defined as the teacher's 'doubting, full/partial disagreement, challenging or rejecting a statement'.[21]

These are consistent with the following higher frequency teacher talk moves associated with greater test score gains in the EEF project:

- Revoicing (teacher verifies own understanding of a student's contribution, which requires a student response, e.g. 'So, are you saying. . . ?', 'Then I guess you think. . . ?').
- Rephrasing (teacher asks a student to repeat or reformulate own or another student's contribution, e.g. 'Can you say that again. . . ?', 'In your own words, what did X say?').

- Evidence of reasoning (teacher stays with the same student, or asks another, and requests evidence of reasoning, e.g. 'Why do you think that. . . ?', 'What is your evidence?').
- Challenge (teacher provides a challenge or counter example, e.g. 'Does it always work that way?', 'What if. . . ?', 'Is that always true?').[22]

In our case, however, the range of higher frequency teacher talk moves (and corresponding student talk moves) in the intervention group was bigger. Interestingly, science was the anomaly in both projects. In the Howe *et al* ESRC project, the three moves listed were more productive for English and mathematics outcomes than for science; while in the EEF project it seemed that in science lessons our teachers used more obviously dialogic moves from the outset. We can speculate that the particular character of scientific questioning and reasoning may have been a factor, or – in the case of the Howe *et al* project – that because science is no longer included in the national tests at age 11 its teaching is lower stakes.

Purists and pragmatists

Another paper from the Howe/Hennessy/Mercer ESRC project[23] raises a rather different issue, and it too resonates with this book's approach. Howe's team used their video analysis to test what they claimed is an assumption by enthusiasts for dialogue that there is not much of it around, and that undiluted recitation remains the default. They showed that although recitation is indeed widespread, the classic IRF/IRE discourse structure is often mixed with moves that can be defined as dialogic.

For those of us who have taught, studied teaching and worked with teachers over many years this is hardly a revelation. Very few teachers are methodological purists, and although in many classrooms recitation may be the centre of gravity, the dynamics of classroom talk may orbit fluidly and not always predictably around it. Our approach to dialogic teaching has always acknowledged the fact of, and need for, such practical eclecticism, and views it as a strength rather than a weakness – hence the primacy of the idea of *repertoire*. So our approach actually includes not only recitation but also the much derided rote, because for certain purposes these fit the bill (the repetition that is rote's signature, for example, aids memorisation), and they therefore have their place in the repertoire of teacher-led talk alongside the discussion and dialogue to which we wish to give greater prominence. Eschewing all educational dichotomies as I have insisted we should, we should therefore also resist the polarising of recitation and dialogue. However, some advocates of dialogue, spurred by proselytising zeal, do just that, seeking an exclusivity in dialogue which is matched by their implacable opposition to recitation. Dialogue is thereby idealised, recitation parodied, and only the two are on offer. That is tough for teachers working in real-life classroom settings, for it may oversimplify the way they work, underestimate the quality of what they achieve, and set standards to which they are expected to aspire which are not so much unattainable as inappropriate.

The inclusiveness of our approach to dialogic teaching is, I believe, distinctive. Yet, in some commentaries that inclusiveness, and the idea of a generous repertoire that straddles patterns of talk that are both more *and less* dialogic, is missed. I go so far as to suggest that one reason why my *Towards Dialogic Teaching* proved so popular with teachers is that it spoke not to some unattainable dialogic ideal but to teaching as it is, to its often messy realities, to the tensions, compromises, frustrations and dilemmas that are intrinsic to the job.[24]

Principle, not recipe

Few people have put better than Martin Nystrand and Adam Gamoran the case for inclusivity, flexible repertoire, and the need for teaching, however configured, to be driven by pedagogical principle rather than technical recipe (and conversely the need to understand that supposedly dialogic moves may not live up to their billing). They therefore deserve to be quoted at length. The italics are theirs.

> The results of our study suggest that authentic questions, discussion, small-group work, and interaction, though important, do not categorically produce learning; indeed we observed many classes where this was not the case. We also found that recitation is not categorically ineffective; rather, its effectiveness varies depending on whether and how teachers expand IRE sequences. The underlying epistemology of classroom interaction defines the bottom line for learning: what ultimately counts is *the extent to which instruction requires students to think, not just report someone else's thinking* . . . Authentic questions, discussion and small group work have important instructional potential, but unless they are used in relation to serious instructional goals and, more important, unless they assign significant and serious epistemic roles to students that the students themselves can value, they may be little more than pleasant diversions.[25]

Or, as Michaels and O'Connor succinctly conclude from the evaluation of their Talk Science Project: 'The simple deployment of talk moves does not ensure coherence in classroom discussions or robust student learning.'[26]

Note that Nystrand's 'bottom line' (which he repeats in his 2019 autobiography[27]) is *not* an 'ingredient x' in the expected sense of one or more specific talk moves. Instead, it expresses the *quality and dynamics* of the interaction to be aimed for, allowing for the possibility that these can be approached by different routes.

If readers detect a certain ambivalence in the discussion so far, they are right, for the evidence seems to point simultaneously in two directions. On the one hand we have the proposition, born of pragmatism, understanding of the dilemmas, tensions and compromises of teaching as it is lived, and an essentially holistic stance on dialogic pedagogy, that what makes the difference is the transformation of classroom culture and relationships. That transformation can be effected by various means, but its trajectory always needs to be towards student engagement, empowerment and meta-cognition, or ensuring that students have a significant stake in the manner of their learning and the way it is conceived and discussed. It is this that unites Barnes's and Mercer's 'exploratory talk'; Resnick's 'I can learn'; her 'culture of argumentation'; the meta-cognitive capacities fostered by the three EEF projects; Nystrand's 'bottom line' of getting students to think for themselves rather than report or repeat what others have thought, said and written; Galton's insight from creative practitioners on the democratisation of classroom discourse; the preoccupation of Matusov, Boyd and Markarian with dialogic stance; Wegerif's idea of 'dialogic space'; and, as the corollary of all these, 'I can teach' – the teacher's confidence to offer students much greater agency in their talking and learning than is traditionally allowed, without feeling threatened or de-skilled, and the added confidence that comes from seeing that for all parties this works.

All this supports the principles of teacher repertoire, agency, choice and judgement that are central to this book's version of dialogic teaching. Among the various models of dialogic teaching jostling for space in an increasingly crowded educational market, there is no 'best buy'.

The third turn and the unquestioned answer

On the other hand, the evidence also takes us to a more specific destination. From the Howe/Hennessy/Mercer ESRC study we conclude that teacher talk moves which encourage students to elaborate their own and each other's ideas have particular potency, and this is confirmed by the video analysis in the EEF project, which showed the significantly higher incidence among intervention group teachers – those whose students made greater learning gains – of revoicing, rephrasing of student contributions, seeking evidence of the student's reasoning, challenging students' responses and inviting students to justify them; and of the consequential repertoire of talk displayed by the students: explanation, analysis, argumentation, challenge and justification. In similar vein, Nystrand is right to warn against presuming too much of dialogue and too little of recitation, as are Boyd and Rubin,[28] but he also argues that transformative learning is most likely when teachers 'ask authentic questions *and follow up student responses*'[29] (my italics).

This second strand of evidence points unerringly to a particular moment in the typical exchange: the third turn, or, whether the exchange is teacher-student or student-student, what happens after a question has been posed and an answer has been given. In recitation, the third turn is mostly predictable: 'F' or 'E', feedback or evaluation, both usually of a minimal kind. So while among discourse analysts 'initiation' (I) and 'response' (R) are treated neutrally as to intent and character, 'F' and 'E' carry specifically judgemental baggage from the outset.

But does it have to be like that? Neutrality would be sustained if 'F' and 'E' were replaced by a question mark, and indeed that would signal that this is the critical moment of choice: the moment when an exchange can stop or continue, when it can open up the student's thinking or close it down, when feedback can be replaced by feed-forward: IR(?). This is in line with the conclusion of Nystrand and Gamoran that 'recitation is not categorically ineffective; rather, its effectiveness varies depending on whether and how teachers expand IRE sequences'.[30] This, again, supports our principle of repertoire, and our warning about polarising recitation and dialogue.

From his classroom observations and recordings Neil Mercer has extrapolated five recurrent teacher moves that have their counterparts in everyday conversation, seek to 'build the future on the foundations of the past' and begin to fill the third-turn space in 'IR?'. They are:

- *recapitulation*: summarising and reviewing what has been said or done earlier;
- *exhortation*: encouraging students to 'think' or 'remember' what has been said or done earlier;
- *elicitation*: asking a question or questions intended to encourage students to reflect on what they have heard;
- *repetition*: repeating a student's answer, either to affirm it or encourage alternatives;
- *reformulation*: paraphrasing a student's response to make it more accessible to others or to improve upon it.[31]

I have re-ordered these (in Mercer's list exhortation comes last) so as to distinguish the two free-standing moves from those – repetition and reformulation – which are embedded in the three-part exchange structure as third-turn alternatives to F and E. (Elicitation can be either.) In fact, they may become so habitual that unless we are careful they may lose their power to stimulate and advance children's thinking. Thus, as Edwards and Mercer note, elicitations may be *cued* – that is, a question may incorporate a clue to its required answer – so heavily that answering questions degenerates into a mere word-completion ritual.[32] Repetition – like praise – may become so habitual, with every final word or phrase of the student repeated by the teacher, that it seems more like a verbal tic than a meaningful response. (Having become aware of this by viewing their lesson videos, teachers in the EEF project became perhaps overly self-conscious about it.) And reformulation may leave children wondering whether their answers are being celebrated, dismissed or charitably salvaged. In such circumstances, the paralinguistic is as eloquent as the linguistic.

No less important, of these five commonly-observed moves only elicitation and reformulation have potential to take a specific answer or statement forward, assuming that they are used deliberately and unambiguously. Yet on their own they hardly constitute a dialogic repertoire. It is not sufficient, then, to repeat or reformulate a pupil's contribution: what is said needs to be reflected upon, discussed, even argued about, and the dialogic element lies partly in getting pupils themselves to do this. Here the activities which accompany questioning in Palincsar and Brown's 'reciprocal teaching' – clarifying, summarising and predicting – may begin to break the question-answer-repetition mould of this barely-extended variant of recitation.[33]

Sarah Michaels and Cathy O'Connor have invested particularly heavily in this moment. They agree that repetition on its own may achieve little, and treat what they call 'revoicing' (cf. Mercer's 'reformulation') as a more productive alternative to the E (evaluation) move of IRE, because it 'contains a cue to the addressee to accept, reject, or clarify the speaker's interpretation of the addressee's prior utterance'[34] and it can 'create a sense of engagement, or helping the insecure or struggling student make their contribution in ways that can be heard and appreciated by others'.[35]

Of course, the cue needs to be acted on, and the insecure or indeed secure student needs to feel comfortable in taking up the teacher's invitation, and then in challenging the revoicing if it is deemed inaccurate or inadequate. In the fascinating paper quoted in the previous paragraph, O'Connor and Michaels recount their painstaking efforts to build on their initial insights about the potential of revoicing and how, through various projects and iterations over many years, these yielded the nine 'talk moves' in their *Talk Science Primer*,[36] all of which elaborate the third turn rather than the first or second, and therefore take as their starting point whatever the student has said and in different ways build on this to nudge the talking and thinking forward. These moves are comparable to, but go well beyond, the 'elaboration invitations' in the Howe, Hennessy and Mercer project.[37] They resonate, too, with the emphasis on *uptake* in the studies of Nystrand and his colleagues, uptake being either 'the incorporation of a previous answer into a subsequent question'[38] or 'when one conversant . . . asks someone else . . . about something the other person said'.[39] Nystrand stresses that 'to qualify as uptake, a question must incorporate a previous answer, not a previous question' because only then can it establish 'intertextual links between speakers . . . [and] promote coherence within the discourse'.[40]

The importance of the work of Michaels and O'Connor here is that it transforms descriptive categories into procedural and linguistic options that have been successfully trialled by teachers: 'say more', 'revoice', 'rephrase', 'add on', 'ask for evidence of reasoning', 'challenge' and so on.[41] Michaels and O'Connor argue that such moves enable the student

> to explicate his or her reasoning so the teacher gains a better sense of the student's understanding and all students can work with it. In the process of responding . . . the student also gains metacognitive and communicative skills that will support more robust reasoning in future turns.[42]

Which also takes us back to our claim that dialogic teaching empowers the teacher as well as the student because by giving him or her access to the student's thinking it facilitates a precision in assessment for learning that the closed third turn denies. (Like Philosophy for Children, assessment for learning – AfL – is a field whose ideas display synergy with those that inform dialogic teaching.)[43]

Elsewhere, joining forces with Jie Park and Renee Affolter, Michaels and O'Connor justify their claim that the third turn is pivotal for classroom talk in general and dialogic teaching in particular. Once again, the relevance of their approach to the stance taken here is such that I need to quote them at length:

> Why not focus on the teacher's first turn, and the quality of teachers' questions in starting a conversational sequence? Or why not focus on the second turn, exploring in detail what a student says that was prompted by the first turn? Why not focus on an interactive episode as a whole, instead of an utterance? The reason is that the third turn has a special status . . . The third turn in everyday conversation or the classroom looks both backwards and forward in a unique way . . . The third turn is where a lot of interesting things happen, things that can position students very differently, with respect to the teacher, their peers, and the academic content under consideration.[44]

That properly cautious phrase 'can position' reminds us that nothing is inevitable. The intention of a cued elicitation, which mirrors the mouthing of the prompter in the theatre wings, is transparent enough: it tells the student exactly what to say. But Mercer's recapitulation/reformulation and Michaels and O'Connor's revoice/rephrase may serve opposing purposes. In the spirit of dialogue they may indeed 'help pupils listen carefully to one another . . . share, expand and clarify their thinking';[45] or, in the guise of helpful scaffolding, they may revoice/rephrase in order to keep the student's thinking in line with the teacher's and effect a 'cognitive take-over'.[46] The latter is the risk or tendency that Segal and Lefstein call 'exuberant voiceless participation'.[47]

Yet provided that we remain alive to Austin's distinctions between an utterance's 'locutionary', 'illocutionary' and 'perlocutionary' force – or the difference between the face meaning, actual intention and consequences of what we say to students[48] – there is indeed an inexorable logic in all this, over and above what the research evidence suggests. For it is the third turn that makes talk dialogic rather than monologic, or fails to do so. A dyadic question and answer (IR) sequence is *dua*logic (two persons) but not *dia*logic, because control of its trajectory rests squarely with the questioner (I). The same applies in the triadic IRF/IRE sequence, because although in commenting on an answer a questioner may stand on the brink of dialogue, the questioner's comment is a unilateral judgement (F/E) and it reinforces rather than diminishes his or her control, so again the talk remains monologic. And it does so epistemically as well as pedagogically. That is to say, the handling of the third turn signals not only whose voices matter, but also the extent to which the knowledge with which teachers and students deal is immutable or negotiable, closed or open, singular in its meaning or capable of different interpretations, to be transmitted and dutifully replayed or open to scrutiny and exploration.

This, too, is the double pedagogical force of Bakhtin's celebrated maxim that 'if an answer does not give rise to a new question from itself, it falls out of the dialogue',[49] for it intimates the dialogue of ideas as well as persons. If there is no uptake or extending move, if an answer does not give rise to a new question, then not only is the sequence's forward learning momentum halted, but the thinking, understanding and misunderstanding embedded in the student's answer, and the teacher's opportunity to probe these to everyone's advantage, will also evaporate. Talk is transitory. Talk that matters is more likely to make its mark if it evokes some kind of response than if it passes unchecked; and student talk really does matter.

In thinking about how our classroom exchanges with students might be improved, we should attend not only to the unanswered question – a familiar enough focus of concern – but also to the unquestioned answer.

Whose question?

But there's a sting in the tail: who controls the third turn and who gets to ask those 'new questions' that in order to keep the dialogue alive every answer should prompt?

In teacher-led discussion, whether whole class or small group, that privilege falls to the teacher. James Dillon reports an exercise in which he observed 721 students engaging in discussion in 27 classrooms and heard questions from just eight of them. That's eight out of 721:

> Questions accounted for over 60 per cent of the teachers' talk and for less than one per cent of the students' talk . . . 80 questions per hour from each teacher and two questions per hour from all the students combined . . . not a single question from 713 adolescents nearing graduation from secondary school.[50]

The massive asymmetry of classroom discourse has been recognised as a near-constant since long before 1963, when 'Between the end of the Chatterley ban/And the Beatles' first LP' life was 'never better' for British poet Philip Larkin but US academic Ned Flanders preferred his self-denying 'law of two-thirds': two thirds of classroom time is devoted to talk, two thirds of this talking time is occupied by the teacher, and two thirds of teacher talk is direct instruction.[51] This asymmetry was one of the spurs to dialogic teaching, and it is useful to juxtapose Flanders and Dillon because, having formulated his 'law', Flanders continued to treat IRF/IRE as the default for his classroom observation instruments, paradoxically encouraging future researchers to give far more attention to the talk of the teacher than to that of the student, even as they cited his critique of this imbalance in what they were observing. Dillon, in contrast, was so determined to break the mould of asymmetric discourse that he inverted the usual convention of starting with teacher talk moves and began one of his books with student questions, arguing that it is they that are most likely to unlock learning.[52]

Yet Dillon also showed how the teaching culture into which students and teachers have been socialised combines with its unequal power relations to make it hard for even the best-intentioned teachers to generate a significant shift in the frequency and character of student questions for as long as they themselves make the initiating moves. So perhaps the most direct way to signal and invite this shift is for the teacher to withdraw so that students have no option but to ask and answer the questions themselves. That, of course, is the essential dynamic of small-group discussion and it is one good reason why, alongside the well-managed third turn in teacher-student exchanges, small-group discussion is essential to the repertoire of dialogic teaching.[53] But if Dillon is right, students and teachers need not only to agree norms or ground rules for discussion in the way that most dialogists advise, but also to ensure that these apply to all parties – for ground rules are more typically confined to how *students* should behave. It is the *teacher's* task, following Dillon again, to 'provide for student questions, make room for them, invite them in, wait patiently for them, welcome the question [and] sustain the asking'.[54]

Conclusion and a meta-analytic footnote

Back, then, to 'ingredient x'. In seeking to understand what it is about dialogic teaching that makes a difference we arrive at both holistic and atomistic explanations. On the one hand, the sum of dialogue's parts yields a classroom culture, a pattern of relationships and a pedagogical and epistemic stance that together foreground and explicitly signal the empowerment of the student as speaker, thinker, reasoner, learner and evaluator. Such empowerment may by attained by various patterns of organisation, most obviously though not inevitably, and certainly not exclusively, by small-group discussion, because when managed well this turns students from answerers into questioners. It was this transformation that enabled Nystrand's students to use peer discussion so strikingly to improve the quality of their writing.[55]

On the other hand, studies that have attempted to isolate the points of maximum leverage in student-*teacher* talk converge on the third turn and the various moves through which, at that critical moment, teachers aim more directly to steer the empowerment to which I have referred. The two categories of explanation are complementary, so while it is clear that we should be aiming for nothing less than the comprehensively dialogic classroom, there is considerable practical value in knowing where, in the way we handle the classroom talk from which so much else flows, we and our students might concentrate our efforts:

overall dialogic stance and classroom culture, students as questioners, student-student small-group discussion, opening up the relationship between talking, reading and writing, enhanced teacher-student exchanges focusing closely on the third turn . . . and more.

There is one piece missing from this explanatory jigsaw: evidence from studies that lie outside the domain of dialogic pedagogy. For to confine our quest for explanations of the power of dialogue to the dialogic literature is to risk missing something important. An obvious port of call is John Hattie's synthesis of 800 meta-analyses of research on the relationship between specific teaching approaches and student learning outcomes.[56]

Hattie's study is as controversial as it is vast, for its judgements of efficacy are based on effect sizes and the research paradigms that produce them, and a great deal of research offering different but equally valuable insight into teaching is thereby ruled out; and his decision to set the bar at an effect size of 0.40 across 800 meta-analyses and over 50,000 individual studies of different kinds, topics and scales may also be regarded as problematic. Further, his synthesis covers relatively few randomised control trials and for these the Education Endowment Foundation (EEF) treats as statistically significant effect sizes lower than 0.40, as one of its senior staff argues:

> Don't take the magnitude of effect sizes at face value. Huge effect sizes (more than +1.00) are most likely the results of poor experiments, but a small size (+0.10) from a large, well-run trial might still be educationally important. Compare like with like.[57]

Hattie's conclusions are mostly congruent with our own, though on the basis of the studies he reviews he is cautious about small-group learning and downright sceptical about the teacher as facilitator. However, he elaborates neither strategy in terms that the advocates of small-group discussion or P4C, as discussed here, would recognise, equating both with lack of teacher guidance. His preference, again on the basis of the studies reviewed, is for teachers taking a proactive and active role, and he is intensely critical of the general disdain for direct instruction, on the grounds that more often than not it is based on a chalk-and-talk caricature of what actually takes place when the teacher consciously guides the student's learning. Direct instruction, as Hattie defines it, is not a parody of recitation but an approach where:

> The teacher decides the learning intentions and success criteria, makes them transparent to the students, demonstrates them by modelling [and] evaluates if they understand. . .[58]

But while Hattie finds high effect sizes for specific strategies that are part of dialogic teaching as discussed here – reciprocal teaching, feedback, meta-cognition, self-questioning – it is his overall conclusion that speaks most directly to our approach. Uncannily echoing our preoccupation with the third turn, and indeed with transfer, he says:

> The art of teaching, and its major successes, relate to 'what happens next' – the manner in which the teacher reacts to how the student interprets, accommodates, rejects, and/or reinvents the content and skills, how the student relates and applies the content to other tasks.[59]

Then, providing a strikingly dialogic corrective to the top-down view of feedback as embodied in classic IRF, Hattie says (his italics):

> It was only when I discovered that feedback was most powerful when it is from the *student to the teacher* that I started to understand it better. When teachers seek . . . feedback from students as to what students know, what they understand, where they make errors, when they have misconceptions, when they are not engaged – then teaching and learning can be synchronised and powerful. Feedback to teachers makes learning visible.[60]

This is of a piece with Dillon's insistence on the need for students to ask their own questions, and with my discussion elsewhere of voice.[61] Reciprocal teaching finally escapes from the bonds or habits of recitation, actual or disguised, when it entails reciprocal questioning and feedback as well as, or as part of, the extending moves in the third turn. Hattie doesn't go quite that far, but he justly celebrates, under the banner of 'visible teaching – visible learning', those moments when 'teachers see learning through the eyes of the student and . . . students see themselves as their own teachers'.[62]

Squaring the circle between direct instruction and students as their own teachers, Hattie would probably argue, is not as problematic as it may seem, for he reconceptualises direct instruction as necessarily reciprocal, and this quality immediately distances it from recitation. Hattie's meta-analytic syntheses certainly reinforce several 'ingredient x' specifics that we have discussed here, but equally they are in line with our belief in the importance of a *stance* that is identifiably dialogic and pervades the entire enterprise in which teachers and students are jointly engaged.

Notes

1 https://educationendowmentfoundation.org.uk/news/eef-publishes-four-new-independent-evaluations/, 7 July 2017 (accessed May 2018).
2 McKeown and Beck 2015; Nystrand 2019.
3 Resnick 2015, 444–7.
4 Rosenthal and Jacobson 1968.
5 Resnick 2015, 446.
6 Resnick 2015, 446; Resnick *et al* 2010.
7 Mercer 2000.
8 Vygotsky 1963, 30. Joan Simon, who undertook one of the first English translations of Vygotsky's work, and did so in consultation with Luria, told me that Luria believed that 'potential' development is a better translation than the usual 'proximal'.

9 Resnick 2015, 446.
10 Resnick 2015, 447.
11 Galton 2008.
12 Interested readers will need to check out the full dialogic teaching framework in Alexander 2020, chapter 7, but we can at least divulge the six principles. *Collective* (the classroom is a site of joint learning and enquiry, and whether in groups or as a class students and teachers are willing and able to address learning tasks together). *Supportive* (students feel able to express ideas freely, without risk of embarrassment over contributions that are hesitant or tentative, or that may be judged 'wrong', and they help each other to reach common understandings). *Reciprocal* (participants listen to each other, share ideas, ask questions and consider alternative viewpoints; and teachers ensure that they have ample opportunities to do so). *Deliberative* (participants discuss and seek to resolve different points of view, they present and evaluate arguments, and they work towards reasoned positions and outcomes). *Cumulative* (participants build on their own and each other's contributions and chain them into coherent lines of thinking and understanding). *Purposeful* (classroom talk, though sometimes open-ended, is nevertheless structured with specific learning goals in view).
13 Nystrand *et al* 1997.
14 Doyle 1983; Pollard 1985; Galton 2008.
15 Edwards 1992, 235.
16 See note 12.
17 Bruner 1978, 1996, 2006.
18 Galton 2008, 38.
19 Alexander *et al* 2017; Hardman 2019, 2020.
20 Alexander *et al* 2017, 8–9; see also Hardman 2019, 2020.
21 Howe *et al* 2019, 15.
22 Alexander *et al* 2017, 11.
23 Vrikki *et al* 2018.
24 Alexander 2017a. I first explored the notion of teaching as intrinsically dilemma-bound in a video-based enquiry with a group of teachers in the mid-1980s (Alexander 1988, reprinted in Alexander *et al* 1995). With John Willcocks and Nick Nelson I revisited the idea in a mid-1990s study of educational change and professional response (Alexander *et al* 1996), returning to it yet again in a commentary on a lesson video and transcript for (Lefstein and Snell 2014, 72–4) entitled 'Triumphs and dilemmas of dialogue'.
25 Nystrand and Gamoran 1997, 72.
26 Michaels and O'Connor 2015, 358.
27 Nystrand 2019, 91–2.
28 Boyd and Rubin 2006.
29 Nystrand 2019, 107.
30 Nystrand and Gamoran 1997, 72.
31 Mercer 2000, 52–6.
32 Edwards and Mercer 1987, 142–6.
33 Palincsar and Brown 1984; Brown and Palincsar 1989.
34 O'Connor and Michaels 2018.
35 O'Connor and Michaels 2018.
36 Michaels and O'Connor 2012.
37 Howe *et al* 2019.
38 Nystrand and Gamoran 1997, 37–8.
39 Nystrand *et al* 2003, 145.
40 Nystrand *et al* 2003, 146.
41 Michaels and O'Connor 2012, 11.
42 Michaels and O'Connor 2015, 348.
43 Black *et al* 2003.
44 Park *et al* 2017, 18.
45 Michaels and O'Connor 2012, 11.

46 Edwards and Westgate 1994, 144.
47 Segal and Lefstein 2015, 1.
48 Austin 1962.
49 Bakhtin 1986, 168.
50 Dillon 1988, 9.
51 Cited and discussed in Dunkin and Biddle 1974, 54–7. Apologies to the memories of Philip Larkin and D.H. Lawrence.
52 Dillon 1988, 6–41.
53 Barnes and Todd 1977, 1995.
54 Dillon 1988, 24.
55 Nystrand 2019, 89; Nystrand *et al* 1997.
56 Hattie 2009.
57 Haslam 2018. For the EEF effect size/months' progress conversion table see: https://educationendowmentfoundation.org.uk/evidence-summaries/about-the-toolkits/attainment/ (accessed July 2019). Comparing like with like, in the case of EEF trials, must include methodological anomalies such as: the absence of pre-test; missing data; the insistence that even if they withdraw from a project before it starts and are in no way involved in it, schools that provisionally agree to take part must be included in the analysis; and a professional development programme that in our case was confined by the terms of the grant to a much shorter period than the research evidence on effective professional development advises. EEF admits that all of these are likely to cause effects to be underestimated (Jay *et al* 2017).
58 Hattie 2009, 206.
59 Hattie 2009, 2.
60 Hattie 2009, 173.
61 Alexander 2020, 53–60. See also this book, 269–72.
62 Hattie 2009, 238.

18 Dialogic pedagogy in a post-truth world

Keynote at the EARLI Conference on *Argumentation and Inquiry as Venues for Civic Education*, Jerusalem (2018). Published as 'Whose discourse? Dialogic pedagogy in a post-truth world' for *Dialogic Pedagogy: an international online journal*, 7 (2019).[1] An abbreviated version appears in the *Routledge International Handbook of Research in Dialogic Education* (eds Mercer *et al* 2020), while a Danish translation of the full version is in *Dialogisk pædagogik, kreativitet og læring* (eds Dysthe *et al* 2020).

In their wide-ranging evidence review, Park, Michaels, Affolter and O'Connor confirm that dialogic pedagogy accelerates learning across students, grades and knowledge domains; but noting that such talk remains uncommon they warn of 'a lack of shared conceptualisations of what [it] is and how best to characterise it'.[2] Yet an earlier review by Howe and Abedin claimed a 'shared conceptual core' with merely 'divergence around the edges'.[3]

The difference between these two assessments could be accounted for by the fact that one was undertaken four years after the other, by which time the rapid expansion of the field and its literature may have amplified rather than reduced conceptual divergence. Or it could mean that such differences as exist are so fundamental that not even the authors of literature reviews can escape them. George Bernard Shaw may or may not have aphorised that 'The biggest single problem in communication is the illusion that it has taken place', but if authorities cannot agree on whether they agree we should take note.

Dialogue comes to most European languages via Latin from the Greek *dialogos*, a conversation, and for some people conversation is all that dialogue ever means. But dialogue is also the exchange of ideas, while when heightened by conscious effort it enables us to expose, explore and resolve competing points of view. Similarly, 'argument' may be a mere statement or proposition, but it may also signify the making and testing of a case, a well-tempered debate between opposing viewpoints, or indeed an ill-tempered quarrel. In many languages other than English the words for argument in these contrasting senses are different, so there is less room for ambiguity. But the community of educational dialogue and argumentation is international, and translation, especially in the realm of ideas, is not an exact science, so we should treat such keywords with caution.

DOI: 10.4324/9781315169378-21

Back, therefore, to 'dialogue' as conversation. The simple definition becomes a complex concept at the point when conversation acquires a purpose. Thereafter, dialogue is stance as well as process. In classrooms the stance is self-evidently relational, certainly epistemological, probably ethical and conceivably ideological, and, both separately and in combination, these properties intimate a barely containable plurality. Some members of the research community seek, evidentially or conceptually, to impose order by describing dialogue; others prescribe the form it should take. As for 'dialogic teaching', it has both multiple stipulative definitions and a vaguely generic one. Stipulatively, I have used the term my way since the early 2000s, others use it their way, and whether the twain or many shall meet is a matter of chance. Generically, 'dialogic teaching' may signify no more than talk that replaces IRF/IRE[4] by discussion, without specifying that discussion's purpose or character. Indeed, used without explanation the term 'dialogic teaching' may be little more than virtue signalling: IRF/IRE bad, dialogic teaching good.

The definitional differences that are most likely to confound even the illusion of communication are those that stem from disciplinary affiliations. The fact that talk, dialogic or otherwise, interests cognitive psychologists, sociologists, anthropologists, philosophers, psycholinguists, sociolinguists, ethnolinguists, pragmatists, comparative linguists, discourse analysts and conversation analysts (among others), might justify celebration that its importance is so widely recognised, except that this plurality reduces prospects for mutual understanding still further.

For disciplinary perspective, or what Park *et al*, following Emig, call a 'governing gaze',[5] determines what we look at, how we look at it, and what, having looked, we see. Then, in application, it shapes our view of what dialogue ought to be about. Some seek to validate the dialogic claim by reference to student performance in standardised tests. Others hold that dialogue, argumentation and discussion serve very different purposes of equal educational significance; while a case can be made for regarding these kinds of talk as of intrinsic value to the development of mind and culture regardless of what schools choose to teach and test. Dialogue, in short, may be a means or an end, a way of doing or of being.[6] It may be a pedagogy narrowly defined, a necessary educational goal which is at once pedagogical, epistemic and ethical, as commended in the Cambridge Primary Review,[7] or indeed an education in itself.[8]

Attempting to make sense of all this, Lefstein and Snell[9] posit six quasi-paradigmatic dialogic concepts – or perhaps stances – each with its own questions, values and goals, and for good measure its own guru: dialogue as the interplay of voices (Bakhtin), as critique (Socrates), as thinking together (Vygotsky), as relationship (Buber), as empowerment (Freire), and as interactional form (no guru specified). Lefstein and Snell then juxtapose these stances with four models of dialogic practice: Nystrand's dialogically organised instruction,[10] Mercer's exploratory talk,[11] the 'accountable talk' of Resnick, Michaels and O'Connor,[12] and my own version of dialogic teaching.

Next, seeking to expose disagreement as well as consensus, Kim and Wilkinson compare the versions or visions of dialogic pedagogy of Freire, Burbules, Nystrand, Wells, Wegerif, Matusov, Mercer, Boyd, Reznitskaya, Mortimer and Scott, Juzwik, Lefstein and myself before identifying three 'points of contention' that underlie the differences that emerge: the balance of significance given to linguistic *form* and *function* and the way, as explored by Boyd and Markarian,[13] that this relationship is perceived; the degree to which talk is embedded in the wider classroom culture or detached from it; and whether dialogic pedagogy is viewed as a specific way of organising classroom talk or as a general approach that can be implemented in different ways.[14]

Conceptual differences such as those exposed in these reviews are marginal, *pace* Howe and Abedin, only if one concedes that dialogic pedagogy is little more than technique; a view perhaps reinforced by the use of standardised tests as the default measure of its effectiveness. Since it is evident that dialogic pedagogy can do, be and produce much more than this, the extent of a 'shared conceptual core' remains open to question.

A collision of discourses

So what else can dialogue be and do? I now stir the definitional waters (and mix my metaphors) by registering what I see as a widening chasm between the ways of talking and reasoning that are cultivated inside the school, whether dialogic or non-dialogic, and those that students encounter outside it. Indeed, I want to propose that while the gradualist agenda for talk reform at scale extrapolated from the reviews cited – clarify concepts, extend evidence, consolidate proof of concept(s), disseminate practice, improve training – pursues the leisurely logic of academic enquiry, it makes educational as opposed to technical sense only if it also confronts this sociocultural collision of discourses, and recognises the urgency of doing so.

Let me elaborate. For some students the norms of pedagogical, curricular and wider cultural discourse may be more or less in harmony. Others experience well-researched dissonances relating to class, race and gender; and they discover how academic and everyday registers diverge – inevitably so, for opening up new ways of knowing, understanding and hence of naming, expressing and communicating is the essence of schooling.

But divergence has lately morphed into confrontation. On the one hand we have the sedimented habits and values embodied in school curriculum domains and the more or less rational and courteous ways of accessing, interrogating and verifying the knowledge that such domains embody. But on the other hand we witness the raucous free-for-all of social media, the ascendancy of ephemeral and anonymous online content over the verifiable and attributable knowledge of book and laboratory, the mischievous anarchy of fake news, the reduction of judgemental nuance to the binary 'like'/'dislike', the trolling and abuse that for many people have replaced discussion and debate; and the sense not so much that truth claims are open to question, as of course they always should be, as that for many in the public and political spheres truth is no longer a standard to which they feel morally obliged to aspire.

As if to prove his immunity from this basic moral standard and pronounce the Overton window well and truly shattered, a democratically-elected American president was able to make, according to the *Washington Post*, 30,573 'false or misleading claims' during his four-year term of office, or an average of 21 falsehoods each day, yet still remain president.[15] These culminated in the 'Big Lie' of his claiming, against all the evidence, that the re-election in 2020 that he believed was his right was stolen from him, and then whipping up his supporters to impose his presidency by force. Just how close they came to succeeding was revealed six months later by the *New York Times* in a painstaking 40-minute video of footage of the storming of the Capitol Building compiled from CCTV and numerous smartphones.[16]

At the time of writing, Trump's case is egregious but far from unique, for in extreme form it displays tendencies that have afflicted the leadership of many other countries that call themselves democratic, as well as those whose regimes are openly autocratic: the bullying braggadocio and narcissism of the would-be alpha male; the manipulation of information; the appeals to people's worst instincts rather than their best; the stoking and exploitation of racism, misogyny and homophobia; the sustained attacks on the press, judiciary and other institutions of civil society that provide the checks and balances that good government requires. And, insidiously but dangerously, the erosion of what Levitsky and Ziblatt call the 'soft guardrails' of democracy:

> mutual toleration, or the understanding that competing parties accept one another as legitimate rivals; and forbearance, or the idea that politicians should exercise restraint in deploying their institutional prerogatives.[17]

The target here was Trump and Trumpism, which at the time of writing are hitting the headlines less frequently than they did between 2016 and 2021; though they have not gone away, and indeed are re-grouping for the 2022 midterm and the 2024 presidential. But Levitsky and Ziblatt could equally have been referring to the UK, where fact-checkers have been working overtime on the sayings and doings of the Conservative government's front bench[18] and Peter Oborne has warned that 'with Trump gone, [Boris] Johnson became the only leader of a Western liberal democracy openly set on challenging international norms', quoting the former British ambassador to the US who remarked 'how fascinated Johnson had seemed by Trump and his use of language':

> the limited vocabulary, the simplicity of the messaging, the disdain for political correctness, the sometimes incendiary imagery, and the at best intermittent relationship with facts and the truth.[19]

In the UK, as in the United States, party loyalty now overrides procedural custom and constitutional obligation; as does the 'tribal epistemology' of elevating partisan narrative, however ludicrous, above objective evidence.[20] Just as all but a handful of Republicans have stuck with Trump's lies, most Conservative MPs have acquiesced in Johnson's mendacity and his refusal, when found out, to do as the Ministerial Code requires.

But MPs of all parties have at least begun to register some of the challenges posed by the political use of social media. In 2018, a parliamentary select committee documented extensive evidence that digital media had been exploited to play to voters' fears and prejudices and influence their voting plans and behaviour in the 2016 US presidential election, the 2016 UK Brexit referendum, and elections in France, Germany, Spain, Africa and Latin America. Meanwhile, there was growing concern about the extent to which social media had come to dominate children's lives, skew their development and exploit their vulnerability.[21] The committee concluded:

> Urgent action needs to be taken . . . to build resilience against misinformation and disinformation into our democratic system . . . Our democracy is at risk. Our education system should [equip] children with the necessary tools to live in our digital world, so that their mental health, emotional well-being and faculty for critical thinking are protected . . . Digital literacy should be the fourth pillar of education, alongside reading, writing and maths.[22]

Children must certainly acquire the knowledge and skills necessary for coping in a digital world, but I am less sanguine about bolting digital literacy onto a curriculum that in other respects remains untouched. Conspicuously unchallenged is the belief that the so-called '3Rs' are the three immovable 'pillars' of school education; and that this hoary definition, which shackled Britain's schools for the urban masses in the nineteenth century but goes back 1400 years to St Augustine's 'legere et scribere et numerare', can be made fit for the twenty-first century by adding another 'literacy' but without challenging the assumption that oracy is merely incidental.

Some see the task in terms of what England's national curriculum calls PSHE (personal, social and health education); others reach for the nostrums of civic education. Traditionally restricted to imparting received wisdom about the institutions of government and the values that are held to underpin them (in Britain officially defined as 'democracy, the rule of law, individual liberty, and . . . respect for and tolerance of those with different faiths and beliefs, and . . . those without faith'),[23] this version of civic education sanitises politics and idealises citizenship. Some might add that it confirms the school as instrument of cultural and economic reproduction,[24] if not as full-blown 'ideological state apparatus'.[25] There is little space in the traditional and somewhat Hirschian view of civic education for the awkward question, let alone for the critical pedagogy of a Freire or Giroux.[26]

The handling of talk in schools may be no less hegemonic. In Britain, exclusive and expensive private schools used to train the nation's future leaders in the art of public speaking and adversarial debate so as to send them into the world articulate, confident and ready to take control. This tradition goes back centuries to when classical and then renaissance rhetoric were fundamental to a gentleman's education.[27] Meanwhile, schools for the ungentlemanly major-ity (of either gender) pinned their faith on the 3Rs and at all costs avoided unleashing the subversive possibilities of talk. In Britain, the contrast between private education for leadership and state education for followership is still evident in the social and educational profiles of senior politicians, the private/state school opposition of liberal and instrumental curricula, and the struggle to persuade government to give spoken language the prominence in state schools that it deserves.

Such conditions highlight the challenge facing those who believe, following Dewey,[28] that a deliberative democracy requires a deliberative pedagogy. For, as Kakutani says, 'Without commonly agreed-upon facts . . . there can be no rational debate . . . Without truth, democracy is hobbled.'[29] Equally, when immediately after the Second World War George Orwell warned that 'The present political chaos is connected with the decay of language',[30] he fore-shadowed our own present, for the abuse of public language is symptomatic of what in some countries is a democratic malaise and in others is a crisis. And in considering where all this might lead we recall Hannah Arendt:

> The ideal subject of totalitarian rule is not the convinced Nazi or the con-vinced Communist, but people for whom the distinction between fact and fiction . . . and . . . between true and false . . . no longer exists.[31]

In light of all this, I suggest that consideration of the future of dialogic peda-gogy might encompass not only conceptual clarification, evidence of impact, strategies for professional development, but also four new imperatives. They are *language, voice, argument* and, as both subset and goal of the latter, *truth*. These provide the focus for the remainder of this chapter.

Language

Cued by Orwell, we nominate language as the pivot. Language makes us human, powers thought, evokes learning, conveys culture, coheres community, and – for better or worse – tempers or inflames public discourse.

We approach this first post-truth imperative by way of a pedagogy that explicitly links spoken language with democratic education and engagement. 'Accountable talk' was first proposed by Resnick during the 1990s[32] and devel-oped with Michaels and O'Connor, who preferred the term 'academically productive talk'.[33] It has three interdependent facets. *Accountability to community,* later modified to *accountability to the learning community,* establishes and main-tains the culture of classroom talk that is essential to collective sense-making and learning – listening, respecting others' ideas, building on each other's con-tributions and so on. *Accountability to standards of reasoning* 'emphasises logical connections and the drawing of reasonable conclusions'. *Accountability to knowledge* requires that speakers base what they say on 'facts, written evidence or other publicly accessible information that all . . . can access'.[34]

This triple insistence on accountability – communal, rational, epistemic – speaks to the conduct of public and policy discourse no less than to that of teaching and learning. Michaels, O'Connor and Resnick acknowledge, as this chapter does, the mismatch between what we strive for within classrooms and what students may encounter outside them; and 'though . . . we have made some progress in . . . classrooms . . . there is much we still do not know about how best to set up the conditions for truly democratic discourse on a wide scale'.[35] Yet accountable talk remains a powerful ideal. It links classrooms with democratic practice not indirectly or by exhortation as in traditional civic education, but by being of itself participatory and deliberative; and it has been applied through a battery of talk moves for the third turn in ways that are both practical and successful.[36] But its authors also speak of unfinished business, and in that spirit I propose a fourth strand: *accountability to language*, and specifically accountability to spoken language.

What do I mean by this? In the first instance, talk must be the object of learning as well as its medium. In the 2014–17 EEF dialogic teaching project 'talking about talk' was the first of 11 cycles in a 20-week programme combining professional development with teaching and video analysis, and it remained prominent throughout. Similarly, Dawes, Mercer and Wegerif initiated their *Thinking Together* programme with a group of five lessons fronted by 'talk about talk'.[37]

Out of such foundational activities can come, alongside ground rules for classroom talk of the kind with which we are all familiar, a heightened awareness of talk's possibilities; of the interplay between linguistic and paralinguistic aspects; of the dynamics of turn-taking; of code, register, accent and dialect and their social ramifications; of the relationship between discourse form, function and context; of the language of argumentation; and, salient here, of the nature, uses and impact of rhetoric.

Such metalinguistic understanding is sensitised and deepened through audio and video. Teachers in several of our projects have shared and discussed with their students the lesson videos they initially intended for their own self-study, with striking results. These teachers literally 'made talk visible' to their students.[38] Ever the pioneer, Cazden was doing this, though with audio, several decades ago.[39]

However, video-prompted 'talk about talk', if untutored, may concentrate more on talk's paralinguistic features than its structure and meaning, or what we see rather than what we hear.[40] Carter's work on the grammar of talk rebalances the focus. Using computer corpora of naturalistic spoken English, he shows how written and spoken forms are different not only in obvious respects like formality and fluency but also in their structure, yet that sufficient consistencies emerge from corpus analysis of discourse markers, word order, ellipsis, deixis and incremental rather than subordinate clauses for the word 'grammar' to be appropriate.[41]

Carter's grammar of talk is descriptive, not normative. It is an aid to understanding the relationship between conversational structure and meaning, not a manual for 'correct' speaking, and in a country like the UK where debates about 'correct' or 'standard' English are sharply politicised this proviso requires emphasis. A grammar of talk begins to do for talk what literary analysis does for text. But it is only a beginning, and if talk is as important as we believe then we might also consider whether tools of discourse analysis used for researching the talk of teachers and students might feature in the education of students themselves, and indeed the place in the school curriculum of linguistic analysis of the kind hitherto confined to universities. These possibilities are now being actively canvassed in the UK.[42]

Talking about talk applies equally in the context of democratic education, for leaving aside the question of whether we live in an Orwellian age of language decay, talk is the medium through which politicians engage with the electorate, even if at one stage removed via tweets and television debates. In the UK I have charted four signature discourses through which policies may be advocated and contrary views marginalised. The *discourse of derision* uses ridicule or abuse to discredit or at least neutralise ideas and evidence that are politically inconvenient.[43] The *discourse of dichotomy* reduces complex issues to a binary choice between caricatured alternatives and the politics of them and us. The *discourse of myth* peddles inflated claims while belittling what others have achieved in order to lower the baseline against which delivery on policy promises will be set. And if the discourse of myth is about the destruction of the past, the *discourse of meaninglessness* destroys language itself, for it evades or obfuscates meaning, parades the old as new, but once unpicked collapses into a tangle of cliché and tautology.[44]

The discourses of derision, dichotomy, myth and meaninglessness transparently flout Grice's maxims governing the relation between logic and conversation: *quantity* (a contribution should give as much information as is needed and no more), *quality* (it should be well-founded and true), *relation* (it should be relevant) and *manner* (it should be clear and orderly in delivery).[45]

Of course, such negative discourses may be offset by the judicious language, serious argument, defensible evidence and intelligibility to which politicians of integrity remain committed. Yet this everyday contrast underlines the argument that examining how political language works should be part of students' democratic education; just as, in their education as a whole, talk should be the object as well as the means of their study. Equally, having recourse to generic tests of the argumentative power and validity of language as used, such as those cited here by Grice and (below) by Walton and Toulmin, or with a specific focus on dialogic pedagogy,[46] or by the proponents of philosophy for children,[47] can make talk a powerful tool for cultural and civic engagement no less than for learning more narrowly defined.

Voice

Of 1 September 1939, that fateful day when Hitler's forces surged into Poland, W.H. Auden lamented that voice was all he had – all that any of us have – to 'undo the folded lie . . . the lie of Authority whose buildings grope the sky'.[48] Today he would have something to say about that other demagogue whose grotesquely gilded skyscrapers allegorised the brazen extravagance of his far from folded lies; whose groping was animal no less than celestial, and whose followers stormed the Washington Capitol in an almost-successful attempt to overthrow the elected government – in which mission, in 2022 or 2024, they may yet succeed. But voice, here, is what matters. Citizenship is the exercise of voice as well as vote. Citizens use their voices to name and nail the lie, to argue for what they believe is right and against what they believe is wrong. Voice is where democracy starts, and voice is what autocracy seeks to stifle.

Like our other keywords, 'voice' has several meanings. In life we speak, shout, scream, whisper or sing, and these contrasting physical exercises of our vocal cords express intentions, opinions, ideas, emotions, wants and needs: indeed, who we are. Grammarians distinguish the active and passive voices of verbs, and stylists argue over their proper use. Writers explore the vocal interplay of author, narrator and character and the different writer/reader relationships afforded by using the first, third or second person pronoun to subjectify voice, objectify it or render it ambiguous.

Within classrooms Segal and Lefstein[49] differentiate four senses of 'voice': having the opportunity to speak; expressing one's own ideas; speaking on one's own terms; and being heeded. These stages in the progress of the classroom exchange, from permission to speak to acknowledgement of what is spoken, are about ownership and rights. Together, they prompt four questions. What do we do to encourage our students to speak? How do we ensure that what they say is treated equitably and respectfully? When they speak, whose voices do we hear? And how do we handle the contributions that don't follow our agenda?

Such questions are partly addressed in the literature on turns and turn-taking, ground rules, communities of discourse and communicative rights and competences,[50] so I concentrate here on the question about voice in the sense of ownership of what is said. Segal and Lefstein tell us that students in their study

> enthusiastically contribute to lively classroom discussion and often frame these discussions as dialogical responses that build on each other's ideas, but at the level of *voice* the discussion is mostly univocal, since most student contributions are aligned with the official voice of the teacher and the curriculum and in the rare instances where they emerge, independent student voices fall out of the conversation.[51]

The authors call this 'exuberant voiceless participation', using voice in their sense of ownership of what is uttered.[52] While they acknowledge Bakhtin's much quoted maxim that 'the word in language is half someone else's',[53] they find their observed teachers and students caught between competing episte-mologies: on the one hand the principle of co-construction, on the other hand the 'official knowledge' of the school curriculum. This dilemma, say Segal and Lefstein, is translated into teaching that may be dialogic in form but monologic in function. Discussion, however lively and promising, reductively yields what the teacher expects and is therefore, in the authors' second and third senses, 'voiceless'.

The paradox of apparently open pedagogy mediating a closed curriculum was noted many years ago in a piece by Atkinson and Delamont entertainingly entitled 'Mock-ups and cock-ups: the stage management of guided discovery instruction'.[54] Yet I am not convinced that matters are this clear-cut, for if Bakhtin is right, then nobody, including the teacher, has an independent voice. Teachers initiate their students into ways of thinking and knowing developed by others, and their task is in large measure cultural transmission, and indeed – if we accept Basil Bernstein's classic definition of pedagogic discourse as 'a relay for power relations external to [the classroom]'[55] – social control. Viewed thus, even the goal of developing students' autonomous thinking, notwithstanding the confident claims of dialogists, is normative.

Yet while freedom is never absolute it can be tempered. The path from the official curriculum to the curriculum as enacted and experienced in the class-room is rarely linear. Governments may specify, but schools translate what is specified, teachers transpose it and together teachers and students transform or domesticate it. It is through pedagogy that a paper curriculum gains life and meaning, and in this matter the agency of teachers and students is critical. Sim-ilarly, students learn more outside school than their teachers may credit,[56] and each student's unique out-of-school biography predisposes classroom contribu-tions to the curriculum as translated and transposed that may be as much their own as the teacher's; though what each student brings to the learning encoun-ter enters the dialogue only if the teacher allows it. But when the teacher does allow the student's voice in Segal and Lefstein's senses of speaking on one's own terms and being heeded, I see no contradiction between the dialogic dynamic and the school's obligation to advance the student's understanding in ways that have been culturally developed and are collectively understood.

If teaching may be dialogic in form but not necessarily in function, it may also be monologic in form but in its content more dialogic than at first sight it appears, for example when the teacher uses the expository mode convention-ally associated with 'traditional' teaching to introduce ideas of different kinds and from different sources in order to encourage corresponding dissonance in the mind of the student.[57] This teaching mode reminds us to differentiate inner from outer speech as well as, again, to avoid confusing form with function.[58] Curriculum domains represent centuries of cumulative co-construction and are inherently dialogic; and while teaching that is behaviourally dialogic may explicate and celebrate the epistemic dialogue and monologic teaching may mask it, neither consequence is inevitable. Here we can note Mortimer and

Scott's discussion of the tension between authoritative and dialogic interactions in science teaching[59]; and Nystrand's insistence that the bottom line is not the presence or absence of discussion, small-group work and so on but the extent to which teaching, however configured, 'requires students to think, not just report someone else's thinking'.[60] We should avoid treating dialogue and monologue as mutually exclusive. Epistemic and pedagogical dimensions transect; boundaries may be blurred.

No less important than the overall balance of teacher and student voice is the matter of vocal equity among students themselves. However, re-casting equity as voice underlines its complexity. Consider this:

> It is difficult for a woman to define her feelings in language which is chiefly made by men to express theirs.[61]

At first sight this expresses a very modern consciousness about voice and patriarchy, and Dale Spender puts the matter almost identically:

> Women have been obliged to use a language not of their own making . . . women [have been allowed] to express themselves, but only in male terms.[62]

But what I quoted first was in fact written nearly 150 years ago, in 1874. And it was written by a man, British novelist Thomas Hardy, putting the sentiment about man-made language into the mouth of a woman, Bathsheba Everdene in *Far from the Madding Crowd*. So which version of Spender's or Hardy's or Bathsheba's statement about language and gender is 'man made'? And while Spender offers explicitly feminist critique, what exactly is Hardy up to? Does he empathise with women's situation, or does he reinforce male dominance by attributing to men more power than they have? And does Dale Spender unwittingly do the same? Is it in fact male arrogance to assert that language is 'man made', and double arrogance for a male novelist to have that assertion voiced by a woman? Or by using the voice of character rather than narrator does Hardy simply leave such teasing questions to us, the readers?

I float the matter in this equivocating way because my final concern about voice is this. Many countries are deeply divided by inequalities of income, opportunity, education, class, race and of course gender. Among the promises of dialogic teaching is that it distributes classroom talk more equitably, first between teacher and students collectively, then among students themselves; and that this redistribution will contribute to the larger cause of reducing social inequality. That is why the UK Education Endowment Foundation was keen to support our trial of dialogic teaching with children meeting the criteria of social and economic disadvantage.

Yet while dialogic teaching can be shown to shift the balance of classroom talk towards students collectively, we must ask how far it equalises the voices of specific groups and individuals. If the word is indeed 'half someone else's' does this maxim apply to every student equally, or is it the case that for some students theirs remains a 'silenced dialogue'?[63] And, as shown in the 2016 and 2021 reports on sexual abuse in schools and colleges, the consequences of such silence, whether voluntary, peer-enforced, pedagogically-induced, or because of schools' underestimation of the gravity of the problem, can be devastating.[64] Indeed, Maria Miller, chair of the House of Commons Committee that produced the 2016 report, lambasted Ofsted – which produced the 2021 report – for failing to act on her committee's report when it was published, and hence failing to safeguard girls' safety – and, because their experiences were belittled or ignored, their voices.[65]

In reconciling cultural transmission, equity and the development of the student's autonomous (or normatively autonomous) thinking, much – as we saw in chapter 17 – hangs on the third move in the spoken exchange. Here the seminal work of Michaels and O'Connor[66] reminds us that the third move has the power to ensure that the student's voice, once invited, does not 'fall out of the dialogue'.[67] So to assess whether an exchange is genuinely dialogic, and whether it promotes student equity and autonomy, we might treat the third move as an indicator, while being ever mindful of the danger of inferring cognitive function from oral form. But, as this brief excursion reminds us, there are deeper and more intractable cultural forces at play which even the most dialogically-attuned and equitably-committed teacher may find it hard to erode.

Argument

In English, 'argument' suggests bellicosity as well as rationality, and this, apparently, is how many students view it.[68] The norms of deliberative discourse are not instinctive but need to be made explicit and translated into ground rules.[69] Argumentation is an acquired skill, and helping students to move from mere disagreement to evidentiary discussion is a necessary educational task.[70]

It is hardly surprising if students view argument as conflict. They witness the media turning complex issues into battling binaries. They join a twittersphere that thrives on intolerance. They see politicians asserting cases rather than demonstrating them, using evidence selectively, and gleefully stoking disagreement into conflict. But the manipulation of evidence is among the oldest tricks in the political game, so rather than deplore this as an aberration students should learn that political and academic argument have different goals and conventions; and that when argument is about persuasion and power rather than truth, evidence gives way to rhetoric, and rhetoric has its own rules.[71]

Cicero, master of political rhetoric, said, 'Wisdom without eloquence does little benefit'; though he did have the grace to add, 'But eloquence without wisdom does much harm.'[72] Pertinently, there has been a revival of interest in classical rhetoric and its modern variants, especially in university English departments.[73] The last great flowering was during the Renaissance, when the key texts of Aristotle, Cicero and Quintilian were rediscovered and in schools and universities the practice of rhetoric was as essential as the study of arithmetic, geometry and astronomy.[74] Rhetoric, too, guided and framed renaissance poetic discourse. Some of Shakespeare's greatest speeches and bouts of oral fencing, for example in *Hamlet* where they culminate fatally in its physical form, can be properly understood only if one has a grasp of the rhetorical devices and figures of speech with many in Shakespeare's audiences were familiar. Is this territory to which dialogic pedagogy might return us?

In any event, we cannot be content to frame our discussion of dialogic pedagogy and civic education by polarising academic and political argument as if each were one-dimensional. Walton, for instance, proposes seven types of dialogic argumentation, each with its own goals, moves, questions and responses: persuasion, inquiry, discovery, negotiation, information exchange, deliberation and eristic argument.[75] The first six are reasoned and rule-bound, and only eristic argument (from the Greek word for 'strife') aims to win by whatever means are available. Political argument can and often does entail negotiation, inquiry and deliberation, but the eristic is always there as the last resort or, for some, the first.

Prominent in eristic argument are the well-known fallacies of syllogistic reasoning: equivocation, or exploiting ambiguity; begging the question; ad verecundiam, or citing an 'authority' who may be nothing of the sort; ad hominem, attacking the person rather than the argument; ad baculum, or threatening dire consequences if one's views aren't accepted; and so on. Some of these classic fallacies are numbered among Schopenhauer's '38 ways to win an argument',[76] which start from the proposition that logic pursues truth but eristic aims only for victory. Schopenhauer's list, published in 1831 but still resonant, includes alongside the familiar syllogistic fallacies some decidedly contemporary echoes: 'make your opponent angry', 'generalise from the specific', 'claim victory despite defeat', 'persuade the audience, not the opponent', 'interrupt or divert the dispute if you think you are losing', 'puzzle or bewilder your opponent by mere bombast' and 'be personal, insulting and rude'.

Just as academic and political argument are not mutually exclusive but overlap on a continuum, so academic argument is not one mode but many. Scientific, mathematical and historical reasoning, to take three obvious paradigms, are manifestly different. Less frequently considered in the dialogic pedagogy literature is argument in the artistic and literary spheres. How do we make or test the case for a work of art, music or literature? Between the 1930s and 1970s the influential Cambridge literary critic F.R. Leavis taught his students to attend as closely as possible to text, investigating and assessing the technical, linguistic and stylistic ingredients of prose, poetry and drama and locating them in historical context, so that they could distinguish the technically original and inventive from the mediocre or routine, and assign dates to samples of writing without knowing the author, which, like 'blind' student grading, certainly aids objectivity.

But moving from assessments of artistic technique and style to judgements of artistic merit is more problematic. Here Leavis relied on his famous question 'This is so, isn't it?' which puts a literary work's moral seriousness and psychological or experiential authenticity on the line alongside its technical and imaginative mastery. But 'This is so, isn't it?' was always followed by 'Yes, but. . .', an obligatory riposte that demands both convincing justification and rigorous scepticism about every judgement ventured – the literary equivalent of Popper's theory of scientific conjectures and refutations, perhaps;[77] though it doesn't deal with the objection that the formula appears to ascribe to the reader or critic, *a priori*, the maturity, experience and psychological insight needed to judge the correspondence between life as lived and portrayed. Of course, this process interrogates evidence of a kind and in a way that would be unlikely to satisfy a physicist, but that is the point: the modes of argument and justification in the arts and sciences are different but not necessarily of unequal validity.

As Reznitskaya, Wilkinson and their colleagues have shown,[78] Toulmin offers a kind of reconciliation, granted that evidence and authenticity are not categorically matching sides of the same coin and, as Charles Taylor notes, the latter is particularly difficult to pin down.[79] Noting that different kinds of question or claim call for different treatment, Toulmin proposes a generic 'lay-out' of six elements of argumentation applicable to most circumstances: *claim* (what has to be established or proved); *ground* (facts, evidence, data or reasoning in support of the claim); *warrant* (justification for the grounds cited); *backing* (additional or alternative support); *qualifier* (limitations on the claim); and *rebuttal* (counter-arguments).[80] This applies as well to Leavis's approach to literary judgement as to the scientific/mathematical examples that Toulmin cites, such as 'whether . . . Fröhlich's theory of super-conductivity is really satisfactory, when the next eclipse of the moon will take place, or the exact nature of the relation between the squares on the different sides of a right-angled triangle'.[81]

This is the briefest of canters across a vast and complex field to which others have devoted the depth and breadth that it deserves;[82] while Reznitskaya and Wilkinson have devised an 'argumentation rating tool' that identifies four key criteria of 'quality argumentation' and tracks these through 11 'facilitation practices'.[83] Learning in general, and learning for democratic engagement in particular, require us to be able to make, understand and test arguments of different kinds. The task is larger than even a totally reconfigured civic education programme can accomplish. It requires us to think about dialogue and democratic education across the curriculum as a whole, and hence in epistemic as well as pedagogical terms. Approached through dialogue rather than recitation, curriculum domains come into their own as ways of arguing as well as knowing, and taken together they can enhance the student's capacity to make, understand, critique and challenge argument outside as well as inside the classroom.

Truth and trust

'Comment is free, but facts are sacred' was the mantra of C.P. Scott, legendary one-time editor of the then *Manchester Guardian*. Nowadays the boundary between objective fact and subjective opinion is more blurred than in 1921, and not only in the media and body politic: in academic life, too, it is contested.

Indeed, academics may be unwittingly implicated in attacks on received truth by epistemic nihilists in the White House and Westminster. 'People have had enough of experts', declared England's former Education Secretary Michael Gove of those who cited evidence to challenge populist claims about migration and economic impact promulgated by Brexit advocates in 2016;[84] and 'truth isn't truth' said presidential attorney Rudi Giulani, to gasps of outrage even louder than those that greeted Kellyanne Conway when she defended as 'alternative fact' President Trump's exaggeration of the size of the crowd at his 2017 inauguration.[85] But Kakutani shows how such tropes do not so much come out of the blue as take to extremes the post-modernist rejection of the enlightenment belief in objective reality, provable truth, stable linguistic constructs and reason itself.[86]

Habermas noted that there is an inherent contradiction in using traditional methods of reasoning and arguing to attack those same methods of reasoning and arguing.[87] If the methods are invalid, so is the critique. The concept 'fake news' is truly fake news. Yet if there are different ways of knowing and making sense, which there manifestly are – look no further than the school curriculum – and if these embody different tests of truth, then truth itself may also be plural, epistemically if not morally.

Some of Jerome Bruner's most interesting work towards the end of his long life provides a perspective on these matters, though he was no post-modernist. He reduces humankind's ways of investigating, knowing and understanding to two modes:

> One verifies by appeal to formal verification procedures and empirical truth. The other establishes *not* truth but truthlikeness or verisimilitude . . . One mode is centered around the narrow epistemological question of how to know the truth; the other around the broader and more inclusive question of the meaning of experience.[88]

Bruner named the first mode logico-scientific or 'paradigmatic' and the second mode 'narrative', which recalls anthropologist Clifford Geertz's definition of culture as 'the stories we tell ourselves about ourselves'.[89] (Not coincidental: the admiration of these two giants was mutual.)[90] But apart from the obvious cases of, say, mathematics and science, assigning school subjects to one or other of Bruner's modes isn't straightforward. History, being both evidential and narrative, can be in either mode or both, while locating the social sciences, despite their name, is equally problematic; and in mentioning F.R. Leavis earlier I noted his exemplifying the educated literary response as a combination of subjective/intersubjective judgement and evidence from textual scrutiny. Leavis's 'common pursuit of true judgement' placed him closer to the toughness of philosophical analysis than to the genially idiosyncratic study of literature as pursued by others of his generation.[91] And it's interesting to note that this most combative and uncompromising of academics got on rather well with Ludwig Wittgenstein.[92]

Bruner's paradigmatic/narrative distinction might appear to reinforce the old opposition of 'fact' and 'fiction', or of what is supposedly true and what is manifestly made up. But would those to whom Margaret Attwood's *The Hand-maid's Tale* speaks so vividly allow that because it's a work of fiction it doesn't deal in truth? Would we be happy for this sweeping judgement to be passed on all those poets, novelists and dramatists, and indeed artists and musicians, whose illuminating insights into the human condition take us beyond the reach of the social sciences, and *show* inner lives rather than merely attach labels to them? (Leavis again: 'This is so, isn't it . . . Yes, but. . .'). In the words of Scottish novelist Ali Smith:

> Fiction and lies are the opposite of each other . . . Lies go out of their way to distort, or to turn you away from, the truth. Fiction is one of our ways to get to truths that are really difficult to talk about, that we haven't yet been able to articulate, or see; truths that we come to articulate via a story.[93]

Not fact versus fiction, then, but fact and fiction versus lies, with both fact and fiction aspiring to truth, albeit to truths of different kinds, while lies fabricate it. Or, to recall our earlier discussion, fiction as a quest for the authentic. But once again there's a problem of definition – fiction as something made up, and fiction as literary genre. Ali Smith is talking about fiction as literary genre, but the colloquial opposition of fact and fiction fails to make that distinction, thereby denying the truths that serious fiction, as opposed to mere entertainment, explore and expose, and relegating Bruner's narrative mode and Geertz's 'stories we tell ourselves about ourselves' to the outer circle of trust.

But let us be clear. When commentators complain of 'truth decay' and 'the death of truth' they speak not of a universal epistemic and moral collapse but of a localised political or media malaise, or in academic circles a post-modernist turn. To most people truth really does matter, and they see it in terms of trust as much as evidence. Today's truth decay is about the behaviour of the body politic and some sections of the print and digital media. It is about people who destroy trust by spreading falsehood and giving comfort to the cynical relativism of 'fake news' and the 'alternative fact'. For the rest of us, including teachers and students, keeping faith with the enlightenment may be the best we can do. Indeed at a time when the leader of the world's most powerful nation dismisses as a hoax what the world's most distinguished scientists accept – incontrovertible evidence of potentially catastrophic climate change and biodiversity loss – we have no alternative.

Conclusion

Democracy is fragile and history cautions us against complacency about its prospects. Playing on voters' worst instincts and deepest fears self-styled 'strong' leaders fan the flames of division and intolerance, marginalise dissenting voices, debase language and argument, and treat truth with contempt. The collision of this discourse with what is aspired towards in schools and universities is reminiscent of the darker decades of the twentieth century, Eric Hobsbawm's 'age of extremes',[94] when H.G. Wells warned that 'human history becomes more and more a race between education and catastrophe',[95] and Joseph Stalin retorted: 'Education is a weapon whose effects depend on who holds it in his hands and at whom it is aimed.'[96]

The scenario, then, is hardly new, but with a screen in every hand allied to a highly addictive technology, twenty-first-century mass communication possesses power and penetration far beyond what was conceivable in the 20th. Yet, by the same token, the sheer volume of information now accessible affords countervailing opportunities to challenge and correct, and tracking every purveyor of fake news or alternative facts is a fact checker.

At the end of his vast and prescient 1990s trilogy *The Information Age*, Manuel Castells concluded that although the enlightenment dream seems forever frustrated by the 'extraordinary gap between our technological overdevelopment and our social underdevelopment', it nevertheless remains within reach; for 'there is no eternal evil in human nature' and 'there is nothing that cannot be changed by conscious, purposive social action'.[97] Dialogue is not a panacea, but it is indeed 'purposive social action' as well as a vital ingredient of effective teaching and a worthy educational end in itself, and hence a manifesto for hope. Dialogue, as Mead, Bakhtin, Taylor and many others agree,[98] is intrinsic to the human condition, to how we perceive, think, define ourselves, relate to others and are defined by them; and dialogue is essential to our responses – scientific, artistic, cultural and educational – to the crises of democracy, climate, ecology and survival with which we are urgently confronted; but only if dialogue attends, rigorously and assertively, to those of its ingredients that, *ipso facto*, are currently under sustained attack: language, voice, argument and truth.

Postscript

When I penned the first version of this chapter, in 2018, I noted that Donald Trump's case was far from unique. But at that stage the extent to which Britain's prime minister would apparently model himself on Trump, and the record of serial lying linked to Brexit, the 2019 general election and the 2020–21 pandemic, had yet to be exposed. Thanks to journalists,[99] fact-checkers[100] and – we must hope – Hansard (which should have recorded for posterity the government's efforts to circumvent binding legislation and ministers' refusal to do what the Ministerial Code requires) the UK picture is now all too clear. What in 2018 Michiko Kakutani wrote of Trump – his 'lies, his efforts to redefine reality . . . his attacks on the press, the judiciary. . .'[101] applies equally to Britain's (or rather England's) leadership, though as yet Johnson's supporters haven't stormed the Palace of Westminster.

The erosion of democracy, and of the carefully-modulated checks and balances on which it depends, obviously matters to all of us. But in education, as

I have tried to show here and in other chapters, there are added resonances. It is noteworthy, for example, that the impoverishment of the national curriculum discussed in Chapters 10–13 coincided with, and was facilitated by, Michael Gove's abolition of education's equivalent of the wider constitutional checks and balances: QCDA, successor to the QCA and a line of 'arm's-length' non-departmental bodies going back to Education Reform Act of 1988. (This was the same Michael Gove who had no time for experts and, according to Peter Oborne, was equally disdainful of truth.[102]) As Mike Baker reminds us, during the 1980s cross-party unease about the totalitarian resonances of a national curriculum ensured that it would be devised not by ministers but by an independent consultative body whose proposals would be laid before Parliament and debated and voted upon in both houses.[103] But in 2010 these protections, and with them broadly-based and non-partisan expertise, were at a stroke replaced by ministerial fiat grounded in the narrowest of prejudice and backed not by evidence and argument but by populist and personal attacks on a mythical enemy:

> The Blob – the network of educational gurus in and around our universities who praised each others' research, sat on committees that drafted politically correct curricula, drew gifted young teachers away from their vocation and instead directed them towards ideologically driven theory.[104]

But the deeper problem is epistemological. It touches on the efforts of teachers to help students to acquire, understand and interrogate knowledge, to search for truth on the basis of reasoning, argument and evidence. This quest, at the heart of what education is about, is now subverted by those in Westminster who should be its ultimate guardians. In place of the epistemology of truth and falsehood we have the 'tribal epistemology' of them and us:

> Information is evaluated not on conformity to common standards of evidence or correspondence to a common understanding of the world, but on whether it supports the tribe's values and goals and is vouchsafed by tribal leaders.[105]

Notes

1. Alexander 2019b.
2. Park *et al* 2017.
3. Howe and Abedin 2013.
4. *Initiation – response – feedback* (or *evaluation*): the traditional default for teacher-student exchanges.
5. Park *et al* 2017.
6. Matusov 2018.
7. Alexander 2010a, 199.
8. Alexander 2006b.
9. Lefstein and Snell 2014.

10 Nystrand *et al* 1997.
11 Mercer and Littleton 2007; Mercer and Dawes 2008.
12 Resnick *et al* 2010.
13 Boyd and Markarian 2015.
14 Kim and Wilkinson 2019.
15 Kessler *et al* 2018; *Washington Post* 2021.
16 *New York Times* 2021.
17 Levitsky and Ziblatt 2018, 9.
18 https://fullfact.org (accessed June 2021).
19 Kim Darroch (sacked by Johnson as British ambassador to the US at Trump's request), quoted in Oborne 2021, 173–4.
20 Roberts 2017.
21 O'Keefe and Pearson 2011; Savage 2019.
22 House of Commons 2018, 3 and 62–3.
23 Ofsted 2018.
24 Bowles and Gintis 1976; Bourdieu and Passeron 1990.
25 Althusser 1976.
26 Hirsch 1987; Freire 1970; Giroux 2011.
27 Simon 1966; Kennedy 1999.
28 Dewey 1916.
29 Kakutani 2018, 172–3.
30 Orwell 1968, 139.
31 Arendt 2004, 474.
32 Resnick *et al* 2010.
33 Michaels and O'Connor 2015; Park *et al* 2017.
34 Michaels *et al* 2008.
35 Michaels *et al* 2008.
36 Michaels and O'Connor 2012, 2015.
37 Dawes *et al* 2004.
38 QCA 2004, 4.
39 Cazden 2001, 7.
40 Discussed more fully in Alexander 2020, 171–4.
41 Carter 1997; McCarthy and Carter 2001.
42 Crystal 2018; Committee for Linguistics in Education 2019.
43 Kenway 1990; Ball 1990.
44 Alexander 2008b, 2010b.
45 Grice 1975.
46 Reznitskaya and Wilkinson 2017.
47 Lipman 2003; Fisher 2008; Gregory 2007.
48 'September 1, 1939'. In Auden 1940.
49 Segal and Lefstein 2015.
50 Edwards and Westgate 1994; Mercer 2000.
51 Segal and Lefstein 2015, 1.
52 See also Segal *et al* 2016; Lefstein *et al* 2018.
53 Bakhtin 1986, 170.
54 Atkinson and Delamont 1977.
55 Bernstein 1990, 168.
56 Mayall 2010.
57 See the case study of one such teacher in Alexander 2008b, 154–72.
58 Wells 1999; Boyd and Markarian 2015.
59 Mortimer and Scott 2003.
60 Nystrand *et al* 1997, 72.
61 Hardy 1916, 414.

62 Spender 1980, 12.
63 Delpit 1988; Edwards 1989.
64 House of Commons 2016; Ofsted 2021b.
65 Weale 2021.
66 Michaels and O'Connor 2012, 2015.
67 Bakhtin 1986, 168.
68 Osborne 2015, 406; Kuhn *et al* 2011.
69 Mercer and Dawes 2008.
70 Reznitskaya and Wilkinson 2017.
71 Condor *et al* 2013.
72 Kennedy 1999, 94.
73 Welch 1990.
74 Simon 1966.
75 Walton 2013.
76 Schopenhauer 2004.
77 Popper 1963.
78 Reznitskaya and Wilkinson 2017; Reznitskaya *et al* 2009.
79 Taylor 1991.
80 Toulmin 2003.
81 Toulmin 2003, 12–13.
82 E.g. Schwarz and Baker 2017.
83 Reznitskaya and Wilkinson 2017, 40–6.
84 Michael Gove on Sky News, 3 June 2016. https://fullfact.org/blog/2016/sep/has-public-really-had-enough-experts/ (accessed May 2021).
85 Giuliani: www.bbc.co.uk/news/world-us-canada-45241838.
    Conway: www.bbc.co.uk/news/uk-scotland-scotland-politics-38764003 (accessed May 2021).
86 Kakutani 2018.
87 Habermas 1987.
88 Bruner 2006, 116.
89 Geertz 1973.
90 Mattingly *et al* 2008.
91 Tanner 1975; Joyce 1988.
92 McKillop 1995.
93 Smith 2018.
94 Hobsbawm 1995.
95 Wells 1920.
96 Stalin and Wells 1937. The juxtaposition of these quotations is not contrived. H.G. Wells met and interviewed Stalin in 1934, and the encounter produced the quoted response from Stalin. See *New Statesman*, 18 April 2014.
97 Castells 1998, 359–60.
98 Mead 1962; Bakhtin 1981; Taylor 1991.
99 For example, Harding *et al* 2021; and especially Oborne 2021.
100 https://boris-johnson-lies.com; https://fullfact.org (accessed June 2021).
101 Kakutani 2018, 167.
102 Oborne 2021, 27, 32, 76, 116, 117, 123, 144.
103 Baker 2013.
104 Gove 2013b.
105 Roberts 2017.

Part 4

Education for all

19 Towards a comparative pedagogy

Cowen, R. and Kazamias, A.M. (eds) *International Handbook of Comparative Education*, Vol 2, 923–41 (2009). An earlier version appeared in *Comparative Education*, 37(4), 507–523 (2001). This chapter, which reaches back to the *Culture and Pedagogy* project, highlights some of the linguistic, cultural and conceptual difficulties facing those who engage in international comparison in education. These, as I show in Chapters 20–21, become even more problematic when such comparison becomes a tool of policy, and when comparison is compromised by nationalistic competition.

The neglect of pedagogy in comparative enquiry

Pedagogy is the most startlingly prominent of the educational themes which British comparativists have ignored. In the special millennial issue of the leading UK journal *Comparative Education* Angela Little recorded that just 6.1 per cent of the journal's articles between 1977 and 1998 dealt with 'curricular content and the learner's experience' as compared with nearly 31 per cent on themes such as educational reform and development;[1] Cowen asserted that 'we are nowhere near coming fully to grips with the themes of curriculum, pedagogic styles and evaluation as powerful message systems which form identities in specific educational sites';[2] and Broadfoot argued that future comparative studies of education should place much greater emphasis 'on the process of learning itself rather than, as at present, on the organisation and provision of education'.[3]

If the omission is so obvious, one might reasonably enquire why comparativists have not remedied it. There may be a simple practical explanation. Policy analysis, especially when it is grounded in documentation rather than fieldwork, is a more manageable option than classroom research. Cheaper, speedier and more comfortable too: who would exchange their library or internet connection for time-consuming and occasionally hair-raising journeys encumbered by video and audio recorders, cameras, tripods, observation schedules, interview schedules, clothing, food and all the other necessary apparatus of 'thick description' – not to mention the complex negotiations which nowadays are required before one can observe teachers or talk to children?

As a less uncharitable possibility, and echoing Brian Simon's 'Why no pedagogy in England?',[4] we might suggest that a country without an indigenous 'science of teaching' is hardly likely to nurture pedagogical comparison:

DOI: 10.4324/9781315169378-23

cherry-picking and policy borrowing maybe, but not serious comparative enquiry.

Or perhaps pedagogy is one of those aspects of comparative education which demands expertise over and above knowledge of the countries compared, their cultures, systems and policies. I rather think it is, especially given the condition which Simon identified. Michael Crossley argues:

> If the well documented pitfalls of comparative education are not to be re-encountered, it is important that those new to such research engage with the literatures that are central to the field. Similarly, it is important for those who see themselves as comparativists to embrace the opportunities presented by such a widening of research networks and discourses.[5]

A certain imbalance in the force of these two imperatives is detectable here: non-comparativists must 'engage with the literature' (presumably because their ignorance is greater), but comparativists need only to 'embrace opportunities'. There may well be evidence of ill-judged comparison among the 'new' educational comparers, but we can also find examples of superficial or even ill-conceived analysis of particular educational phenomena in the mainstream comparative literature. Unless one is content to confine oneself to that superficial A *vs* B juxtaposing of national educational systems which used to be the staple diet of university comparative education courses but, mercifully, is now much less common, then meaningful educational comparison is never less than a magnificent challenge, for it requires engagement with several distinct literatures and modes of analysis simultaneously. One can hardly study comparative law or literature without knowing at least as much about law or literature as about the countries and cultures involved and the business of making comparisons; the same goes for comparative education.

This is why this chapter's title refers to 'comparative pedagogy'. Pedagogy is a complex field of practice, theory and research in its own right. The challenge of comparative pedagogy is to marry the study of education elsewhere with the study of teaching and learning in a way that respects both of these fields of enquiry yet also creates something which is more than the sum of their parts.

New territories, old maps

Little's framework for classifying journal articles on comparative education[6] differentiated *context* (the country or countries studied), *content* (using the thematic classification reproduced inside the journal's back cover) and *comparison* (the number of countries compared). Trying to place my own *Culture and Pedagogy*[7] within this framework underlines pedagogy's marginal status in mainstream comparative discourse. This study used documentary, interview, observational, video and photographic data collected at the levels of system, school and classroom between 1994 and 1998. The study's 'context' was England, France, India, Russia and the United States.

So far so good, even though five-country studies are relatively unusual. (Edmund King's seven-nation study remains the classic example of this genre.)[8] Its 'content' straddled at least six of Little's 13 themes without sitting comfortably within any of them, and the educational phase with which it dealt – primary education – did not appear at all in that framework (nor, strikingly, did the terms 'teaching' or 'learning', let alone 'culture' or 'pedagogy'). Its 'comparison' was across five countries (a rarity) and included both North and South (a rarity overall, and a novelty in Little's five-country category).

Apart from the fact that, as already noted, pedagogy is a neglected field in comparative enquiry, there is a further reason why the content of this research maps so imperfectly onto Little's framework: the framework does not accommodate studies which cross one important boundary hitherto unmentioned, that between the macro and the micro. *Culture and Pedagogy* – as the title suggests – illustrates Sadler's hoary maxim about the inseparability of the worlds inside and outside the school,[9] yet Little's framework seems to imply that comparative studies must be either national *or* local, about policy *or* practice, the system *or* the classroom, rather than about their interaction. In this respect, comparativists may be somewhat behind the larger social science game, in which the relationship between social structure, culture and human agency has been 'at the heart of sociological theorising' for well over a century.[10]

Thus, pedagogy does not begin and end in the classroom. It is comprehended only once one locates practice within the concentric circles of local and national, and of classroom, school, system and state, and only if one steers constantly back and forth between these, exploring the way that what teachers and students do in classrooms reflects the values of the wider society. That was one of the challenges which the *Culture and Pedagogy* research sought to address.

Another challenge for a comparative pedagogy is to engage with the interface between present and past, to enact the principle that if one is to understand anything about education elsewhere one's perspective should be powerfully informed by history. So while the comparative journey in *Culture and Pedagogy* culminates in a detailed examination of teacher-pupil discourse – for language is at once the most powerful tool of human learning and the quintessential expression of culture and identity – it starts with accounts of the historical roots and developments of primary education in each of the five countries, paying particular attention to the emergence of those core and abiding values, traditions and habits which shape, enable and constrain pedagogical development.

Defining pedagogy

So far a definition of pedagogy has been inferred. It is time to be more explicit. One of the values of comparativism is that it alerts one to the way that the apparently bedrock terms in a particular discourse are nothing of the sort.

Thus it may well matter, in the context of the strong investment in citizenship which is part of French public education, that *éduquer* means to bring up as well as formally to educate and that *bien éduqué* means well brought up or well-mannered rather than well schooled ('educate' in English has both senses too, but the latter now predominates); or that the root of the Russian word for education, *obrazovanie*, means 'form' or 'image' rather than, as in our Latinate version, a 'leading out', and is thus closer to the German *Bildung* than to 'education'; or that *obrazovanie* is inseparable from *vospitanie*, an idea which has no equivalent in English because it combines personal development, private and public morality, and civic commitment, while in England these tend to be treated as separate and even conflicting domains; or that *obuchenie*, which is usually translated as teacher-led 'instruction', signals learning as well as teaching.[11] It is almost certainly significant that in English (and American) education 'development' is viewed as a physiological and psychological process which takes place independently of formal schooling whereas Russian teachers define 'development' transitively, as a task which requires their active intervention: in the one context development is 'natural' while in the other it is more akin to acculturation. Similarly, in the Anglo-American tradition the most able child is defined as the one with the greatest potential, while in Russia's Soviet pedagogical legacy it is the least able, because he/she has furthest to travel towards goals which are held to be common for all children.[12]

Such terms hint at more than the comparativist's need to be sensitive to the problems of language and translation. They also subtly align the educational agenda along culturally-distinctive lines even before one starts investigating the detail of policy and practice. In the cases exemplified here, both *l'éducation* and *vospitanie* inject suggestions of public morality and the common good into the discourse in ways which subliminally influence the recurring discussions about school goals and curricula in France and Russia; while the Russian notions of 'potential' and 'development' each imply – and indeed impose – strong teacher agency and responsibility in a way which their more passive and individualistic English and American connotations do not. The notion of teacher as 'facilitator', which is so central to the Anglo-Saxon progressive tradition, would make little headway in those continental European countries in which teacher intervention and instruction are seen as essential to school learning.

The consciousness intimated here also implies a model of pedagogy, and a course for comparative pedagogical analysis, which are as far removed as they can be from the polarising of 'teacher-centred' (or 'subject-centred') and 'child-centred' teaching which too often remains the stock-in-trade of such accounts of pedagogy as are available in the comparative literature.[13] Mainstream pedagogical research abandoned this dichotomy years ago; mainstream comparative research should do likewise. Perhaps the most damaging residue of this sort of thinking can still be found in the reports of some development education consultants and NGOs, which happily commend Western 'child-centred' pedagogy to non-Western governments without regard for local cultural and educational circumstances, or for recent advances in the psychology of learning and teaching, or for the findings of pedagogical research on the decidedly questionable record of child-centred teaching in Western classrooms.

That touch of waspishness apart, we would do well to be no less cautious about another boundary problem here. In the literature on culturally-located views and models of teaching, generalised 'Asian', 'Pacific Rim', 'Western', 'non-Western' and 'European' 'models' of teaching and learning feature prominently and confidently.[14] If we recognise that the geographical and cultural coverage of 'Asian' is too broad to have descriptive validity for the analysis of teaching, we should be no less aware of the hegemonic overtones of 'Western'. Does 'Western' encompass South as well as North America? Does it include some European countries while excluding others? With its implied validation of a particular worldview, tellingly captured after 2003 in the Old/New Europe name-calling of the Bush administration, 'Western' may well exacerbate rather than supplant the pedagogy of opposition, fuelling a self-righteous occidentalism every bit as pernicious as Said's orientalism.[15]

As our core educational concept, 'pedagogy' lies linguistically and culturally on sands at least as treacherous as these. In the Anglo-American tradition, pedagogy is subsidiary to curriculum, sometimes inferring little more than 'teaching method'. 'Curriculum' itself has both a broad sense (everything that a school does) and a narrow one (what is formally required to be taught) which comes closer to continental European 'didactics' without capturing the sense in *la didactique* or *die Didaktik* of a quasi-science comprising subject knowledge and the principles by which it is imparted. Curriculum is more prominent in educational discourse in systems where it is contested, less where it is imposed or accepted as a given. In the central European tradition, it is the other way round: pedagogy moves centre-stage and frames everything else, including curriculum – in so far as *that* word is used – and didactics.[16]

Because the range of meanings attaching to pedagogy varies so much in English – quite apart from differences between English and other languages – we have to be stipulative, and in a way which allows us to use the term for comparative analysis. I prefer to eschew the greater ambiguities of 'curriculum' and the resulting tendency to downgrade pedagogy, and use the latter term to encompass the larger field. I distinguish pedagogy as *discourse* from teaching as *act*, yet I make them inseparable. Pedagogy, then, encompasses both the act of teaching and its contingent theories and debates. Pedagogy is the discourse with which one needs to engage in order both to teach intelligently and make sense of teaching – for discourse and act are interdependent, and there can be no teaching without pedagogy or pedagogy without teaching.

A *comparative* pedagogy takes this discourse not one stage but several stages further. Pedagogy relates the act of teaching to the ideas which inform and explain it. Comparative pedagogy identifies, explores and explains similarities and differences in pedagogy, as concept, discourse and practice, across designated units of comparison such as nation states. It thereby exploits opportunities which only proper comparison can provide: teasing out what is universal in pedagogy from what is culturally or geographically specific; informing the development of pedagogic theory; and extending the vocabulary and repertoire of pedagogic practice.

We can now propose three conditions for a comparative pedagogy. First, it should incorporate a defensible rationale and methodology for comparing across sites, cultures, nations and/or regions. Second, it should combine procedures for studying teaching empirically with ways of accessing the values, ideas and debates which inform, shape and explain it. Third, because these values, ideas and debates are part of a wider educational discourse and – typically – are located in the context of public national education systems as well as schools and classrooms, a comparative pedagogy should access these different levels, contexts and constituencies and examine how they relate to each other and inform the discourse of pedagogy and the act of teaching.

Frameworks for a comparative pedagogy

If pedagogy is shaped by national culture and history, and by the migration of ideas and practices across national borders, as well as by more immediate practical exigencies and constraints such as policy and resources, is it possible to postulate a model of pedagogy, and a framework for studying it, which both accommodates its many forms and variations and rises above the constraints of value and circumstance? Can we devise an analytical model which will serve the needs of the empirical researcher in any context? This was the challenge we had to take up in the *Culture and Pedagogy* project, for we needed to make sense of disparate classroom data in a way which showed no obvious bias towards particular, culturally-specific accounts of learning and teaching.

The resulting framework has three parts. The first deals with the observable act of teaching; the second with the ideas which inform it; the third with the macro-micro relationship which links classroom transaction to national policy via the curriculum.

We start, though, with a definition:

> Pedagogy is the observable act of teaching together with its attendant discourse of educational theories, values, evidence and justifications. It is what one needs to know, and the skills one needs to command, in order to make and justify the many different kinds of decisions of which teaching is constituted.

With this our colours are nailed firmly to the international mast. In Britain, if the word is used at all, 'pedagogy' signals merely the teaching act, and the act's informing ideas stand in an at best uneasy relationship to it, as so much 'theory' to be 'applied' (or not). But, unfortunately for the theory/practice dualists, the theory is there whether they like it or not, unless of course they are prepared to claim that teaching is a mindless activity. The task is to explicate the theory, which in teaching we know to be a complex amalgam of sedimented experience, personal values and beliefs, re-interpretations of published research, and policy more or less dutifully enacted.

Pedagogy as act

Many years ago anthropologist Edmund Leach argued that the more complex the model, the less likely it is to be useful.[17] With that warning in mind, we start by reducing teaching to its barest essentials: *Teaching, in any setting, is the act of using method x to enable students to learn y.*

In so skeletal a form the proposition is difficult to contest, and if this is so we extract from it two no less basic questions to steer empirical enquiry: What are students expected to learn? What method does the teacher use to ensure that they do so?

'Method' needs to be unpacked if it is to be useful as an analytical category which can cross the boundaries of space and time. Any teaching method combines *tasks*, *activities*, *interactions* and *judgements*. Their function is represented by four further questions: In a given teaching session or unit what *learning tasks* do students encounter? What *activities* do they undertake in order to address these learning tasks? Through what *interactions* does the teacher present, organise and sustain the learning tasks and activities? By what means, and on the basis of what criteria, does the teacher *evaluate* the nature and level of the tasks and activities which each student shall undertake (*differentiation*), and the kinds of learning which students achieve (*assessment*)?

Task, activity, interaction and evaluation are the building blocks of teaching as act. However, as they stand they lack the wherewithal for coherence and meaning. To our first proposition, therefore, we must add a second. This unpacks 'in any setting', the remaining phrase in the first proposition: *Teaching has structure and form; it is situated in, and governed by, space, time and patterns of pupil organisation; and it is undertaken for a purpose.*

Structure and form in teaching are most clearly and distinctively manifested in the *lesson*. Lessons and their constituent teaching acts are framed and governed by *time*, by *space* (the way the classroom is disposed, organised and resourced) and by the chosen forms of *student organisation* (whole class, small group or individual).

But teaching is framed conceptually and ethically, as well as temporally and spatially. A lesson is part of a larger *curriculum* embodying educational purposes and values, and reflecting assumptions about what knowledge and understanding are of most worth to the individual and to society. This is part of the force of 'teaching . . . is undertaken for a purpose'.

One element remains. Teaching is not a series of random encounters. Together, students and teachers create and are defined by a microculture. They develop procedures for regulating the complex dynamics of student-teacher and student-student relationships, the equivalent of law, custom, convention and public morality in civil society. This element we define as *routine, rule* and *ritual*.

Frame	Form	Act
Space		Task
Student organisation		Activity
Time	Lesson	
Curriculum		Interaction
Routine, rule and ritual		Evaluation

Figure 19.1 Pedagogy as act

This part of the pedagogical framework is schematised in Figure 19.1 and was applied over the six classroom-focused chapters in *Culture and Pedagogy*.[18] The various elements are grouped under the headings of *frame, form* and *act*. The core acts of teaching (task, activity, interaction and evaluation) are framed by classroom organisation ('space'), pupil organisation, time and curriculum, and by classroom routines, rules and rituals. They are given form in the lesson or teaching session.

Choices then have to be made about how one analyses each of the elements. These dictate further questions about analytical categories, research methods and technologies which for reasons of space cannot be addressed here. Suffice it to say that in the *Culture and Pedagogy* research each element was broken down into several analytical sub-units, the main research tools were observation, video and interview, and the core data comprised fieldnotes, interview transcripts, lesson transcripts, photographs, teaching documents and some 130 hours of videotape. However, this information is relevant here only in so far as it demonstrates that the framework actually works. The comparative analysis of teaching in *Culture and Pedagogy* starts with the basic disposition of the framing and regulatory elements of curriculum, space, pupil organisation, time and routine/rule/ritual, and works through each of the others before finishing with a sustained analysis of patterns of classroom interaction and the dynamics and content of teacher-pupil discourse. The same framework could be used to inform a rather different research methodology. The point at issue here is conceptual rather than technical: it concerns not the relative advantages of, say, systematic observation using pre-coded interaction categories to produce quantifiable data and the use of transcripts to sustain close-grained qualitative analysis of discourse, but the viability of this as a framework for researching teaching in any context and by any means.

Pedagogy as ideas

The second part of our framework for the comparative study of pedagogy attends to the ideas, values and beliefs by which the act of teaching is informed and justified. These can be grouped into three domains, as shown in Figure 19.2.

Classroom level: ideas which *enable* teaching

• *Students*	• characteristics, development, needs, differences
• *Learning*	• nature, facilitation, achievement and assessment
• *Teaching*	• nature, scope, planning, execution and evaluation
• *Curriculum*	• modes and domains of knowing, doing, creating, investigating and making sense

School/system-level: ideas which *formalise and legitimate* teaching

• *School*	• e.g. organisation, governance, ethos
• *Curriculum*	• e.g. aims, content, structure
• *Assessment*	• e.g. tests, qualifications; summative, formative
• *Other policies*	• e.g. equity, inclusion; teacher quality, expertise, training and deployment

Cultural/societal level: ideas which *locate* teaching

• *Culture*	• the stories we tell ourselves about ourselves
• *Self*	• what it is to be a person; identity and identities

Figure 19.2 Pedagogy as ideas

Private assumptions and beliefs about teaching are not distinguished here from public accounts of the kind which teachers meet while being trained, for all are a kind of theory. The object here is not to differentiate theory which is public or private, espoused or in use[19] but the themes with which such theories deal. Pedagogy has at its core ideas about learners, learning and teaching, and these are shaped and modified by context, policy and culture. Where the first domain *enables* teaching and the second *formalises* and *legitimates* it by reference to policy and infrastructure, the third domain *locates* it – and children themselves – in time, place and the social world, and anchors it firmly to the questions of human identity and social purpose without which teaching makes little sense. Such ideas enlarge the act of teaching to pedagogy and notions of what it is to be educated.

Macro and micro

The element in the framework in Figure 19.1 which most explicitly links macro with micro, in the narrower sense of policy and school rather than culture and professional agency, is the curriculum. In most systems curriculum is centrally prescribed, either at national level or, as in a federal and decentralised system like the United States, at the levels of state and school district. In rather fewer public education systems is control of the curriculum vested solely in the school.

In fact, the curriculum is probably best viewed as a series of *translations*, *transpositions* and *transformations* from its initial status as a set of formal requirements. At the beginning of this process of metamorphosis is the national or state curriculum. At its end is the array of understandings in respect of each specified curriculum goal and domain which the student acquires as a result of his or her classroom activities and encounters. In between is a succession of shifts, sometimes bold, sometimes slight, as curriculum moves from specification to transaction, and as teachers and students interpret, modify and add to the meanings which it embodies. Sometimes the change may be slight, as when a school takes a required syllabus or programme of study and maps it onto the timetable. This we might call a *translation*. Then a school or teacher may adjust the nomenclature and move parts of one curriculum domain into another to effect a *transposition*, which then leads to a sequence of lesson plans. But the real change, the *transformation*, comes when the curriculum passes from document into action and is broken down into learning tasks and activities and expressed and negotiated as teacher-student interactions and transactions.

However faithful to government, state or school requirements a teacher remains, teaching is always an act of curriculum transformation. In this sense, therefore, curriculum is a 'framing' component of the act of teaching, as suggested by Figure 19.1, only before it is transformed into task, activity, interaction, discourse and outcome. From that point on it becomes inseparable from each of these. In the classroom, curriculum *is* task, activity, interaction and discourse, and they are curriculum.

Figure 19.3 schematises this process, and ties it into the families of 'frame', 'form' and 'act' from the model of teaching in Figure 19.1. Together with Figure 19.2, the frameworks provide a basis for constructing a reasonably comprehensive empirical account of pedagogy at the level of action, and for engaging with the attendant discourses.

Of course, the macro-micro relationship is about much more than state-school curriculum transmission or transformation. For a start, the process is

Specification	National, state or local curriculum	1	
Translation	School curriculum	2	**Frame**
Transposition	Age/grade/class curriculum	3	
	Lesson plan	4	
Transformation	Lesson	5	**Form**
	Task	6	
	Activity	7	**Act**
	Interaction	8	
	Evaluation	9	

Figure 19.3 Curriculum metamorphosis

complicated by the existence of more levels than bipolar formulations like 'macro-micro' or 'centralisation-decentralisation' allow. Regional and local tiers of government have their own designated powers, or strive to compensate for their lack of these by exploiting their closeness to the action, and local agency manifests itself in many other guises, both formal and informal, beyond the governmental and administrative. In the *Five Cultures* data, the importance of these intermediate levels and agencies provided a corrective to Margaret Archer's classic account of the development of state education systems.[20] A proper explanatory account of pedagogical discourse needs to engage with this more complex arena of control and action if it is to move out of the straitjacket of linear models of teaching as policy-enactment and education as unmodified cultural transmission. Here the work of Giroux or Apple provides the necessary moderation to the stricter reproductionist line taken by Bowles and Gintis or Bourdieu and Passeron.[21]

Such an account also needs to treat the somewhat mechanistic concept of 'levels' itself with a certain caution, for once we view pedagogic practice through the profoundly important lens of values we find – as Margaret Archer shows in her later work[22] – that the relationship between structure, culture and (pedagogic) agency is more complex still.

Values

Values, then, spill out untidily at every point in the analysis of pedagogy, and it is one of the abiding weaknesses of much mainstream research on teaching, including the rare accounts that appear in the comparative education literature, that it tends to play down their significance in shaping and explaining observable practice. Latterly, the idea of 'value-free' teaching has been given a powerful boost by the endorsement by several Anglophone governments of school effectiveness research (which reduces teaching to technique and culture to one not particularly important 'factor' among many) and by its adoption, across the full spectrum of public policy, of the crudely utilitarian criterion 'what works'. Teaching is an intentional and moral activity: it is undertaken for a purpose and is validated by reference to educational goals and social principles as well as to operational efficacy. In any culture it requires attention to a range of considerations and imperatives: pragmatic, certainly, but also empirical, ethical and conceptual.[23]

Clearly, a value-sanitised pedagogy is not possible. It makes as little sense as a culture-free comparative education. Yet values can all too easily be neglected, and the problem may reflect the accident of technique rather than conscious design. Thus, an account of classroom interaction in Kenyan primary schools[24] uses Sinclair and Coulthard's discourse analysis system, which reduces spoken discourse to a hierarchy of ranks, transactions, moves and acts with little regard to its meaning and none to its sociolinguistic context.[25] The Kenyan study is illuminating, yet if the chosen procedure is problematic in linguistic terms, it may be doubly so in a comparative study of teachers in one country undertaken by researchers from another.

In the rather different setting of a seminar on the American East Coast, a participant viewed one of the *Culture and Pedagogy* lesson videotapes[26] and condemned the featured teacher for 'wasting time' when she negotiated with her students rather than directed them. The teacher concerned was highly experienced, and perfectly capable of delivering a traditional lesson and imposing her will upon the children. But she chose not to, because her educational goals included the development of personal autonomy and choice and she believed it necessary for children to learn, the hard way if necessary, how to master time rather than have it master them. (For time, as we found in this research, is a value in education as well as a measure of it, and it was viewed and used in very different ways in the five countries.[27]). This teacher was expressing in her practice not only her private values, but also those embodied in the policies of her school, school district and state. These values should have been the seminar participant's first port of call.

The issue here was not one of simple professional competence but of how, in a culture which stands so overtly for individual freedom of action, the diverging individualities of 25 students in one classroom can be reconciled with ostensibly common learning goals. For this example was but the tip of a values iceberg, a continuum in which the observed American pedagogy stood at the opposite extreme to what we observed in Russia and India. On the one hand, confusion, contradiction and inconsistency in values; on the other, clarity, coherence and consistency (inside the classroom at least, for what we saw on the streets of post-Soviet Russia told a different story, but then our teacher respondents were very clear that their task was to hold the line against the rising tide of *anomie*). It is this inherent cultural dissonance, as much as simple executive competence, which explains many of the startling contrasts in the practice, and in the apparent efficiency of the practice, with which such values were associated.

This example, too, may help us with our earlier asides about cultural borrowing and lending. For perhaps it is the degree of compatibility at the level of values which sets the limits to what can be successfully transferred at the level of practice. A pedagogy predicated on teacher authority, induction into subject disciplines, general culture and citizenship will sit uneasily, at best, with one which celebrates classroom democracy, personal knowledge, cultural pluralism, and antipathy to the apparatus of the state. And *vice versa*. This simple proposition, which can readily be tested in practice, eludes the policy borrowers, who presume that 'what works' in one country will work in another. Thus until Russian education succumbed to resource starvation following the economic crisis of the mid-1990s, Russian children continued for a while to outperform those of the United States in mathematics and science, despite the massive disparity in funding between the two countries' education systems.[28] Yet in those early years after the collapse of the Soviet Union the World Bank and OECD dismissed Russian teaching as 'authoritarian' and 'old-fashioned' and pressed for a more 'democratic' and 'student-centred' pedagogy.[29]

Temporal and spatial continuities

So the explication of values is *a sine qua non* for a comparative pedagogy. Such analysis can reveal continuities as well as differences. Thus, although an off-spring of revolution, French public education retains features which recall its pre-revolutionary and ecclesiastical origins,[30] and the conjunction of institutional secularism and individual liberty is not without its tensions, as is shown by the recurrent crises over *l'affaire du foulard* (the scarf in this case is the Muslim *hijab*, occasionally the *chador*). The more obvious Soviet trappings of Russian education have been shed, but the abiding commitment to *vospitanie*, and the emphasis in schools and classrooms on collective action and responsibility allied to unambiguous teacher authority, not to mention the methods of teaching, show all the more clearly that the continuities here are Tsarist as well as Soviet. The continuities in India reach back even further, and we found at least four traditions – two of them indigenous (Brahmanic and post-Independence) and two imposed (colonialist and missionary) - combining to shape contemporary primary practice in that vast and complex country.[31]

In England, the twin legacies of elementary school minimalism and progressive idealism offset government attempts at root-and-branch modernisation. The one still shapes school structures and curriculum priorities (and government is as much in its thrall as are teachers), while the other continues to influence professional consciousness and classroom practice. Indeed, in seeking to win over a disgruntled teaching force the UK government's post-2003 Primary National Strategy sought to soften its statist image by appealing directly to the progressivist virtues of 'enjoyment', 'creativity' and 'flexibility', complete with large print and pictures of smiling children. Some saw through this ploy; many others did not.[32]

Jerome Bruner reminds us, too, that in our pedagogical theorising 'we are still drawing rich sustenance from our more distant, pre-positivist past. Chomsky acknowledges his debt to Descartes, Piaget is inconceivable without Kant, Vygotsky without Hegel and Marx, and "learning theory" was constructed on foundations laid by John Locke'.[33]

This kind of intellectual layering or genealogy was most strongly visible in Russian pedagogy, partly because of the overall consistency of practice and partly because those whom we interviewed were themselves fully aware of the roots of their thinking; for this is a pedagogy in which – unlike in England – education theory and history are held to be important. Thus, if Russian pedagogy owes much, via Vygotsky and his disciples, to Hegel and Marx, it owes no less to a tradition of pedagogic rationality which reaches back via Ushinsky to Comenius and Francis Bacon. And it is a familiar truth that Lenin and Stalin built directly on the Tsarist legacy of political autocracy, nationalism and religious orthodoxy, thus securing fundamental continuities amidst the chaos.[34] In interview, one of our Russian teachers spoke readily about the influence on her pedagogy of Vygotsky (1896–1934), Ushinsky (1824–71) and Kamenski (Comenius, 1592–1670), not to mention a host of post-Vygotskians such as

Davydov, Elkonin and Leontiev and academics at the local pedagogical university. How many British teachers have this depth of historical awareness – let alone such interest in what, beyond personal values, public policies and classroom circumstances, might inform their teaching?

Temporal continuities such as these shape contemporary educational practice and set limits to the character and speed of its further development, notwithstanding the ahistorical zeal of government modernisers. The spatial continuities, casually crossing national borders without so much as a nod to Sadler, are detectable in a study involving several countries to an extent that is not possible, or plausible, in a study involving just two. These continuities place within our reach an important prize, that of differentiating the universal in pedagogy from the culturally-specific.

Versions of teaching

Again, it is not possible to list all the cross-cultural resonances we encountered in the *Five Cultures* research. However, overarching these were six versions of teaching and three primordial values which can be briefly summarised.

- *Teaching as transmission* sees education primarily as a process of instructing children to absorb, replicate and apply basic information and skills.
- *Teaching as initiation* sees education as the means of providing access to, and passing on from one generation to the next, the culture's stock of high-status knowledge, for example in literature, the arts, humanities and the sciences.
- *Teaching as negotiation* reflects the Deweyan idea that teachers and students jointly create knowledge and understanding in an ostensibly democratic learning community, rather than relate to one another as authoritative source of knowledge and its passive recipient.
- *Teaching as facilitation* guides the teacher by principles which are developmental (and, more specifically, Piagetian) rather than cultural or epistemological. The teacher respects and nurtures individual differences, and waits until children are ready to move on instead of pressing them to do so.
- *Teaching as acceleration*, in contrast, implements the Vygotskian principle that education is planned and guided acculturation rather than facilitated 'natural' development, and indeed that the teacher seeks to outpace development rather than follow it.
- *Teaching as technique*, finally, is relatively neutral in its stance on society, knowledge and the child. Here the important issue is the efficiency of teaching regardless of the context of values, and to that end imperatives like structure, economic use of time and space, carefully graduated tasks, regular assessment and clear feedback are more pressing than ideas such as democracy, autonomy, development or the disciplines.

The first is ubiquitous, but in the *Five Cultures* data it was most prominent in the rote learning and recitation teaching of mainstream Indian pedagogy. French classrooms provided the archetype of the second, but it also surfaced in

Russia and India, and – though often under professional protest at the primary stage – in England and the United States (its more secure pedigree in English education perhaps lies with Matthew Arnold and the independent and grammar school traditions). Teachers in the United States frequently argued and sought to enact both the third and the fourth versions of teaching, often with explicit obeisance to John Dewey and Jean Piaget. Those in England, subject to the pressures of the governments' literacy and numeracy strategies, still made much of developmental readiness and facilitation though rather less of democracy. Drawing explicitly on Vygotsky's maxim that 'the only good teaching is that which outpaces development', our Russian teachers illustrated the pedagogy of intervention and acceleration (version 5) which was diametrically opposed to facilitation and developmental readiness. At the same time, they, like teachers across a wide swathe of continental Europe, drew on the older Comenian tradition (version 6) of highly structured lessons, whole-class teaching, the breaking down of learning tasks into small graduated steps, and the maintenance of economy in organisation, action and the use of time and space.[35]

The trajectory of pedagogical reform shows interesting permutations on these. Thus, under the Government of India's District Primary Education Programme (DPEP) and its successor Sarva Shiksha Abhiyan (SSA), Indian teachers were urged to become more democratic and developmental (versions 3 and 4).[36] The language of developmentalism and facilitation also found its way into policy documents in France and Russia.[37] In contrast, English teachers were being urged to emulate the continental tradition represented by version 6, notably through the espousal of 'interactive whole-class teaching' in the UK government's literacy and numeracy strategies.[38] These are deliberate acts of pedagogical importation. How far the alien can accommodate to the indigenous remains to be seen.

A distinctly continental European tradition has already been inferred. The *Five Cultures* data enables the idea of broad pedagogical traditions which cut across national boundaries to be consolidated. In this research, the great cultural divide was the English Channel, not the Atlantic. There was a discernible Anglo-American nexus of pedagogical values and practices, just as there was a discernible continental European one, with Russia at one highly formalised extreme and France – more eclectic and less ritualised, though still firmly grounded in structure and *les disciplines* – at the other. India's pedagogy was both Asian and European, as its history would suggest.

Primordial values

Teachers in the five-nation study also articulated, enacted or steered an uncertain path between three versions of human relations: *individualism, community* and *collectivism*.

- *Individualism* puts self above others and personal rights before collective responsibilities. It emphasises unconstrained freedom of action and thought.

- *Community* centres on human interdependence, caring for others, sharing and collaborating.
- *Collectivism* also emphasises human interdependence, but only in so far as it serves the larger needs of society, or the state (the two are not identical), as a whole.

Within the observed classrooms, a commitment to individualism was manifested in intellectual or social differentiation, divergent rather than uniform learning outcomes, and a view of knowledge as personal and unique rather than imposed from above in the form of disciplines or subjects. Community was reflected in collaborative learning tasks, often in small groups, in 'caring and sharing' rather than competing, and in an emphasis on the affective rather than the cognitive. Collectivism was reflected in common knowledge, common ideals, a single curriculum for all, national culture rather than pluralism and multi-culture, and on learning together rather than in isolation or in small groups.

These values were pervasive at national, school and classroom levels. We are familiar with the contrast between the supposedly egocentric cultures of the west, with the United States as the gas-guzzling arch villain, and the supposedly holistic, sociocentric cultures of south and east Asia. Though there is evidence to support this opposition,[39] it is all too easy to demonise one pole and romanticise – or orientalise – the other. But I think when it comes to pedagogy the tripartite distinction holds up, and it seems by no means accidental that so much discussion of teaching methods should have centred on the relative merits of whole-class teaching, group and individual work.

In France this debate can be traced back to arguments at the start of the nineteenth century about the relative merits of *l'enseignement simultané*, *l'enseignement mutuel* and *l'enseignement individuel*.[40] As a post-revolutionary instrument for fostering civic commitment and national identity as well as literacy, *l'enseignement simultané* won. Only now, reflecting decentralisation and the rising tide of individualism, has its hegemony begun to be questioned.

Individualism, community and collectivism are – as child, group and class – the organisational nodes of pedagogy because they are the social nodes of human relations. However, divorcing teaching as technique from the discourse of pedagogy as we so often do, we may have failed to understand that such core values and value-dissonances pervade social relations inside the classroom no less than outside it; and hence we may have failed to understand why it is that undifferentiated learning, whole-class teaching and the principle of bringing the whole class along together 'fit' more successfully in many other cultures than they do in England or the United States, and why teachers in these two countries have sometimes approached this pedagogical formula with suspicion. For individualism and collectivism arise inside the classroom not as a clinical choice between alternative teaching strategies so much as a value-dilemma which may be fundamental to a society's history and culture.

But the scenario is not one of singularity. Human consciousness and human relations involve the interplay of all three values; and though one may be dominant, they may all in reality be present and exist in uneasy tension. Nowhere was this tension more evident than in the United States, where we found teachers seeking to reconcile – and indeed to foster as equivalent values – individual self-fulfilment with commitment to the greater collective good; self-effacing sharing and caring with fierce competitiveness; and environmentalism with consumerism. Meanwhile, in the world outside the school rampant individualism competed with the traditional American commitment to communal consciousness and local decision-making; and patriotism grappled with anti-statism. As the teacher interviews and lesson transcripts show, such tensions were manifested at every level from formal educational goals to the everyday discourse of teachers and children.[41]

Conclusion

If globalisation dictates a stronger comparative and international presence in educational research generally, there is a no less urgent need for comparativists to come to grips with the very core of the educational enterprise, pedagogy. Such an enterprise, however, demands as much rigour in the framing and analysis of pedagogy as in the act of comparing. In this chapter I have drawn on a five-nation comparative study of primary education to postulate principles and frameworks for a new comparative pedagogy. Pedagogy is defined stipulatively as the act of teaching together with its attendant discourses, ideas and values. The analysis of this discourse requires both that we engage with culture, values and ideas at the levels of classroom, school and system, and that we have a viable and comprehensive framework for the empirical study of teaching and learning. The interlocking models of pedagogy, teaching and curriculum in Figures 19.1–19.3, which were initially developed to frame the *Culture and Pedagogy* data analysis, link national culture, structure and policy with classroom agency; but they also allow for the structure-agency relationship to be played out within the micro-cultures of school and classroom.

The focus here is not on the detailed findings of the *Culture and Pedagogy* research but on the potential of its kind of analytical framework to support the overdue development of a comparative pedagogy. But in arguing the centrality of culture, history and values to a proper analysis of pedagogy, and in applying the chosen frameworks, tools and perspectives to five countries rather than just one or two, we can open up other important domains: that of the balance of change and continuity in educational thinking and practice over time, and of pedagogical diversity and commonality across geographical boundaries. In so doing, we are not only forced to re-assess the Sadlerian resistance to educational import-export; we also come closer to identifying the true universals in teaching and learning. A properly-conceived comparative pedagogy can both enhance our understanding of the interplay of education and culture and help us to improve the quality of educational provision.

Notes

1 Little 2000, 283.
2 Cowen 2000, 340.
3 Broadfoot 2000, 368.
4 Simon 1981b.
5 Crossley 2000, 324.
6 Little 2000.
7 Alexander 2001a.
8 King 1979.
9 'In studying foreign systems of education we should not forget that the things outside the schools matter even more than the things inside the schools, and govern and interpret the things inside' (Sadler 1900, 50).
10 Archer 2000, 1.
11 Joan Simon discusses the challenge of translating Russian terms like *obuchenie* and *obrazovanie* in Simon and Simon 1963.
12 Muckle 1988; Alexander 2001a, 368–70.
13 Alexander 2006a.
14 Reynolds and Farrell 1996; Stevenson and Stigler 1992; Clarke 2001.
15 Said 1979.
16 Alexander 2001a, 540–56; Moon 1998.
17 Leach 1964.
18 Alexander 2001a, 265–528.
19 Argyris and Schön 1974.
20 Archer 1979.
21 Giroux 1983; Apple 1995; Bowles and Gintis 1976; Bourdieu and Passeron 1990.
22 Archer 1989.
23 Politics of good practice. In Alexander 1997, 267–87.
24 Ackers and Hardman 2001.
25 Sinclair and Coulthard 1992.
26 With the permission of the teacher concerned. The ethics of using video as a research tool must always be taken seriously.
27 Alexander 2001a, 411–26.
28 Ruddock 2000; World Bank 2000.
29 World Bank 1996; OECD 1998b.
30 Sharpe 1997.
31 Kumar 1991.
32 DfES 2003; Alexander 2004a.
33 Bruner 1990, x–xi.
34 Lloyd 1998; Hobsbawm 1995.
35 Comenius 1657, 312–34.
36 Government of India 1998.
37 Ministère de l'Education Nationale 1998; Ministry of General and Professional Education 2000.
38 DfEE 1998a, 1999.
39 Shweder 1991.
40 Reboul-Sherrer 1989. Historically, *l'enseignement simultané*, *l'enseignement mutuel* and *l'enseignement individuel* denoted teaching that is simultaneous (i.e. whole-class teaching as we understand it), mutual (in this case peer-peer, so not unlike collaborative pair or group work) and individual (one to one, which could mean that the student worked with the teacher or, as under the monitorial system, an older or more advanced student).
41 Alexander 2001a, 201–6 and 490–515.

20 World beating or world sustaining?

' "World class schools" – noble aspiration or globalised hokum?' British Association for International and Comparative Education (BAICE) Presidential Address at the 10th UKFIET Conference on Education and Development, Oxford, 2009. Reprinted in *Compare 40(6)*, 801–818 (2010). An edited German version appeared in *Kulturvergleich in der Qualitativen Forschung* (eds Hummrich and Rademacher 2013), and an abbreviated version formed part of the keynote *Visiones Sobre Educacíon, Caminos de Reforma* at Universidad Gabriela Mistral, Santiago, Chile (2012).

'What do rich countries do?' The question was posed by Keith Lewin, one of my BAICE presidential predecessors, as a test of how far in their own backyards affluent nations rise to the challenges of access, enrolment, retention, quality, equity and governance on which they regularly pontificate to less affluent nations in the context of Education for All (EFA).

The answer, it would seem, is that a growing number of rich nations become obsessed with what other rich nations do, extrapolating from their competitors' success in pursuit of the accolade of 'world class'. With access, enrolment and retention more or less taken care of, and 'world class' defined almost exclusively in terms of tests of student attainment in a narrow spectrum of learning, they devote rather less attention to quality, equity and governance, which, arguably, are the hallmarks of an education system which is civilised as well as competitive.

The symptom and problem are usefully illustrated by the British government's 2009 pre-legislative White Paper *Building a 21st Century Schools System*. 'My ambition,' said Education Secretary of State Ed Balls in the paper's introduction, 'is for [England] to have the best school system in the world . . . schools are central to our . . . vision . . . to make this the best place in the world to grow up.'[1]

Some might consider the government's ambition both praiseworthy and necessary if a trifle unrealistic. After all, England does tolerably well in international surveys of student educational achievement like PISA, PIRLS and TIMSS; but certain countries in northern Europe and south-east Asia consistently do better. Even as I write, government advisers and media commentators are pondering the secret of Finland's success, asking which Finnish policies they should copy, and devising ever crueller ways to make poor Michael Sadler turn in his grave.[2]

DOI: 10.4324/9781315169378-24

Meanwhile, in a league table somewhat more attuned to those other EFA criteria, quality and equity, the UK came last in the 2007 UNICEF report on childhood wellbeing in the world's 21 richest nations.[3] Aggravating and to a considerable degree explaining Britain's low ranking in the UNICEF study was a *per capita* income gap which in the UK was wider than in most other high-GDP countries apart from the United States.[4] Moreover, as the British government's chief statistician told *The Guardian* in 2008:

> Britain grew richer during Tony Blair's decade in power, but for large sections of the population it did not become fairer . . . The income gap between high- and low-earners was not affected by the measures introduced while Gordon Brown was chancellor to raise the living standards of the poor.[5]

So what do rich nations do? In England's case, the long tail of student underachievement, which offsets the nation's otherwise respectable ranking in the international surveys, maps with considerable precision onto the demography of income, unemployment, health, risk and ethnicity. Conversely, as is shown in Wilkinson's and Pickett's groundbreaking reassessment of the international data on income, health, education and social wellbeing, more equal societies are not only happier but more successful, and the relationship is causal rather than coincidental.[6]

Thus it was that the Cambridge Primary Review's 2006–9 enquiry into the condition and future of English primary education identified poverty and inequality as far more genuine and urgent crises of British childhood than the 'cult of celebrity' on which the media have tended to fixate;[7] while closing the overlapping and contingent gaps in wealth, wellbeing and educational attainment headed the list of policy priorities which the Review presented to the leaders of the political parties contesting the May 2010 general election.[8]

This is the background to the chapter's examination of the idea and reality of 'world class' education. I shall examine the way that in education 'world class' tends to be defined and measured, the problems which are revealed by the prevailing definition, criteria and methods, and the wider educational and indeed moral questions which the 'world class' enterprise raises. I shall also refer, by way of case study, to a publication which epitomises the 'world class' educational quest and which bears the characteristic title *How the world's best-performing school systems come out on top*, otherwise known as the McKinsey report.[9] As a blueprint for educational reform and the achievement of world-class schools, the McKinsey report on education was embraced in Britain with a degree of political enthusiasm matched only by the speed with which the same politicians rejected the McKinsey report on health.

Talking of which, Britain's National Health Service (NHS) has also been infected by the 'world class' bug (if you will pardon the tasteless metaphor). McKinsey's brief from the Department of Health was to advise on 'how commissioners might achieve world class NHS productivity',[10] and 'world class commissioning', we were told, 'will be the delivery vehicle for world class clinical services and a world class NHS'.[11] When the phrase 'world class' is used three times in one sentence we might ask whether it amounts to anything at all. Indeed, in her 2002 study of the relationship between education and economic growth, Alison Wolf comments that 'In recent years, the term "world class . . ." has become a political and marketing slogan, with little attempt to define its meaning.'[12] It is in the category of meaningless slogans that we might place the stated aim of England's Qualifications and Curriculum Development Agency (QCDA) 'to develop a modern, world class curriculum that will inspire and challenge all learners and prepare them for the future'.[13] QCDA could hardly set out to develop an outdated, parochial curriculum that would bore and alienate learners and prepare them for the past, though there are no doubt some disaffected students who would find this recipe closer to their experience.

International usage

In fact, 'world class' is rather more than a slogan, for it has teeth — and they bite. Every few years, the research of academics and departments at British universities is assessed on behalf of the UK government against criteria such as 'recognised nationally', 'recognised internationally', 'internationally excellent' and of course 'world leading'. Internationally, similar exercises rank the world's universities using criteria such as Nobel Prizes, highly-cited researchers, and papers appearing in the Science and Social Science Citation Indices. A place in the THES-QS 'top 100 universities' ranking is eagerly sought. In 2009 the winners were Harvard, Cambridge, Yale, UCL, Imperial, Oxford and Chicago.[14] The 2009 Shanghai Academic Ranking of World Universities (ARWU) 'top 500' list was again headed by Harvard, with Stanford, Berkeley, Cambridge, MIT and Caltech close behind.[15]

Both lists were, and always are, dominated by American universities. Thus the Toronto *Globe and Mail* asked, on behalf of its envious Canadian readers, 'How *do* the Americans do it?' – answering, without missing a beat, 'money, of course . . . a significant world-class university is a billion-dollar a year operation, minimum'.[16] Never mind, according to statistics provided by *The Economist*, that the United States also outperforms Canada on less desirable indicators such as alcohol consumption, childhood obesity and the proportion of its population in prison; and never mind that Canada is in the happy, or dare I say euphoric, position of outperforming the United States not just in school-level educational achievement but also in cannabis use per head of population.[17] Never mind that Canada was much higher up the 2007 UNICEF league table of childhood wellbeing than the United States. Never mind Canada's superior performance on any number of contrary indicators of educational quality and social wellbeing: world class universities are what matter.

But, significantly, America's dominance of the world university league tables isn't matched at school level: 22nd in maths and 19th in science in PISA 2006; 11th at grade 8 and 9th at grade 4 in TIMSS 2007. In that discrepancy may lie uncomfortable truths about what money cannot buy, and about what, for the 50 per cent of Americans who do not go to university, money could be spent on but is not. So, in his presidential nomination acceptance speech at the Democratic Party convention in August 2008, Barack Obama said, 'Now is the time to finally meet our moral obligation to provide every child a world-class education, because it will take nothing less to compete in the global economy.' In response, there are few United States school boards which haven't by now adopted the term 'world class', often in bafflingly diverse ways. Go to Australia, Britain, Canada, New Zealand, the United States – any Anglophone country – and you will find yourself inspired or irritated by the same aspirational rhetoric, and by the associated anxiety: '*Can* our schools become world-class?' quavers the Toronto *Globe and Mail*.

But if we pursue 'world-class' across linguistic boundaries something different begins to emerge. On German websites *Weltklasse-Erziehung* turns out to be not an educational clarion call but merely a translation of 'world class education' as commended in Obama's nomination acceptance speech. On Russian websites 'world class education' takes one to the World Bank's attempts to encourage the 'modernisation' of Russian schools and universities on American lines. So is 'world class' just another symptom of globalisation as westernisation, or – as our French friends would no doubt have it – *l'impérialisme anglo-saxon*?

But explore the French connection further and you'll find a concept of education *au niveau mondial* – at global level – which has little to do with McKinsey's 'How the best-performing school systems come out on top' and rather more to do with global consciousness. At this point, we note two contrasting definitions: world class as beating or conquering the world and world class as understanding, engaging with and indeed sustaining the world; between competition and co-operation; between education for national supremacy and education for global interdependence.

American cable television magnate Glenn R. Jones may well be right that education is now the biggest market in the world. It is in that knowledge that education systems find themselves competing to secure market dominance in terms of the best students and researchers, and it is why they feel obliged to frame their outcomes as tightly-focused and marketable skills rather than pursue old-fashioned notions of a liberal education. '"Economically valuable skills" is our mantra', says the Leitch Report, commissioned by the UK government to address the question of how a small and crowded country like Britain, with limited natural resources, can remain economically competitive;[18] and the mantra is dutifully repeated by many or most of Britain's university vice-chancellors.

Yet the alternative perspective is also gathering strength, and it is no less driven by global awareness. Here, some very different league tables command our attention: for example, the ranking from 1st to 179th place on the UN Human Development Index (HDI) which bands nations by 'high', 'medium' and 'low' human development with its composite measure of life expectancy, education and *per capita* GDP, and for 2007–8 placed Iceland in triumphant first place.[19] That was before the meltdown of Iceland's banking system eerily foreshadowed the melting of its glaciers.

Talking of global warming, the subtitle of the 2007–8 HDI report – *Human solidarity in a divided world* – effectively captures the gulf between the two versions of 'world class':

> Climate change is the defining human development challenge of the 21st century . . . In a divided but ecologically interdependent world, it challenges all people to reflect upon how we manage the environment of the one thing that we share in common: planet Earth. It challenges us to reflect on social justice across countries and generations . . . It challenges political leaders and people in rich nations to acknowledge their historic responsibility for the problem . . . It challenges the entire human community to undertake prompt and strong collective action based on shared values and a common vision.[20]

'Shared values and a common vision': worlds apart, one might suggest, from 'How the best-performing school systems come out on top.'

Then there are those league tables that fill the second half of UNESCO's annual Education for All global monitoring reports (GMRs) that track the world's halting progress towards the UN Millennium Development Goal of achieving universal primary education by 2015[21]; league tables which cover every factor and indicator that we imagine can be contingent on the achievement of the six subsidiary EFA goals, provided – a big proviso – that they can be quantified and measured. On the other hand, the discussion of EFA is vastly more sophisticated and sensitive than that which commonly attends the idea of 'world class' schools.

Until fairly recently, these two worlds and two kinds of consciousness remained resolutely apart, and the builders of Western education systems left it to their international development colleagues, and to donors and NGOs, to worry about the millions of children and families for whom any education, let alone a supposedly world class education, was beyond reach. But now, connections are being made, and we find a growing interest in the national curricula of many countries in a concept of citizenship which is global rather than merely national. Thus, for example, from Scotland's national curriculum:

> The global dimension recognises that we now live in an interdependent global society. It incorporates key concepts of human rights, diversity, conflict resolution, social justice, interdependence and sustainable development in international context. It is an essential component of developing responsible global citizens.[22]

I am aware of the reservations of those like Lynn Davies who ask whether 'global citizenship' may be just too vast and abstract a concept for useful purchase at classroom level.[23] It's for that reason that in the Cambridge Primary

Review we present global citizenship not as an attribute apart but as the proper extension of citizenship more locally defined;[24] and we tie it back into pedagogy in the same way that the 2005 EPPI review showed how understanding of citizenship as *action* (as opposed to information about the institutions of governance and the rhetoric of democracy by which such institutions are officially justified) starts with the dynamics of the classroom and the extent and manner in which children are involved in decisions about their own learning.[25] Yet there's clearly a danger that global citizenship, like 'world class' this and that, will satisfy a feel-good requirement but achieve little else.

The genealogy of 'world class' education

Although visions of world domination have driven nations and their leaders ever since my Macedonian namesake set out for Iran and India in 334 BCE, its emergence as an *educational* ambition is more recent. The context of Michael Sadler's objections to misplaced policy borrowing at the end of the nineteenth century was rivalry within the narrow geographical frame of just two countries, Britain and Germany. By the 1980s the field was much broader. The OECD started amassing indicators of inputs, outputs, processes and resources for its international series *Education at a Glance*, first published in 1992. Then there was the International Association for the Evaluation of Educational Achievement (IEA). Though it originated at a UNESCO meeting as far back as 1958 and was legally incorporated in 1967, its early efforts made little impact. In 1992, the so-called 'three wise men' report on English primary education surveyed the then available IEA and IAEP reports for evidence on how the attainment of English primary pupils compared with that from other countries, but found the data to be too sparse, inconclusive and methodologically problematic to be useful.[26] Only with PISA and TIMSS, from 1999 onwards, do we seem to have entered an era where expert analysts are prepared to take the international achievement data seriously, and even then they invariably add notes of caution, as – to their credit – do the authors of the survey reports themselves.

Meanwhile, following the 1983 report *A Nation at Risk* and the 1991 national educational goals, the 1994 *Educate America Act* launched world class education – in the sense of global supremacy – with its famous but doomed declaration that 'By the year 2000, United States students will be first in the world in mathematics and science achievement.' Whoever proposed 'the best school system in the world' and 'the best place in the world to grow up' for Ed Balls's confident introduction to the 2009 White Paper should perhaps have reminded him of this cautionary tale from across the Atlantic. But then, you can be sure that the person who drafted the White Paper was neither a comparativist nor a historian.

What above all has facilitated and encouraged the supremacist view of world class education in high-income countries is the growing availability of data which positively invite the league table treatment. Those data have been mainly provided by the IEA and OECD, who between them have produced the achievement studies in mathematics, science, reading literacy, citizenship and technology which announce themselves by bewildering acronyms like FIMS, SIMS, FISS, SISS, TIMSS, TIMSS-R, PIRLS, ICCS, SITES, TEDS-M and of course PISA.

In England, the study which set the seal on the trend was the review *Worlds Apart? A review of international surveys of educational achievement involving England*, which Ofsted, England's national schools inspectorate, commissioned from David Reynolds and Shaun Farrell.[27] Published only four years after the so-called 'three wise men' report had concluded that such data were not yet safe as a tool of policy,[28] the Reynolds study proceeded not just to identify trends but also to propose causes and solutions, framing the entire analysis by the assumptions and methods of what Reynolds and his colleagues called the 'discipline' of school effectiveness research.

In 1996, I published a detailed critique of the Ofsted study, and the ISERP school effectiveness project on which it drew, and I have since elaborated that critique.[29] I don't intend to repeat it here except briefly to mention some of its salient points:

- The quality and effectiveness of whole schools and entire education systems is reduced to a statistical calculation of gain in output over input.
- The measures of input and output used are extremely restricted in relation to what we know from other sources about the contexts, conditions, processes and outcomes of schooling and learning. Output measures are confined to students' test scores in limited aspects of a narrow range of subjects, and these are taken as proxies for pupil attainment across the entire curriculum.
- The 'process' measures which are added to the mix in order to calculate what aspects of education make a difference are no less restricted, for they must satisfy the basic requirement of measurability. Hence the fixation on measures like time on task – which the late Nate Gage called 'a psychologically empty concept'.[30] As we cross cultures, we find time in teaching and learning, notwithstanding its arithmetic constancy, is also culturally elastic. Time is a value in education, not just a measure of it.[31]
- Culture – which is absolutely central to the proper pursuit of educational comparison – is reduced to one 'factor' among many, something which is external to school life rather than that which creates it and gives it meaning.
- The literature on which the paradigm draws represents a very narrow segment of the wider literatures on comparative and international education and on school and classroom processes.

As if to celebrate these limitations, the 1996 *Worlds Apart* study said, of the work of those who tend to be members of BAICE:

The frankly inept contribution which the comparative education discipline has made over time . . . the presence of a large body of theories, without any apparent empirical backing . . . a large range of descriptive case studies of individual schools which it is impossible to synchronise together because there are no common measures of outcomes or processes utilised . . . descriptions of the range of educational, political, economic and cultural phenomena within different countries, with no attempt ever made to assess the contribution of the educational system as against that of other factors.[32]

There is certainly a problem – which Angela Little noted from her systematic analysis of the comparative literature a few years ago[33] – of a preponderance of one-country studies that are not really comparative at all. But the literature has also demarcated with considerable care the different kinds and paradigms of comparative research and the uses to which it may legitimately be put and it is clear that comparativists are as interested as the next person in cause, consequence and practical application.

Of course, criticisms of particular comparative approaches and studies are merited and necessary, and I myself entered the field deeply concerned at the almost total omission from comparative enquiry, until very recently, of *pedagogy* – this being the crucial point at which culture, history, policy and ideas about education come together as observable action and felt experience in the classroom.[34] Comparative pedagogy was a grave, even epic omission. But it's notable that in 2003 the now sadly-defunct BICSE – the Board on International Comparative Studies in Education of the United States National Academy of Sciences – also found the Ofsted report's 'them and us' methodological dichotomy of large and small scale, quantitative and qualitative, decidedly unhelpful and came up instead with three main types of study, characterised by purpose rather than scale or method.

Type I studies typically include large-scale surveys that aim to compare educational outcomes at various levels . . . Type II studies are designed to inform one or more particular . . . education policies by studying specific topics relevant to those policies and their implementation in other countries. Type III studies are not designed to make direct comparisons . . . in terms of specific policies or educational outcomes. Rather, they aim to further understanding of educational processes in different cultural and national contexts.[35]

Type I includes the large-scale international student achievement studies like TIMSS, PISA and PIRLS. Type II covers the policy-directed studies, outside the context of achievement testing, commissioned by national governments or international agencies (the *Worlds Apart* study of Reynolds and Farrell, commissioned by Ofsted, is an example). Type III includes the majority of academic comparative studies. The EFA global monitoring reports would, I suppose, represent a combination of Types I and II.

BICSE has no doubt where the power and perceived policy relevance lies, for while the majority of comparative education studies are Type III, Type

I and II studies receive most of the funding, and the funding difference per study is truly vast. Type I and II studies are a multi-million-dollar business. Type III studies scrape together what they can from hard-pressed funding bodies. Yet, the BICSE report goes on, in terms which contrast sharply with the comments of Reynolds and Farrell:

> Although they vastly outnumber Type I and Type II studies, Type III studies often do not come to the attention of policy makers or the public. This is a loss, since many are rich in narrative detail and paint a more engaging and provocative portrait of education in other countries than do the summary bar charts and graphs typical of many larger studies. Ethnographic and case studies, in particular, can explore cultural context in depth and, in turn, help elucidate the way education is organised and understood in different cultures.[36]

Before I turn, as I said I would, to the McKinsey report as the current manifestation of the kind of thinking that informed the 1996 *Worlds Apart* report, we might ask whether those who work within this paradigm have modified their position, perhaps heeding BICSE's conclusion. Sadly, the answer would appear to be 'no'. In a later study Reynolds and his colleagues moved from disdain to defiance:

> In the United Kingdom the recent attacks upon the school effectiveness paradigm . . . have extended to attacks upon the ISERP study and the thinking behind it . . . Their arguments appear to be frankly non-rational to a marked degree . . . Throughout their writing is an intellectual temerity and doubt about 'what works' that probably reflects *simple* ignorance of the literature . . . Perhaps the critics are *simply* taking refuge in 'context specificity' rather than facing an intellectual challenge . . . that is *simply* beyond them . . . If attention is paid to them, the critics may, wittingly or unwittingly, be damaging the prospects of educational advance, since countries that restrict the search for 'good practice' only to those educational settings within their own boundaries, of necessity miss potentially valuable practices from outside their own boundaries.[37]

Once an academic resorts to *ad hominem* attacks you know that he or she has nowhere else to go (my added italics register the not-so-subliminal message that comparativists are simpletons). If comparativists try to understand the character and power of context and culture, it's not so that they can 'take refuge in context specificity' and deny the applications of what they study, but rather so that they can understand why 'what works' works there but may or may not work here; and so that they can move beyond copying the surface features of 'what works' to a proper understanding of the thinking which informs it. That thinking is embedded not just in culture but also in history, and comparativists also know that history is a tale of the international traffic in *ideas* as well as people and commodities. Sadler's famous injunction against international cherry-picking (though he used the metaphor of picking flowers) is not a denial of history or an intellectual trade embargo but a note of caution about the need to temper conscious acts of educational import and export with proper understanding. For, as I have noted elsewhere:

> Cultural borrowing happens; it has always happened. Few countries remain hermetically sealed in the development of their educational systems, and for centuries there has been a lively international traffic in educational ideas and practices. So, for example, Pestalozzi mingles with Tagore, Krishnamurti and the Elmhirsts in both English and Indian progressivism; Dewey turns up briefly in China, the Soviet Union and Turkey as well more lastingly in England and the United States; both the German *Gymnasium* and the American high school help shape the development of Russian schooling; Kay Shuttleworth imports or exports the *Ecole Normale* from France to England and India; Jan Komensky (Comenius) journeys tirelessly from Moravia to Heidelberg, Amsterdam, Prague, Berlin, Paris, Stockholm, London and points between and beyond, and his principles of common vernacular schooling and carefully graduated whole class teaching, not to mention his textbooks, embed themselves deeply and lastingly in the pedagogy of many countries of central, eastern and northern Europe; and the monitorial systems of Bell and Lancaster seed themselves just about everywhere from their probable roots in what was then Madras.[38]

And so onwards, upwards or backwards to the 2007 report, *How the best-performing school systems come out on top*, from the multi-national management consultancy McKinsey. It is difficult not to be influenced by the report's physical format, though I shall try. It's so large that one has to stand up to read it – an act of enforced deference which I somewhat resent. Its cover is solidly constructed of cardboard of the same robust grade as is used for eco-coffins. Inside, as in *Worlds Apart*, the baseline for McKinsey's comparative analysis is the international student achievement survey, and here too culture is mentioned only to be dismissed:

> International comparisons such as . . . PISA . . . make it now possible to regularly and directly compare the quality of education outcomes across education systems . . . But measuring performance does not automatically lead to insights as to what policy and practice can do to help students to learn better, teachers to teach better, and schools to operate more effectively. This is where McKinsey's report comes in . . . With a focus on issues that transcends [sic] cultural and socio-economic contexts, such as getting the right people to become teachers, developing those people into effective instructors, and putting in place targeted support . . . the report allows policy-makers to learn about features of successful systems without copying systems in their entirety.[39]

The quest for universals in education is an interesting and I believe necessary one. Certainly it informed my own comparative study of primary education in England, France, India, Russia and the United States.[40] But you achieve an account of what might arguably be deemed universal only by staying as close as possible to national and local culture, not by sidelining it in the way of reports such as this. Otherwise all you get is reduction to the banalities of McKinsey's conclusion:

> The experiences of these top ten school systems suggest that three things matter most: 1) getting the right people to become teachers, 2) developing them into effective instructors and, 3) ensuring that the system is able to deliver the best possible instruction for every child.[41]

I don't know how much this report cost – McKinsey charged the UK tax-payer £1.27 million for the report on health service reform which the British government promptly rejected, so no doubt the McKinsey study of world class schools cost something similar. But I'm not sure that if I were told, after all the words, pictures, paper and coffin-grade cardboard, that children need good teachers, good teacher training and good teaching, I would gladly reach for my credit card, still less when I look at the bibliography and discover the same wilful isolation from the richness of the mainstream comparative literature which characterises other examples of the genre. Even worse, McKinsey says that good teaching matters – which it certainly does – but then announces: 'We have chosen *not* to focus on pedagogy or curricula, however important these subjects might be in themselves. These subjects are well-debated in the literature.'[42]

I note these omissions for the most basic of methodological reasons. If research from the school effectiveness stable stands or falls on the validity and reliability of the student attainment measures by which it judges effectiveness, then in seeking to understand what makes a school effective, such research also stands or falls on its capacity to engage in a conceptually valid and empirically defensible way with what schools and teachers do with the students whose attainment they seek to advance. It simply isn't good enough, in a study entitled *How the World's Best-Performing Systems Come Out on Top*, where the word 'how' surely signals the intention to explain, to say, 'The quality of teaching is what makes the most difference, but we not going to discuss teaching or define quality.' What kind of an explanation is that?

For the rest, I'm afraid it's the familiar story. Here are three further examples of the frailty of this much-praised product of the world-class education industry, illustrating its failure at the levels of *conceptualisation*, *veracity* and *meaningfulness*.

First, McKinsey insists that 'All of the top-performing systems . . . recognise that they cannot improve what they do not measure.'[43] Now there's an interesting one, not just because of its absolute faith in measurement but because of how it translates at the level of the school, where it looks like a counsel of despair. Are teachers not capable of improving children's learning unless they measure it? What of the majority of the curriculum which in the English primary system is not measured? Are primary science, art, humanities, music and personal education incapable of improvement because they are not tested? Are only literacy and numeracy amenable to improvement? Or does McKinsey really mean 'assess' rather than 'measure', in which case we might agree that the improvement and assessment of learning go hand in hand? And is McKinsey really saying, not so subliminally, that what is *not* measured is of no importance? And what would McKinsey make of Wynne Harlen's finding, after carefully surveying published research on the relationship between testing and standards for the Cambridge Primary Review, that testing may *measure* standards but does not of itself *raise* them, except obliquely and temporarily?[44] What raises standards is good teaching. But then McKinsey opts not to discuss teaching.

My second example has to do with truth. McKinsey talks confidently about how the 25 school systems which it has chosen to benchmark actually work. Thus:

> Singapore's school system is managed from the centre and they have used this to drive through improvements in performance. In England, policymakers have relatively less control over its more decentralised school system, so they have used standards, funding, public accountability and strong support mechanisms to create the conditions under which improvement can occur.[45]

The comparison is interesting: Singapore's state school system has just 331 schools to England's 24,360, so in this particular context does the comparison have any point? Even more interesting is the claim about 'decentralised' England, for other sources suggest that since 1987, and especially since 1997, England's school system has become one of the most highly centralised among all rich nations, delegating budgets but controlling from the centre what matters most – curriculum, assessment, quality assurance, pedagogy and teacher training – to an extent which prompted advisers to the Cambridge Primary Review to suggest that England's primary schools were subject to a 'state theory of learning' ordained by government and its agencies and enforced and policed by Ofsted, the Training and Development Agency (TDA) and local authority SIPs.[46] This was a grave and unpalatable charge, but one which after careful assessment of the evidence the Cambridge Primary Review felt obliged to uphold.[47]

So McKinsey falls at the hurdles of conceptualisation and veracity. It also has a problem with language and meaning. Most of the time one is merely bemused by its densely-deployed management jargon, but from time to time even that dissolves into utter meaninglessness. Thus: 'Top-performing school systems leverage a substantial and growing knowledge about what constitutes effective school leadership to develop their principals into drivers of improvement in instruction.'[48]

Taking stock

Let me work towards my conclusion by summarising the position so far. The phrase 'world class' has become both a linguistic adjunct to globalisation and the stated aspiration of national governments worldwide, especially in rich Anglophone countries. It is an aspiration which covers a wide range of aspects of national life, from economic performance to public services like health and education.

When it is anything more than an unthinking cliché, and often it isn't, 'world class' is defined in relation to measurable educational outputs, whether these be research productivity and international academic visibility in universities, or, in schools, student performance in international achievement surveys such as TIMSS, PISA and PIRLS.

The assessment procedures which are used in these surveys lend themselves readily to translation into league tables of nations, just as in England the national tests have been used to generate league tables of schools, and in the UK as a whole the Research Excellence Framework (REF) has produced league tables of universities, university departments and indeed individual academics.

Linked with these developments, at school level, has been a particular approach to educational enquiry which goes by the name of school effectiveness research. This treats the national and international test scores as valid and reliable measures of school and school system effectiveness, and draws on the older tradition of process–product research to find correlates for educational input and process which will explain what it is in classrooms, schools and systems which generates effectiveness as measured at the level of outcome; and what it is that makes one school or one system more or less effective than another. Because the exercise is a statistical one, the input and process correlates which are chosen, like the outcome measures, are limited to those aspects of education which are measurable.

The enterprise as a whole, therefore, is massively skewed away from aspects of education which are not measured, either because they are unmeasurable or because they are not deemed significant enough to justify the effort. Instead, what are measured at the levels of input, process and output are taken as proxies for the whole – thus, for example, opportunity to learn and time on task as proxy for the complexities of pedagogy, and basic literacy and numeracy as a proxy for the entire curriculum. This preoccupation becomes a self-fulfilling prophecy: the curriculum as taught tends to shrink until it becomes indistinguishable from the tested proxy, while the measurable aspects of pedagogy – time on task, for example – are pursued as ends in themselves.

Aggravating these distortions is an unwillingness of those operating within this paradigm not just to look at other aspects of education but also to consider other kinds of research which might illuminate their understanding of what they are researching, as commended, for example, in the 2003 BICSE report referred to earlier.

The paradigm leads, inevitably, to confident but questionable claims about cause, effect, what 'works' and what does not, extending outwards from the process-product relationship within education to the relationship between particular educational outcomes and a nation's economic performance. The literature tells us, however, that establishing causality in both areas is a minefield. Meanwhile, 'what works' educationally may be no more than what works methodologically. Reductionism is the name of the game.

The skewing of judgements on standards and effectiveness may also distort what schools actually do, since armed with their limited data policymakers subject schools to pressure to 'drive up standards' only in and through what is measured. Hence, in England, Labour's so-called 'standards agenda' of mandatory literacy and numeracy strategies for every teacher, reinforced by key stage tests and teacher training, and policed for compliance by Ofsted inspection.

At international level, the world-class aspiration produces an essentially supremacist ethic and 'world class' comes to mean 'world beating'. At national level, school league tables praise, name and shame, and there are uncomfortable tensions between the rhetorics of competition and inclusion.

In sharp contrast are two other kinds of globally-oriented development. First, there are those who, with an eye to the fragility of international relations and the global ecosystem, see a world class education not as one which enables one country merely to *beat* the others, but as engendering the capacity to *understand*, *engage with* and indeed *sustain* the world while nevertheless being economically successful and productive. Out of this has come a range of curricular and educational developments which are of considerable significance and potential but remain well below the radar of the supremacist view of world class schooling and its attendant measures of educational effectiveness. Second, there are those who out of a commitment to equity, social justice and national prosperity, and impelled by the inequalities that generated Jomtien, Dakar, the UN Millennium Development Goals and Education for All, study very different league tables of human development and educational progress and use them to target policies and resources which will reduce the gap between those at the league tables' upper and lower ends.

The two world-views ought to meet in a recognition of the inseparability of education from other aspects of national life, but they don't. School effectiveness detaches schools and systems from culture and context while education for development not only understands the power of these but also recognises that the advancement of education must go hand in hand with efforts to reduce poverty, gender disparity and discrimination, and improve health, wellbeing and childcare. (As I noted in the introduction, this understanding informs the 2021 EPI and EHI reports on post-Covid recovery, but not, apparently UK government thinking.)[49]

However – and this point is crucial – both world-views encounter acute difficulties in relation to what we mean by the *quality* of education. In the first tradition, quality actually doesn't feature, and the notion of 'standards' is preferred, standards being defined as testable and tested outcomes rather than experienced processes. In education for development, both quality and process are now deemed hugely important, as is equity, and they are a necessary corrective to the earlier though necessary preoccupation with access, enrolment and retention. At the same time, I have to say that there is the same urge to reduce quality to quantity in order that it can be indicated and measured; the same tendency to reduce the proper scope and complexity of educational process and outcome to a small number of proxies; and the same risk that the entire enterprise will be seriously distorted both in the way it is perceived and understood and in what – in the language of the McKinsey report – are defined as the essential levers or drivers of educational improvement. We need good system-level data, and inevitably it must be quantified for speedy analysis, but I don't think that in the development context we've yet solved the problem of how to quantify educational quality in a way which does justice to those aspects of pedagogy which really do make a difference – the quality of classroom interaction, for example.[50]

Conclusion: small, rich or equal?

For those interested in cause and effect and the so-called drivers and levers of educational improvement, here are two further thoughts on Finland, the country which on the basis of its students' performance in TIMMS and PISA currently heads the league table of 'world class' education systems.

What makes Finnish schooling so effective? McKinsey, as we've seen, settles for good teachers, teacher training and teaching. Others dig deeper, highlighting, alongside teachers' motivation, entry level and qualifications, factors such as relative cultural and linguistic homogeneity; low rates of immigration; high levels of student engagement with reading outside school; universal entitlement to high quality pre-school education coupled with a relatively late start to formal schooling and an emphasis on thoroughly preparing children, socially and linguistically, for learning in school; decentralised decision-making and a high degree of institutional and professional autonomy.[51]

Beyond these, Finland has two features which tend not to be acknowledged by the architects and defenders of high-stakes standards drives such as those in England and the United States:

- a paramount commitment to social and educational equity through a genuinely comprehensive school system of consistently high quality, with a minimal private sector which co-exists rather than competes with the public sector;
- no national tests, no league tables, no draconian national system of inspection, no national teaching strategies, and indeed none of the so-called 'levers' of systemic reform in which the British government has invested so much.[52]

My second comment on Finland might look like statistical mischief-making but has a serious purpose. If we look at Ruzzi's synthesis of all the international achievement survey results from 1995 to 2003,[53] we find that at the top of the combined league table there is disproportionate representation from countries which – like Finland – have small populations and are relatively homogenous culturally and linguistically. If we take the 19 countries which between them take the top 12 places in reading, maths and science, their average population is just 18.1 million. Remove Japan, the one country in the list with a large population, and that average national population drops to 12.1 million, which in global terms is truly minute. The McKinsey report doesn't say that the best performing school systems come out on top because they are small and rich, but if you play the game of educational cause and consequence at this simple level that's what you might conclude.

It *is* grossly simplistic. Yet take the case of the United States, which doesn't feature at all in Ruzzi's league tables despite its massive educational purchasing power. It has a population of over 332 million (Finland has 5.5 million). It is culturally highly diverse. There is considerable variation in educational funding and provision between individual states and school boards. There are massive disparities in the wealth, health and prospects of its citizens, and considerable divergence in matters of value and identity. On some measures it is the most unequal of all the rich countries. It seems reasonable to suggest that in this case size, diversity and inequality militate against wealth, and that if money can buy a world-class university system, at least as judged by the chosen measures of research productivity used in the THES and Shanghai league tables, it takes much more than money to achieve a world class school system. For while university systems cater for the relatively privileged, school systems cater for all. Culture, social structure, history, values, and policies in the wider economic and social spheres matter too – a great deal.

On this basis, Japan's appearance among the 'small, rich and educationally successful' nations in Ruzzi's table is not the anomaly it might seem, for in terms of the income difference between a country's rich and poor, Japan is one of the more equal of the world's 23 richest nations.[54] Wealthy and educationally successful Singapore is bottom of the same list but it has only 5.9 million inhabitants. So there's a constellation of factors in which wealth, demography, equity and relative equality all play a part alongside the school and education system factors on which McKinsey concentrates, though in the end it's culture that determines how wealth is disposed, how education is conceived and how much or little equality matters. For Wilkinson and Pickett, however, the latter is the key:

> Greater equality, as well as improving the wellbeing of the whole population, is also the key to national standards of achievement and how countries perform in lots of different fields . . . There is not one policy for reducing inequality in health or the educational performance of school children, and another for raising national standards of performance . . . If . . . a country wants higher average levels of educational achievement among its school children, it must address the underlying inequality which creates a steeper social gradient in educational achievement.[55]

In 2021, the debate about post-Covid recovery confirms even more strongly the force of this thesis. Health, income, housing and educational inequalities continued to coincide, and the equality gap was even more cruelly underlined in striking regional differences in the death rate and life expectancy referred to in this book's introduction.

The McKinsey report rightly says: 'The quality of an education system cannot exceed the quality of its teachers.'[56] But remember also Ernest Boyer: 'A report card on public education is a report card on the nation. Schools can rise no higher than the communities that support them.'[57]

What I have discussed here illustrates some significant and profoundly unhelpful divisions in the international discourse of education. The long-standing divide between the paradigms of comparative and development education is still with us, though it is less pronounced than it used to be, and the way UKFIET and BAICE come together every two years is a testament to such convergence, or at least to hope that it can be achieved. But other divisions are less readily bridged. There's the aggressively-defended barrier between the international school effectiveness movement and mainstream comparative research; and between the versions of 'world class' which I've explored here, between education for supremacy and education for viability, interdependence and sustainability. If the coming global crisis really is one of human survival, then this last gulf needs to be bridged, and urgently.

Finally, there is the gap between national and international consciousness in the wider education community. It is encouraging that global citizenship, despite its problematic nature conceptually, is being explored as an essential part of the school curriculum in an increasing number of countries; that the menu of modern foreign languages is now far longer than it used to be, and that many Western school students are now learning languages like Mandarin Chinese and Arabic which would have been unthinkable as school subjects only a few years ago; that international student exchanges are increasingly commonplace; and that there is a growing interest in international schools and the International Baccalaureate. But it remains the case, in Britain at least, that too often it is left for comparativists to bring an international dimension to national educational research; and that comparativists too often exist at one stage removed from other education academics.

In the Cambridge Primary Review we sought to make the global dimension natural and inevitable rather than laboured; as intrinsic to the analysis of English education as the gathering of statistics on schools and local authorities; and as proper a component of the curriculum as the 3Rs. What is required, in the context of globalisation, migration, poverty, inequality, cultural fluidity, geo-political tension and, above all, the crises of climate change and human survival, is an educational consciousness which is instinctively and inevitably international, and which understands that the imperatives are moral as well as economic. It's from that consciousness that truly world class education will emerge.

Notes

1 DCSF 2009, 2.
2 Sadler 1900, 50, again: 'No other nation, by imitating a little bit of German organisation, can thus hope to achieve a true reproduction of the spirit of German institutions . . . All good and true education is an expression of national life and character.'
3 UNICEF 2007.
4 Wilkinson and Pickett 2010.
5 Carvel 2008.
6 Wilkinson and Pickett 2010.
7 Alexander 2010a, 488.
8 Cambridge Primary Review 2010.
9 Barber and Mourshed 2007.
10 McKinsey 2009.
11 Britnell 2007.
12 Wolf 2002.
13 QCDA 2009.
14 THE 2009. In 2021 the top seven were: Oxford, Stanford, Harvard, Caltech, MIT, Cambridge, Berkeley (THE 2021).
15 CWCU 2009.
16 Usher 2006.
17 *The Economist* 2009.
18 H.M. Treasury 2006.
19 UNDP 2008.
20 UNDP 2008.
21 UNESCO 2008. Chapter 22 in this volume discusses the 2014 GMR.
22 Scottish Government 2008.
23 Davies 2006.
24 Alexander 2010a, 267–80.
25 Deakin Crick *et al* 2005.
26 Alexander *et al* 1992, 11–17.
27 Reynolds and Farrell 1996.
28 Alexander *et al* 1992, 15–17.
29 Alexander 1996, 2001a, 2008a.
30 Gage 1978, 75.
31 Alexander 2001a, 425.
32 Reynolds and Farrell 1996, 53.
33 Little 2000.
34 Alexander 2001a, 2001b. See this volume, Chapter 19.
35 National Research Council 2003, 13.
36 National Research Council 2003, 23–4.
37 Reynolds *et al* 2002, 287–8.
38 Alexander 2001a, 508.
39 Barber and Mourshed 2007, 6.
40 Alexander 2001a.
41 Barber and Mourshed 2007, 2.
42 Barber and Mourshed 2007, 8.
43 Barber and Mourshed 2007, 36.
44 Harlen 2007.
45 Barber and Mourshed 2007, 40.
46 Balarin and Lauder 2008.
47 Alexander 2010a, 291–9. See this volume, Chapter 7.
48 Barber and Mourshed 2007, 30.
49 Crenna-Jennings *et al* 2021; Marmot *et al* 2021.

50 The problem of indicators and measures of quality in the context of Education for All (EFA), especially in the domain of pedagogy, is explored in Alexander 2008b, 2015b. See this volume, Chapter 22.
51 Lyytinen 2002; Fredriksson 2006.
52 Eurydice 2009.
53 Ruzzi 2006.
54 Wilkinson and Pickettt 2010, 17.
55 Wilkinson and Pickett 2010, 29–30.
56 Barber and Mourshed 2007, 40.
57 Boyer 1983.

21 Moral panic and miracle cures

'Moral panic and miracle cures: what can we really learn from international comparison?' The 2011 SERA Lecture, delivered at the annual conference of the Scottish Educational Research Association in Stirling. Published in *Scottish Educational Review*, 44(1), 4–21 (2012) and here slightly extended. A shorter version provided a keynote at *From Regulation to Trust: education in the 21st century*, the Third Van Leer International Conference on Education, Jerusalem, May 2012, and was published in Hebrew that year in *Educational Echoes*.

The current 'age of austerity' responds not only to the behaviour of maverick bankers but also to seismic changes in the global economy and the growing economic might relative to Europe and the United States of Brazil, India and above all China. With Shanghai, South Korea, Hong Kong and Singapore all now apparently untouchable at the top of the PISA league tables of student achievement in reading, mathematics and science, it's hardly surprising that Britain's policymakers believe that these Asian education systems have something to teach us.

That is both sensible and responsible. It's *how* policymakers study education elsewhere and how they translate into policy what they discover that's the problem. Policy responses frequently display one or more of three tendencies: extreme selectivity in the evidence admitted and the methodology preferred; a misplaced faith in the capacity of centrally-directed interventions to transform grassroots classroom practice and hence raise standards; and a preference for interventions that are high stakes and draconian – 'tough' is the usual epithet – presumably on the grounds that having publicly registered a problem policymakers believe that only the firmest of firm government hands will impress the electorate.

I make no apology for returning to a theme that has preoccupied me, on and off, since the mid-1990s.[1] For despite all that we know about the pitfalls of cause/effect attribution in the educational and economic spheres, successive governments have found it hard to resist the naive belief that raising test scores in literacy and numeracy will elevate a country's economic performance, and that copying other nations' educational policies will both raise standards and pull us out of recession. The prevailing term is 'leverage'. It's a revealing metaphor: depress one end of the lever (high-calory literacy and numeracy, high-octane

DOI: 10.4324/9781315169378-25

school leadership, high-stakes tests) and up goes the other (improved educational standards and economic performance). If only it were that simple.[2]

Thus the 'moral panic' of this chapter's title is economic no less than educational, and the 'miracle cures' are the policies which politicians and school improvement experts nominate as the key ingredients in the success of the countries in question. Import these, they assert, and our problems will be solved.

Of course, what we are witnessing here in the millennial context of globalisation, economic turbulence and international re-alignment isn't new. At the end of the nineteenth century, as students of comparative education know well, Michael Sadler famously warned:

> In studying foreign systems of education we should not forget that the things outside the schools matter even more than the things inside the schools, and govern and interpret the things inside . . . The practical value of studying in a right spirit and with scholarly accuracy the working of foreign systems of education is that it will result in our being better fitted to study and understand our own . . . No other nation, by imitating a little bit of German organisation, can thus hope to achieve a true reproduction of the spirit of German institutions . . . All good and true education is an expression of national life and character.[3]

At the turn of the twentieth century all eyes were on German industrial might – with good reason as it turned out just 14 years later. Sadler's point was obvious and I'd have thought incontrovertible. National education systems are deeply embedded in national culture. Indeed education is one of the main vehicles for mediating, transmitting and sustaining a culture. So, as I've argued elsewhere, 'no educational policy or practice can be properly understood except by reference to the web of inherited ideas and values, habits and customs, institutions and world views, that make one country distinct from another'.[4]

This means that while, in Sadler's words, 'All *good and true* education is an expression of national life and character', it is also the case, as Basil Bernstein neatly expressed the matter 50 years ago, that 'education cannot compensate for society'.[5] That is to say, if a national education system is not 'good and true' then we must seek explanations in our society as well as our schools.

Thus it is, as is well known but insufficiently acknowledged, that the gap in student achievement between high and low-attainers is wider in Britain than many other rich nations in part because it maps with depressing precision onto the gaps in income, health and wellbeing which are also wider in Britain than in most other rich nations. As Wilkinson and Pickett demonstrate in their epidemiological study *The Sprit Level*, unequal societies have unequal education systems and unequal educational outcomes.[6] Britain and the United States illustrate these interlocking inequalities *par excellence*, though in this context 'excellence' is hardly the right word.

Obvious all this may be, yet it is not obvious enough to the current crop of educational policy advisers who advocate policy borrowing on what I believe is a culturally reckless scale and are applauded by their governments for doing so; and who find it politically more expedient to counter Britain's patchy educational performance by commending the educational policies of Singapore than by making the economic and social policies of Britain more equitable.

To be fair, though historical awareness is something that such discourse conspicuously lacks, history also sets limits to the purist Sadler line, for 'cultural borrowing happens; it has always happened. Few countries remain hermetically sealed in the development of their educational systems, and for centuries there has been a lively international traffic in educational ideas and practices.'[7]

The question begged by this apparent paradox is this: if culture is central to education, and cultural transplants are on the face of it doomed to failure or at best limited success, what exactly is the character of that educational thinking and practice which, over the past thousand years or so, has successfully migrated from one country to another and embedded itself there? By the end of this chapter I hope to have answered this, in part by reference to my own efforts to apply lessons of international comparison to the improvement of classroom practice in England. But we might also note the real force of Sadler's claim that 'the practical value of studying in a right spirit and with scholarly accuracy the working of foreign systems of education is that *it will result in our being better fitted to study and understand our own*' (my italics). The prime purpose of comparative international study, Sadler insists, is to understand ourselves, not to copy others. Or as David Raffe argues, 'policy learning' is a more valid and effective pursuit than 'policy borrowing'.[8]

In this chapter I examine the current educational manifestations of moral panic and miracle cures by considering four questions:

- What kinds of evidence are policymakers most interested in?
- What do they do with the findings?
- What is wrong with what they do?
- How might they make better use of international comparison?

What kinds of evidence are policymakers most interested in?

The official answer to this question is 'evidence which will help them develop worthwhile and effective policies'. The cynical answer is 'evidence which is carefully selected to justify policies that have already been determined'. This invokes the familiar jibe that what is presented as 'evidence-based policy' is likely to be policy-based evidence. The jibe may sound cheap, but it has substance – as is shown by the experience of the Cambridge Primary Review.[9]

But beyond policymakers' preference for evidence that supports chosen policies rather than challenges them, there is also a tendency to pay greater attention to some research paradigms and forms of data than to others. Take, for example, data from international comparison. Among the many typologies of comparative international research – descriptive/prescriptive, quantitative/qualitative, single country/two or more countries, macro/micro/macro-micro and so on – one of the most useful in the context of its policy applications has come from the National Research Council (NRC) of the US National Academies. Through its Board on International Comparative Studies in Education (BICSE – sadly no longer extant, though its work continues), the NRC has both advised and commented on US participation in the international student achievement surveys over many years.

The 2003 NRC/BICSE report differentiates the three types of comparative study mentioned in Chapter 20.[10] Type I studies include large-scale international student achievement studies like TIMSS, PISA and PIRLS. Examples of Type II are the reports from Ofsted, McKinsey and Cambridge Assessment which adopt the desk review format first to explain countries' differential performance in the student achievement surveys and then to propose policy responses.[11] Type III includes the majority of work in the published corpus of academic comparative education, and Type III studies range from pedestrian accounts of the education system of countries x or y to truly illuminating comparative studies of classroom life and what shapes it. Good examples of the latter are Joseph Tobin's *Preschool in Three Cultures* and *Preschool in Three Cultures Revisited*, and the Bristol group's *World of Difference?* exploration of the experience of being a learner in three European countries.[12] Tobin's 'in three cultures' signals the much greater effort entailed here than in the standard description of educational system x or y produced by the academic hacks of comparative education, and its 'polyvocal ethnography'[13] achieves deeper and richer strata of analysis than typical Type 1 measures can ever attain.

Type III territory is admittedly uneven, and the scale, range and methods of its instances are variable, but what all such studies have in common is that though some may have significant policy applications, the imperatives of policy are not their principal impetus. Rather, their goal is the advancement of understanding of other countries, their education systems, schools and classrooms, for its own sake. But even when Type III studies do have policy applications they tend to be ignored by government because, in that phrase redolent of ministerial complacency and civil servant defensiveness that we encountered during the Cambridge Primary Review, they are 'not invented here'. Which is to say, if they are not commissioned or approved by government, or if they cannot comfortably be plagiarised, then they are assumed to have nothing to offer.

Thus it is that governments confirm and recycle their own world-views and policies, and the unexamined follies that attend some of them. Yet it must also be acknowledged that the failure of policymakers to attend to Type III studies is partly the fault of the academic community itself. Such studies may lie buried in low-circulation, closed-access and overpriced academic journals, and too few education academics accept the need to communicate their work in accessible form to policymakers and practitioners. Many, indeed, prefer to remain within their institutional cocoons and are fearful of sticking their heads above the parapet.

What do policymakers do with the evidence?

Having funded and studied Type I studies like TIMSS and PISA, and having commissioned or welcomed Type II literature reviews that seek to explain the resulting league tables and propose what to do about them, and having ignored the Type III studies which may offer the insight they desperately need but would prefer not to be inconvenienced by, what do our policymakers do next? I answer that question by referring to three high-profile examples of Type II.

In 1996 Ofsted, England's national schools inspectorate, published a report commissioned from David Reynolds and Sean Farrell entitled *Worlds Apart? A review of international surveys of educational achievement involving England*. This reviewed England's performance in the international student achievement surveys published up to that point. It then proposed reasons for England's generally poor performance, and identified solutions. Its principal conclusion was that the complex pedagogy of English primary classrooms, with its emphasis on grouping and individualisation, accentuated the already wide differences between pupils. To counter this the authors recommended

> high quantities of whole-class interactive instruction, in which the teacher attempts to ensure the entire class have grasped the information being given . . . the use of the same textbooks by all children . . . mechanisms to ensure that the range of achievement is kept small.[14]

The judgements about pedagogical complexity and children growing apart were pertinent and indeed had been anticipated in a number of earlier Type III observational studies of primary classrooms,[15] though the real political appeal of *Worlds Apart?* to right-leaning governments, whether Conservative or New Labour, was its apparent invitation to go back to basics with didactic whole-class teaching and standardised textbooks.

Next, in 2007, the multi-billion-dollar international management consultancy McKinsey published the first of three reports from a team headed by Michael Barber, formerly Prime Minister Blair's Head of Delivery, on what the education systems that performed best in PISA could teach those which by this single debatable criterion are judged less successful. Its provocative title was *How the world's best-performing education systems come out on top*. From the ten top performers in PISA 2003 it concluded that what mattered most was (i) getting the right people to become teachers, (ii) developing them into effective instructors, and (iii) ensuring that the system is able to deliver the best possible instruction for every child.[16] In the course of its expensive quest for this damp squib the McKinsey report delivered further stunning insights such as: 'The quality of an education system cannot exceed the quality of its teachers', and 'High performance requires every child to succeed.' To such compound tautologies McKinsey added linguistic gems like: 'Top-performing systems leverage a substantial and growing knowledge about what constitutes effective school leadership to develop their principals into drivers of instruction.'[17] Two further reports followed from the same stable and in similar methodological and linguistic vein: *How the world's most-improved school systems keep getting better*[18] and *Capturing the leadership premium: how the world's top school systems are building leadership capacity for the future.*[19] The second McKinsey report looked at 20 rapidly-improving systems, the third at eight. 'Systems' in all three reports was defined very loosely indeed, allowing comparisons, which some would balk at, between Japan (a country with a population of 126 million), Alberta (a Canadian province with 3.3 million) and Aspire (a charter school system in the state of California with just 40 schools).

The third case is the report by Tim Oates, of the examination agency Cambridge Assessment, which has a foreword by England's Secretary of State for Education, no less, and is entitled *Could do better? Using international comparisons to refine the national curriculum in England.*[20] Notice the preference in these Type II studies for titles which have the appropriate back to basics ring of old-fashioned school reports – 'worlds apart', 'how to come out on top', 'could do better', 'most improved' – though what these titles more immediately bring to mind is the more entertaining if not significant educational report of my childhood, by one Nigel Molesworth: *How to be topp: a guide to sukcess for tiny pupils, including all there is to kno about space.*[21]

But I digress. With Oates as with the others, the international student achievement surveys (in this case PISA 2009) provide the 'benchmark' and on the basis of a curious range of sources, with not a single significant Type III study in sight, Oates concludes that 'in all high-performing systems, the fundamentals of subjects are strongly emphasised, have substantial time allocation and are the focus of considerable attention'.[22]

Oates goes on to list 13 'control factors for transnational analysis'. His list is so long and diffuse that it confronts governments with the choice of ignoring it or adopting it in full, which would require them to take over every school in the land. Conspicuous by its absence from the list of 'control factors' (ominous phrase) is culture: more on this anon.

Thus we have three reports, all enjoying classic Type II political patronage (in McKinsey's case by many more governments than that of the UK), all starting from and giving unquestioning credence to the same kind of dataset – international student achievement surveys covering a limited range of outcomes in relation to the totality of what most schools seek to achieve – yet, interestingly, each reaching different conclusions. Looking at high-performing systems as these are defined by their showing on the international league tables of student achievement, educational improvement requires, variously: more whole-class teaching coupled with standardised textbooks (Reynolds), better teaching, teacher training and school leadership (McKinsey), and a drastically pared-down curriculum which concentrates on what is deemed 'essential knowledge in the key subject disciplines' (Oates).[23] Whole-class teaching (Reynolds) and a narrow subject-based curriculum (Oates) fall into my category of 'miracle cures'. The McKinsey recommendation of better teachers, teacher training and school leadership is decidedly unmiraculous since it is a statement of the obvious.

What have policymakers done with these three studies? The 1996 Ofsted study's advocacy of whole-class teaching and standardised textbooks contributed directly to the pedagogy of the national literacy and numeracy strategies introduced by the Labour government in 1998–9. For a decade these were imposed on every primary teacher in England and policed by Ofsted, only to be abandoned by the coalition government in 2010. The Oates paper led to Oates's appointment as leader of the 'Expert Panel' which was asked to advise the UK government on how to slim down England's national curriculum to what is 'essential'. In December 2011 this group produced their report (DfE 2011a). Notwithstanding its attempt at educational rationale, the slimming-down exercise is chiefly one of placing more subjects below a line notionally marked 'essential' than were below that line in the previous version of England's national curriculum. Crucially, 'essential' is not defined, except by reference to what 'high-performing jurisdictions' do.[24]

The impact of McKinsey is more diffuse. It can be seen, for example, in the UK government's raising of the academic entry bar for trainee teachers (in England), though nowhere near as high as Finland, the country which is cited in this context. However, while saying that good teaching is what makes the difference, McKinsey had nothing whatever to say about pedagogy as such, so its reports have no obvious classroom purchase, and in any case the focus is on systems rather than classrooms. But the McKinsey brand is evident in the current elevation of school leaders from head teachers, who by their traditionally modest English title were *primus inter pares*, to heroic figures who turn round failing schools and stamp their sharp-suited presence on the mere mortals who actually do the teaching. The latter – as John Bangs of the England's National Union of Teachers has observed – seem in danger of being forgotten altogether.[25] Instead, what appears to be emerging as sanctioned policy is a staffing structure for schools – especially large secondaries – which is decidedly top-heavy. Stephanie Northen has charted this trend, which in one 1300-pupil secondary school has yielded a principal, a senior vice-principal, two vice-principals, eight assistant principals and a finance director, all commanding the kinds of salaries which hitherto have been confined to the business sector – whose style, clearly, all this seeks to replicate.[26]

Incidentally, this decidedly Anglo-Saxon view of school leadership has become another post-PISA miracle cure, recommended by McKinsey for universal consumption despite the fact that in many countries – including top-performing Finland – school heads/principals/directors have a much more modest role than in Britain and are by no means free to impose their will on other teachers.

What is wrong with what policymakers do with international evidence?

If Type II policy extrapolations could be shown to have raised standards there would be no grounds for complaint. So far, however, it's not at all clear that this is so, and the reasons for this lies partly in the methods the authors use and the inferences they draw.

As to the Type I datasets which provide Type II studies with their benchmarks, from the methodologically shaky IEA and IAEP studies of the 1970s to the later iterations of PISA, these have become more reliable and culture-fair, and the most recent PISA commentaries produced by OECD demonstrate commendable awareness of the challenges of cross-cultural testing and the inferential and explanatory caveats that need to be entered and heeded.[27]

In this sense, the problem isn't so much PISA as what, faced by the resulting league tables and the surrounding media noise, policymakers and their advisers do with what PISA provides. Hence my particular concern about the Type II data extrapolations and the disproportionate influence they exert. For the political attraction of Type II studies is that they select, mediate, repackage and re-interpret the research of others, presenting it in a form which they believe policymakers will find palatable both politically and stylistically. Being gate-keepers rather than creators of evidence, Type II studies are acutely vulnerable to the charge of methodological myopia and/or ideological bias.

There are now available some pertinent critiques of the Ofsted and McKinsey studies though as yet there's disappointingly little on the Oates paper. Although it seems to me that the 1996 Ofsted *Worlds Apart?* report[28] is the best of the bunch, both because it has genuine grounding in what actually happens in schools and classrooms and because it sounds appropriate notes of caution to which the McKinsey and Oates reports are immune, I remain critical of this one too. Here, for example, the quality and effectiveness of whole schools and entire education systems is reduced to a statistical calculation of gain in output over input. The chosen measures of input and output are extremely restricted in relation to what we know from other sources about the contexts, conditions, processes and outcomes of schooling and learning. Output measures are confined to students' test scores in limited aspects of a narrow range of subjects, and these are taken as proxies for pupil attainment across the entire curriculum. The 'process' measures which are added to the mix in order to calculate what aspects of education make a difference are no less restricted, for they must satisfy the basic requirement of measurability – hence the fixation on measures like time on task. Most egregiously, culture – which is absolutely central to the proper pursuit of transnational educational comparison and illumination – is reduced to one 'factor' among many, something which is external to school life rather than that which creates it and gives it meaning. Finally, the literature on which the paradigm draws represents a very narrow segment of the wider literatures on comparative and international education and on school and classroom processes.[29]

All these criticisms apply *a fortiori* to the Oates and McKinsey reports. In Chapter 20, I argued that McKinsey falls well short of the kind of analysis which is required by a study purporting to explain how PISA high-flyers achieve their success. For example, McKinsey says that the quality of teaching matters most, and we'd probably agree that it is critical, though the balance of within-classroom and other factors is very much open to debate. Yet, almost perversely it seems, the authors offer no account or analysis of teaching whatever, conceptually or empirically. Further, like the 1996 Ofsted study, McKinsey's methodological repertoire and vocabulary start and end with the input-output preoccupations of school effectiveness research, and the authors display unshakeable faith in the power and validity of testing. 'All of the top-performing systems', say McKinsey, 'recognise that they cannot improve what they do not measure',[30] which presumably means that the curriculum beyond English, maths and science is beyond redemption (and indeed of no account). Further, McKinsey relies almost totally on official information about its chosen education systems, which can be pretty unreliable because the ministries that supply it have an interest in presenting their systems and policies in the best possible light. Put these objections together and you have a study which is almost bound to be weak, conceptually and methodologically. Add to the mix the report's abundance of cliché and leaden English, and you have a document that falls at the hurdles of veracity, validity and meaningfulness.

Since, in spite of or possibly because of these failings, McKinsey's three education reports proved so influential internationally, we might press the critique further. David Raffe argues that the second McKinsey report remains locked within the policy 'bubble'; that it is a particularly flawed example of policy borrowing; that it makes light of all-important educational processes and contexts; and that it applies exceptionally narrow criteria of systemic educational success.[31] But the most devastating criticisms come from Frank Coffield.[32] His central charge is that McKinsey's analysis is culpably mono-factorial when it has long been understood that socio-economic factors have a significant impact on students' motivation, engagement, learning and attainment, especially in a country whose economic and social disparities are as great as they are in Britain. The first McKinsey report, continues Coffield, is methodologically flawed, 'disablingly selective' in its data and explanatory frame, superficial in its account of 'best practice' and how this can be disseminated, and seduced by its own rhetoric on leadership. Coffield likes the second McKinsey report a bit better than the first, though still not a lot, but castigates it for an impoverished view of teaching and learning, a thin evidence base, implausible arguments about the mechanisms and processes of school improvement, technocratic and authoritarian language and a pervasive neglect of culture and political context. Yet, Coffield notes, the UK coalition government's 2010 White Paper *The Importance of Teaching*[33] approvingly quotes McKinsey no fewer than seven times in its first 20 pages. Coffield sees McKinsey as

> the work of 'global' policy analysts, remote from the complexities of classrooms and the discomfiting findings of researchers which pose such difficulties for politicians in search of quick 'transformations' of school systems before the next election. They espouse a . . . model of schooling . . . characterised by relentless pressure, competition, line managers, customer services, data for performance management, accountability and value for money; and professional autonomy for teachers only when granted

by the centre . . . Their notion of teaching is narrowly conceived and technocratic . . . Their model remains unsophisticated, impracticable and undemocratic . . . Their recommendations are educationally and socially dysfunctional and should not be part of school reform in a democracy.[34]

Strong stuff indeed, though in my view not unjustified. The paradox is that McKinsey's authoritarian and micro-managerial nostrums are welcomed by the same government that says it wants to give teaching back to teachers after 13 years of what contributors to the Cambridge Primary Review called a 'state theory of learning'.[35]

To the criticisms of Raffe and Coffield I would add others that seem to me to be no less fundamental. Thus, Type II comparative studies of the kind I have exemplified are desk-based and therefore lack the vital asset of first-hand empirical data systematically and transparently presented, and analysed in accordance with methodological procedures that are publicly recognised or, if they are experimental, are at least open to scrutiny. The three studies exemplified here are notable for a high degree of selectivity, arbitrariness and bias in the literature on which they draw and in the way they handle it. That, I'm afraid, may be part of their attraction in policy circles, because they select their evidence to prove a point or come up with a politically-acceptable solution rather than demonstrate the complexity which properly-conducted comparative analyses and literature reviews are likely to reveal.

Aside from the results of PISA tests, the core database for these studies is information that has been generated by governments or their agencies. From such material – high on political rhetoric, low on classroom practice, devoid of cultural context, cleansed of problematic realities – they then construct edifices for school improvement and systemic reform. Disarmingly straightforward and carefully pitched to appeal to political instincts, these studies are eagerly taken up in the corridors of power.

The ready acceptance of official statements and the neglect of school and classroom practice are all the more serious when we note from Hogan's work in Singapore that in a system which outperforms most others in PISA – and whose policies both Barber and Oates urge governments elsewhere to copy – there is a substantial gap between the prescribed and the enacted curriculum despite the existence of mechanisms to secure coherence and control, and the sources of this gap are 'multiple, mutually reinforcing, resilient and intractable'. Hogan adds that using system-level curriculum specifications and controls as levers for reform, as Oates recommends, ignores what really makes the difference.[36] Yet Oates's entire thesis centres on the curriculum as officially specified, and its hegemony and presumed efficacy are such that this considerable limitation isn't even mentioned. Similarly, one of the key supporting documents for England's national curriculum review is subtitled *What can we learn from the English, mathematics and science curricula of high-performing jurisdictions?* and consists of an exhaustive analysis of official syllabuses in nine systems.[37] For policymakers, 'curriculum' is what they prescribe, not what teachers do.

And what of the measures that prompt policymakers to summon the dispensers of miracle cures? PISA assesses the attainment of 15-year-olds in aspects of reading, mathematics and science. Its spectrum of 'key competencies', though clearly essential, is actually quite limited. But to its credit, and unlike some who use it as a badge of national superiority or a stick with which to beat teachers, PISA itself more realistically and modestly acknowledges that its tests cover just 'some of the knowledge and skills that are essential for full participation in society'.[38] PISA is right, and Reynolds, Barber, Oates and gullible government ministers worldwide should pay attention: the TIMMS and PISA surveys are not a sufficient basis for describing an education system as a whole as 'high performing'.

Next, we return to what some call 'cherry-picking', a tendency that publicly all deplore but many continue to pursue. This has a statistical variant: false correlation, or a version of the philosophers' 'fallacy of division'. X may well be a common feature of high-performing education systems a, b, c, d and e, but that doesn't demonstrate a cause-effect relationship between feature and performance. And if x is also a common feature of *low*-performing systems g, h, i, j and k, then the claimed relationship is clearly inadmissible. In 1996, the Ofsted *Worlds Apart* study found that in its chosen high-performing systems (at that stage as judged by TIMSS results) whole-class teaching was the main teaching method used.[39] Reynolds and Farrell therefore concluded that whole-class teaching was one of the keys to delivering high standards, hence its commendation in the Labour government's national literacy and numeracy strategies introduced in 1998 and 1999. However, had they looked at other systems they would have discovered that whole-class teaching is the international pedagogical default, as prevalent in low-performing systems as high, so actually there is no correlation.

The same applies to Oates's claim that the key ingredient of success in PISA is a curriculum concentrating on what is deemed to be 'essential knowledge in key subjects'. In fact, like whole-class teaching and as the Benavot studies and INCA curriculum databases show, a curriculum constructed in terms of 'essential knowledge in the key subjects' is the basis of most of the world's national curriculum specifications, PISA successes and failures alike, though of course they may differ in their view of which subjects are 'key' and what knowledge is 'essential'.[40] In short, far from being unique to high-performing systems, Westminster's current curriculum holy grail of a narrow range of subjects dominated by literacy, numeracy and science is a global curriculum commonplace. So, as with whole-class teaching, there is no correlation between this account of curriculum structure and student achievement scores in TIMSS, PISA or PIRLS. The issue, of course, is what schools and teachers *do* with national curriculum specifications, which is about pedagogy, the area which the Oates and McKinsey studies ignore, much more than curriculum. Hogan's recent findings on the prescribed/enacted curriculum in Singapore confirm this.[41] For Oates, pedagogy is relegated to the status of one 'control factor' among many, acquiring the same lowly and almost incidental status as culture in the Reynolds and Farrell study.

Once we move beyond the restricted range of system and school variables deployed in these Type II studies, we encounter wider social, cultural, demographic and economic conditions which directly and massively influence the educational performance of a country's students. In a recent critique of such studies I show that while we can rightly conclude that teachers and teaching make a considerable difference (true but banal and probably not worth McKinsey-level expenditure and hype), extra-educational factors like country size, per capita GDP, demographic homogeneity and relative equality may well correlate no less convincingly with PISA performance. Indeed, a glance at the top end of the PISA league tables shows that the systems in question are mostly small, rich or preferably both, and to these factors we can add two others from Wilkinson's and Pickett's epidemiological study *The Spirit Level*: equity and relative equality.[42] Interestingly, in their most recent survey PISA too confirms the significance of equity as a factor in national performance.[43]

So there's a constellation of factors in which wealth, demography, equity and relative equality all play a part alongside the particular school and education system factors on which our three Type II studies concentrate, though in the end it is culture that determines how wealth is disposed, how education is conceived and how much or little equality matters. On all such matters, the Ofsted, McKinsey and Cambridge Assessment reports are strangely silent.

How might policymakers make better use of international comparison?

The obvious but perhaps uncharitable answer is that policymakers should use researchers who are less prone to the errors I have exemplified and who are more careful in the inferences they draw, the explanations they offer and the policy options they recommend, and who tell policymakers what they need rather than wish to hear. The second thing to say is that once one entertains a wider range of explanatory factors in international student achievement than the limited spectrum considered by the three Type II studies of educational cause and effect that I have exemplified, the possibilities for genuinely useful international comparison increase dramatically.

For example, in 2007 UNICEF published a study placing the UK at the bottom of a league table of children's wellbeing in 21 rich nations, using indicators for income, health and safety, family and peers, behaviour and risk, and of course education, plus one for the subjective judgement of children themselves.[44] A follow-up study explored the reasons for Britain's poor showing in the 2007 study by comparing the UK, Spain and Sweden. It concluded that a materialistic and commercial culture is deeply embedded in the UK and in concepts of good parenting in a way that is not seen in Spain and Sweden, and this culture reinforces inequality, adversely affects family time and relationships, and overall has a negative impact on children's wellbeing.[45] Since we know that the maps of attainment and social equity broadly coincide, we have in such studies clues to how schooling, through the values and relationships it fosters as well as through its quality of teaching, might raise the standards of both attainment and wellbeing.

Here are some further examples. My Cambridge colleague John Gray undertook a meta-analysis of adolescent wellbeing, using international data, which showed that while the Netherlands and Finland both ranked high on PISA, Dutch students were much happier at school than their Finnish contemporaries. He also argued that McKinsey-style comparisons between the UK and Hong Kong or Singapore are fruitless because the cultures are so utterly different and the educational systems are not remotely comparable in scale. He therefore suggested that if we really wish to use international comparison for policy transfer we should look not at Hong Kong, Singapore or even Finland, but at the Netherlands, because it is successful in the interlocking areas of attainment and wellbeing and it is culturally not so different from the UK.[46]

Another Cambridge colleague takes an alternative but no less intriguing view. Like myself, David Hargreaves sees culture as central to the understanding of differences in educational structure, content, process and outcome, but doesn't follow Gray's line on how we should act on that understanding. For Hargreaves, the world's educational and economic centre of gravity in the twenty-first century will be China, and since Shanghai-China outperforms most other countries in PISA it is essential that we investigate what it is about Chinese culture that accounts for this and what we can extrapolate not so much from the education system as from the culture that shapes it. This inevitably leads him to the resilience and pervasiveness of Confucianism, whose values he suggests might profitably inform our own schools' collective identity and their approach to self-improvement.[47]

Though Confucius invariably features in explanatory accounts of East Asian approaches to education,[48] this is a novel, and on the face of it startling, response to Sadler's maxim that 'all good and true education is an expression of national life and character': import the culture, not the policies. On the other hand, Hargreaves makes a useful distinction between policy *replication*, *adaptation*, *grafting* and *redesign* and suggests that only the last of these has much chance of success, though it is also considerably more difficult to achieve than the other three.[49] This is closer to my own argument that policy learning from international comparison should be about explicating and where appropriate emulating *values and principles* rather than importing and copying *policies or practices*. But this requires a comparative methodology capable of distinguishing the lived-in values and principles of education in action from the erzatz or cosmetic claims of policy and official documents, and this points us decisively away from study Types I and II, and as decisively towards the aspirations, if not always the achievements, of Type III.

Then there's the important line of research from Yariv Feniger and Adam Lefstein in Israel.[50] They are deeply critical of what they call the 'education systems hypothesis' that informs McKinsey and some other influential studies I have referred to – and indeed the commentaries of PISA boss Andreas Schleicher himself[51] – on the grounds that it attributes too much to policy levers like high-stakes testing and too little to history and culture. (Here one might interpose the suggestion that those who operate exclusively in the world of policy are probably likely to overstate its impact, if only because that's all they know.) Feniger and Lefstein argue that if randomised control experiments were possible in this area then they would support the alternative 'cultural-historical' hypothesis about what has the greatest impact on student attainment. They test the hypothesis by taking immigrant children – those who were either born in the host country or immigrated there before starting school – and comparing their test scores with those of their indigenous peers from both their host and their source countries. Looking at children of Turkish and Chinese origin, that is children whose source countries perform very differently in PISA, Feniger and Lefstein show that 'the mean achievement of immigrants is closer to students in their country of origin than to students in their host country'. The decisive factor, then, is culture, especially as it bears on parental attitudes, values and expectations, but culture also perhaps as magnified by the pedagogy of the host countries, whose teachers have heard a great deal about high-achieving East Asian students and raise their expectations accordingly.

From Belgorod to Barking, from Kursk to Kirkby: principled policy learning at work

I have an obligation to take up the challenge I have issued. In 2001, I published my own Type III study. *Culture and Pedagogy* is a large-scale exploration of the relationship between history, culture, policy, schooling and classroom practice in primary education in England, France, India, Russia and the United States.[52] The study culminates in close-grained analysis of interaction and discourse in the classrooms of these countries, drawing on a dataset that includes 130 hours of videotape, transcripts of 166 lessons in over 100 schools, together with field-notes, photographs, interview transcripts, official documents, teachers' lesson plans, students' written work, and much else. The discourse analysis is the culmination of the study in the literal sense that this is where it ends, but more fundamentally because it is through language, and especially spoken language, that culture, teaching and learning are most decisively yet subtly mediated.

So when at the end of the study I asked 'What can English pedagogy learn from France, India, Russia and the United States?',[53] I sounded the familiar warnings about policy borrowing but then argued that precisely because spoken language is so central to both human learning and collective culture and identity, and precisely because the differences I had observed were so striking, classroom talk surely has potential for policy learning which is richer and more apt than the systemic structures and policies commended by McKinsey, or the dozens of national curriculum statements collated by the 2010–12 DfE national curriculum review. Accordingly I embarked on the task which led to what I called 'dialogic teaching' being progressively elaborated, refined, adopted in many schools and teacher education programmes, and finally evaluated by the Education Endowment Foundation.[54]

As we saw in Chapters 15–18, dialogic teaching is one response among several to the imperatives of classroom talk analysis and reform. To this collective effort I have been able to add cross-cultural perspectives and pedagogical principles which at first glance may seem alien but when appropriately applied work rather well.

Here is just one example. From Russian and French classrooms I was able to identify and then challenge the then pervasive belief in many English classrooms – manifested in both teachers' accounts of their practice and video recordings and transcripts of their classroom discourse – that the main function of classroom talk is *social* rather than *cognitive*, or that it is about boosting the child's confidence and 'communication skills' more than getting him or her to think. This view of talk conditions the organisational principle that in a given lesson as many students as possible must be persuaded to say something. Once one calculates the logistics of this strategy in relation to class size and lesson time, it's evident that it is more likely to secure participation in a lesson's social round than in the learning the lesson seeks to advance, because such participation is likely to be restricted to brief exchanges that have shallow cognitive content and impact. In the Russian and to a lesser degree the French classrooms – and since then I have observed this approach in several other countries – teachers consciously opted for extended and more probing exchanges with a smaller number of pupils in a given lesson, ensuring that over a longer period, say a day or a week rather than a single lesson, every pupil had such an opportunity. As a matter of fact, these teachers also believed in maximising student participation, but the maximisation they aimed for was qualitative rather than quantitative.

As we saw in Chapter 17, such extended and reciprocal rather than brief and one-sided exchanges, in which the third turn opens doors rather than closes them, and student contributions are justified, probed and built on, are more likely to achieve the goal of scaffolded understanding than round-the-class question and answer. However, they require commitment to a second principle, that of collectivity, the idea that students are not lonely individuals in a crowd as famously portrayed by Philip Jackson from observation in American elementary school classrooms,[55] but members of a learning community who listen to and learn from each other, and who speak as co-contributors to a shared enterprise.

I have two video clips which I have used with teachers to illustrate this very particular finding from international comparative analysis, one from Kursk in southern Russia and the other from England's rural North Yorkshire. On the face of it, the teaching is utterly different. The Kursk teacher retains the brisk, authoritative manner and unbreachable social distance which run deep in Russian pedagogy and culture. The English teacher operates in a more informal, approachable and – yes – more English way. But what the two teachers have in common is the way they manage time and events to create space for teacher-student exchanges which are extended and carefully structured, and to which the rest of the class have learned that they must listen intently with a view to both learning and joining in; and it must be emphasised that the North Yorkshire teacher started moving in this direction only after she had watched, pondered and discussed the Kursk tape and transcript and others from the same dataset. For her, the idea of staying with one child over several cumulative exchanges ran counter to her inherited belief, and to the wider 'folk pedagogy'[56] of English primary education, that in a given lesson every child must say something, and that the function of such talk is communicative and social as much as, or even more than, cognitive. Yet despite having made this fundamental change, her teaching remained resolutely English rather than Russian. She and her students applied and domesticated the principle but did not copy the practice. For not only was the practice visibly alien, but transplanted as it stood it would have conveyed messages about the nature of knowledge and teacher authority that the English teacher would have found unacceptable.

I was so impressed with the quality of classroom talk and the intensity of pupil engagement that this teacher orchestrated that with her permission I invited Kevan Collins[57] – then director of the government's primary strategy – to meet her and observe her at work. He was equally impressed, and when later he become Chief Executive of the Education Endowment Foundation he encouraged me to subject dialogic teaching to randomised control trial. Which I did.[58]

Current efforts to reform classroom talk provide, I think, a useful example of principled learning from education elsewhere. Central to my account of dialogic teaching are not specific strategies to be copied, but repertoires which the teacher deploys according to circumstance and need. These are framed and guided by justifications, values and principles that come together as a dialogic stance, and they steer and validate the practice, whatever form it takes.

Conclusion

The example of the talk that lies at the heart of pedagogy may help us understand why the ideas of Comenius travelled so far and so successfully from their roots in seventeenth-century Moravia and are still discernible in the pedagogies of many of the world's countries. It is true that Comenius produced prescriptive textbooks to advance his theories of education and pedagogy, but it is the principles rather than the materials that proved most durable. And how revolutionary they were at a time when education was largely confined to boys from wealthy families and Latin was the medium of instruction. Thus, on the nature of the education system:

- There should be universally-available education for both boys and girls, and for all children regardless of income or social position.
- The school system should start with education within the family up to the age of six, and be followed by elementary school, secondary school and university.

- Teaching should be in the pupils' mother tongue.
- Lifelong education should be available for adults.[59]

And on pedagogy (from Keatinge's 1896 translation of Comenius's *Great Didactic*):

> There should be one teacher for each class . . . Time should be carefully divided, so that each day and each hour may have its appointed task . . . The same exercise should be given to the whole class . . . Everything should be taught thoroughly, briefly, and pithily, that the understanding may be, as it were, unlocked with one key . . . All things that are naturally connected ought to be taught in combination . . . Every subject should be taught in definitely graded steps, that the work of one day may thus expand that of the previous day, and lead up to that of the morrow.[60]

And foreshadowing the dialogic teaching principles referred to in Chapter 16:

> The scholars should be given leave to ask questions on any point that they wish explained. . . [They] should ask the question openly. In this way the whole class will benefit, as much by the question as by the answer.[61]

There, in a treatise from a time and place far removed from ours, are two of the principles of dialogic teaching: collectivity and reciprocity. If we add to such principles the illustrated textbooks and the use of natural and man-made objects to stimulate children's interest and advance their understanding – objects we can still view in the Comenius Pedagogical Museum in Prague and the Franckesche Stiftungen in Halle in Saxony – we begin to understand the continuing significance of this founder of modern pedagogy.

Mention of Germany and the Czech Republic, neither of which country has a seat at the PISA top table or is deemed by the current wave of policy borrowers to have educational systems, policies or practices from which we can learn, takes me to my closing questions. Others must answer them.

First, we know that Singapore, Hong Kong, Korea, Shanghai-China and Finland do well in PISA tests of student attainment in reading, maths and science. But what else do their students learn, and how well? Do these systems provide their children with an education which is about significantly more than passing tests in three subjects? And if the wider curriculum in top-performing PISA systems were to be measured as assiduously as the reading, maths and science are measured, would the same countries still head the league table?

Second, we are asked to subscribe to a view of 'world class' schooling as *outperforming* other countries. The uncomplicated but undeniably imperialist goal, shared by the policy supremacists and their unacknowledged alter ego Nigel Molesworth, is *How to Be Topp*. But in a world facing the crises of climate change, resource depletion, over-population, environmental degradation and geo-political instability, is this really how 'world class' should be defined? Should we not consider the merits of 'world class' as sustaining the world rather than beating it? As fostering international interdependence rather than national supremacy?

Third, if we take this rather different view of education, adopting a broader, richer and more humane vision than that espoused by McKinsey's executives and their Westminster and Washington cheerleaders, have we selected the right countries from which to learn about what makes for a 'world class' education?

Fourth, is it not at least possible that this whole current PISA-led obsession does a grave injustice to countries, schools and teachers that care no less passionately about educational standards but for whom standards mean more than test performance – and ultimately therefore to the cause of education itself?

Finally, national curricula are increasingly being reconfigured to respond less to national culture, values and needs than the claims of 'international benchmarking' and 'world class' educational standards – the latter equated with test scores in a limited spectrum of human learning. The curriculum narrows to what is tested, the summative function of assessment is elevated over its formative contribution to children's understanding and progress, and the larger questions of purpose and value, which in democratic societies ought to be central to educational debate, are neglected.

Afterword: once more to Finland

Like so many others, I have become fascinated by Finnish education, though my fascination predates that country's PISA-driven celebrity. As one of the Ofsted team making a comparative study of the education of 6-year-olds in Denmark, England and Finland, I first visited Finnish schools in 2002, observed in classrooms, and talked with students and teachers.[62] I was struck not only by features with which we are all now familiar – for example, a teaching profession to which entry is highly competitive, which requires masters-level training, and which enjoys considerable classroom autonomy – but also by aspects which are less frequently noted, such as the intermingling of students of different ages within the common schools and of students and older members of the community in local libraries. This absence of age-based segregation is very different from what one finds elsewhere, and it speaks to a distinctive notion of community.

Since then, so much has been written about Finland's PISA 'miracle' that its government has had to intervene to control the number of visitors to its schools.[63] The miracle cures the visitors bring back with them depend on their diagnosis. The chair of England's national curriculum review 'expert panel' argued, somewhat against the emerging consensus, that 'Finland's success can be traced to highly centralised control in previous decades, including control of textbooks'.[64] At a conference in 2012 (see Chapter 10) I queried that claim. Its author responded that he had been quoted out of context and as a consequence his views had been misrepresented. The one charge doesn't necessarily follow the other, for the quoted statement seems to be capable of only one reading, namely that Finland's success can be traced to highly centralised control in previous decades, including control of textbooks. Yet, because it is important to be accurate as well as fair on such matters I decided to seek further clarification about educational cause and effect in Finland from some of that country's leading experts, including Pasi Sahlberg. I now summarise their views.

First, because of substantial national differences on a number of significant dimensions – population size, culture, demography, language, educational goals and priorities, education system structure and structure, and so on – all educational comparisons between Finland and England should be made with extreme caution.

Second, it is not legitimate to claim, as do some – especially in the United States – who find Sahlberg's 'Finnish lessons' politically unacceptable, that such differences wholly invalidate this particular exercise in learning from comparing.

Third, the assertion that 'Finland's current success can be traced to highly centralised control in previous decades, including control of textbooks' contains an element of truth in as far as Finland's system was, and in some respects remains, centralised, and textbooks have been a significant part of the mix. However, it is emphatically not correct to claim or imply a direct cause-effect relationship between centralisation, textbooks and PISA success in Finland.

Further, even if there had been an initial impact of centralised measures, including textbooks, during the 1960s and 1970s, it is naive to presume that this could continue to have a significant impact half a century later, by which time the teachers concerned had retired, Finland's education system and policies had evolved far beyond the 1960s vision, and the measures for assessing impact had changed out of all recognition. (On the latter point, the international measures available during the 1970s and 1980s were the few and suspect IEA and IAEP surveys, followed during the late 1990s by TIMSS, and only from 2000 by the more reliable PISA surveys.)

The central point, however, is that Finland's reforms centred on the introduction of the *peruskoulu*, or nine-year municipal comprehensive school, in place of the earlier mix of primary schools, grammar schools and civic schools. The aim of these reforms was not to raise standards in as then unheard-of tests but to secure equality of educational opportunity and equity in educational experience and outcome, and 'to build a more socially just society with higher educational levels for all'.[65] In other words, it was believed – and was later confirmed not just by Wilkinson and Pickett's epidemiological studies[66] but also by OECD itself from the PISA data of many more countries than Finland – that narrowing the equity gap is not only a social and educational good in itself but also enhances attainment. This is precisely the line that the Cambridge Primary Review took when, at the top of the list of policy priorities for the new British government in 2010, it placed this:

Policy priority 1. Accelerate the drive to reduce England's gross and overlapping gaps in wealth, wellbeing and educational attainment, all of them far wider in England than most other developed countries. Understand that teachers can do only so much to close the attainment gap for as long as the lives of so many children are blighted by poverty and disadvantage. Excellence requires equity.[67]

Although the UK government's Pupil Premium acknowledged this relationship, England's educational reforms since 1998 have generally prioritised two rather different objectives, which the Finns see as working against each other. The first is to raise measured educational standards in literacy and numeracy. The second is to increase parental choice of schooling through marketisation and competition. Both elements consciously follow the American model of charter schools and high-stakes testing that was subsequently disowned as a failure by one of its leading initial advocates, not least because it widened rather than narrowed the equity gap (Ravitch 2010). To the Finns, as I have reported, these policies are in direct opposition, and they are therefore not at all surprised that the achievement gap in England (as in the United States) remains as wide as ever. For them, as for OECD itself,[68] equity is the key.

The other key is teaching quality, and here there are further contrasts. What Finland has done is to front-load system reform by concentrating on what it sees as the two essential prerequisites for a high-achieving school system: equity and teaching quality. The Finns are categorical in their belief that it is the combination of these, going back to the *peruskoulu* legislation of the 1960s and building on it through reforms to teacher recruitment and training, that has produced the high standards that Finland has achieved not just in PISA but across the curriculum as a whole. For their part, England's governments have rejected equity in favour of 'choice' and competition, and have introduced quality controls or levers which operate much further down the line than in Finland, and arguably are applied too late to make a real and lasting difference. These are headed by high-stakes testing and inspection which, it will be noted, focus on outcomes rather than input and process. The government's one 'Finnish lesson' to date, marginally raising the bar for graduate entrants to teacher training, is a very modest adjustment compared with what is required of teachers in Finland. So the front loading is too weak and the controls or levers are applied too late.

My Finnish informants suggest that the contrasting reform standpoints in the two education systems can be summarised as follows:

Finland: *peruskoulu* (municipal comprehensive schools) + highly trained teachers = equity + standards.

England: marketisation/competition + high-stakes testing/inspection = choice + standards.

On this, Pasi Sahlberg told me:

> My feeling is that in Finland we have so many young Finns interested in teaching because equity and equality of outcomes are so high in the list of key objectives in education here . . . I am quite convinced that the strong equity focus in Finland has been the driving force and the magnet for

people to choose teaching. Marketization plus testing would be a rapid killer here, as it has been with our Scandinavian neighbours.[69]

And, of course, the greater the attraction of teaching to high calibre applicants, the higher the teacher training entry and qualifications bar can be raised, yielding direct and positive gains in educational standards: a virtuous circle.

Finally, commentators point to a 'Finland paradox': success in PISA but a refusal to follow the standard OECD reform package; consistently high student achievement but resistance to the apparatus of centrally-directed tests and inspections; belief in the importance of highly-trained teachers but a high degree of professional autonomy; pride in schools' success but a dislike of academic competition between schools. In other words, Finland succeeds by *avoiding* the very strategies for school and system improvement to which recent UK governments have been most heavily committed.[70]

Notes

1 Alexander 1996, 2001a, 2006a, 2008b, 2011a (and more).
2 Wolf 2002.
3 Sadler 1900, 50.
4 Alexander 2001a, 5.
5 Bernstein 1970, 344.
6 Wilkinson and Pickett 2010; Pickett and Vanderbloemen 2015.
7 Alexander 2001a, 171.
8 Raffe 2011a.
9 See this volume, Chapters 2–7.
10 NRC 2003, 13.
11 Reynolds and Farrell 1996; Barber and Mourshed 2007; Mourshed *et al* 2010; Barber *et al* 2011; Oates 2010.
12 Tobin *et al* 1989, 2009; Osborn *et al* 2003.
13 Tobin 1999.
14 Reynolds and Farrell 1996, 55.
15 Galton and Simon 1980; Mortimore *et al* 1988; Alexander 1997.
16 Barber and Mourshed 2007, 2.
17 Barber and Mourshed 2007, 4 and 30.
18 Mourshed *et al* 2010.
19 Barber *et al* 2011.
20 Oates 2010.
21 By Geoffrey Willans and Ronald Searle.
22 Oates 2010.
23 As cited in the remit for England's 2010–12 national curriculum review: DfE 2010a.
24 See this volume, Chapters 10 and 11.
25 Bangs 2011.
26 Northen 2011.
27 OECD 2010a, 2010b, 2010c, 2010d, 2011a, 2011b.
28 Reynolds and Farrell 1996.
29 Alexander 2001a, 29–30 and 36–9.
30 Barber and Mourshed 2007, 36.
31 Raffe 2011b.
32 Coffield 2012.

33 DfE 2010b.
34 Coffield 2012.
35 Balarin and Lauder 2010.
36 Hogan *et al* 2012; Hogan, Kwek *et al* 2012; Hogan, Towndrow *et al* 2012.
37 DfE 2011b.
38 OECD 2012.
39 Reynolds and Farrell 1996.
40 Benavot *et al* 1991; Benavot 2008.
41 Hogan, Towndrow *et al* 2012.
42 Wilkinson and Pickett 2010. See conclusion to the previous chapter.
43 OECD 2010d, 9–11.
44 UNICEF 2007.
45 UNICEF 2011.
46 Gray *et al* 2011.
47 Hargreaves 2011.
48 Watkins and Biggs 1996; Tobin *et al* 1989, 2009; Li 2012.
49 Hargreaves 2012, 6–7.
50 Feniger and Lefstein 2014.
51 Schleicher and Stewart 2008.
52 Alexander 2001a.
53 Alexander 2001a, 563.
54 Alexander 2020. See this volume, Chapters 15–18.
55 Jackson 1968.
56 Bruner 1996.
57 The same Kevan Collins whom we met in this book's introduction as England's post-Covid Education Recovery Commissioner.
58 See Chapter 16.
59 Pánková 2010.
60 Comenius 1896 [1657], 312–34.
61 Comenius 1896 [1657], 320.
62 Ofsted 2003.
63 Meyer and Benavot 2013a, 15.
64 Oates 2012.
65 Sahlberg 2011, 1.
66 See note 49.
67 Cambridge Primary Review 2010.
68 See note 50.
69 Pasi Sahlberg to Robin Alexander, personal communication, 28 May 2012. The Scandinavian neighbour is in Sweden.
70 Meyer and Benavot 2013b; Varjo *et al* 2013.

22 In pursuit of quality

'Teaching and learning for all: the quality imperative revisited'. Keynote at the 2014 Oslo conference launching the UNESCO 2013–14 Education for All (EFA) Global Monitoring Report on progress towards UN Millennium Development Goal 2, *Achieve universal primary education by 2015*. Published in *International Journal of Educational Development*, 40 (2015), and McGrath, S. and Gu, Q. (eds) *Routledge Handbook of International Education and Development* (2016).

Quality: now you see it . . .

Like its predecessors, the 2013–14 Global Monitoring Report *Teaching and Learning: achieving quality for all* – hereafter GMR 2014[1] – is impressive in the scale of its evidence, the progress it documents, the warnings it issues, and the humanity of its endeavour.

Quality has been an EFA goal since the 2000 Dakar framework declared it to be 'at the heart of education' and a fundamental determinant of student enrolment, retention and achievement;[2] while, along with quality, learning featured a decade earlier in no fewer than three of the six Jomtien goals.[3] Yet despite these early emphases, quality in the global monitoring reports, and quality in teaching and learning in particular, have since then been surprisingly elusive. In part this may have reflected a preoccupation with those EFA goals whose urgency has seemed the more pressing because their pathology and progress are readily computed. With at least 57 million children still out of primary school, half of them in 32 countries suffering conflict, and only 13 out of 90 countries likely to achieve universal primary school completion by 2015, we understand why this is so.[4] Add secondary education and the picture is starker still: 258 million children aged 6–17 out of school.[5] Numbers offer headlines and dramatic immediacy. 'Quality' does not.

Paradoxically, quality may also be elusive because it is ubiquitous. For instance, a consistent argument in the GMRs has been the inseparability of quality from equity, because until an education system is equitable in terms of access, enrolment, gender parity, retention and completion it can hardly be described as being of good quality, even if for some children, in some schools, the experience of learning is rewarding and high standards are achieved. We are justifiably disturbed by the finding of GMR 2014 that

DOI: 10.4324/9781315169378-26

while the richest boys may on present trends achieve universal primary education by 2021, the poorest girls will not catch up until 2086. Quality for some is not education for all.

Indeed, quality pervades all six EFA goals.[6] The first GMR called quality a 'composite goal' and one of the strengths of these annual reports is that though each of them has had a specific theme – gender, literacy, early childhood, governance, the marginalized, conflict, quality, inequality – each has begun by tracking progress towards all six goals as a reminder of the way they are intertwined and must be simultaneously pursued if EFA is to be achieved.[7]

But quality's very pervasiveness may have encouraged the view that it requires no further elucidation. So it becomes all the more important to examine how quality has been handled in the EFA monitoring process and how this 'composite' goal has been translated into working indicators and measures in the two GMRs – 2005 and 2014 – which have included quality in their titles and remits, for these, *post hoc* if not *a priori*, may reveal the definition we seek. Having uncovered that definition, and mindful of the pedagogical orientation of GMR 2014, we can then apply three tests:

- Does the account of quality in EFA attend to what in teaching and learning really matters?
- Are the classroom processes and outcomes that are truly transformative for our children adequately captured in the EFA goals, objectives and targets, the EFA monitoring indicators and measures, and the evidence on which EFA thinking and policy draw?
- If not, what are the implications for the UN's education mission after 2015, and if learning is to be a target, how should it be defined, indicated and assessed?

In attempting to address these questions I first return to the analysis undertaken for the UK Department for International Development (DfID) in 2007[8] during a period when I was making regular visits to India in connection with the Government of India's ambitious EFA initiative, Sarva Shiksha Abhiyan (SSA), and its predecessor the District Primary Education Programme (DPEP). The choice of title for this chapter should now be clear.[9] In the sense that it reengages with quality, teaching and learning, GMR 2014 revisits GMR 2005, *The Quality Imperative*;[10] and this first revisiting allows a second: a reassessment of my earlier concerns about how quality, teaching and learning have been handled in the GMR process as a whole.

In 2007, one of those concerns was the striking neglect of pedagogy, despite the fact that pedagogy is at the very heart of education and without pedagogy discussion of educational quality makes little sense. Another was the gulf between the evidence on both quality and pedagogy cited in the EFA GMRs and the much larger body of evidence about these matters that appears in the research literature: one world but two discourses. To counter these tendencies I end this chapter with an example showing how the EFA movement and its post-2015 successor could increase their effective purchase on the declared priority of advancing quality in teaching and learning if they were prepared to foster a more inclusive discourse and consult a less exclusive literature.

Input, output, proxies and process

Here, briefly summarised, are the problems identified in the 2007 analysis.

First, the quest for indicators and measures of quality produced an understandable preoccupation with *input* and *output* – pupil/teacher ratio, balance of male and female teachers, balance of trained and untrained teachers, expenditure per pupil as per cent of GDP, net enrolment ratio, adult literacy rate, survival rate to grade 5 – but this was at the expense of indicators of *process*. Output is in part determined by process but is not synonymous with it.

Second, when attempts were made to plug the gap, the identified process elements appeared to reflect not teaching and learning as either experienced or researched but those few random aspects of classroom life that were deemed measurable, regardless of whether they had the significance that their selection implies. Hence, for example, the foregrounding of learning time, time on task and class size.

Third, the very act of isolating such aspects validated them in the eyes of those – governments, administrators, donors – who had the money and power to make them matter, and set in train policies for embedding them ever more exclusively, whether or not this response was justified by the evidence. In this way, the monitoring distorted both what it monitored and the decisions and interventions to which it led. By way of illustration of the risky consequences of this approach we might note that in Lockheed's and Verspoor's influential 1991 World Bank cost-benefit analysis of investments for improving primary education in developing countries, pre-service teacher education and midday meals were rejected as 'blind alleys'.[11] Today we take a very different view of the efficacy of both interventions.

Fourth, in an attempt to engage more comprehensively with process, some frameworks posited unashamedly qualitative variables such as 'high expectations', 'strong leadership', 'positive teacher attitudes', 'appropriate use of language', 'committed and motivated teachers', 'appropriate teaching and learning materials', 'meaningful assessment', 'effective management of physical assets' and the ubiquitous 'active teaching methods' and 'child-friendly environment'.[12] But each of these modifiers – high, strong, positive, appropriate, committed, meaningful, effective, active, child-friendly – lacks objective meaning and is open to many interpretations, not just across cultures but also within them, while the overall selection is no less arbitrary notwithstanding its abundance of adjectives.

Fifth, in the absence of watertight measures, compensatory use was made of proxies. 'Survival rate to grade 5', as the proxy indicator of quality in the EFA Education Development Index (EDI), is a prominent example.[13] This approach is not confined to EFA. Many governments, and certainly the world's media, treat the performance of a sample of 15-year-olds in the PISA tests at a single moment in their educational journey as a valid and reliable measure of the performance of entire education systems. Some proxy.

As a not entirely flippant aside I find the use of 'survival' in this context bizarre as well as evidentially ambiguous. 'Survival' allows two very different takes, one of them suggesting that education is to be endured rather than enjoyed: (i) 'How good was your education?' 'Excellent: I survived to grade 5.' (ii) 'How good was your education?' 'Terrible: I survived to grade 5 but then could take no more and left school.'

This brings me to three overarching problems, which like the tendencies summarised earlier seem to apply no less in 2015 than in 2007.

Quality: a mantra in need of definition

First, there remains a conspicuous lack of precision in the use of the keyword 'quality' itself. Though 'quality' is often used quasi-adjectivally, as in 'quality healthcare', 'quality teaching', 'quality learning' and so on, it is actually a noun. The adjectival use of 'quality', as in 'quality education – is no more than a slogan, offering limited purchase on what quality actually entails. But even when used as a noun, 'quality' is multi-faceted, for it can mean an attribute – as in 'the qualities we look for in a teacher' – or a degree of excellence, as when we say teaching is of outstanding quality, in which case 'outstanding' needs to be defined. So 'quality' – as in *Teaching and Learning: quality for all* – can describe, prescribe or evaluate.

In the debate about quality in EFA this basic distinction has too often been blurred. That is to say, some have been happy to use supposed indicators of quality in teaching and learning – quality in the sense of a standard to aim for – without adequately exploring and describing those qualities or attributes of which teaching and learning are actually constituted. When we favour prescription over description we risk producing a prospectus for quality which is arbitrary or biased. So I suggest that the task of improving the quality of teaching and learning requires closer attention to the description and analysis of quality and rather less to soundbites like 'child-friendly teaching' and 'active learning'.

Indicators and measures: not the same

The second overarching problem is a confusion between *indicators* and *measures*. The terms are frequently treated as interchangeable when they are not. Here I concede that I may well be in a minority within the EFA community (though not, I'm happy to say, outside it) for at a 2014 London seminar of the great and good in development education an indicator was defined *ex cathedra* as 'a precise metric from identified databases that assesses if a target is being reached', and nobody thought or dared to disagree. But this definition is stipulative and context-bound and I prefer to argue that if we have the luxury of two terms we should not squander the clarity and nuancing this allows by treating them as synonymous.

Thus, measures measure, indicators indicate: they do different jobs. A measure is a procedure, device or unit for measuring and is irrevocably tied to quantity. An indicator is a more complex and variable clue about whether something is happening and if so to what extent. Approaching clouds indicate the imminence of rain but they do not guarantee it and they certainly don't measure it. A noisy classroom may indicate lack of student concentration but it does not conclusively prove it, still less measure the precise balance of student attention and inattention; indeed, there are those who say that a noisy classroom indicates active learning, but that's another story.

Take, as one familiar and ostensibly absolute measure of learning in school effectiveness studies, time on task – or what, to distinguish it from available instructional time, Hattie and Yates call 'engaged time'.[14] This is often no more than an indicator, and a less than conclusive one at that, for it depends only up to a point on objectively-measured time and rather more on an inferential response to students' observable behaviour. A student who appears to be attending to the teacher, or reading, and hence 'on task', may in reality be daydreaming; or if not wholly off-task then (as happens to all of us) concentrating for only some of the time apparently committed, and with only some of his or her available attention. Who then, from the coding categories offered by conventional classroom observation schedules, is able to calibrate the proportion of actual instructional time when in Hattie's terms the student is not only engaged but also learning?

These difficulties sustain Gage's claim that time on task is a 'psychologically empty quantitative concept'.[15] As it happens, Hattie's survey of 800 student achievement meta-analyses found time on task also to be a poor indicator of both learning and attainment,[16] for what matters is the *nature* of the engagement, not its quantity. Unpacking this relationship further, my own observation of teaching across cultures required me to differentiate the related measure of *pace*, which in UK school inspections is treated as monolithic and unproblematic, by reference to five elements:

- *organizational pace* (the speed at which lesson preparations, transitions and conclusions are handled);
- *task pace* (the speed at which learning tasks and their contingent activities are undertaken);
- *interactive pace* (the pace of teacher-student and student-student exchanges, and contingent matters such as maintaining focus and the handling of cues and turns);
- *cognitive* or *semantic pace* (the speed at which conceptual ground is covered in classroom interaction, or the ratio of new material to old and of task demand to task outcome);
- *learning pace* (how fast students actually learn).[17]

Time, as the *Culture and Pedagogy* study also observed, 'is a value, not merely a unit of measurement'.[18] Of course, the methodological challenge of mental/ behavioural inference is at least as old as the discipline of psychology, and time on task is just one of its manifestations. Small wonder that some have chosen to measure learning by focusing exclusively on behaviour *qua* behaviour. That the problem is at once methodological and conceptual is amply demonstrated in Lefstein and Snell's more recent take on the problem of pace as identified here.[19]

Notwithstanding all this, but for reasons we know and understand, what can be measured is privileged in policy circles over what cannot. But this is a dubious and indeed pyrrhic elevation if what is measured has limited indicative power and what is important is marginalised or ignored. Some indicators can be translated into measures, some cannot, but let's talk about the full spectrum of what *needs* to be indicated before we start talking about measures. I accept that national education systems, and international education efforts such as EFA, entail massive expenditure and huge populations and therefore require metrics that are as precise as possible and cannot be content with high-inference indicators. But if this imperative excludes what is most important then we have a problem.

To keep open the prospects for engaging with what really matters in teaching and learning I believe that we should sharpen rather than blunt the distinction between indicators and measures, treating the identification of indicators as the necessary first step in the formulation of measures. If it is indeed the case that much that is essential to the quality and outcomes of learning can be indicated but not be measured, we should not arbitrarily exclude such attributes or grasp at proxies which may be conveniently measurable but barely relevant. Instead, we should leave the unmeasurable indicators in place, develop and refine them *in their own terms* as qualitative devices for making qualitative judgements, and look for appropriate ways of using them to support our tasks of monitoring, development and improvement.

A more radical and creative discussion of EFA indicators is needed than the GMRs have so far provided; one that proceeds from the 'quality imperative' of teaching and learning as they irreducibly *are*, rather from numerical convenience. Hard data are not necessarily useful data.

The task I have outlined applies as much to the assessment of the learning of individual children as to the monitoring of schools and education systems. We can measure children's mathematical attainment and certain aspects of their basic literacy development. However, GMR 2014 argues, and its argument is welcome, that while the so-called basics are essential, the fractured nature of our world and the tragedies of poverty and conflict require schools to promote a global citizenship that addresses

> issues such as environmental sustainability and peace-building – which require core transferable skills such as critical thinking, communication, co-operation, problem-solving, conflict-resolution, leadership and

advocacy – and the promotion of core values such as tolerance, appreciation of diversity and civic responsibility.[20]

Here we are firmly in the territory of non-measurable indicators. So we must
find other ways to describe and assess children's learning in these vital areas.
A single testable target or indicator for 'learning' across the board – as is proposed for EFA post-2015 – may not suffice, unless it can be proved that, say,
numeracy correlates with tolerance, appreciation of diversity and civic responsibility. Actually, this isn't as far-fetched as it may seem for as GMR 2014
reminds us, the entire EFA effort is predicated on evidence that education,
and especially literacy, reduces poverty, boosts growth, increases employment
prospects, enhances health, reduces child mortality, narrows the gender gap and
much else.[21] Even more to the point, a British review of research on citizenship education showed that the skills in question are most effectively developed
when they are embedded in the teaching process rather than merely conceived
as outcomes,[22] and this I also take to be the force of the references in GMR
2014 to critical thinking, communication, problem-solving and so on. This,
once again, underlines the need for GMRs to engage with classroom process,
for that's where citizenship starts.

Pedagogy: one thing needful

This takes me to the third overarching problem predicated on my earlier analysis. Brian Simon, the UK's most distinguished educational historian, famously
asked: 'Why no pedagogy in England?'[23] and we might ask: 'Why no pedagogy
in the GMRs?' If pedagogy is both the act of teaching and the ideas, values,
knowledge and evidence that shape and justify it, if it is what the teacher needs
to know in order to make valid, effective and defensible classroom decisions,[24]
and if once access and enrolment have been achieved it is what delivers the
learning outcomes towards which EFA is directed, then it should have pride of
place in a report entitled *Teaching and Learning: quality for all*. But it does not.

In EFA 2002, repeated in subsequent GMRs, there is a table entitled 'an
input-process-outcome framework for assessing education quality'.[25] At least
process is included: all too often it remains securely locked in its black box.
But that is as far as it goes, for in this framework 'process' comprises just two
elements, 'school climate' and 'teaching/learning'. The school climate indicators – high expectations, strong leadership, positive teacher attitudes, safe and
gender-sensitive environments, incentives for good results, flexibility/auton-
omy – are preconditions or contextual factors rather than processes; and the
teaching/learning indicators are confined to 'sufficient learning time', 'active
teaching methods', 'integrated systems for assessment and feedback', 'appropriate class size' and 'appropriate use of language'.

Apart from the fact that these indicators display, in their use of adjectives
like 'high', 'strong', 'positive', 'sufficient', 'active' and 'appropriate', the problem of prescription in the guise of description that I referred to earlier, and

uncalibrated prescription at that, most of them are also about context and conditions rather than processes. Only 'active teaching methods' and 'appropriate use of language' come close, but without further explication these do not amount to much.

In fact, the striking feature of the GMRs is that they do not so much engage with pedagogy as circle around it. Like knowledge itself, pedagogy is a very deep pool. Perhaps UNESCO is afraid of falling in.

Quality and pedagogy: have the GMRs progressed?

What has changed during the GMR cycle? I should say immediately that while GMR 2005 was confined to the indicators that have been a constant since Dakar, it was an exception to some of the tendencies I've mentioned. It reviewed definitions of quality from Jomtien, Dakar, the UN Convention on the Rights of the Child and elsewhere, comparing humanist, behaviourist, critical, indigenous and adult education approaches. It also took us back to the 1996 Delors report, *Learning: the treasure within*, whose simple but powerful distinction between learning 'to know', 'to do', 'to live together' and 'to be' deserves to be revisited.[26]

All this was timely and helpful. However, GMR 2005 then proposed a 'framework for understanding education quality' in the hope of combining and reconciling the differences which its discussion had exposed.[27] In fact, apart from juggling the boxes and providing a more detailed elaboration of contextual factors, and in spite of the excellent accompanying discussion of the nature of quality, the quality framework in GMR 2005 was not very different from that in GMR 2002, and its account of teaching and learning – which it revealingly renamed 'inputs' rather than 'process' – was almost identical. Learning as an input? Only if you view teaching as no more than transmission.

The chronology is interesting, too. GMR 2002 offered 'a framework for *assessing* education quality' while three years later GMR 2005 gave us 'a framework for *understanding* education quality'.[28] Surely it should have been the other way round, for you can't assess something without first understanding it. Does this back-to-front chronology illustrate a wider tendency in EFA monitoring, I wonder?

What happens when we fast forward to GMR 2014? Here I can find no exploration, comparable to that provided by GMR 2005, of what educational 'quality' means. I assume that this is because it would look odd still to be debating such matters after ten reports and just one year before GMR 2015, the final report in the series. So in the assessment of progress towards EFA Goal 6, quality is characterised by the 'key indicators' of pupil/teacher ratio at the pre-primary, primary and secondary stages, the continuing teacher gender imbalance and the availability of textbooks.[29] To these is added a section on the need to strengthen international and regional assessments.[30]

All of these are important, but are they sufficient? And where, once again, are the processes of teaching and learning which GMR 2014 itself acknowledges are so vital to the EFA effort? 'Strong national policies that make teaching and learning a high priority are essential', says the report, 'to ensure that all children in school actually obtain the skills and knowledge they are meant to acquire.'[31] Just so. However, in the next paragraph expectations that at last we are getting somewhere are dashed when 'teach*ing* quality' becomes 'teach*er* quality' (my italics in each case) and this unexplained but significant shift from act to agent is then consolidated in the report's detailed discussion of teacher numbers, recruitment, qualifications, subject knowledge, training, retention and governance.

The emphasis on teachers is supremely important. Without teachers there is no teaching, and without good teachers the learning potential of many children will remain untapped. The association between teacher quality and learning outcomes is both self-evident and empirically demonstrable. But what are teachers to teach and how? And on what aspects of their teaching should their training concentrate, and why? And can we answer these questions if the nature of teaching has been inadequately conceived?

GMR 2014 does engage with some of these questions. It emphasises training for pupil diversity, gender parity and children with learning difficulties. It argues the need to compensate for teachers' poor subject knowledge and the importance of tools for classroom diagnosis and assessment, especially in relation to children at risk.[32] And then, in its crucial seventh and final chapter, 'Curriculum and assessment strategies that improve learning' it at last enters the classroom.[33] So 14 years after Dakar are we there at last? Have we finally reached pedagogy?

Yes and no, but mainly no. The discussions of both curriculum and assessment are, within the limits they set themselves, useful. As I've noted, GMR 2014 departs from the exclusive preoccupation with literacy and numeracy and argues the need for a wider curriculum and transferable skills. However, it sticks to the received view, dating back to the nineteenth century, that literacy and numeracy are and forever should remain the sole 'basics' of education, regardless of time, location, culture or national circumstance.

In this matter, the case for literacy remains exceptionally strong as both a tool for individual empowerment and a lever for social and economic progress, and successive GMRs have convincingly documented its impact in these terms. But, heretical though some may find the thought, the case for continuing to give numeracy parity with literacy is neither proved nor even considered. The habit of history, it seems, is sufficient justification, and because 'literacy-and-numeracy' has become in effect a single curriculum component, numeracy gets a free ride. Thus we are offered a curriculum in which only literacy, numeracy and citizenship are deemed 'basic'. But where, some beneficiaries of citizenship education might ask, are science or IT? And where, given the reference to transferable skills for citizenship, is the no less compelling evidence on transfer of learning through the arts?[34] Questioning fixed curriculum mindsets is surely as necessary a part of the GMR exercise as revisiting habitual assumptions about what constitutes a valid educational indicator, and if the task is thought to be necessary in rich countries,[35] why not elsewhere?

Commendation with reservation also applies to the treatment of assessment. GMR 2014 breaks new ground in EFA circles (though only there) by discussing formative as well as summative assessment, or what in the UK is called 'assessment for learning'. But here the discussion is again frustrated by the GMR's limited apprehension of pedagogy. Effective assessment for learning is more than the tools, boxes and packs that in this context GMR 2014 recommends from examples in Uganda, Liberia, South Africa, Colombia and India, which indeed their evaluations show to be effective in terms of both diagnosis and outcomes.[36] More fundamentally, assessment for learning is the very stuff of which effective teaching is made: the day-to-day, minute-by-minute observations and interactions through which good teachers constantly monitor children's learning and progress, affording the feedback which will build on their understandings and probe and remedy their misunderstandings.

On this vital matter GMR 2014, like its predecessors, has little to say. Once again we trip over the black box or meet the timorous figures circling the deep pool of pedagogy. Curriculum prescribed but not enacted; summative assessment but not formative; input and outcome but not process.

Why no pedagogy in the global monitoring reports?

If I am right that pedagogy is the missing ingredient in accounts of educational quality in these global monitoring reports, and that where pedagogic process appears its treatment is confined to random indicators, and that these tend to circle the teaching-learning process rather than engage with it, then as a prerequisite for improving matters in the post-2015 agenda we must urgently ask why this should be so. *Why* no pedagogy?

One answer is that when the availability and competence of teachers is a major challenge, as the GMRs show that it is, then it makes sense to focus on teachers rather than teaching, invest heavily in teacher recruitment, training and retention, and develop textbooks and classroom materials which in 1960s US parlance are 'teacher proof' and will enable even the minimally-trained teacher to do a reasonable job. On that basis, it may be thought that there's more to be gained from providing such materials than advocating more sophisticated and interactive models of teaching, especially in the context of large classes and multi-grade teaching. In these situations, textbooks and TLMs provide a predictable and reliable foundation for the teacher's work, effective even when the teacher is absent. For, as GMR 2014 reminds us, teacher absenteeism remains a major impediment to EFA.[37]

This argument is persuasive, though we must ask whether it is right for all circumstances and all teachers, and to what extent it should inform the EFA agenda after 2015. Making teaching 'teacher proof' may safeguard educational minima and compensate for teachers' poor training or erratic attendance, but it can be disempowering and, for competent and talented teachers, demeaning.

But is there another explanation for the neglect of process? I think there is, and it resides in the literature and evidence on which, since 2002, the GMRs have drawn.

A head count of the 680 or so published sources listed at the end of GMR 2014 reveals that in a report promisingly entitled *Teaching and Learning* the titles of only 40 of the cited publications – a mere 6 per cent – refer, directly or indirectly, to the report's claimed focus. A somewhat larger proportion deal with teacher supply, training and retention, and a much larger proportion still are macro-level national or cross-national studies of education policies, programmes, strategies, governance, funding and outcomes.[38]

That apparently skewed citation profile encourages us to dig deeper. A decade ago, a review undertaken for the US National Research Council (NRC) identified three main types of international comparative study in education. Type 1 are large-scale policy-directed statistical studies of educational achievement, expenditure and other matters of the kind that emanate from OECD, the World Bank and the UN. Type 2 are desk-based extrapolations from international data aimed at identifying policy options and solutions. Type 3 include the majority of studies in the published corpus of academic comparative, international and development education. These range from broadly descriptive accounts of individual education systems to the 'thick description' of close-grained cross-national and cross-cultural comparative studies of school and classroom life and the forces that shape it.[39]

Types 1, 2 and 3 add up to a literature of considerable variety and richness. However, the NRC report adds that while the majority of published comparative education studies are Type 3, and while many Type 3 studies have significant policy applications, it's the Type 1 and 2 studies that receive most of the funding, political patronage and publicity. The neglect of Type 3 evidence reinforces the remoteness of policymakers and the policy process from schooling as it is experienced by teachers and children, and increases the risk that high-cost and high-stakes interventions relating to teachers, teaching and learning may be misconceived or misdirected.

Following the NRC analysis, what we may have, then – not universally or inevitably, but too frequently – is a six-fold problem of evidential selectivity in the corridors of power. First, the preferred evidence is top-down. It reflects the world, the preoccupations, the priorities and the experiences of policymakers rather than those of teachers and children. Second, it may privilege a supposedly international but essentially western perspective over an indigenous one. Third, its view of school and classroom life may be generalised, coarse-grained, un-nuanced and perhaps simplistic. Fourth, its understandable pursuit of what can be measured removes from the agenda and consciousness of policymakers those vital aspects of education that quantification cannot access. Fifth, it ignores a substantial tranche of evidence of which, in the interests of competent and democratic policy making, policymakers, or at least their advisers, have a duty to be aware. Sixth, it is self-sealing and self-reinforcing. Reading UK government publications I am constantly struck by the extent to which they refer only to other government publications. Such circularity in evidence, argument and policy is always dangerous, *a fortiori* in the context of global education.

It would be impolite of me to accuse GMR 2014 of these tendencies, but given what I have said about the balance of published sources listed at the end of the report the possibility at least deserves consideration, for GMR 2014, like all the GMRs, leans more towards Type 1 evidence than Type 3. In doing so, is it missing something important? I think it is.

Engaging with pedagogy: conceptual and empirical possibilities

I want now to show how in the elusive area of pedagogy such evidential selectivity and imbalance can be avoided and how we can then greatly enhance the debate about the quality of teaching and learning in EFA. I shall deal with the matter first conceptually, then empirically.

The genealogy of the teaching-learning framework in GMR 2002, which was modified in GMR 2005 and remains influential in EFA, is clear: 1960s US process-product research was transmuted into 1990s transatlantic school effectiveness research and domesticated by international agencies like the World Bank.[40] It atomises rather than synthesises, includes only what can be easily measured, views teaching as simple transmission and so concentrates much more on the teacher than the learner, and treats culture not as an all-pervasive feature to be handled with care, sensitivity and humility but as just another variable to be factored and crunched.

I would not claim that my own alternative is impervious to critique, still less that it is the one to adopt, but it least it provides a contrast. Striving to develop a framework for the analysis of both quantitative and qualitative classroom data from five very different education systems in Europe, North America and Asia, I started with what I believed were irreducible propositions about the nature of teaching, as it is in any context. From these I derived a two-part framework or matrix comprising the *act* of teaching and the *ideas* that inform it.

Teaching as act identifies the cross-cultural *structural invariants* of teaching. This part of the framework has been shown to be not only comprehensive but also as culture-fair as any such cultural artefact can be. In 2014–15, for example, a research team at Ben Gurion University used it to analyse Israeli pedagogy.[41] Teaching as ideas accesses the *cultural variables* that shape, breathe life and meaning into, and indeed define these invariants and thus demonstrate the extent to which (as I showed earlier) even the most securely quantifiable of them is culturally loaded.

In my own cross-cultural studies I found that such ideas concerned not just the nature and purposes of learning, knowledge and teaching – transmission, induction, negotiation, facilitation, acceleration and so on – but even more fundamentally what I called 'primordial values' about the relationship of the individual to others and to society which translate into culturally-distinctive classroom routines and patterns of organisation. This could take us into discussion of so-called 'western' and 'non-western' models of teaching for which there isn't space in this chapter, except to note that to portray the cultural diversity of teaching and learning as conceived and enacted across 196 nations and thousands of cultures and sub-cultures as a simple choice between 'western' and 'non-western' is crude in the extreme. Note, too, that this dichotomy makes 'western' the default and 'non-western' the aberration.[42] Edward Said would have had something to say about that.[43]

There is no way that the inherited GMR paradigm can capture any of this. What the comparison of these frameworks also signals is another important question: are there universals in teaching and learning that apply across cultures and contexts, or is everything culturally unique? In my own work I strenuously argue that culture and history are the keys to understanding and comparing national education systems. But I also believe from what we know about human development and education across cultures that there is a level at which pedagogic universals can be defined. My complementary frameworks for teaching as act and ideas try to capture these. (See pp 288–99).

Frameworks like those I have exemplified expose the conceptual incompleteness of the input-output models in GMR 2002. Above all, the classroom interaction through which both learning and teaching are mediated is almost absent from the GMR frameworks. Let us therefore stay with interaction, mindful of the NRC's judgement that policy-directed studies lean too exclusively on Type 1 and 2 research and ignore Type 3 – a judgement which, in relation to the interactive heart of teaching and learning is borne out by the bibliography of GMR 2014. Where, then, can we go to plug this gap?

There is a considerable literature on classroom interaction in general and educationally productive talk in particular, but I'll mention by way of example just two major sources that have the virtue of being comprehensive, methodologically diverse, cross-cultural, cross-national and rigorously empirical. Further, their publication dates coincide neatly with our consideration of the post 2015 agenda.

The first is a collection of research papers arising from an international conference on classroom talk which was convened in 2011 at the University of Pittsburgh, USA, under the auspices of AERA.[44] This brought together many of the world's leading researchers in the areas of pedagogy and linguistics to establish whether, after several decades of research, we have proof of concept that high quality classroom talk not only engages children's attention and participation – as we have known for a long time that it does – but also raises their standards of achievement in tests of literacy, numeracy and science.

The answer to that question was conclusively affirmative. There is now a critical mass of randomised control studies in different countries showing that high quality classroom talk enhances understanding, accelerates learning and raises measured standards. This finding is also confirmed in Hattie's synthesis of 800 meta-analyses relating to student achievement in respect of interactive strategies such as reciprocal teaching, peer tutoring, student verbalisation and feedback.[45] Such strategies, in Hattie's words, make children's learning visible to the teacher and hence amenable to appropriate diagnosis, assessment and intervention (Hattie, 173–8). The quest for indicators of visible learning would be a useful exercise for the team of GMR 2015. 'Visible' and 'measurable' are not, however, synonymous.

The other study counters the claim that because the research I have cited comes from classrooms in high-income countries it cannot fairly be expected to apply in the context of education for development. This second study is a review of research on pedagogy, curriculum, teaching practices and teacher education in developing countries which the UK government's Department for International Development (DfID) commissioned from the University of Sussex.[46] Having trawled 489 studies from middle- and low-income countries, the Sussex team examined 54 of these in depth. While acknowledging the methodological limitations of some of the studies the Sussex team neverthe-less felt able to conclude that classroom interaction is the pedagogical key. They highlighted as feasible and proven strategies for effective teaching in these contexts inclusive and supportive communication, varied teacher questioning, informative feedback, building on student responses, student questioning, and other elements of what I call dialogic teaching.

All the studies in these important US and UK collections, which together include classroom research from high-, middle- and low-income countries, are Type 3. Being Type 3 and engaging with teaching as it happens, they show not just that high quality classroom talk makes a difference but how it can be improved. But only a handful of the studies in the Sussex report, and none of those from the AERA symposium, found their way into the vast bibliographies of GMR 2005 and 2014, dominated as these were by Types 1 and 2. In the UK, meanwhile, a major research and development project capitalises on such evidence to develop, test and evaluate the capacity of talk-rich teaching strate-gies to close the achievement gap between some of Britain's most disadvan-taged children and their more advantaged peers.[47]

Conclusion: what is to be done?

And so we return to my initial questions:

- Does the account of quality in EFA attend to what really matters in teach-ing and learning?
- Are the classroom processes and outcomes that are truly transformative for our children adequately captured in the EFA goals, objectives and targets, the EFA monitoring indicators and measures, and the evidence on which EFA thinking and policy draw?
- If not, what are the implications for EFA after 2015, and if learning is to be a target, how should it be defined, indicated and assessed?

I submit that in respect of the monitoring of quality in teaching and learning in EFA we have a problem which is both conceptual and empirical. Neither quality nor pedagogy are adequately conceived, and some of the world's most important and relevant evidence on teaching, learning and their improvement has been ignored. Classroom interaction is the most prominent and perhaps crucial aspect of pedagogy, among several, to suffer this fate, and the example outlined shows that its omission is both grave and unnecessary.

How can this unsatisfactory situation be addressed?

First, education for the period post-2015 needs a radical and properly informed debate about indicators and measures in relation to the black box, or black hole, of teaching and learning, for classrooms are the true front line in the quest for educational quality. The proper sequence, surely, is not to make do with the odd measure that happens to have featured in a number of school effectiveness studies but to start with a rounded account of the educational process and the purposes it serves, then range comprehensively and eclectically across the full spectrum of relevant research and extrapolate what the evidence shows can safely be regarded as key indicators of quality, and only then proceed to the question of how those indicators that have been shown to have pre-eminent influence on the quality and outcomes of learning can be translated into measures. In all cases, both indicators and measures should resonate clearly with goals. It is all too common for education planners grandly to espouse goal x and then signal through what is tested that outcome y is what really matters.

Second, where an indicator has empirical provenance but cannot readily be translated into a simple measure, other ways should be found to keep it in the frame. Under no circumstances should an indicator that peer-reviewed research has shown to be critical to effective teaching and standards of learning be dropped at this stage merely because it cannot be quantified. We have to find other ways of handling it. We need a more creative and less doctrinal approach to the whole question of indicators and measures, exploiting, as I have suggested, the methodological possibilities that the vocabulary encourages. In any case, the objectivity of quantitative measures is often overstated, while there are established procedures for assuring inter-judge reliability in the use of so-called subjective assessments. Again, I warn against paradigm wars.

Third, to cover the evidence as it needs to be covered, teams working on the defining and monitoring of quality in education post 2015 should become more relevantly multi-disciplinary than, in the EFA context, they appear to have been thus far.

Fourth, let's accept that although much Type 3 evidence comes from and relates to high-income jurisdictions and systems, the DfID review of research on pedagogy, curriculum and teacher education in developing countries shows that there's now a fair Type 3 corpus from middle- and low-income contexts too. One of the post-2015 tasks, I suggest, should be to expand that corpus and make it as reliable as possible. In any case, there's sufficient evidence from cross-national studies of teaching and learning, and from Hattie-style meta-analyses of classroom research, to show that there are universals to which in any event we should attend; for example, teacher professional content knowledge (not the same as subject knowledge), the character and degree of cognitive challenge afforded by teacher-student interaction, and the quality of the information conveyed in teacher-student and student-teacher feedback.

Fifth, having identified which processes matter most and having nominated them as essential indicators, we will find from Type 3 research that some of them are more amenable to measurement than may be thought. That goes especially for the teacher-student interaction that lies at the heart of teaching.

Sixth, in light of all this, we therefore need to explore targets and indicators for both learning and teaching. Learning needs a process indicator as well as an outcome one, and on the basis of what we know about the crucial conditions for learning, we might try *student engagement.* Similarly if teaching has to be reduced to just one indicator, on the basis of what we know about the characteristics of effective teaching from both Hattie's meta-analysis of studies in high-income countries and the 2013 DfID literature review, we might try *reciprocity* in teacher-student interaction. As it happens, both engagement and oral reciprocity are amenable to measurement, so mine is not a completely hopeless cause. Having said that, they are also susceptible to the same problems of behavioural inference that I discussed earlier in relation to time on task, which underlines the need for continuing caution and vigilance.

Finally, here is the double and troubling dilemma. We want teaching and learning, *as they happen and are experienced,* to gain the prominence in global education that they deserve and need in the interests of equity and progress. But the modality and discourse highlight targets, indicators and metrics. So we should start by exploring how far what matters in teaching and learning is amenable to such treatment, noting that on the basis of the reductionism we have witnessed thus far, the prospect of a single global measure of the quality of teaching applied across all cultural and pedagogical contexts is nothing if not deeply alarming. Quite apart from the totalitarian resonance of such an idea, or the possibility – nay, probability – that the measure would be plain wrong, teaching is a quintessentially local activity; and I say this having argued that there are observable structural invariants in teaching and learning that are encountered across cultures and systems.

This also means that while generalised process quality targets may be volunteered on the basis of what the evidence tells us makes a difference, it is only at classroom level that they can be feasibly monitored. The trick will be to give process and the quality of process the prominence they deserve without allowing the resulting indicator(s) to tyrannise and debase what they purport to advance and improve; and to find a way to add this essential local dimension to development and monitoring processes that are no less essentially about global and national development.

There are many barriers to achieving education for all, but evidence should not be one of them. Quality in teaching and learning is a global imperative. It demands a global community of discourse. The concept note from the EFA GMR team[48] preparing for the post-2015 Sustainable Development Goals (SDGs) is somewhat self-congratulatory about the methodology of GMR 2014 and seemingly impervious to critique of the kind offered here. Nevertheless, we have to hope that UNESCO and its advisers will approach education in the context of the SDGs with a commitment to make much more inclusive use of the abundant evidence on pedagogy that is now available in order to exert maximum impact on quality where it matters: in the classroom. Stop tiptoeing around the pool of pedagogy. Take the plunge.[49]

Notes

1 UNESCO 2014.
2 UNESCO 2000.
3 UNESCO 1990.
4 UNESCO 2014.
5 Updated in UNESCO 2019.
6 The EFA goals are: (1) Early childhood care and education; (2) Universal primary education; (3) Youth and adult skills; (4) Adult literacy; (5) Gender parity and equity; (6) Quality of education.
7 The ten previous GMRs, from 2002–12, are listed on p (iv) of GMR 2014.
8 Alexander 2008c.
9 The title of the Oslo keynote was 'Teaching and learning for all: the quality imperative revisited'.
10 UNESCO 2004 (hereafter GMR 2005).
11 Lockheed and Verspoor 1991, 87.
12 Alexander 2008c, 3–6.
13 UNESCO 2008, 244–51.
14 Hattie and Yates 2014, 37.
15 Gage 1978, 75. For a cross-national and cross-cultural discussion of time as a far from objective pedagogical 'indicator', see Alexander 2001a, 391–426.
16 Hattie 2009, 184–5; Hattie and Yates 2014, 43.
17 Alexander 2001a, 418–26.
18 Alexander 2001a, 425.
19 Lefstein and Snell 2013.
20 UNESCO 2014, 295.
21 UNESCO 2014, 144ff.
22 Deakin Crick *et al* 2005.
23 Simon 1981b. His 'Why no pedagogy?' critique was revisited a quarter of a century later in 'Still no pedagogy?' (Alexander 2004a).
24 Alexander 2008b, 47. See this volume, Chapter 20. My definition is more continental European than Anglo-American, and contrasts with the tradition, reaching back to the 1960s US/UK curriculum builders, in which curriculum is paramount and pedagogy subsidiary. The neglect of pedagogy in the GMRs may relate to this legacy as well as to other problems this chapter identifies.
25 UNESCO 2002, 81.
26 Delors *et al* 1996.
27 UNESCO 2004, 36.
28 UNESCO 2002, 81; UNESCO 2004, 36.
29 UNESCO 2014, 84–9.
30 UNESCO 2014, 89–99.
31 UNESCO 2014, 217.
32 UNESCO 2014, 233–41.
33 UNESCO 2014, 276–97.
34 See, for example, the evidence assembled for the (US) President's Commission on the Arts and Humanities 2011.

35 Alexander 2010a, 174–278.

36 UNESCO 2014, 288–9.

37 UNESCO 2014, 267.

38 UNESCO 2014, 410–43. I cannot of course claim to have read every one of the cited publications, and am basing this assertion on scrutiny of their titles, authors and publishing details. But it's an analysis I have applied elsewhere: see, for example, Chapters 20 and 21 in this volume.

39 National Research Council 2003. 'Thick description', the ethnographer's credo, was first coined by the philosopher Gilbert Ryle but popularised by anthropologist Clifford Geertz (1973, 3–30).

40 For analysis and critique of this paradigm: Alexander 2001a, 26–40, 2008b, 9–42.

41 For an early paper from this project: Lefstein 2013.

42 These matters are discussed in a paper first presented at the 2002 AERA Annual conference and later revised for Alexander 2008b, chapter 4.

43 Said 1985.

44 Resnick *et al* 2015.

45 Hattie 2009.

46 Westbrook *et al* 2013.

47 *Classroom talk, social disadvantage and educational attainment: closing the gap, raising standards.* A joint project of the Cambridge Primary Review Trust and the University of York, funded from 2014–17 by the UK Educational Endowment Foundation. See this volume, Chapter 16.

48 UNESCO 2015.

49 The UN Sustainable Development Goal (SDG) 4 is 'Quality education: ensure inclusive and equitable quality education and promote lifelong learning opportunities for all'. SDG 4 has ten targets and 11 indicators. These frequently use the word 'quality' ('By 2030, ensure that all girls and boys complete free, equitable and quality primary and secondary education leading to relevant and Goal-4 effective learning outcomes . . . By 2030, ensure that all girls and boys have access to quality early childhood development, care and pre-primary education so that they are ready for primary education . . . By 2030, ensure equal access for all women and men to affordable and quality technical, vocational and tertiary education, including university. . .'), but the force of the word seems little more than rhetorical, and the problems of definitions, indicators, measures, proxies and the treatment of pedagogy have been allowed to persist.

Bibliography

Aaronovitch, D. (2008) Do old-style subjects deaden young minds? *The Times*, 9 December.

Ackers, J. and Hardman, F. (2001) Classroom interaction in Kenyan primary schools. *Compare 31*(2), 245–62.

Adams, R. (2017) Proportion of students taking arts subjects falls to lowest level in decade. *The Guardian*, 21 September.

Adey, P. and Shayer, M. (1993) An exploration of long-term far-transfer effects following an extended intervention programme in the high school science curriculum. *Cognition and Instruction 11*(1), 1–29.

Adonis, A. (2007) DCSF response to media coverage of Cambridge primary review interim reports 4/1, 4/2 and 3/4. Quoted by *Reuters*, 2 November.

Ainscow, M., Dyson, A., Hopwood, L. and Thomson, S. (2016) *Primary Schools Responding to Diversity: Barriers and Possibilities*. CPRT Research Survey 8. York: Cambridge Primary Review Trust.

Alexander, R.J. (1984) *Primary Teaching*. London: Cassell.

Alexander, R.J. (1988) Garden or jungle? Teacher development and informal primary education. In W.A.L. Blyth (ed) *Informal Primary Education Today: Essays and Studies*. London: Falmer Press, 148–88.

Alexander, R.J. (1992) Holding the middle ground. *Times Educational Supplement*, 31 January.

Alexander, R.J. (1996) *Other Primary Schools and Ours: Hazards of International Comparison*. University of Warwick: CREPE.

Alexander, R.J. (1997) *Policy and Practice in Primary Education: Local Initiative, National Agenda*. London: Routledge.

Alexander, R.J. (2001a) *Culture and Pedagogy: International Comparisons in Primary Education*. Oxford: Blackwell.

Alexander, R.J. (2001b) Border crossings: towards a comparative pedagogy. *Comparative Education 37*(4), 507–23.

Alexander, R.J. (2003) *Talk for Learning: The First Year*. Northallerton: North Yorkshire County Council. www.robinalexander.org.uk/docs/NYorks_EVAL_REP_03.pdf.

Alexander, R.J. (2004a) Still no pedagogy? Principle, pragmatism and compliance in primary education. *Cambridge Journal of Education 34*(1), 7–33.

Alexander, R.J. (2004b) *Towards Dialogic Teaching: Rethinking Classroom Talk* (1st edition). York: Dialogos.

Alexander, R.J. (2005a) *Talk for Learning: The Second Year*. Northallerton: North Yorkshire County Council. www.robinalexander.org.uk/docs/TLP_Eval_Report_04.pdf.

Alexander, R.J. (2005b) *Teaching Through Dialogue: The First Year*. London: Barking and Dagenham Council. www.robinalexander.org.uk/bardagreport05.pdf.

Alexander, R.J. (2006a) Dichotomous pedagogies and the promise of cross-cultural comparison. In A.H. Halsey, P. Brown, H. Lauder and J. Dilabough (eds) *Education: Globalisation and Social Change*. Oxford: Oxford University Press, 722–33.

Alexander, R.J. (2006b) *Education as Dialogue: Moral and Pedagogical Choices for a Runaway World*. Hong Kong and York: Hong Kong Institute of Education with Dialogos.

Alexander, R.J. (2007) Where there is no vision. . . *Forum 49*(1 & 2), 87–99.

Alexander, R.J. (2008a) Testaments to the power of 10. *Times Educational Supplement*, 16 May.

Alexander, R.J. (2008b) *Essays on Pedagogy*. London: Routledge.

Alexander, R.J. (2008c) *Education for All, the Quality Imperative and the Problem of Pedagogy*. CREATE Pathways to Access Research Monograph 20. London: CREATE.

Alexander, R.J. (2009a) Ministers fail to learn lessons. *The Guardian*, 24 October.

Alexander, R.J. (2009b) Plowden, truth and myth: a warning. Keynote address, College of Teachers Awards Ceremony. www.robinalexander.org.uk/wp-content/uploads/2012/05/Plowden-truth-and-myth.pdf.

Alexander, R.J. (2009c) Towards a comparative pedagogy. In R. Cowen and A.M. Kazamias (eds) *International Handbook of Comparative Education*. New York: Springer, 922–41.

Alexander, R.J. (ed) (2010a) *Children, Their World, Their Education Final Report and Recommendations of the Cambridge Primary Review*. London: Routledge.

Alexander, R.J. (2010b) World class schools: noble aspiration or globalised hokum? (BAICE Presidential Address). *Compare 40*(6), 801–18.

Alexander, R.J. (2010c) Speaking but not listening? Accountable talk in an unaccountable context. *Literacy* 44(3), 103–11.

Alexander, R.J. (2011a) Evidence, rhetoric and collateral damage: the problematic pursuit of 'world class' standards. *Cambridge Journal of Education* 41(3), 265–86.

Alexander, R.J. (2011b) Legacies, policies and prospects: one year on from the Cambridge primary review. *Forum 53*(1), 71–91.

Alexander, R.J. (2011c) Primary schools need a broad curriculum. *The Guardian*, 15 March.

Alexander, R.J. (2011d) Evidence from the US tells us arts belong at the heart of the curriculum – but it's our last chance to make this happen. *Times Educational Supplement*, 5 September.

Alexander, R.J. (2011e) Could do even better? Making the most of international comparison as a tool of policy. Paper for the Department of Education, November.

Alexander, R.J. (2012a) Improving oracy and classroom talk in English schools: achievements and challenges. Paper for the Department for Education (DfE) seminar on Oracy, the National Curriculum and Educational Standards, 20 February. http://robinalexander.org.uk/wp-content/uploads/2019/12/DfE-oracy-120220-Alexander-FINAL0.pdf (accessed May 2021).

Alexander, R.J. (2012b) Entitlement, freedom, minimalism and essential knowledge: can the curriculum circle be squared? Paper for the CPPS Westminster seminar, 23 April.

Alexander, R.J. (2012c) Citing Finland's educational reforms in support of those proposed for England: a warning. Paper for the Department for Education, May.

Alexander, R.J. (2012d) Neither national nor a curriculum? *Forum 54*(3), 369–84.

Alexander, R.J. (2012e) Moral panic, miracle cures and educational policy: what can we really learn from international comparison? *Scottish Educational Review 44*(1), 4–21.

Alexander, R.J. (2012f) Strengthening curriculum capacity in primary schools: definitions, levels, roles and options. Paper for the Department for Education, January.

Alexander, R.J. (2013) *Curriculum Freedom, Capacity and Leadership in the Primary School*. NCSL Expert Perspective. Nottingham: National College for School Leadership.

Alexander, R.J. (2014a) The best that has been thought and said? *Forum 56*(1), 157–66.

Alexander, R.J. (2014b) Evidence, policy and the reform of primary education. *Forum 56*(3), 349–75.

Alexander, R.J. (ed) (2015a) *The CPRT/IEE Dialogic Teaching Project, Trial Stage, 2015–16: Handbook for Schools*. York: Cambridge Primary Review Trust and University of York.

Alexander, R.J. (ed) (2015b) *The CPRT/IEE Dialogic Teaching Project, Trial Stage, 2015–16: Planning and Review Forms for Mentors*. York: Cambridge Primary Review Trust and University of York.

Alexander, R.J. (2015c) Dialogic pedagogy at scale: oblique perspectives. In L.B. Resnick, C.S.C. Asterhan, and S.N. Clarke (eds) *Socializing Intelligence Through Academic Talk and Dialogue*. Washington DC: AERA, 429–40.

Alexander, R.J. (2015d) Teaching and learning for all: the quality imperative revisited. *International Journal of Educational Development 41*(1), 250–8.

Alexander, R.J. (2016a) What's the point? Select committee ponders the meaning of education. *Forum 58*(2), 155–66.

Alexander, R.J. (2016b) Teaching and learning for all: the quality imperative revisited. In S. McGrath and Q. Gy (eds) *The Routledge Handbook of International Education and Development*. London: Routledge, 118–32.

Alexander, R.J. (2017a) *Towards Dialogic Teaching: Rethinking Classroom Talk* (5th edition). York: Dialogos.

Alexander, R.J. (2017b) Dialogic teaching and the study of classroom talk: a developmental bibliography. www.robinalexander.org.uk/wp-content/uploads/2017/01/Alexander-dialogic-teaching-bibliography.pdf.

Alexander, R.J. (2018) Developing dialogic teaching: genesis, process, trial. *Research Papers in Education 33*(5), 561–98.

Alexander, R.J. (2019a) *Submission to the All-Party Parliamentary Group on Oracy from Professor Robin Alexander*. Cambridge: Wolfson College.

Alexander, R.J. (2019b) Whose discourse? Dialogic pedagogy for a post-truth world. *Dialogic Pedagogy Journal* 7, E1–E19. http://robinalexander.org.uk/wp-content/uploads/2019/12/Alexander-DPJ-2019.pdf (accessed May 2021).

Alexander, R.J. (2020) *A Dialogic Teaching Companion*. London: Routledge.

Alexander, R.J., Doddington, C., Gray, J., Hargreaves, L. and Kershner, R. (eds) (2010) *The Cambridge Primary Review Research Surveys*. London: Routledge.

Alexander, R.J. and Flutter, J. (2009) *Towards a New Primary Curriculum: A Report from the Cambridge Primary Review*. Cambridge: University of Cambridge Faculty of Education. https://cprtrust.org.uk/cpr/cpr-publications/interim-reports/ (accessed May 2021).

Alexander, R.J., Hardman, F., Hardman, J., Rajab, T. and Longmore, M. (2017) *Changing Talk, Changing Thinking: Interim Report from the in-House Evaluation of the CPRT/UoY Dialogic Teaching Project*. York: University of York.

Alexander, R.J. and Hargreaves, L. (2007) *Community Soundings: The Cambridge Primary Review Regional Witness Sessions*. Cambridge: University of Cambridge Faculty of Education. https://cprtrust.org.uk/wp-content/uploads/2014/06/Comm-soundings-briefing-REVISED-2014.pdf (accessed May 2021).

Alexander, R.J., Rose, J., and Woodhead, C. (1992) *Curriculum Organisation and Classroom Practice in Primary Schools: A Discussion Paper*. London: DES.

Alexander, R.J. and Willcocks, J. (1995) Task, time and talk. In R.J. Alexander *Versions of Primary Education*. London: Routledge, 103–219.

Alexander, R.J., with contributions from J. Willcocks, K. Kinder and N. Nelson, (1995) *Versions of Primary Education*. London: Routledge.

Alexander, R.J., Willcocks, J. and Nelson, N. (1996) Discourse, pedagogy and the national curriculum: change and continuity in primary schools. *Research Papers in Education, 11*(1), 83–122.

Althusser, L. (1976) *On the Reproduction of Capitalism: Ideology and Ideological State Apparatuses*, trans. and ed. G.M. Goshgarian. Brooklyn, NY: Verso.

Apple, M.W. (1995) *Education and Power*. London: Routledge.

Archer, M.S. (1979) *Social Origins of Educational Systems*. London: Sage.

Archer, M.S. (1989) *Culture and Agency: The Place of Culture in Social Theory*. Cambridge: Cambridge University Press.

Archer, M.S. (2000) *Being Human: The Problem of Agency*. Cambridge: Cambridge University Press.

Arendt, H. (2004) *The Origins of Totalitarianism*. New York: Schocken Books.

Argyris, C. and Schön, D. (1974) *Theory in Practice: Increasing Professional Effectiveness*. San Francisco: Jossey-Bass.

Armstrong, M. (1980) *Closely Observed Children*. London: Writers and Readers.

Armstrong, M. (2006) *Children Writing Stories*. London: Open University Press.

Armstrong, M. (2011) *What Children Know: Essays on Children's Literary and Visual Art*. Lulu. com.

Arnold, M. (1869) Culture and anarchy. In S. Collini (ed) *Culture and Anarchy and Other Writings*. Cambridge: Cambridge University Press.

Arnold, M. (1960) The twice-revised code. In R.H. Super (ed) *The Complete Prose Works of Matthew Arnold*. Ann Arbor: University of Michigan Press.

Atkinson, P. and Delamont, M. (1977) Mock-ups and cock-ups: The stage management of guided discovery instruction. In P. Woods and M. Hammersley (eds) *School Experience: Explorations in the Sociology of Education*. London: Croom Helm, 87–108.

Auden, W.H. (1940) *Another Time*. London: Faber and Faber.

Austin, J.L. (1962) *How to Do Things with Words*. Oxford: Oxford University Press.

Bakare, L. and Adams, R. (2021) Plan for 50% funding cut to arts subjects at universities 'catastrophic'. *The Guardian*, 6 May.

Baker, M. (2009) When is a review not really a review? Comparing Sir Jim Rose's review of the primary curriculum with the Plowden Report of 1967. *The Guardian*, 18 May.

Baker, M. (2013) Gove takes control of the curriculum. *The Guardian*, 15 June.

Bakhtin, M.M. (1981) *The Dialogic Imagination*. Austin, TX: University of Texas.

Bakhtin, M.M. (1986) *Speech Genres and Other Late Essays*. Austin, TX: University of Texas.

Balarin, M. and Lauder, H. (2008) *The Governance and Administration of English Primary Education*. Cambridge Primary Review Research Survey 10/2. In Alexander, R.J., Doddington, C., Gray, J., Hargreaves, L. and Kershner, R. (eds) (2010) *The Cambridge Primary Review Research Surveys*. London: Routledge, 733–50.

Ball, S.J. (1990) *Politics and Policy-making in Education*. London: Routledge.

Ball, S.J. (2012) *Politics and Policy-Making in Education: Explorations in Sociology*. London: Routledge.

Ball, S.J. (2018) The tragedy of state education in England: reluctance, compromise and muddle – a system in disarray. *Journal of the British Academy 6*, 207–38.

Ball, S.J., Maguire, M. and Braun, A. (2011) *How Schools Do Policy: Policy Enactments in Secondary Schools*. London: Routledge.

Balls, E. (2008) Secretary of State's response to media coverage of Cambridge primary review interim reports 9/1, 3/1 and 3/3. Reported in *The Independent*, 29 February.

Bangs, J. (2011) Oral Statement to the New Visions for Education Group. London: NVEG.

Bangs, J., MacBeath, J. and Galton, M. (2010) *Reinventing Schools, Reforming Teaching: From Political Visions to Classroom Reality*. London: Routledge.

Barber, M. (2001) Large-scale education reform in England: a work in progress. Paper for the Managing Education Reform conference, Moscow, 19-30 October.

Barber, M. (2007) *Instruction to Deliver: Fighting to Transform Britain's Public Services*. London: Politico's.

Barber, M. (2011) *Deliverology: From Idea to Implementation*. London: McKinsey. www.mckinsey.com/industries/public-and-social-sector/our-insights/deliverology-from-idea-to-implementation (accessed June 2021).

Barber, M. and Mourshed, M. (2007) *How the World's Best-Performing School Systems Come Out on Top*. Dubai: McKinsey and Company.

Barber, M., Whelan, F. and Clark, M. (2011) *Capturing the Leadership Premium: How the World's Top School Systems Are Building Leadership Capacity for the Future*. Dubai: McKinsey and Company.

Barnes, D. (1988) The politics of oracy. In M. MacLure, T. Phillips and A. Wilkinson (eds) *Oracy Matters: The Development of Talking and Listening in Education*. Milton Keynes: Open University Press.

Barnes, D., Britton, J. and Rosen, H. (1969) *Language, the Learner and the School*. Harmondsworth: Penguin Books.

Barnes, D. and Todd, F. (1977) *Communication and Learning in Small Groups*. London: Routledge and Kegan Paul.

Barnes, D. and Todd, F. (1995) *Communication and Learning Revisited: Making Meaning Through Talk*. Portsmouth, NH: Heinemann.

Bayliss, V. (1999) *Opening Minds: Education for the 21st Century*. London: RSA.

Benavot, A. (2008) The organisation of school knowledge: official curricula in global perspective. In J. Resnick (ed) *The Production of Knowledge in the Global Era*. Rotterdam and Taipei: Sense Publishers.

Benavot, A., Cha, Y-K., Kames, D., Meyer, J.W. and Wong, S-Y. (1991) Knowledge for the masses: world models and national curricula, 1920–1986. *American Sociological Review 56*.

Berliner, D.C. (2002) Educational research: the hardest science of all. *Educational Researcher 31*, 18–20.

Berliner, D.C. (2004) Expert teachers: their characteristics, development and accomplishments. *Bulletin of Science, Technology and Society 24*(3), 200–12.

Berliner, D.C. (2012) Effects of inequality and poverty vs teachers and schooling on America's youth. *Teachers College Record 116*(1).

Berliner, D.C. and Biddle, B.J. (1995) *The Manufactured Crisis: Myths, Fraud and the Attack on America's Public Schools*. Cambridge MA: Perseus Books.

Berliner, D.C., Glass, G.V. and associates (2014) *50 Myths and Lies that Threaten America's Public Schools*. New York: Teachers College Press.

Bernstein, B. (1970) Education cannot compensate for society. *New Society*, 26 February, 344–7.

Bernstein, B. (1990) *The Structuring of Pedagogic Discourse*. Class, Codes and Control, Vol. 4. London: Routledge.

Black, P., Harrison, C., Lee, C., Marshall, B. and Wiliam, D. (2003) *Assessment for Learning: Putting it into Practice*. Maidenhead: Open University Press.

Black, P. and Wiliam, D. (1998) *Inside the Black Box*. Slough: NFER-Nelson.

Blatchford, P., Bassett, P., Brown, P. and Martin, C. (2008) *Deployment and Impact of Support Staff in Schools and the Impact of the National Agreement.* London: University of London Institute of Education.

Board of Education (1931) *Report of the Consultative Committee on the Primary School.* The Hadow Report. London: HMSO.

Bond, L., Smith, T., Baker, W.K. and Hattie, J.A. (2000) *The Certification System for the National Board for Professional Teaching Standards: A Construct and Consequential Validity Study.* Greensborough: University of Greensborough.

Bourdieu, P. and Passeron, J.-C. (1990) *Reproduction in Education, Society and Culture.* London: Sage.

Bourn, D., Hunt, F., Blum, N. and Lawson, H. (2016) *Primary Education for Global Learning and Sustainability.* CPRT Research Survey 5. York: Cambridge Primary Review Trust.

Bowe, R., Ball, S.J. and Gold, A. (2017) *Reforming Education and Changing Schools: Case Studies in Policy Sociology.* London: Routledge.

Bowles, S. and Gintis, H. (1976) *Schooling in Capitalist America: Educational Reform and the Contradictions of Economic Life.* London: Routledge.

Boyd, M.P. and Markarian, W.C. (2015) Dialogic teaching and dialogic stance: Moving beyond interactional form. *Research in the Teaching of English* 49(3), 279–96.

Boyd, M.P. and Rubin, D. (2006) How contingent questioning promotes extended student talk: a function of display questions. *Journal of Literacy Research* 38(2), 141–69.

Boyer, E.L. (1983) *High School: A Report on Secondary Education in America.* New York: Harper and Row.

Brighouse, T. and Waters, M. (2022) *About our Schools: Improving on Previous Best.* London: Crown House.

British Educational Research Association (BERA) (2012) Background to Michael Gove's response to the report of the expert panel for the national curriculum review in England. www.bera.ac.uk/bera-in-the-news/background-to-michael-goves-response-to-the-report-of-the-expert-panel-for-the-national-curriculum-review-in-England (accessed May 2021).

Britnell, M. (2007) World class commissioning: NHS sets out to lead the world. *Health Service Journal*, 8 November.

Britton, J. (1969) Talking to learn. In D. Barnes, J. Britton and H. Rosen (eds) *Language, the Learner and the School.* Harmondsworth: Penguin Books.

Broadfoot, P. (2000) Comparative education for the 21st century: retrospect and prospect. *Comparative Education* 36(3), 357–72.

Brown, A. and Palincsar, A.S. (1989) Guided co-operative learning and individual knowledge acquisition. In L.B. Resnick (ed) *Knowing, Learning and Instruction.* Hillsdale, NJ: Erlbaum, 393–490.

Brown, M. and White, J. (2012) An unstable framework: critical perspectives on the framework for the national curriculum. www.newvisionsforeducation.org.uk/2012/04/05/an-unstable-framework/.

Bruner, J.S. (1978) The role of dialogue in language acquisition. In A. Sinclair, R. Jarvella and W. Levelt (eds) *The Child's Conception of Language.* New York: Springer.

Bruner, J.S. (1983) *Child's Talk: Learning to Use Language.* Oxford: Oxford University Press.

Bruner, J.S. (1990) *Acts of Meaning.* Cambridge, MA: Harvard University Press.

Bruner, J.S. (1996) *The Culture of Education.* Cambridge, MA: Harvard University Press.

Bruner, J.S. (2006) *In Search of Pedagogy.* Vol. 1. London: Routledge.

Bruner, J.S. and Haste, H.E. (1987) *Making Sense: The Child's Construction of the World.* London: Routledge.

Burgess, H. (2010) Primary workforce management and reform. In R.J. Alexander, C. Doddington, J. Gray, L. Hargreaves and R. Kershner (eds) *The Cambridge Primary Review Research Surveys*. London: Routledge, 649–701.

Burnett, C. (2016) *The Digital Age and Its Implications for Learning and Teaching in the Primary School*. CPRT Research Survey 7. York: Cambridge Primary Review Trust.

Calderhead, J. (1993) *The Contribution of Research on Teachers' Thinking to the Professional Development of Teachers*. London: Routledge.

Cambridge Primary Review (2007) *Community Soundings: The Cambridge Primary Review Regional Witness Sessions* (briefing). Cambridge: University of Cambridge Faculty of Education. https://cprtrust.org.uk/wp-content/uploads/2014/06/Comm-soundings-briefing-revised-2014.pdf (accessed May 2021).

Cambridge Primary Review (2009) *The Final Report* (briefing). Cambridge: University of Cambridge Faculty of Education. https://cprtrust.org.uk/wp-content/uploads/2014/06/final_report_briefing_revised_5_14.pdf (accessed May 2021).

Cambridge Primary Review (2010) *After the Election: Policy Priorities for Primary Education* (briefing). Cambridge: University of Cambridge Faculty of Education. https://cprtrust.org.uk/wp-content/uploads/2014/06/policy-priorities-briefing-revised-2.pdf (accessed May 2021).

Cambridge Primary Review (2011) *National Curriculum Review: Response to the DfE Call for Evidence*. Cambridge: Cambridge Primary Review, 14 April. https://cprtrust.org.uk/about_cprt/cprt-publications/ (accessed May 2021).

Cambridge Primary Review (2012) *National Curriculum Review: Response to the Proposals in the Secretary of State's Letter of 11 June 2012*. Cambridge: Cambridge Primary Review. https://cprtrust.org.uk/about_cprt/cprt-publications/ (accessed May 2021).

Cambridge Primary Review Trust (2016) What is education for? Submission to the house of commons education committee inquiry into the purpose and quality of education in England. https://cprtrust.org.uk/wp-content/uploads/2016/01/HoC-Purposes-Inquiry-CPRT-logo-1.pdf (accessed May 2021).

Carter, R. (1997) *Investigating English Discourse: Language, Literacy and Literature*. London: Routledge.

Carvel, J. (2008) Poverty gap has not narrowed under Labour. *The Guardian*, 3 April.

Castells, M. (1997) *The Power of Identity*. The Information Age: Economy, Society and Culture, Vol. 2. Oxford, Blackwell.

Castells, M. (1998) *End of Millennium*. The Information Age: Economy, Society and Culture, Vol. 3. Oxford: Blackwell.

Cazden, C.B. (2001) *Classroom Discourse: The Language of Teaching and Learning*. Portsmouth, NH: Heinemann.

Center for World Class Universities/Institute of Higher Education of Shanghai Jiao Tong University (2009) Academic ranking of world universities. www.arwu.org/ARWU2009.jsp.

Central Advisory Council for Education (England) (1967) *Children and Their Primary Schools*. (The Plowden Report). London: HMSO.

Centre for Economics and Business Research (2020) *Contribution of the Arts and Culture Industry to the UK Economy: A Cebr Report for Arts Council England*. London: Cebr.

Chawla-Duggan, R. and Lowe, J. (2010) Aims for primary education: changing global contexts. In R.J. Alexander, C. Doddington, J. Gray, L. Hargreaves and R. Kershner (eds) *The Cambridge Primary Review Research Surveys*. London: Routledge, 261–81.

Civil Service (UK) (2010) Statutory guidance: the civil service code. www.gov.uk/government/publications/civil-service-code/the-civil-service-code (accessed May 2021).

Clarke, P. (2001) *Teaching and Learning: The Culture of Pedagogy*. New Delhi: Sage.

Clegg, N. and Laws, D. (2013) Raising ambitions and standards for primary schools. *DfE Press Release*, 17 July.

Coaker, V. (2009) Cambridge primary review woolly and unclear on schools' accountability. *DCSF Press Release*, 16 October.

Coffield, F. (2012) Why the McKinsey reports will not improve school systems. *Journal of Education Policy* 27(1), 131–49.

Coffield, F., Ball, S., Taylor, R. and Scott, P. (2008) Letter to *The Independent*, 2 June.

Comenius, J.A. (1657) [1896] *The Great Didactic*, trans. M.W. Keatinge. London: A. & C. Black.

Committee for Linguistics in Education (2019) Language analysis in schools. http://clie.org.uk/language_analysis/ (accessed 7 February 2019).

Condor, S., Tileaga, C. and Billig, M. (2013) Political rhetoric. In L. Huddy, D.O. Sears and J.S. Levy (eds) *The Oxford Handbook of Political Psychology*. Oxford: Oxford University Press. DOI: 10.1093/oxfordhb/9780199760107.013.0009 (accessed February 2019).

Cowen, R. (2000) Comparing futures or comparing pasts? *Comparative Education* 36(3), 333–42.

Cox, B. and Dyson, A.E. (1971) *The Black Papers on Education*. London: Davis-Poynter.

Craske, J. (2021) Logic rhetoric and 'the blob': populist logic in the Conservative reforms to English schooling. *British Educational Research Journal* 47(2), 279–98.

Crenna-Jennings, W., Perera, N. and Sibieta, L. (2021) *Education Recovery and Resilience in England. Phase 1 Report*. London: Education Policy Institute.

Crossley, M. (2000) Bridging cultures and traditions in the reconceptualisation of comparative and international education. *Comparative Education* 36(3), 319–32.

Crossley, M. and Jarvis, P. (2001) Context matters. *Comparative Education* 37(4), 405–8.

Crystal, D. (2018) The case for language analysis in schools. Paper for the event UKLO and Language Analysis. British Academy, 27 February. http://clie.org.uk/2018-2meeting/ (accessed 7 February 2019).

Cunningham, P. (1988) *Curriculum Change in the Primary School Since 1945: Dissemination of the Progressive Ideal*. London: Falmer.

Cunningham, P. and Raymont, P. (2008) *Quality Assurance in English Primary Education*. Cambridge Primary Review Research Survey 4/3. In Alexander, R.J., Doddington, C., Gray, J., Hargreaves, L. and Kershner, R. (eds) (2010) *The Cambridge Primary Review Research Surveys*. London: Routledge, 767–91.

Daily Mail (2009) Stalinist control over teaching condemned, 16 October.

Dale, R. (1997) The state and the governance of education. In A.H. Halsey, H. Lauder, P. Brown and A.S. Wells (eds) *Education, Culture, Economy, Society*. Oxford: Oxford University Press, 273–82.

Davies, L. (2006) Global citizenship: abstraction or framework for action? *Educational Review* 58(1), 5–25.

Dawes, L., Mercer, N. and Wegerif, R. (2004) *Thinking Together: A Programme of Activities for Developing Speaking and Listening*. Birmingham: Imaginative Minds.

Day, M. (2007) Why Britain has the best-trained teachers ever. *The Guardian*, 16 May.

DCSF (2007) DCSF spokesperson quoted in the *Times Educational Supplement*, 2 November.

DCSF (2009) Cambridge Primary Review woolly and unclear on schools' accountability. Press release issued in the name of Schools Minister Vernon Coaker, 16 October.

Deakin Crick, R., Taylor, M., Ritchie, S., Samuel, E. and Durant, K. (2005) *A Systematic Review of the Impact of Citizenship Education on Student Learning and Achievement*. London: EPPI-Centre, UCL Institute of Education.

Dearden, R.S. (1976) *Problems in Primary Education.* London: Routledge and Kegan Paul.

Dearing, R. (1993) *The National Curriculum and Its Assessment: Interim Report.* York and London: NCC and SEAC.

Delors, J., Al Mufti, I., Amagi, I., Carneiro, R., Chung, F., Geremek, B., Gorham, W., Kornhauser, A., Manley, M., Padrón Quero, M., Savané, M.A., Singh, K., Stavenhagen, R., Myong, Won Suhr, and Nanzhao, Zhou (1996) *Learning: The Treasure within. Report to UNESCO of the International Commission on Education for the Twenty-First Century.* Paris: UNESCO.

Delpit, L. (1988) The silenced dialogue: power and pedagogy in educating other people's children. *Harvard Educational Review 58*(3), 280–99.

Department for Children, Schools and Families (2007) DCSF spokesperson quoted in *Times Educational Supplement*, 2 November.

Department for Children, Schools and Families (2008) *Narrowing the Gap.* London: DCSF with LGA and I&DEA.

Department for Children, Schools and Families (2009) *Your Child, Your Schools, Our Future: Building a 21st Century Schools System.* London: DCSF.

Department for Digital, Culture, Media and Sport (2012a) *Cultural Education in England: An Independent Review by Darren Henley for the Department for Culture, Media and Sport and the Department for Education.* London: DCMS/DfE.

Department for Digital, Culture, Media and Sport (2012b) *The Government's Response to Darren Henley's Review of Cultural Education.* London: DCMS/DfE.

Department for Digital, Culture, Media and Sport (2016) Creative industries worth almost £10 million an hour to UK economy. www.gov.uk/government/news/creative-industries-worth-almost-10-million-an-hour-to-economy (accessed May 2021).

Department for Digital, Culture, Media and Sport (2020) UK's creative industries contribute almost £13 million to the UK economy every hour. www.gov.uk/government/news/uks-creative-industries-contributes-almost-13-million-to-the-uk-economy-every-hour (accessed May 2021).

Department for Education (2010a) *Remit for the Review of the National Curriculum in England.* London: DfE.

Department for Education (2010b) *The Importance of Teaching: The Schools White Paper 2010.* London: DfE.

Department for Education (2011a) *Review of the National Curriculum in England: Report on Subject Breadth in International Jurisdictions.* London: DfE.

Department for Education (2011b) *Review of the National Curriculum in England: What Can We Learn from the English, Mathematics and Science Curricula of High-Performing Jurisdictions?* London: DfE.

Department for Education (2011c) *Review of the National Curriculum: Summary Report of the Call for Evidence.* London: DfE.

Department for Education (2011d) *The Framework for the National Curriculum: A Report by the Expert Panel for the National Curriculum Review.* London: DfE.

Department for Education (2011e) *Independent Review of Key Stage 2 Testing, Assessment and Accountability: Final Report.* Bew Report. London: DfE.

Department for Education (2013a) *Freedom of Information Response, Case Reference 2013/0047506.* London: DfE.

Department for Education (2013b) *The National Curriculum in England: Framework Document.* London: DfE.

Department for Education (2014) Pupil Premium: funding for schools and alternative provision. www.gov.uk/pupil-premium-information-for-schools-and-alternative-provision-settings (accessed May 2014).

Department for Education (2021) Education recovery commissioner: role specification and terms of reference. https://assets.publishing.service.gov.uk/government/uploads/system/uploads/attachment_data/file/960070/Terms_of_reference.pdf (accessed May 2021).

Department for Education and Employment (1998a) *The National Literacy Strategy: Framework for Teaching*. London: DfEE.

Department for Education and Employment (1998b) *The Learning Age: A Renaissance for a New Britain*. London: DfEE.

Department for Education and Employment (1999) *The National Numeracy Strategy: Framework for Teaching Mathematics from Reception to Year 6*. London: DfEE.

Department for Education and Skills (2003) *Excellence and Enjoyment: A Strategy for Primary Schools*. London: DfES.

Department of Education and Science (1975) *A Language for Life: Report of the Committee of Inquiry Appointed by the Secretary of State for Education and Science and the chairmanship of Sir Alan Bullock FBA*. London: HMSO.

Department of Education and Science (1977) *Local Authority Arrangements for the School Curriculum*. Circular 14/77. London: DES.

Department of Education and Science (1978) *Primary Education in England: A Survey by HM Inspectors of Schools*. London: HMSO.

Department of Education and Science (1979) *Aspects of Secondary Education in England: A Survey by HM Inspectors of Schools*. London: HMSO.

Department of Education and Science (1981) *The School Curriculum*. London: DES.

Department of Education and Science (1982) *Education 5 to 9: An Illustrative Survey of 80 First Schools in England*. London: HMSO.

Department of Education and Science (1983) *9–13 Middle Schools: An Illustrative Survey*. London: HMSO.

Department of Education and Science (1985) *Better Schools*. London: HMSO.

Department of Education and Science (1988) *Report of the Committee of Inquiry into the Teaching of English Language*. The Kingman Report. London: HMSO.

Department of Education and Science (1989) *Report of the English Working Party 5 to 16*. The Cox Report. London: HMSO.

Dewey, J. (1916) *Democracy and Education: An Introduction to the Philosophy of Education*. New York: Collier Macmillan.

Dillon, J.T. (1988) *Questioning and Teaching: A Manual of Practice*. Eugene, OR: Resource Publications.

Douglas, J.W.B. (1964) *The Home and the School*. London: McGibbon & Kee.

Doyle, W. (1983) Academic work. *Review of Educational Research 53*, 159–99.

Dreyfus, H.L. and Dreyfus, S.E. (1986) *Mind Over Machine*. New York: Free Press.

Drummond, M-J. (1989) *Four Year Olds in Primary Schools*. London: Taylor and Francis.

Drummond, M-J. (2003) *Assessing Children's Learning*. London: David Fulton.

Dunkin, M.J. and Biddle, B.J. (1974) *The Study of Teaching*. New York: Holt, Rinehart and Winston.

Dysthe, O., Ness, I.J. and Kirkegaard, P.O. (eds) (2020) *Dialogisk Paedagogik Kreativitet og Laering*. Aarhus: Klim.

Earl, L., Watson, N., Levin, B, Leithwood, K. *et al* (2003a) *Watching and Learning 2: OISE/UT Evaluation of the Implementation of the National Literacy and Numeracy Strategies*. Toronto: Ontario Institute for Studies in Education.

Earl, L., Watson, N., Levin, B, Leithwood, K. *et al* (2003b) *Watching and Learning 3: Final Report of the External Evaluation of England's National Literacy and Numeracy Strategies*. Toronto: Ontario Institute for Studies in Education.

Economist, The (2009) *The Economist Pocket World in Figures 2009*. London: Profile Books.

Education Endowment Foundation (2019) *Improving Literacy in Secondary Schools: Guidance Report*. London: EEF.

Education Policy Institute (2021) *EPI Newsletter, June 2021*.

Edwards, A.D. (1992) Teacher talk and pupil competence. In K. Norman (ed) *Thinking Voices: The Work of the National Oracy Project*. London: Hodder.

Edwards, A.D. and Mercer, N. (1987) *Common Knowledge: The Development of Understanding in the Classroom*. London: Routledge.

Edwards, A.D. and Westgate, D.P.G. (1994) *Investigating Classroom Talk* (2nd edition). London: Falmer Press.

Edwards, J. (1989) *Language and Disadvantage* (2nd edition). London: Cole and Whurr.

Eisner, E.W. (1969) Instructional and expressive objectives: their formulation and use in curriculum. In W.J. Popham, E.W. Eisner, H.J. Sullivan and L.L. Tyler (eds) *Instructional Objectives*. AERA Monograph Series on Curriculum Evaluation 3. Chicago: Rand McNally.

Eisner, E.W. (2005) *Reinventing Schools: The Selected Works of Elliot W. Eisner*. London: Routledge.

Ericsson, K.A. (ed) (1996) *The Road to Excellence: The Acquisition of Expert Performance in the Arts and Sciences, Sports and Games*. London: Lawrence Erlbaum.

Eurydice (2009) *National Summary Sheets on Education Systems in Europe and Ongoing Reforms: Finland*. Slough: NFER.

Feniger, Y. and Lefstein, A. (2014) How not to reason with PISA data: an ironic investigation. *Journal of Education Policy 29*(6), 845–85.

Fisher, R. (2008) *Teaching Thinking: Philosophical Enquiry in the Classroom*. London: Continuum.

Flanders, N.A. (1960) *Interaction Analysis in the Classroom: A Manual for Observers*. Ann Arbor: University of Michigan.

Flynn, J.R. (1987) Massive IQ gains in 14 nations: what IQ tests really measure. *Psychological Bulletin 101*(2), 17–91.

Fredriksson, P. (2006) What is so special about education in Finland? Paper for the EU Presidency Conference, Helsinki.

Freire, P. (1970) *Pedagogy of the Oppressed*. London: Bloomsbury.

Gage, N. (1978) *The Scientific Basis of the Art of Teaching*. New York: Teachers College Press.

Galton, M. (1995) *Crisis in the Primary Classroom*. London: David Fulton.

Galton, M. (2007) *Learning and Teaching in the Primary Classroom*. London: Sage.

Galton, M. (2008) *Creative Practitioners in Schools and Classrooms*. Cambridge: University of Cambridge Faculty of Education.

Galton, M., Hargreaves, L., Comber, C., Wall, D. and Pell, A. (1999) *Inside the Primary Classroom: 20 Years on*. London: Routledge.

Galton, M. and Simon, B. (eds) (1980) *Progress and Performance in the Primary Classroom*. London: Routledge.

Galton, M., Simon, B. and Croll, P. (1980) *Inside the Primary Classroom*. London: Routledge.

Gardner, H. (2006) *The Development and Education of the Mind*. London: Routledge.

Geertz, C. (1973) *The Interpretation of Cultures: Selected Essays*. New York: Basic Books.

Geertz, C. (1983) *Local Knowledge: Further Essays in Interpretive Anthropology*. New York: Basic Books.

George, M. (2019) Tech revolution could make arts 'more important than maths'. *Times Educational Supplement*, 26 February.

Ginsburg, A. and Smith, M.S. (2016) *Do Randomised Control Trials Meet the 'Gold Standard'? A Study of the Usefulness of RCTs in the What Works Clearinghouse.* Washington, DC: American Enterprise Institute.

Giroux, H.A. (1983) *Theory and Resistance in Education.* London: Heinemann.

Giroux, H.A. (2011) *On Critical Pedagogy Today.* London: Bloomsbury.

Goody, J. (1987) *The Interface Between the Written and the Oral.* Cambridge: Cambridge University Press.

Goswami, U. (2015) *Children's Cognitive Development and Learning.* CPRT Research Survey 3. York: Cambridge Primary Review Trust.

Gove, M. (2011) House of commons oral answers to questions, 7 February. www.publications.parliament.uk/pa/cm201011/cmhansrd/cm110207/debtext/110207–0001.htm (accessed February 2011).

Gove, M. (2012) Letter accompanying draft national curriculum programmes of study for English, mathematics and science, 11 June. https://webarchive.nationalarchives.gov.uk/20130105103711/http://media.education.gov.uk/assets/files/pdf/l/secretary%20of%20state%20letter%20to%20tim%20oates%20regarding%20the%20national%20curriculum%20review%2011%20june%202012.pdf (accessed May 2021).

Gove, M. (2013a) The progressive betrayal. Speech to the Social Market Foundation, 5 February, www.smf.co.uk/media/news/michael-gove-speaks-smf/ (accessed May 2014).

Gove, M. (2013b) I refuse to surrender to the Marxist teachers hell-bent on destroying our schools: education secretary berates 'the new enemies of promise' for opposing his plans. *Daily Mail,* 22 March.

Gove, M. (2013c) Start schooling later than age five, say experts. *Daily Telegraph,* 11 September.

Government of India (1998) *DPEP Moves On: Towards Universalising Basic Education.* New Delhi: Government of India Ministry of Human Resource Development.

Government Office for Science (2008) *Mental Capital and Wellbeing: Making the Most of Ourselves in the 1st Century.* London: Government Office for Science.

Gray, J., Galton, M., McLaughlin, C., Clarke, B. and Symonds, J. (2011) *The Supportive School: Wellbeing and the Young Adolescent.* Newcastle upon Tyne: Cambridge Scholars Publishing.

Green, A. (1990) *Education and State Formation: The Rise of Education Systems in England, France and the USA.* London: Macmillan.

Gregory, M.R. (2007) Normative dialogue types in philosophy for children. *Gifted Education International 22,* 160–71.

Grice, H.P. (1975) Logic and conversation. In P. Cole and J. Morgan (eds) *Syntax and Semantics, Volume 3, Speech Acts.* New York: Academic Press.

Gulbenkian Foundation (1982) *The Arts in Schools: Principles, Practice and Provision.* London: Gulbenkian Foundation.

Habermas, J. (1987) *The Philosophical Discourse of Modernity,* trans. F. Lawrence. Cambridge: Cambridge University Press.

Harding, L., Elgot, J. and Sparrow, A. (2021) Accusations of lying pile up against Boris Johnson. Does it matter? *The Guardian,* 30 April.

Hardman, J. (2019) Developing and supporting implementation of a dialogic pedagogy in primary schools in England. *Teaching and Teacher Education 86.*

Hardman, J. (2020) Analysing talk moves in whole class teaching. In N. Mercer, R. Wegerif and L. Major (eds) *The Routledge International Handbook of Research on Dialogic Education.* London: Routledge, 152–66.

Hardman, F., Smith, F. and Wall, K. (2003) 'Interactive whole class teaching' in the national literacy strategy. *Cambridge Journal of Education 33*(2), 197–215.

Hardy, T. (1916) *Far from the Madding Crowd*. London: Macmillan.

Hargreaves, D.H. (2004) *Learning for Life: The Foundations for Lifelong Learning*. Bristol: Policy Press.

Hargreaves, D.H. (2010) *Creating a Self-Improving School System*. Nottingham: National College for School Leadership.

Hargreaves, D.H. (2011) *Leading a Self-Improving School System*. Nottingham: National College for School Leadership.

Hargreaves, D.H. (2012) *A Self-Improving School System in International Context*. Nottingham: National College for School Leadership.

Harlen, W. (2007) *The Quality of Learning: Assessment Alternatives for Primary Education*. Cambridge Primary Review Research Survey. In Alexander, R.J., Doddington, C., Gray, J., Hargreaves, L. and Kershner, R. (eds) (2010) *The Cambridge Primary Review Research Surveys*. London: Routledge, 484–520.

Harlen, W. (2014) *Assessment, Standards and Quality of Learning in Primary Education*. CPRT Research Survey 1. York: Cambridge Primary Review Trust.

Haslam, J. (2018) Beware of enormous effect sizes. *Schools Week*, 20 December.

Hattie, J. (2009) *Visible Learning: A Synthesis of Over 800 Meta-Analyses Relating to Achievement*. London: Routledge.

Hattie, J. and Yates, G. (2014) *Visible Learning and the Science of How We Learn*. London: Routledge.

Hawkesworth, E. (2007) Attributed DCSF press briefing in response to Cambridge primary review interim reports 5/3, 7/1, 8/1 and 8/2, 23 November. London: DCSF.

Heath, S.B. (1999) *Ways with Words: Language, Life and Work in Communities and Classrooms*. Cambridge: Cambridge University Press.

Higgins, S. Kokatsaki, D. and Coe, R. (2012) *The Teaching and Learning Toolkit: Technical Appendices*. London: Education Endowment Foundation/Sutton Trust. https://v1.educationendowmentfoundation.org.uk/uploads/pdf/Technical_Appendices_(July_2012).pdf (accessed May 2018).

Hinsliff, G. (2021) Is Boris Johnson really going to sacrifice arts degrees for the conservative cause? *The Guardian*, 20 May.

Hirsch, E.D. (1987) *Cultural Literacy: What Every American Needs to Know*. New York: Vintage Books.

Hirsch, E.D. (2007) *The Knowledge Deficit: Closing the Shocking Educational Gap for American Children*. New York: Houghton Mifflin.

HM Treasury (2006) *Prosperity for All in the Global Economy: World Class Skills*. The Leitch Report. London: TSO.

Hobsbawm, E.J. (1995) *Age of Extremes: The Short Twentieth Century 1914–1991*. London, Abacus.

Hobsbawm, E.J. (2007) *Globalisation, Democracy and Terrorism*. London: Little, Brown.

Hofkins, D. and Northen, S. (eds) (2009) *Introducing the Cambridge Primary Review*. Cambridge: University of Cambridge Faculty of Education.

Hogan, D., Chan, M. and Rahim, R. (2012) *Examinations and the Logic of Instructional Practice in Secondary 3 English and Mathematics Classrooms in Singapore*. Singapore: National Institute of Education.

Hogan, D., Kwek, D., Towndrow, P., Abdul Rahim, R., Kiang, T.T., Jing, Y.H. and Chan, M. (2012) *Opaque or Transparent? First Reflections on Visible Learning in Singapore*. Singapore: National Institute of Education.

Hogan, D., Towndrow, P., Rahim, R. and Chan, M. (2012) *Interim Report on Instructional Practices in Singapore in Secondary 3 Mathematics and English, 2004 and 2010.* Singapore: National Institute of Education.

Holmes, E. (1911) *What Is and What Might Be: A Study of Education in General and Elementary Education in Particular.* London: Constable.

Holquist, M. (2002) *Dialogism: Bakhtin and His World.* London: Routledge.

House of Commons (1986) *Achievement in Primary Schools: Third Report from the Education, Science and Arts Committee.* London: HMSO.

House of Commons (2008) *Testing and Assessment: Fifth Special Report of the Children, Schools and Families Committee.* Session 2007–8. London: TSO.

House of Commons (2016) *Sexual Harrassment and Sexual Violence in Schools: Report from the Women and Equalities Committee.* London: House of Commons.

House of Commons (2018) *Disinformation and 'Fake News': Interim Report from the Digital, Culture, Media and Sport Committee.* London: House of Commons.

Howe, C. and Abedin, M. (2013) Classroom dialogue: a systematic review across four decades of research. *Cambridge Journal of Education* 43(3), 325–56.

Howe, C., Hennessy, S., Mercer, N., Vrikki, M. and Wheatley, L. (2019) Teacher-student dialogue during classroom teaching: does it really impact on student outcomes? *Journal of the Learning Sciences.* DOI: 10.1080/10508406.2019.1573730.

Hummrich, M. and Rademacher, S. (eds) (2013) *Kulturvergleich in der qualitativen Forschung.* Wiesbaden: Springer VS.

Jackson, B. and Marsden, D. (1962) *Education and the Working Class.* London: Routledge and Kegan Paul.

Jackson, P.W. (1968) *Life in Classrooms.* New York: Holt, Rinehart and Winston.

James, M. (2012) *'For the Record': Some (Lesser Known) Factual Background to the Work of the Expert Panel for the National Curriculum Review in England 2010–12.* London: BERA.

James, M. and Pollard, A. (2008) *Learning and Teaching in Primary Schools: Insights from TLRP.* Cambridge Primary Review Research Survey 2/4. In Alexander, R.J., Doddington, C., Gray, J., Hargreaves, L. and Kershner, R. (eds) (2010) *The Cambridge Primary Review Research Surveys.* London: Routledge, 525–47.

James, M. and Pollard, A. (2011) TLRP's ten principles for effective pedagogy: rationale, development, evidence, argument and impact. *Research Papers in Education* 26(3), 275–328.

Jay, T., Taylor, R., Moore, N., Burnett, C., Merchant, G., Thomas, P., Willis, B. and Stevens, A. (2017) *Dialogic Teaching: Evaluation Report and Executive Summary.* London: Education Endowment Foundation with Sheffield Hallam University.

Jerrim, J. (2011) *England's 'Plummeting' PISA Test Scores between 2000 and 2009: Is the Performance of Our Secondary School Pupils Really in Decline?* DoQSS Working Paper 11–09. London: University of London Institute of Education.

Jopling, M. and Vincent, S. (2016) *Vulnerable Children: Needs and Provision in the Primary Phase.* CPRT Research Survey 6. York: Cambridge Primary Review Trust.

Joseph Rowntree Charitable Trust (2006) *Power to the People: The Report of Power, an Independent Inquiry into Britain's Democracy.* New York: Joseph Rowntree Foundation.

Joyce, C. (ed) (1988) *Leavis and Philosophy.* Bishopstone: Edgeways Books.

Joyce, H. (2009) Competing visions: academics and ministers differ on what is to be done. *The Economist,* 20 February.

Kakutani, M. (2018) *The Death of Truth.* London: William Collins.

Keeble, R. (2016) *Effective Teaching Practice 2016.* London: Teaching Schools Council.

Kennedy, G.A. (1999) *Classical Rhetoric and its Christian and Secular Tradition.* Chapel Hill: University of North Carolina Press.

Kenway, J. (1990) Education and the right's discursive politics: private versus state schooling. In S. Ball (ed) *Foucault and Education: Disciplines and Knowledge*. London: Routledge.

Kessler, G., Rizzo, S. and Kelly, M. (2018) President Trump has made over 5000 false or misleading claims. *Washington Post*, 13 September.

Kidson, M. and Norris, E. (2015) *Implementing the London Challenge*. London: Institute for Government with the Joseph Rowntree Foundation.

Kim, M-Y. and Wilkinson, I.A.G. (2019) What is dialogic teaching? Constructing, deconstructing and reconstructing a pedagogy of classroom talk. *Language, Learning and Social Interaction 21*, 70–86.

King, E.J. (1979) *Other Schools and Ours: Comparative Studies for Today*. London: Holt, Rinehart & Winston.

Koedinger, K.R. and Wiese, E.S. (2015) Accounting for socializing intelligence with the knowledge-learning-instruction framework. In L.B. Resnick, C.S.C. Asterhan and S.N. Clarke (eds) *Socializing Intelligence Through Academic Talk and Dialogue*. Washington, DC: AERA, 275–88.

Kogan, M. (1971) *The Politics of Education: Edward Boyle and Anthony Crosland in conversation with Maurice Kogan*. Harmondsworth: Penguin Books.

Kuhn, D., Wang, Y. and Li, H. (2011) Why argue? Developing understanding of the purposes and values of argumentative discourse. *Discourse Processes 48*(1), 26–49.

Kuhn, D. and Zillmer, N. (2015) Developing norms of discourse. In L.B. Resnick, C.S.C. Asterhan, and S.N. Clarke (eds) *Socializing Intelligence Through Academic Talk and Dialogue*. Washington, DC: AERA, 77–86.

Kumar, K. (1991) *Political Agenda of Education: A Study of Colonialist and Nationalist Ideas*. New Delhi: Sage.

Lawton, D. (1980) *The Politics of the School Curriculum*. London: Routledge and Kegan Paul.

Lawton, D. (1983) *Curriculum Studies and Educational Planning*. London: Hodder and Stoughton.

Leach, E. (1964) Models. *New Society*, 14 June.

Leach, F. and Preston, R. (2001) Editorial. *Compare 31*(2), 149–50.

Lefstein, A. (2010) More helpful as problem than solution: some implications of situating dialogue in classrooms. In K. Littleton and C. Howe (eds) *Educational Dialogues: Understanding and Promoting Productive Interaction*. London: Taylor and Francis.

Lefstein, A. (2013) The rules of pedagogical discourse in Israel: has the time come to break them? Paper presented to the Israel Ministry of Education, 10 October.

Lefstein, A., Pollak, I. and Segal, A. (2018) Compelling student voice: dialogic practices of public confession. *Discourse: Studies in the Cultural Politics of Education*. DOI 10.1080/01596306.2018.1473341.

Lefstein, A. and Snell, J. (2011) Classroom discourse: the promise and complexity of dialogic practice. In S. Ellis and E. McCartney (eds) *Applied Linguistics and Primary School Teaching*. Cambridge: Cambridge University Press, 165–85.

Lefstein, A. and Snell, J. (2013) Beyond a unitary conception of pedagogic pace: quantitative measurement and ethnographic experience. *British Educational Research Journal 39*(1), 73–106.

Lefstein, A. and Snell, J. (2014) *Better Than Best Practice: Developing Teaching and Learning Through Dialogue*. London: Routledge.

Levitsky, S. and Ziblatt, D. (2018) *How Democracies Die*. New York: Crown.

Li, J. (2012) *Cultural Foundations of Learning: East and West*. New York: Cambridge University Press.

Lipman, M. (2003) *Thinking in Education* (2nd edition). New York: Cambridge University Press.

Little, A. (2000) Development studies and comparative education: context, content, comparison and contributors. *Comparative Education* 36(3), 279–96.

Lloyd, J. (1998) *Birth of a Nation: An Anatomy of Russia.* London: Michael Joseph.

Lockheed, M., Verspoor, A. and associates (1991) *Improving Primary Education in Developing Countries.* Washington, DC: Oxford University Press for the World Bank.

Lord, P., Sharp, C., Mehta, P. and Featherstone, G. (2015) *Evaluation of In Harmony, Year 2.* Slough: NFER.

Lovett, W. (1840) Importance of general education, and the modes to be pursued in the different schools. In *Chartism: A New Organization of the People.* http://gerald-massey.org. uk/lovett/b_chartism.htm (accessed May 2014).

Luke, A. and Carrington, V. (2002) Globalisation, literacy, curriculum practice. In R. Fisher, M. Lewis and G. Brooks (eds) *Language and Literacy in Action.* London: Routledge.

Luxton, R.G. and Last, G. (1997) *Under-Achievement and Pedagogy.* London: National Institute of Economic and Social Research, 13–14.

Lyytinen, H.K. (2002) *Why Are Finnish Students Doing So Well in PISA?* Paris: OECD.

Machin, S. and McNally, S. (2010) Aims for primary education: the changing national context. In R.J. Alexander, C. Doddington, J. Gray, L. Hargreaves and R. Kershner (eds) *The Cambridge Primary Review Research Surveys.* London: Routledge, 247–60.

Major, J. (1992) Speech to the Conservative Party Conference, September.

Mansell, W. (2007) *Education by Numbers: The Tyranny of Testing.* London: Politico's.

Mansell, W. (2014a) Community schools lose out on honours. *The Guardian,* 7 January.

Mansell, W. (2014b) DfE offering 'bribes' for schools to convert to academies. *The Guardian,* 13 May.

Mansell, W. (2015) State school honours uneven, as academies notch up another knighthood. *The Guardian,* 23 June.

Mansell, W. (2016) *Academies: Autonomy, Accountability, Quality and Evidence.* CPRT Research Survey 9. York: Cambridge Primary Review Trust.

Mansell, W. and James, M. (2009) *Assessment in Schools: Fit for Purpose?* London: Assessment Reform Group.

Marmot, M., Allen, J., Boyce, T., Goldblatt, P. and Morrison, J. (2021) *Building Back Fairer in Greater Manchester: Health Equity and Dignified Lives.* London: Institute of Health Equity.

Marshall, S. (1963) *An Experiment in Education.* Cambridge: Cambridge University Press.

Mattingly, C., Lutkehaus, N.C. and Throop, C.J. (2008) Bruner's search for meaning: A conversation between psychology and anthropology. *Ethos* 36(1), 1–28.

Matusov, E. (2018) Mapping dialogic pedagogy: instrumental and non-instrumental education. In A. Rose and J. Valsiner (eds) *The Cambridge Handbook of Sociocultural Psychology* (2nd edition). Cambridge: Cambridge University Press, 274–301.

Mayall, B. (2010) Children's lives outside school and their educational impact. In R.J. Alexander, C. Doddington, J. Gray, L. Hargreaves and R. Kershner (eds) *The Cambridge Primary Review Research Surveys.* Abingdon: Routledge, 49–82.

McCarthy, M. and Carter, R. (2001) Ten criteria for a spoken grammar. In E. Hinkel and S. Fotos (eds) *New Perspectives on Grammar Teaching in Second Language Classrooms.* Mahwah, NJ: Lawrence Erlbaum, 5175.

McKeown, M.G. and Beck, I.L. (2015) Effective classroom talk *is* reading comprehension. In L.B. Resnick, C.S.C. Asterhan and S.N. Clarke (eds) *Socializing Intelligence Through Academic Talk and Dialogue.* Washington, DC: AERA, 51–62.

McKillop, I. (1995) *F.R. Leavis: A life in criticism*. London: Allen Lane.

McKinsey and Company (2009) *Achieving World Class Productivity in the NHS 2009/10–2013/14: Detailing the Size of the Opportunity*. Dubai: McKinsey and Company.

McLellan, R., Galton, M., Steward, S. and Page, C. (2012) *The Impact of Creative Partnerships on the Wellbeing of Children and Young People*. Newcastle: CCE.

McNamara, O., Webb, R. and Brundrett, M. (2010) Primary teachers: initial teacher education, continuing professional development and school leadership development. In R.J. Alexander, C. Doddington, J. Gray, L. Hargreaves and R. Kershner (eds) *The Cambridge Primary Review Research Surveys*. London: Routledge, 649–701.

Mead, G.H. (1962) *Mind, Self and Society*, ed. C.W. Morris. Chicago, IL: University of Chicago Press.

Mehan, H. (1979) *Learning Lessons: Social Organization in the Classroom*. Cambridge, MA: Harvard University Press.

Mehan, H. and Cazden, C.B. (2015) The study of classroom discourse: early history and current developments. In L.B. Resnick, C.S.C. Asterhan, and S.N. Clarke (eds) *Socializing Intelligence Through Academic Talk and Dialogue*. Washington, DC: AERA, 13–34.

Mercer, N. (2000) *Words and Minds: How We Use Language to Think Together*. London: Routledge.

Mercer, N. and Dawes, L. (2008) The value of exploratory talk. In N. Mercer and S. Hodgkinson (eds) *Exploring Talk in School*. London: Sage, 55–72.

Mercer, N. and Hodgkinson, S. (eds) (2008) *Exploring Talk in School*. London: Sage.

Mercer, N. and Howe, C. (2010) Children's social development, peer interaction and classroom learning. In R.J. Alexander, C. Doddington, J. Gray, L. Hargreaves and R. Kershner (eds) *The Cambridge Primary Review Research Surveys*, 170–94. London: Routledge.

Mercer, N. and Littleton, K. (2007) *Dialogue and the Development of Children's Thinking: A Sociocultural Approach*. London: Routledge.

Mercer, N., Wegerif, R. and Major, L. (eds) (2020) *The Routledge International Handbook of Research on Dialogic Education*. London: Routledge.

Meyer, H-D. and Benavot, A. (2013a) PISA and the globalization of education governance. In H-D Meyer and A. Benavot (eds) *PISA, Power and Policy: The Emergence of Global Educational governance*. Oxford: Symposium Books, 7–26.

Meyer, H-D. and Benavot, A. (eds) (2013b) *PISA, Power and Policy: The Emergence of Global Educational Governance*. Oxford: Symposium Books.

Michaels, S. and O'Connor, C. (2012) *Talk Science Primer*. Cambridge, MA: TERC.

Michaels, S. and O'Connor, C. (2015) Conceptualizing talk moves as tools: professional development approaches for academically productive discussions. In L.B. Resnick, C.S.C. Asterhan, and S.N. Clarke (eds) *Socializing Intelligence Through Academic Talk and Dialogue*. Washington, DC: AERA, 347–61.

Michaels, S., O'Connor, C. and Resnick, L.B. (2008) Deliberative discourse idealized and realized: accountable talk in the classroom and in civic life. *Studies in Philosophy and Education* 27(4), 283–97.

Ministère de l'Éducation Nationale (1998) *Bâtir l'école du XXI siècle*. Paris: Ministère de l'Éducation Nationale.

Ministerial Council on Education, Employment, Training and Youth Affairs (2008) *Melbourne Declaration on Educational Goals for Young Australians*. Melbourne: Ministerial Council on Education, Employment, Training and Youth Affairs.

Ministry of Education (1958) *Primary Education: Suggestions for the Consideration of Teachers and Others Concerned with the Work of Primary Schools*. London: HMSO.

Ministry of General and Professional Education of the Russian Federation (2000) *National Doctrine of Education in the Russian Federation*. Moscow: Ministry of General and Professional Education.

Moon, R. (1998) *The English Exception: International Perspectives on the Initial Education and Training of Teachers*. London: Universities Council for the Education of Teachers.

Moore, K. and Harkins, C. (2017) *Evaluating Sistema Scotland – Big Noise Torry: Initial Findings Report*. Glasgow: Glasgow Centre for Population Health.

Morgan, N. (2014) Our plan for education. Priestley Lecture, University of Birmingham.

Morgan Jones, M., Abrams, D. and Lahiri, A. (2020) Shape the future: how the social sciences, humanities and the arts can SHAPE a positive, post-pandemic future for peoples, economies and environments. *Journal of the British Academy 8*, 167–266.

Mortimer, E.F. and Scott, P.H. (2003) *Meaning Making in Secondary Science Classrooms*. Buckingham: Open University Press.

Mortimore, P. (2009) Cambridge Review team take heart – your ideas may yet triumph. *The Guardian*, 3 November.

Mortimore, P., Sammons, P., Stoll, L., Lewis, D. and Ecob, R. (1988) *School Matters: The Junior Years*. Wells: Open Books.

Moss, G. (2007) Lessons from the national literacy strategy. Paper presented at the annual conference of the British Educational Research Association, September.

Moss, G. (2009) The politics of literacy in the context of large-scale education reform. *Research Papers in Education 24*(2), 155–74.

Mourshed, M., Chijioke, C. and Barber, M. (2010) *How the World's Most-Improved School Systems Keep Getting Better*. Dubai: McKinsey and Company.

Muckle, J. (1988) *A Guide to the Soviet Curriculum: What the Russian Child Is Taught in School*. London: Croom Helm.

National Advisory Committee on Creative and Cultural Education (1999) *All Our Futures: Creativity, Culture and Education*. London: DfEE.

National Commission on Education (1993) *Learning to Succeed: A Radical Look at Education Today and a Strategy for the Future*. Report of the Paul Hamlyn Foundation National Commission on Education. London: Heinemann.

National Research Council (2003) *Understanding Others, Educating Ourselves: Getting More from International Comparative Studies in Education*, eds. C. Chabbott and E.J. Elliott. Washington, DC: The National Academies Press.

Neisser, U.E. (1998) *The Rising Curve: Long-Term Gains in IQ and Related Measures*. Washington, DC: American Psychological Association.

Nevill, C. (2016) *Do EEF Trials Meet the New 'Gold Standard'?* London: Education Endowment Foundation.

New York Times (2021) Inside the Capitol riot: an exclusive video investigation. *New York Times*, 30 June. www.nytimes.com/2021/06/30/us/jan-6-capitol-attack-takeaways.html ?referringSource=articleShare (accessed July 2021).

Nichols, S.L. and Berliner, D.C. (2007) *Collateral Damage: How High-Stakes Testing Corrupts America's Schools*. Cambridge, MA: Harvard Education Books.

Noden, P. and West, A. (2010) The funding of English primary education. In R.J. Alexander, C. Doddington, J. Gray, L. Hargreaves and R. Kershner (eds) *The Cambridge Primary Review Research Surveys*. London: Routledge, 751–66.

Norman, G. (2003) RCT = results confounded and trivial: the perils of grand educational experiments. *Medical Education 37*, 582–4.

Norman, K. (ed) (1992) *Thinking Voices: The Work of the National Oracy Project*. London: Hodder.

Northen, S. (2011) Follow my (associate) leader. *The Guardian*, 15 November.

Nystrand, M. (2019) *Twenty Acres: Events That Transform Us*. London and Paris: KiwaiMedia.

Nystrand, M., Gamoran, A., Kachur, R. and Prendergast, C. (1997) *Opening Dialogue: Understanding the Dynamics of Language and Learning in the English Classroom*. New York: Teachers College Press.

Nystrand, M., Wu, L.L., Gamoran, A., Zeiser, S. and Long, D.A. (2003) Questions in time: investigating the structure and dynamics of unfolding classroom discourse. *Discourse Processes 35*(2), 135–98.

Oates, T. (2010) *Could do Better? Using International Comparisons to Refine the National Curriculum in England*. Cambridge: Cambridge Assessment.

Oates, T. (2012) The role of high quality textbooks in raising educational standards – how we need to link textbooks to curriculum and assessment – the evidence from transnational analysis. Submission to the House of Commons Education Committee Inquiry into the Administration of Examinations for 15–19 Year Olds, 3.

Oborne, P. (2021) *The Assault on Truth: Boris Johnson, Donald Trump and the Emergence of a New Moral Barbarism*. London: Simon and Schuster.

O'Connor, C. and Michaels, S. (2018) Supporting teachers in taking up productive talk moves: the long road to professional learning at scale. *International Journal of Education and Research*. DOI: 10.1016/j.ijer.2017.11.003.

Ofsted (1994) *Primary Matters: A Discussion on Teaching and Learning in Primary Schools*. London: Ofsted.

Ofsted (1996) *Subjects and Standards*. London: Ofsted.

Ofsted (1997) *National Curriculum Assessment Results and the Wider Curriculum at Key Stage 2: An Illustrative Survey*. London: Ofsted.

Ofsted (1999) *Handbook for Inspecting Primary and Nursery Schools*. London: Ofsted.

Ofsted (2002a) *The Curriculum in Successful Primary Schools*. London: Ofsted.

Ofsted (2002b) *The National Literacy Strategy: The First Four Years, 1998–2002*. London: Ofsted.

Ofsted (2002c) *The National Numeracy Strategy: The First Three Years, 1999–2002*. London: Ofsted.

Ofsted (2003) *The Education of Six Year Olds in England, Denmark and Finland: A Comparative Study*. London: Ofsted.

Ofsted (2004) *Standards and Quality 2002–3: The Annual Report of Her Majesty's Chief Inspector of Schools*. London: Ofsted.

Ofsted (2006) *Creative Partnerships: Initiative and Impact*. London: Ofsted.

Ofsted (2008) *Improving Primary Teachers' Subject Knowledge Across the Curriculum: A Summary of Evidence from Subject Surveys Excluding English and Mathematics*. London: Ofsted.

Ofsted (2009) *Twenty Outstanding Primary Schools: Excelling Against the Odds*. London: Ofsted.

Ofsted (2010a) *London Challenge*. London: Ofsted.

Ofsted (2010b) *The Annual Report of Her Majesty's Chief Inspector of Education, Childrens' Services and Skills, 2009–10*. London: Ofsted.

Ofsted (2012a) *Music in Schools: Student Progress*. London: Ofsted.

Ofsted (2012b) *Art, Craft and Design Education: Making a Mark*. London: Ofsted.

Ofsted (2012c) *The Evaluation Schedule for the Inspection of Maintained Schools and Academies: Guidance and Grade Descriptors for Inspecting Schools in England under Section 5 of the Education Act 2005, from January 2012*. London: Ofsted.

Ofsted (2012d) *The Framework for School Inspection: Guidance and Grade Descriptors for Inspecting Schools under Section 5 of the Education Act 2005*. London: Ofsted.

Ofsted (2013) *Music in Schools: What Hubs Must Do*. London: Ofsted.

Ofsted (2015a) *Key Stage 3: The Wasted Years?* London: Ofsted.

Ofsted (2015b) *School Inspection Handbook.* London: Ofsted.

Ofsted (2017) *Ofsted Schools Research.* London: Ofsted.

Ofsted (2018) *School Inspection Handbook.* London: Ofsted.

Ofsted (2021a) *School Inspection Handbook (updated April 2021).* London: DfE.

Ofsted (2021b) *Review of Sexual Abuse in Schools and Colleges.* London: DfE www.gov.uk/government/publications/review-of-sexual-abuse-in-schools-and-colleges/review-of-sexual-abuse-in-schools-and-colleges (accessed June 2021).

O'Keefe, G.S. and Clarke-Pearson, K. (2011) The impact of social media on children, adolescents, and families: American Academy of Pediatrics clinical report. *Pediatrics* 127(4). http://pediatrics.aappublications.org/content/127/4/800 (accessed 6 January 2019).

Oracy All-Party Parliamentary Group (2021) *Speak for change: final report and recommendations from the oracy all-party parliamentary group inquiry.* https://oracy.inparliament.uk/sites/oracy.inparliament.uk/files/2021-04/Oracy_APPG_FinalReport_28_04%20%284%29.pdf (accessed May 2021).

Organization for Economic Co-operation and Development (1998a) *Education at a Glance: OECD Indicators 1998.* Paris: OECD.

Organization for Economic Co-operation and Development (1998b) *Review of National Policies for Education: Russian Federation.* Paris: OECD.

Organization for Economic Co-operation and Development (2010a) *PISA 2009 Results: Learning Trends.* Paris: OECD.

Organization for Economic Co-operation and Development (2010b) *PISA 2009 Results: What Makes a School Successful?* Paris: OECD.

Organization for Economic Co-operation and Development (2010c) *PISA 2009 Results: Overcoming Social Background: Equity in Learning Opportunities and Outcomes.* Paris: OECD.

Organization for Economic Co-operation and Development (2010d) *PISA 2009 Results: Executive Summary.* Paris: OECD.

Organization for Economic Co-operation and Development (2011a) *PISA 2009 Results: Quality Time for Students – Learning in and out of School.* Paris: OECD.

Organization for Economic Co-operation and Development (2011b) *PISA 2009 Results: Against the Odds.* Paris: OECD.

Organization for Economic Co-operation and Development (2012) *What PISA Assesses.* Paris: OECD.

Orwell, G. (1968) [1946] Politics and the English language. In S. Orwell and I. Angos (eds) *The Collected Essays, Letters and Journalism of George Orwell.* New York: Harcourt, Brace, Javonovich, 127–39.

Osborn, M., Broadfoot, P., McNess, E., Planel, C., Ravn, B. and Triggs, P. (2003) *A World of Difference? Comparing Learners Across Europe.* Maidenhead: Open University Press.

Osborne, J. (2015) The challenges of scale. In L.B. Resnick, C.S.C. Asterhan and S.N. Clarke (eds) *Socializing Intelligence Through Academic Talk and Dialogue.* Washington, DC: AERA, 403–14.

Palincsar, A.S. and Brown, A.L. (1984) Reciprocal teaching of comprehension-fostering and comprehension-monitoring activities. *Cognition and Instruction 1*, 117–75.

Pánková, M. (ed) (2010) *The Legacy of J.A. Comenius: Traditions and Challenges of the Czech Culture and Education to Europe.* Prague: Pedagogical Museum of J.A. Comenius.

Park, J., Michaels, S., Affolter, R. and O'Connor, C. (2017) *Traditions, Research and Practice Supporting Academically Productive Classroom Discourse.* Oxford Research Encyclopedia of Education, Oxford University Press, December. https://oxfordre.com/education/view/10.1093/acrefore/9780190264093.001.0001/acrefore-9780190264093-e-21 (accessed May 2021).

Paton, G. (2014) Nicky Morgan: pupils 'held back' by overemphasis on the arts. *Daily Telegraph*, 10 November.

Peters, R.S. (Ed.) (1968) *Perspectives on Plowden*. London: Routledge.

Phillips, T. (2005) The tyranny of silence gives extremists a voice. *The Guardian*, 6 October.

Pickett, K. and Vanderbloemen, L. (2015) *Mind the Gap: Tackling Social and Educational Inequality*. CPRT Research Survey 4. York: Cambridge Primary Review Trust.

Pickles, M. (2015) The orchestra fine-tuning the performance of school students. www.bbc.co.uk/news/business-32381815 (accessed May 2021).

Pogrow, S. (2017) The failure of the US education research establishment to identify effective practices: beware 'effective practice' policies. *Education Policy Analysis Archives 25*(5), 2–19.

Pollard, A. (1985) *The Social World of the Primary School*. London: Cassell.

Pollard, A. (2012) Narrowness and imbalance in National Curriculum design. *IoE blog*. http://ioelondonblog.wordpress.com/category/andrew-pollard/ (accessed May 2014).

Popper, K.R. (1963) *Conjectures and Refutations: The Growth of Scientific Knowledge*. London: Routledge and Kegan Paul.

Posner, M.I. and Patoine, B. (2009) *How Arts Training Improves Attention and Cognition*. New York: Cerebrum.

Power Enquiry (2006) *Power to the People: The Report of Power, an Independent Enquiry into Britain's Democracy*. York: Joseph Rowntree Charitable Trust.

President's Committee on the Arts and Humanities (2011) *Reinvesting in Arts Education: Winning America's Future Through Creative Schools*. Washington, DC: PCAH.

Prideaux, (2002) Researching the outcomes of educational interventions: a matter of design. *British Medical Journal 324*, 126–7.

Qualifications and Curriculum Authority (2004) *Introducing the Grammar of Talk*. London: QCA.

Qualifications and Curriculum Authority (2007) *The Curriculum: Taking Stock of Progress*. London: QCA.

Qualifications and Curriculum Development Agency (2009) www.qcda.gov.uk/8665.aspx.

Raffe, D. (2011a) What can we learn from other school systems about improvement? Comments on how the world's most improved school systems keep getting better. Presentation to Parliamentary Research Enquiry, 28 June.

Raffe, D. (2011b) Policy borrowing or policy learning? How (not) to improve education systems. *CES Briefing 57*.

Ravitch, D. (1983) *The Troubled Crusade: American Education 1945-80*. New York: Basic Books.

Ravitch, D. (2010) *The Death and Life of the Great American School System: How Testing and Choice Are Undermining Education*. New York: Basic Books.

Ravitch, D. (2013) *Reign of Error: The Hoax of the Privatisation Movement and the Danger to America's Public Schools*. New York: Knopf.

Reboul-Sherrer, F. (1989) *Les Premiers Instituteurs, 1833–1882*. Paris: Hachette.

Resnick, L.B. (2015) Talking to learn: the promise and challenge of dialogic teaching. In L.B. Resnick, C.S.C. Asterhan and S.N. Clarke (eds) *Socializing Intelligence Through Academic Talk and Dialogue*. Washington, DC: AERA, 441–50.

Resnick, L.B., Asterhan, C.S.C. and Clarke, S.N. (eds) (2014) *Socialising Intelligence Through Academic Talk and Dialogue*. Washington, DC, AERA.

Resnick, L.B., Asterhan, C.S.C. and Clarke, S.N. (2015) Talk, learning and teaching. In L.B. Resnick, C.S.C. Asterhan and S.N. Clarke (eds) *Socializing Intelligence Through Academic Talk and Dialogue*. Washington, DC: AERA, 1–12.

Resnick, L.B., Michaels, S. and O'Connor, C. (2010) How well structured talk builds the mind. In R. Sternberg and D. Preiss (eds) *From Genes to Context: New Discoveries about Learning from Educational Research and Their Applications*. New York: Springer.

Revell, P. (2006) Does anyone ever fail teaching? *The Guardian*, 16 May.

Reynolds, D., Creemers, B., Stringfield, S., Teddlie, C. and Schaffer, G. (2002) *World Class Schools: International Perspectives on School Effectiveness*. London: Routledge.

Reynolds, D. and Farrell, S. (1996) *Worlds Apart? A Review of International Surveys of Educational Achievement Involving England*. London: TSO.

Reznitskaya, A. (2012) Dialogic teaching: rethinking language use during literature discussions. *Reading Teacher* 65(7), 446–56.

Reznitskaya, A. and Gregory, M. (2013) Student thought and classroom language: examining the mechanisms of change in dialogic teaching. *Educational Psychologist* 48(2), 114–33.

Reznitskaya, A., Kuo, L., Glina, M. and Anderson, R.C. (2009) Measuring argumentative reasoning: What's behind the numbers? *Learning and Individual Differences* 19, 219–24.

Reznitskaya, A. and Wilkinson, I. (2017) *The Most Reasonable Answer: Helping Students Build Better Arguments Together*. Cambridge, MA: Harvard University Press.

Richards, C.M. (2012) Framed or fudged? A primary perspective on 'the framework for the national curriculum: a report by the expert panel for the national curriculum review'. *ASPE Newsletter*, March.

Roberts, D. (2017) Donald Trump and the rise of tribal epistemology. *Vox*, 19 May. www.vox.com/policy-and-politics/2017/3/22/14762030/donald-trump-tribal-epistemology (accessed June 2021).

Robinson, C. (2014) *Children, Their Voices and their Experiences of Schools: What Does the Evidence Tell Us?* CPRT Research Survey 2. York: Cambridge Primary Review Trust.

Rose, J. (2008a) *The Independent Review of the Primary Curriculum: Interim Report*. London: DCSF.

Rose, J. (2008b) *Independent Review of the Teaching of Early Reading: Final Report*. London: DfES.

Rose, J. (2009a) Independent Review of the Primary Curriculum: update from Sir Jim Rose. www.dcsf.gov.uk/primarycurriculumreview (accessed February 2009).

Rose, J. (2009b) *The Independent Review of the Primary Curriculum: Final Report*. London: DCSF.

Rosen, H. (1971) Towards a language policy across the curriculum: a discussion document prepared and introduced by Harold Rosen on behalf of the London association for the teaching of English. In D. Barnes, J. Britton and H. Rosen (eds) *Language, the Learner and the School*. London: Penguin, 117–68.

Rosenthal, R. and Jacobson, L. (1968) *Pygmalion in the Classroom: Teacher Expectations and Pupils' Intellectual Development*. New York: Holt.

Rowe, M.B. (1974) Wait time and rewards as instructional variables, their influence on language, logic and fate control. Part One, wait time. *Journal of Research in Science Teaching* 11(2), 81–94.

Rowe, M.B. (1986) Wait time: slowing down may be a way of speeding up. *Journal of Teacher Education* 37(1), 43–50.

Ruddock, G. (2000) *Third International Mathematics and Science Study Repeat (TIMSS-R): First National Report*. London: DfEE.

Ruskin, J. (1859) [1986] The two paths. In J. Ruskin (ed) *Unto This Last and Other Writings*. London: Penguin Books.

Russell, J. (2008) The NUT has cried wolf too often, but this time it's right. *The Guardian*, 26 March.

Ruzzi, B.B. (2006) *International Education Tests: An Overview, 2005.* Washington, DC: NCEE.

Sadler, M. (1900) How can we learn anything of practical value from the study of foreign systems of education? In J.H. Higginson (ed) *Selections from Michael Sadler: Studies in World Citizenship.* Liverpool: Dejall & Meyorre.

Sahlberg, P. (2011) *Finnish Lessons: What Can the World Learn from Educational Change in Finland?* New York: Teachers College Press.

Said, E. (1979) *Orientalism.* London: Vintage.

Sampson, A. (2004) *Who Runs This Place? The Anatomy of Britain in the 21st Century.* London: John Murray.

Sands, P. (2005) *Lawless World: America and the Making and Breaking of Global Rules.* London: Allen Lane.

Savage, M. (2019) Health secretary tells social media firms to protect children after girl's death. *The Guardian,* 26 January. www.theguardian.com/politics/2019/jan/26/matt-hancock-facebook-social-media-suicide-self-harm-young-people (accessed 26 January 2019).

Schleicher, A. and Stewart, V. (2008) Learning from world-class schools. *Educational Leadership 66*(8).

Schön, D.A. (1983) *The Reflective Practitioner: How Professionals Think in Action.* London: Temple Smith.

Schopenhauer, A. (2004) [1831] *The Art of Always Being Right,* ed. A.C.Grayling. London: Gibson Square Books.

Schwarz, B.B. and Baker, M.J. (2017) *Dialogue, Argumentation and Education: History, Theory and Practice.* Cambridge: Cambridge University Press.

Scott, S. (2015) Character education awards process lacks rigour. *SchoolsWeek,* 16 January.

Scottish Government (2008) *Curriculum for Excellence.* https://education.gov.scot/education-scotland/scottish-education-system/policy-for-scottish-education/policy-drivers/cfe-building-from-the-statement-appendix-incl-btc1–5/what-is-curriculum-for-excellence/ (accessed May 2020).

See, B.H. and Kokotsaki, D. (2015) *Impact of Arts Education on the Cognitive and Non-Cognitive Outcomes of School-Aged Children.* London: Education Endowment Foundation.

Segal, A. and Lefstein, A. (2015) *Exuberant Voiceless Participation: Dialogic Sensibilities in the Israeli Primary Classroom.* Working Papers in Urban Language and Literacies 156. London: King's College.

Segal, A., Pollak, A. and Lefstein, A. (2016) Democracy, voice and dialogic pedagogy: the struggle to be heard and heeded. *Language and Education.* DOI: 10.1080/09500 782.2016.1230124.

Sharp, C., Pye, D., Blackmore, J., Brown, E., Eames, A., Easton, C., Filmer-Sankey, C., Tabary, A., Whitby, K., Wilson, R. and Benton, T. (2007) *National Evaluation of Creative Partnerships: Final Report.* Slough: NFER.

Sharpe, K. (1997) The Protestant ethic and the spirit of Catholicism: ideological and instructional constraints on system change in English and French primary schooling. *Comparative Education 33*(3), 329–48.

Shuayb, M. and O'Donnell, S. (2010) Aims and values in primary education: England and other countries. In R.J. Alexander, C. Doddington, J. Gray, L. Hargreaves and R. Kershner (eds) *The Cambridge Primary Review Research Surveys.* London: Routledge, 306–40.

Shulman, L.S. (1987) Knowledge and teaching: foundations of the new reform. *Harvard Educational Review 57*(1), 49–60.

Shweder, R.A. (1991) *Thinking Through Cultures*. Cambridge, MA: Harvard University Press.

Simon, B. (1981a) The primary school revolution: myth or reality? In B. Simon and J. Willcocks (eds) *Research and Practice in the Primary Classroom*. London: Routledge, 7-25.

Simon, B. (1981b) Why no pedagogy in England? In B. Simon and W. Taylor (eds) *Education in the Eighties: The Central Issues*. London: Batsford, 124–45.

Simon, B. (1992) Review article – 'Curriculum organisation and classroom practice in primary schools: a discussion paper.' *Curriculum Journal 3*(1).

Simon, B. and Simon, J. (eds) (1963) *Educational Psychology in the U.S.S.R.* London: Routledge and Kegan Paul.

Simon, J. (1966) *Education and Society in Tudor England*. Cambridge: Cambridge University Press.

Sinclair, J. McH and Coulthard, R.M. (1975) *Towards an Analysis of Discourse*. Oxford: Oxford University Press.

Sinclair, J. McH and Coulthard, R.M. (1992) Towards an analysis of discourse. In M. Coulthard (ed) *Advances in Spoken Discourse Analysis*. London: Routledge, 1–34.

Sippitt, A. (2019) *Political Trust in the UK*. London: Full Fact.

Smith, A. (2018) quoted in media release from the Edinburgh International Book Festival, 21 August. www.edbookfest.co.uk/news/ali-smith-fiction-is-one-of-our-ways-to-get-to-truths-that-are-really-difficult-to-talk-about (accessed 24 September 2018).

Smith, F., Hardman, F., Wall, K. and Mroz, M. (2004) Interactive whole class teaching in the national literacy and numeracy strategies. *British Educational Research Journal 30*(3), 403–19.

Snyder, J. (2014) Teaching kids 'grit' is all the rage. Here's what's wrong with it. *New Republic*, 6 May.

Spender, D. (1980) *Man Made Language*. London: Routledge.

Stalin, J. and Wells, H.G. (1937) *Marxism vs Liberalism: An Interview*. Transcript of interview in 1934. New York: New Century Publishers. www.rationalrevolution.net/special/library/cc835_44.htm (accessed September 2018).

Staufenberg, J. (2017) Entries to EBacc peak as fewer pupils take creative subjects. *SchoolsWeek*, 15 June.

Stern, N. (2007) *The Economics of Climate Change: The Stern Review*. Cambridge: Cambridge University Press.

Stevenson, H.W. and Stigler, J.W. (1992) *The Learning Gap: Why Our Schools Are Failing and What We Can Learn from Japanese and Chinese Education*. New York: Simon and Schuster.

Straw, J. (1987) Speech at second reading of the education reform bill. *Hansard*, 1 December Vol. 123. http://hansard.millbanksystems.com/commons/1987/dec/01/education-reform-bill-1 (accessed May 2014).

Stronach, I., Pickard, A. and Jones, L. (2010) Primary schools: the professional environment. In R.J. Alexander, C. Doddington, J. Gray, L. Hargreaves and R. Kershner (eds) *The Cambridge Primary Review Research Surveys*. London: Routledge, 627–48.

Sullivan, G.M. (2011) Getting off the 'gold standard': randomized control trials and educational research. *Journal of Graduate Medical Education 3*(3), 285–9.

Tanner, M. (1975) Literature and philosophy. *New Universities Quarterly 30*(1).

Taylor, C. (1991) *The Ethics of Authenticity*. Cambridge, MA: Harvard University Press.

TDA (2007) *Professional Standards for Teachers in England from September 2007*. London: TDA.

Thomas, N. (2007) Written submission to the Cambridge Primary Review.

Thornton, M. (1993) The role of government in education. In C. Chitty and B. Simon (eds) *Education Answers Back: Critical Responses to Government Policy*. London: Lawrence and Wishart.

Times Higher Education (2009) Top 200 world universities. www.timeshighereducation. co.uk/hybrid.asp?typeCode=438 (accessed August 2009).

Times Higher Education (2021) THE university rankings 2021. www.timeshighereducation.com/world-university-rankings/2021/world-ranking#!/page/0/length/25/sort_by/rank/sort_order/asc/cols/stats (accessed June 2021).

Tobin, J.J. (1999) Method and meaning in comparative classroom ethnography. In R.J. Alexander, P. Broadfoot and D. Phillips (eds) *Learning from Comparing: New Directions in Comparative Educational Research. Vol 1: Contexts, Classrooms and Outcomes.* Oxford: Symposium Books, 113–34.

Tobin, J.J., Hsueh, Y. and Karasawa, M. (2009) *Preschool in Three Cultures Revisited.* Chicago: University of Chicago Press.

Tobin, J.J., Wu, D.Y.H. and Davidson, D.H. (1989) *Preschool in Three Cultures: Japan, China and the United States.* New Haven: Yale University Press.

Tough, J. (1979) *Talk for Teaching and Learning.* London: Ward Lock Educational.

Tough, P. (2013) *How Children Succeed: Grit, Curiosity and the Hidden Power of Character.* Boston, MA: Mariner Books.

Toulmin, S. (2003) *The Uses of Argument.* Cambridge: Cambridge University Press.

Tymms, P. and Merrell, C. (2007) *Standards and Quality in English Primary Schools Over Time: The National Evidence.* Cambridge Primary Review Research Survey 4/1. In R.J. Alexander, C. Doddington, J. Gray, L. Hargreaves and R. Kershner (eds) *The Cambridge Primary Review Research Surveys,* 435–60. London: Routledge.

UK Parliament (2021a) Written questions, answers and statements, UIN 7928, 26 May. https://questions-statements.parliament.uk/written-questions/detail/2021-05-26/7928 (accessed June 2021).

UK Parliament (2021b) Written questions, answers and statements, UIN 7927, 26 May. https://questions-statements.parliament.uk/written-questions/detail/2021-05-26/7927 (accessed June 2021).

UNESCO (1990) *World Declaration on Education for All: Meeting Basic Learning Needs.* World Conference on Education for all, Jomtien, March 1990. Paris: UNESCO.

UNESCO (2000) *The Dakar Framework for Action: Education for All – Meeting Our Collective Commitments.* Paris: UNESCO.

UNESCO (2002) *Education for All: Is the World on Track?* EFA Global Monitoring Report 2002. Paris: UNESCO.

UNESCO (2004) *Education for All: The Quality Imperative.* EFA Global Monitoring Report 2005. Paris: UNESCO.

UNESCO (2008) *Overcoming Inequality: Why Governance Matters.* EFA Global Monitoring Report 2009. Paris and Oxford: UNESCO and Oxford University Press.

UNESCO (2014) *Teaching and Learning: Achieving Quality for All.* EFA Global Monitoring Report 2013/14. Paris: UNESCO.

UNESCO (2015) Concept note for a 2016 report on *Education, sustainability and the post-2015 development agenda,* prepared by the EFA GMR team. www.unesco.org/new/fileadmin/MULTIMEDIA/HQ/ED/GMR/images/2014/2016_Concept_Note_rev2.pdf (accessed January 2015).

UNESCO (2019) New methodology shows that 258 million children, adolescents and youth are out of school. *UNESCO Institute for Statistics Fact Sheet 56.* http://uis.unesco.org/sites/default/files/documents/new-methodology-shows-258-million-children-adolescents-and-youth-are-out-school.pdf (accessed May 2021).

UNICEF (2007) *Child Poverty in Perspective: An Overview of Child Well-Being in Rich Countries.* Innocenti Report Card 7. Florence: UNICEF Innocenti Research Centre.

UNICEF (2011) *Child Well-being in the UK, Spain and Sweden: The Role of Inequality and Materialism*. London: UNICEF UK.

United Nations Development Programme (2008) *Fighting Climate Change: Human Solidarity in a Divided World*. Human Development Report 2007/8. New York: UNDP.

Usher, A. (2006) Can our schools become world class? *The Globe and Mail*, Toronto. www. theglobeandmail.com/archives/article852033.ece (accessed August 2009).

Varjo, J., Simola, H. and Rinne, R. (2013) Finland's PISA results: an analysis of dynamics in education politics. In H-D. Meyer and A. Benavot (eds) *PISA, Power and Policy: The Emergence of Global Educational Governance*. Oxford: Symposium Books, 51–76.

Vrikki, M., Wheatley, L. Howe, C., Hennessey, S. and Mercer, N. (2018) Dialogic practices in primary school classrooms. *Language and Education*. DOI: 10.1080/09500782. 2018.1509988.

Vygotsky, L.S. (1962) *Thought and Language*. Cambridge, MA: MIT Press.

Vygotsky, L.S. (1963) Learning and mental development at school age. In B. Simon and J. Simon (eds) *Educational Psychology in the U.S.S.R.* London: Routledge and Kegan Paul, 21–34.

Vygotsky, L.S. (1978) *Mind in Society*. Cambridge, MA: Harvard University Press.

Vygotsky, L.S. (1981) The genesis of higher mental functions. In J.V. Wertsch (ed) *The Concept of Activity in Soviet Psychology*. London: M.E. Sharpe.

Walton, D. (2013) *Methods of Argumentation*. Cambridge: Cambridge University Press.

Washington Post (2021) The Fact Checker's ongoing database of the false or misleading claims made by President Trump since assuming office. www.washingtonpost.com/ graphics/politics/trump-claims-database/?noredirect=on&utm_term=.ab9ee6608cc8 (accessed May 2021).

Watkins, D.A. and Biggs, J.B. (1996) *The Chinese Learner: Cultural, Psychological and Contextual Differences*. Hong Kong: Comparative Education Research Centre.

Weale, S. (2016) Art history A level saved after high-profile campaign. *The Guardian*, 1 December.

Weale, S. (2021) Tory MP accuses Ofsted of 'massive failure' over sexual abuse in schools. *The Guardian*, 10 June.

Welch, K.E. (1990) *The Contemporary Reception of Classical Rhetoric: Appropriations of Ancient Discourse*. Hillsdale, NJ: Lawrence Erlbaum.

Wells, H.G. (1920) *The Outline of History*. Vol. 2. London: George Newnes.

Wells, H.G. (1999) *Dialogic Inquiry: Towards a Sociocultural Practice and Theory of Education*. Cambridge: Cambridge University Press.

Westbrook, J., Durrani, N., Brown, R., Orr, D., Pryor, J., Boddy, J. and Salvi, F. (2013) *Pedagogy, Curriculum, Teaching Practices and Teacher Education in Developing Countries*. EPPI Education Rigorous Literature Review. London: IoE.

Whetton, C., Ruddock, G. and Twist, L. (2007) Standards in English primary education: the international national evidence. In R.J. Alexander, C. Doddington, J. Gray, L. Hargreaves and R. Kershner (eds) *The Cambridge Primary Review Research Surveys*. Cambridge Primary Review Research Survey 4/2, 461–83. London: Routledge.

White, J. (2010) Aims as policy in English primary education. In R.J. Alexander, C. Doddington, J. Gray, L. Hargreaves and R. Kershner (eds) *The Cambridge Primary Review Research Surveys*. London: Routledge, 282–305.

White, J. (2015) A caricature of character education? Morgan needs a broader vision. *IoE blog*, 16 January. https://ioelondonblog.wordpress.com/2015/01/16/a-caricature-of-character-education-morgan-needs-a-broader-vision/ (accessed May 2021).

Wilkinson, A. (1965) *Spoken English*. Birmingham: Birmingham University Press.

Wilkinson, R. and Pickett, K. (2010) *The Spirit Level: Why Equality Is Good for Everyone.* London: Penguin Books.

Williams, P. (2008) *Independent Review of Mathematics Teaching in Early Years Settings and Primary Schools.* London: DCSF.

Wolf, A. (2002) *Does Education Matter? Myths About Education and Economic Growth.* London: Penguin.

Wood, D. (1998) *How Children Think and Learn.* Oxford: Blackwell.

World Bank (1996) *Russia: Education in the Transition.* Washington, DC: World Bank.

World Bank (2000) *Entering the 21st Century: World Development Report 1999–2000.* New York: Oxford University Press.

Wragg, E.C. and Brown, G. (1993) *Explaining.* London: Routledge.

Wragg, E.C. and Brown, G. (2001) *Questioning.* London: Routledge.

Wyse, D., McCreery, E. and Torrance, H. (2007) *The Trajectory and Impact of National Reform: Curriculum and Assessment in English Primary Schools*, Cambridge Primary Review Research Survey 3/2. In Alexander, R.J., Doddington, C., Gray, J., Hargreaves, L. and Kershner, R. (eds) (2010) *The Cambridge Primary Review Research Surveys.* London: Routledge, 792–817.

Youde, K. (2010) Music has the power to shape a child's mind. *The Independent*, 21 February.

Young, T. (2014) *Prisoners of the Blob: Why Most Education Experts Are Wrong About Nearly Everything.* London: Civitas.

Index

The index includes authors cited in the text and endnotes, but not all those in the bibliography. Authors' surnames are followed by their initials. The entries for political, public and historical figures adopt common usage, with surnames mostly followed by forenames. The present author's name does not appear.